Gardeners' World

COMPLETE BOOK
OF GARDENING

**Gardeners'
World**

COMPLETE BOOK
OF GARDENING

The essential guide to planting and practical techniques

Alan Titchmarsh

BBC

ACKNOWLEDGEMENTS

My thanks are due to Nicky Copeland, Khadija Manjlai,
Isobel Gillan, Amanda Patton and Sue Phillips for their
invaluable help in the production of this book, and
Jo Whitworth and Tim Sandall for turning up to my garden
with their cameras in all weathers. For their patience I am
indebted, and for their good humour I am grateful.

Published by BBC Worldwide Ltd,
Woodlands, 80 Wood Lane, London W12 0TT

First published 1999
Reprinted twice 1999
This paperback edition first published 2001

ISBN 0 563 38426 3 (hardback)
ISBN 0 563 53401 X (paperback)

Commisioning Editor: Nicky Copeland
Project Editor: Khadija Manjlai
Copy-editor: Julie Hawker
Picture Researcher: Frances Abraham
Designer: Isobel Gillan
Art Editor: Lisa Pettibone
Illustrations: Amanda Patton

Set in Bembo and Gill Sans
Printed and bound by Butler & Tanner Ltd, Frome and London
Colour separations by Radstock Reproductions Ltd,
Midsomer Norton
Jacket printed by Lawrence Allen Ltd, Weston-super-Mare

Contents

Location Gardening

Gardeners' Diary

Introduction

Why do some people find gardening such a worry? Is it because the weeds seem to grow too fast and the plants too slowly? Or is it that they're intimidated by 'proper' gardeners, who spout Latin names and know exactly when and how to do all the jobs that need to be done? Maybe they planted something once and it never grew, so they gave up gardening and turned to hang gliding as being more rewarding.

If you count yourself among the apprehensive types, this book aims to get you out there gardening with the best of them. Approached in the right way – slowly – gardening can be tremendous fun, and the patch of earth outside your back door that was once a dreary lump of mud or a weed-infested jungle can be tamed to become something you really can call a garden.

The secret is not to be intimidated by what other people do in their gardens, but to create a garden that suits *your* lifestyle and meets your needs. If you need a place to relax, and which will need little in the way of maintenance, there are suggestions here of the sort of plants you can use and the ways in which you can use them. If you long for the perfect lawn, this book tells you how to achieve it. If you want a small tree for your garden, this book recommends a selection that will not eat you out of house and home.

When it comes to choosing plants, you can consult the A–Z sections, where those I think best-suited to British gardens are listed. Life is too short, and most borders too small, to give space to plants that are hard to please or mean with their flowers and foliage.

If you are never sure when you should be doing a particular job, there is a diary section to act as a reminder, and information on plants that suit problem spaces. If you select plants at the outset that are compatible with your soil and conditions, rather than struggling to overcome the difficulties posed by an environment that they are known to dislike, you will find that they are much easier to grow. If your soil is heavy, don't grow plants that are native to hot, sandy soils. If the corner you are planting up is shady, pick plants that naturally grow in woodland, not on Mediterranean shores. The book will advise you in every instance.

I started gardening when I was nine. All right, so I'm an oddity, but I have discovered that it is one of life's greatest pleasures and one which becomes even more fulfilling as the years go by. I am for ever discovering new plants that I 'must have', and learning new ways of growing them.

Don't be daunted by the apparently endless supply of different plants; instead, cheer yourself up by realizing that as long as you live you will never know all of them – there is always something new to grow.

And the Latin names? You'll get used to them. They're not nearly so intimidating as you might think. Most people nowadays say hosta rather than plantain lily, and acer rather than Japanese maple. It is simply a matter of habit. Learning a plant name is no harder (and for me a darned sight easier) than learning a person's name. It also means that you can be sure you're getting what you ask for. *Hosta sieboldiana* is the same plant the world over, but blue-leaved plantain lily is not only a mouthful, it's confusing to boot.

I hope this book will help to dispel your worries and inspire you to make a garden that you really enjoy. It aims to take the mystique out of gardening and to reward you for your efforts. There will still be failures and frustrations, but these are always part of life and make the successes that much more pleasurable.

And when you find yourself baffled by a plant that fails to do well, or by your inability to grow something, just remember the words of novelist H.E. Bates: 'Gardening, like love, is a funny thing, and doesn't always yield to analysis.'

GARDENING ESSENTIALS

Before you can begin to make a new garden, there are things to be considered. What do you want from it? Do you have the right tools for the job? What sort of problems are you likely to encounter? This section will help you to make a promising start so that work carried out later on will not be wasted.

Planning a garden

Planning a new garden, or making over an old one, is among the most exciting aspects of gardening. Before you can start you need to take stock of what is available, so you can decide how best to use the plot and which existing features can be given a new lease of life.

The airstrip

We've all seen this type of garden, the sort that is divided in two by a long, straight, concrete path. A lot of older gardens were laid out like this by the builders, and it is amazing how many still have the same garden layout. The idea behind it was to provide a clean, dry surface to reach your washing line, but rotary airers and tumble driers have made them obsolete. If you really hate the straight line of the path, it's possible to take it up using a Kango hammer (a device like a junior pneumatic drill), but you are left with a lot of rubble to clear up and a big hole that needs filling with topsoil before you can grow anything in the space. Digging up the path may not be the easiest solution, but it is the only way to redesign the garden from scratch.

The back yard

Very small gardens are often just too tiny to turn into a traditional garden with lawns and borders. The lawn is the biggest problem. With a tiny lawn, it takes longer to get the mower out than to cut the grass, and since you have nowhere else to walk or put garden seats, it quickly develops bald patches and looks awful. It is better to pave or gravel the whole area, except for a few beds, and turn it into a courtyard garden. Alternatively, make a patio garden with a pool, containers and climbing plants growing on trellis screens. It will cost a bit of money, but you won't need to buy a mower and it will look very stylish and be easy to maintain.

The new garden

Starting with a completely clean slate has its advantages, but your first job will most likely be clearing away the builders' rubble and putting the soil to rights after it has been churned up by heavy machinery. Dig the whole area over deeply, a job that is better done by hand than with a rotary cultivator. Remove any bricks, bags of set cement and rubble, and work in as much organic matter as you can. Use whatever you can get cheapest locally – spent mushroom compost or manure, for instance. If you skimp on the early preparation, you can find you have trouble persuading plants to grow for years, and it works out more expensive in the long run if you have to keep replacing plants.

LEFT: Paving and gravel paths divide up this small plot, making it both accessible and interesting. RIGHT: Stepping-stone slabs laid through pea shingle always look classy.

The 'second-hand' garden

The problem with inheriting a garden is that the last owners created it for themselves, and it may not suit you, your family and the way you want to use it. On the plus side you will probably have gained a few reasonable plants or features you can incorporate into a new design, so at least it won't cost you as much as starting from scratch. There is a lot of sense in the advice about leaving an inherited garden for a year so you can see exactly what you have, otherwise you might be hacking out valuable bulbs or herbaceous plants that are not visible. You can save a lot of time by just asking the outgoing owners what the garden contains.

Front gardens

Front gardens are a bit of a mixed blessing. They are too open to sit and relax in; you may need a lot of the space for parking cars, which restricts what you can do with them, yet they are always on show, and since they are the first thing people see when they visit your house, it's likely you'll want to create a good impression. My advice is go for a simple design that will be quick and easy to keep tidy. Make sure it takes into account what you need from your front garden, as well as providing easy access. Avoid meandering paths because people making deliveries will take the shortest route over the garden anyway. After planting, mulch everything deeply with bark chippings or gravel to give the garden an attractive finish and keep weeding to a minimum.

Take a plant's-eye view of your plot

When you are itching to start creating a new garden, there is nothing worse than someone making you stop and check things out first, but that is exactly what I am going to do. Boring though it sounds, it is the only way to avoid putting plants in the wrong place. Some plants are fussy and won't grow in shady spots, windy corners or certain types of soil. When planning a garden, it is important to know your growing conditions.

First find out what sort of soil you have. Heavy clay soil is the sort that sets so hard when dry you can hardly stick a fork into it, but when it's wet it is sticky and water stays in puddles for hours after heavy rain. Sandy soil is light-coloured and gritty, and rain runs away without leaving puddles; it is very dry in summer and organic matter disappears quickly, so you have to keep adding more. Most garden soils lie somewhere between the two and can easily be turned into a good place for plants. A dark colour indicates a fertile soil with lots of humus, which is usually found in older gardens that have been well looked after. If in doubt about your soil type, see if you can get an experienced gardener, perhaps from your local garden club, to come out and take a look at it for you.

Next 'map' the shady and sunny areas of the garden. Go out in the early morning, at midday and again in the evening to see which parts of the garden are in shadow or sun, and sketch this in on a plan of the garden. On breezy days, see which parts of the garden are sheltered and which get the full force of the wind. Make a note of the prevailing direction and check for any windy corridors where the wind funnels down between buildings, making it hard for plants to survive.

You should also do a soil test (see page 41). You can buy inexpensive kits from the garden centre that tell you if the ground is acid, alkaline or neutral. All of this affects the type of plants you can grow and where they will do best. It will save you a fortune in the long run.

Deciding what to keep and what to scrap

In a 'second-hand' garden it is not always a good idea to clear everything away and start again. If you remove the lot at once, you risk leaving the garden looking very open and exposed with no privacy. Many existing features such as trees and shrubs can be left, and a new garden created around them. Large, established plants provide instant maturity in a newly planted garden. Neglected features like fences or overgrown shrubs can be easily improved. Unproductive, old trees can be given a new lease of life by planting climbers up them, and patchy, weed-infested lawns soon improve out of all recognition with regular cutting and a couple of doses of a combined feed and weed treatment. Some existing features may be difficult to remove, like paving or outbuildings, but again you can often clean them up, or alter their appearance. Old concrete paths, for instance, provide a firm, level base for new paving slabs, or you could put edging tiles along the edge and lay gravel over the concrete. Use the brick base of an old greenhouse as a low wall around a new raised vegetable bed. Take a good look at everything with a critical eye before deciding what to discard.

FRONT GARDEN SOLUTIONS

♦ If you want to park cars in the front garden, use hard surfaces with interesting textures and choose a few striking trees and shrubs. Lots of fiddly little plants will look messy if they flop over the parking space and are squashed. Plan the design to take into account the movement of cars. Group a few plants strategically instead of dotting them about, to create a bold but practical effect.

♦ For a garden that is on a busy road an evergreen border of shrubs or a hedge will offer a bit of privacy and filter out road dust and traffic fumes. If space is very short or you want fairly quick results, grow climbers on chain-link fencing. Use evergreen climbers like cultivars of the honeysuckle *Lonicera japonica* for year-round effect.

♦ Security is often important. To deter vandals or intruders, grow prickly plants like berberis, pyracantha or roses as a hedge or in a border. To keep your pets in fix small-mesh wire netting to posts about 30cm (12in) inside the garden and plant shrubs either side of it.

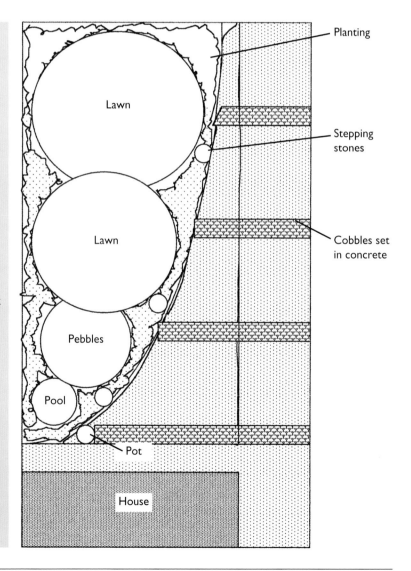

Planting

Stepping stones

Cobbles set in concrete

Lawn

Lawn

Pebbles

Pool

Pot

House

Starting the plan

Even the best garden designers don't expect to sit down and draw up a complete plan in one go, so you shouldn't either. Take your time deciding what new features you want, how you will use the garden and the amount of time you will have to look after it. The trick is to play around with different ideas, sketching several designs on paper before deciding which one you like best.

Start by drawing a rough plan of the garden on squared paper, so you can make it approximately to scale. Mark in the position of the house, showing where all the windows and doors open – this is important as it shows you where you will look out over the garden from. Draw in all the features you plan to keep, such as existing fences, outbuildings, trees and paths, and then, instead of using this to pencil in places you might like to put new features and keep having to rub them out, lay a sheet of tracing paper over the top and use that to try out a new plan. This way you can replace the tracing paper and have several stabs at different ideas without having to redraw the master plan underneath. If you have a home computer, you might prefer to use one of the garden design programmes, which can show you what your garden will eventually look like as they usually produce a three-dimensional picture of the result.

Whichever method you choose to make a plan, it is a very good idea to have one, however rough, combined with your record of garden conditions. This way you can enjoy shopping at garden centres and flower shows, knowing that you'll only bring back plants to which you can give a good home.

Rectangular gardens can look very boring, so here I've used 45-degree angles to offer a bit of perspective. The stone-flagged terrace juts out from the house in a triangle, and away from this shoots a rectangle of gravel flanked with bricks. There is room for a lawn with a curved edge, surrounded by a wrap-around border. A sun deck at the bottom right-hand corner picks up on the triangular theme and offers a place to dine.

I once had to design a garden which was very long and thin. The owners wanted to make it look shorter and wider, so I divided it into three sections with each area having a different feel.

At the end of the bark path a raised, wooden, planked walkway leads between boulder-strewn borders to a decked area which surrounds the once dull brown shed. It was painted a soft yellow with white eaves to give it a colonial feel. Here the owners can sit and enjoy their evening pre-supper drinks, looking down through the three new gardens towards the house.

The next area is reached by passing through a woven-willow archway, flanked by willow screens. Here the feeling is wilder, with a curving, chipped-bark pathway snaking its way between generously planted borders of shrubs and perennials. The mature tree on the left-hand side of the garden was retained to add a bit of height and stature; shade-loving plants are planted under its canopy.

The area nearest to the house is traversed by stepping stones, which are surrounded by a sea of smooth pebbles dotted with groups of larger cobbles. A simple, circular bowl makes a pool, and bamboos and grasses erupt through the stones. The feeling here is one of coolness and Orientalism.

Designs and features

The secret of success in garden design is not to mix styles. Having chosen your style, use hard surfaces to give it form and character and garden features, such as arbours and statues, to link together groups of plants and show them off attractively.

Formal

Formal gardens rely on geometrical shapes for their impact; they have straight hedges and walls, paths with perfect right angles at every bend, and geometric-shaped beds. Think of formal herb gardens, which are laid out on a square or circular theme with paths bisecting them into equal-sized segments, and traditional double borders – two parallel borders planted with herbaceous flowers and a straight path between them. Walled gardens, pergolas, terraces and carpet bedding are also formal features.

A formal garden looks good in a geometrical space, such as a rectangle, ideally enclosed by hedges or walls. But it does not have to be designed to a traditional plan. Modern formal gardens can be based on shapes that overlap and may even be asymmetrical.

Informal

Informal gardens are exactly the opposite. The essence of this sort of garden is that there isn't a straight line in the place. Lawn edges curve gently, beds are cut into natural contours in the land and paths meander round bends with plants spilling over the edges. Think of island beds, cottage gardens and woodland walks. You can have hedges with peepholes cut in them, seats under climber-clad structures, irregularly shaped areas of paving and teardrop-shaped flower beds. Informal gardens are getting even more informal. Now, wild gardens, old-fashioned hay meadows and prairie-style borders are the last word in fashionable informal gardens, where the effect is positively untamed.

Traditional

My idea of a traditional garden is a sort of scaled-down version of a country house garden with a lawn, shrubberies and a herbaceous border, and the fruit and vegetable plot out of sight down at the end. This is the sort you could happily put a 'bit of everything' into and that could include things like a rockery and fishpond, bulbs growing in grass under trees, and a work area with greenhouse, cold frames and compost heaps. Nowadays you'll find a traditional sort of garden has only a few items from the original 'menu', and even these will be scaled down in size. But the colour scheme is tasteful – probably pastel, or a sort of random mixture of colours diluted with plenty of green foliage to prevent clashing. Any furniture is subtle (real wood, or cast-aluminium repro). Planting is based on the tried-and-tested principles of Vita Sackville-West, Gertrude Jekyll and other such icons.

Modern

Young, trendy designers may be like red rags to traditional gardeners, but a lot of their output (seen at Chelsea and Hampton Court Flower Shows) gives a new slant on garden layout. Modern garden designs tend to follow the trends of interior decoration – so paint-effect pots, *trompe l'oeil* and murals on walls, colourful sheds and seats and loud, subtropical-look plants all have their place. A state-of-the-art design can look just right around a contemporary house. But unless you are the sort of person who likes to follow fashion and doesn't mind updating their garden every few years, be warned. A very modern style is likely to go out of fashion quite quickly. Choose an *avant-garde* design that suits the style of your house rather than slavishly following the latest trends, if you want a garden you can live with for some time.

ABOVE: *A concrete cherub sits at one side of a flight of steps leading to a small formal garden.*

ODD-SHAPED GARDENS

Regular-shaped, oblong gardens are less and less common, now that houses are being squeezed into all sorts of odd-shaped parcels of land – someone always has to get the end wedge-shaped plot.

♦ Odd-shaped plots are the easiest to divide into 'garden rooms' as the shape virtually dictates how to carve the area up. It's much harder in a perfectly regular plot.

♦ A long, narrow garden looks best divided into three garden rooms, separated by trellis or hedges with arches leading through from one area to the next, so you cannot see straight to the end of the garden. Avoid having a straight path, as it makes the plot look longer and thinner.

♦ Use mirror acrylic (a shiny, reflective, unbreakable plastic material that you can easily cut to shape) and perspective trellis (which looks as if it goes back into an alcove) to give the illusion of space and make a small or narrow area seem bigger.

♦ Use asymmetric-shaped beds, lawns and features to put detail into an odd-shaped plot and take your mind off the shape, while actually making the most of it.

✎ top tip

If you are really stuck for ideas, get a local garden designer to do an outline plan showing the shape of the beds and lawn or paving, but prepare your own planting plan. Its much cheaper than getting a detailed design. Find a good designer by word of mouth, or ask garden centres if they can recommend someone. You can also get lots of ideas from books on garden design; some provide sample plans for various awkward plots to give you a good start.

DOS AND DON'TS OF DESIGN

✔ Do keep tabs on new trends in garden style by visiting the big flower shows and reading gardening and glossy home interior magazines. There's no need to copy them, but they are a good source of ideas for gradually updating your 'look'.

✗ Don't be afraid to try out new ideas, experiment with new colour schemes, grow new plants you have not tried before – it is all part of the fun of gardening, and if it doesn't quite work out it is easily altered.

✗ Don't try to make enormous changes to the garden every year just for the sake of it or the garden will never look established and will cost you a fortune. But do take the opportunity to 'make over' an old bed when herbaceous plants need dividing.

✔ Do visit other people's gardens and large gardens open to the public, with a camera and notebook, so you can remind yourself of ideas that have taken your fancy. File them in an old shoebox for future reference.

A mirror in a stout wooden frame seen through a brick archway gives the impression the path continues on the other side. This visual trickery is known as trompe l'oeil.

Hard surfaces

To a real enthusiast, gardens are all about plants. But you have only to walk round a few gardens to see that it takes more than plants alone to make an attractive landscape. You need hard surfaces to walk on without getting your feet dirty in wet weather, and to set your garden chairs and table on. You also need them to provide the vital change of colour and texture that breaks up huge expanses of green plants into separate 'ingredients', so your eye can take everything in properly. They contribute to a garden's practicality as well as its design. You don't need to have the same type of hard surface all around the garden. In fact, changing the texture underfoot is a subtle way garden designers have of alerting you to a change of garden theme. Sometimes your feet will spot the change before your eye does. The idea is to team the type of surface to the planting.

Paths and paving

In a woodland garden, you could make a path out of bark chippings edged with fallen logs. On a patio, you'd have paving slabs. In a formal garden, you might like York stone paving. (But watch out as this

Outside the conservatory I made a raised timber deck on which to have morning coffee under the shade of a Gleditsia *'Sunburst'.*

gets very slippery when it's wet – you can water it with tar-oil wash in winter to kill algae and moss, but personally I'd go for a reconstituted stone version with a slight texture to give it a bit of grip.) Conversely, in a cottage garden, you'd probably choose gravel paths for rambling around to look at plants, and a paved path from the garden gate to the front door where you want to go quickly. The type of walking surface actually affects the speed you walk on it and the way you are thinking when you do so.

But there's more to it than that. You can actually make people walk where you want them to, just by your choice of underfoot surfacing. Put cobblestones or granite setts where you want to discourage people from walking – it works because they are slightly uneven and very knobbly, which makes them uncomfortable to tread on. And lay smooth, flat paving where you want people to walk, as it feels comfortable underfoot. (If you put cobbles each side of the slabs, visitors won't step off the path.)

Edging tiles are a neat way to finish off a path, keeping the soil in flower beds and the gravel on gravel paths. They can also help to set the scene for what lies beyond them: Victorian rope-twist tiles suggest a smart country garden, while in a more informal, cottagey setting you might use a row of old, red bricks set edgeways on to make a zigzag

I love the sea, and found this seaside garden easy to make at home with hefty black-painted planks and a supply of pebbles and cobbles from the builders' merchant. A Cornish crab pot finishes it off. Can you hear the seagulls?

edge. And in some situations, instead of a proper path, all you need are 'stepping stones' set into the ground. In an informal herb garden it is pleasing to have stepping stones running through a carpet of low ground-cover plants like scented thymes or chamomile. Or use stepping stones in a lawn, to stop a muddy track being worn through the grass if you have to keep using the same route. Occasional stepping stones also look good in informal borders, as they make a good background for plants (try sinking large terracotta flowerpots into the border, upside down – this is a good way to use up broken ones, incidentally), while allowing you to weed easily.

Decking
Although in Britain it is normal to use stone, gravel or other 'mineral' surfaces for paths and paving, in some parts of the world it is common to use wood. In Scandinavia and the USA, they have big forests and use a lot of timber for building houses, so inevitably it spins off into garden use as decking for what look like wooden patios. These are just coming into fashion in Britain. If your climate is cool and damp, you must choose carefully which sort of timber you use or it won't last long. (Old railway

sleepers have often been used in British landscapes to make 'nursery' paths or rustic bridges over streams or ditches – the sleepers last for years due to all the old oil they are bathed in.) It boils down to using only pressure-treated timber for decking – some firms supply timber imported from Scandinavia, where it is accustomed to a tough climate.

Mosaics
If you want to be trendy, you can make your own mosaics. Use pebbles arranged in patterns (concentric rings look effective, but be sure to use roughly equal-sized pebbles) – though I've seen some very striking examples made of anything from bits of broken coloured tiles arranged Roman style, to seashells, or sunken wine bottles with the bottoms showing. The trick, when making a mosaic, is to lay out your pattern first, before pressing the stones, tiles or what-have-you into cement, so you know where they go.

Play areas and other surfaces
Garden surfaces have more uses than just being walked on. Instead of letting children wreck your lawn, you can now buy a range of safe surfaces to cover a special garden play area for them. At its simplest, you can make a raised edge 15cm (6in) high out of planks and fill it with 8–10cm (3–4in) of bark chippings. Or you can lay rubber granules or rubberized 'underlay' type material to make a games pitch, or graze-proof flooring under swings and slides.

ALTERNATIVE DECORATIONS

Keep a look out for novel ideas for decorating the garden. Natural-looking, woven, basket-style or twiggy plant supports are always attractive, and willow wigwams are a good idea for holding up annual climbers in pots or in a border. Use miniature hazel sheep hurdles to prop up flowers spilling over the edge of the lawn, or to deter the dog from running straight down the path into a special clump of plants. Try bending your own small plant supports out of home-grown bamboo (use slim canes while they are green and flexible) or red dogwood (cornus) stems. To add height to a more traditional border, use upright supports like pillars or metal obelisks to grow permanent climbers such as clematis or pillar roses. Trim forked poles to make 'props' to support low branches of fruit trees that have been bent down under the weight of crops, and grow clematis up them and into the tree for a spot of rustic charm.

✍ top tip

Recycling is fashionable and a cheap, creative way of getting unusual garden decorations. Look in your local junk shops to see what can be given a new lease of life. Old tin baths and mop buckets make good plant containers. A few coats of paint will brighten them up: use acrylic paint and, if necessary, seal with a layer of varnish. Old wicker baskets can be stained, varnished and lined with black plastic, and all sorts of old kitchen pots, pans and bowls make good plant pot holders for the patio. Coloured containers can be made by painting plain terracotta plant pots. Don't throw away broken pots – they can be used for a display of rock plants such as sempervivums surrounded by broken bits of pot.

Statues

Statues are a good way to make a focal point in a formal garden. There is nothing like a a piece of handsome sculpture on a plinth to give a touch of distinction to a recess in a wall or a niche in a clipped evergreen hedge. But they are good in informal settings too. Here, the best way to use them is half hidden by foliage or wreathed in ivy, so they suggest a romantic, secret garden with a faint air of disorder.

You don't have to use classical statues; it's better to choose something that suits the surroundings. In an Oriental-style garden based on gravel and pebbles, a stone lantern or Buddha looks the part. In a Mediterranean-style garden, a large, empty, terracotta olive-oil jar helps to set the scene. Stone mushrooms, which are old staddle-stones, once used for holding up cornstacks so that rats couldn't get in, look good in a country garden. Stand a row along the edge of the drive, or use one on its own at the end of a border, among low-growing flowers. In a romantic cottage garden, an old chimney pot or ancient pump is often used to break up a carpet of plants. But don't always go for the obvious. There is a huge range of modern sculptures including stone guinea fowl, bronze ducks, storks and geese, as well as many abstract creations – you can even make your own out of recycled garden junk.

Pergolas

If you have a long, narrow path or paved area behind the house, this is the ideal place to make a pergola. It is usually a row of timber uprights supporting joists that lean up against the back of the building, but there is no reason why it should be tacked on to a house. A free-standing pergola provides a pretty, covered walkway that also adds height to a flat garden, as well as supporting climbers you might not otherwise have room to grow. Have a pergola constructed for you by a local builder, or buy a kit consisting of pre-cut uprights and cross-pieces you can put together yourself and add to, depending on the space available.

Arches and tunnels

Arches are a very good way of linking different parts of the garden together, particularly if you have an odd-shaped plot or several 'garden rooms'. They make it obvious that you are entering another area with a different style. Construct the arch from material that reflects the style of the garden, such as rustic poles, wrought iron, sawn timber or trellis.

FAR LEFT: A beehive used as an ornament in my gravel garden.
ABOVE: The man we call Juan Carlos – a sculpture presiding over the Mediterranean garden.

You can make arches very cheaply by bending lengths of old metal pipe or builders' reinforcing bars. It doesn't matter what they look like as they'll be hidden by climbers anyway, so no one will know but you. The secret of a good arch is to smother it with lots of plants, but prickles are best avoided. If you do want roses for your arch, choose *Rosa* 'Zéphirine Drouhin', which is virtually thornless.

Trellis

Nowadays trellis is not just a bit of squared or diamond lattice you hang on a wall to grow climbers on – it is available in so many different shapes and sizes that you can create all sorts of wonderful structures from it. Use trellis panels with curved tops to make screens to shelter the patio, divide the garden up, or hide distant eyesores. You can put trellis along the back of a border to support tall plants or climbers or, with

In summer a shady arbour like this one, with its arch of fragrant honeysuckle, is a lovely place under which to sit.

right-angled extensions, to divide a long border into planting bays. I've seen this done with very formal trellis painted in black and white, for a mock-Tudor effect, which made a wonderful backdrop to a rose garden. You can also use trellis panels to cover a garden structure made from a framework of timbers to create a feature that is half-way between a gazebo and an arbour, with plenty of emphasis on climbing plants. All it takes is imagination.

Other structures

Throughout history, decorative structures have played a big part in the scenery of the garden and it's amazing how some of the trends from the past are once again popular. A hundred and fifty years ago Victorian gardening magazines carried adverts asking 'Do you not have a tent?' and showing an illustration of exactly the same sort of canvas-style gazebo that has sprung into fashion today.

Modern tent-style gazebos come in anything from practical plastics for family use, to billowing canvas with interior lighting and a fancy lining for posh parties. They are great for temporary cover, should you need a spot of shelter from the sun, a light breeze or a shower of rain during an al fresco function. Although you can hold them down with tent pegs and stays, they tend to take off in a stiff breeze and are not designed to be left up for long.

A real gazebo is a permanent affair. According to the dictionary, it is a garden structure intended to take advantage of a view: an ideal place to relax in comfort, with all the ambience of the garden but without the weather. You can buy quite elaborate gazebos made from forged metal rather like a bandstand, or timber-built ones which are half-way to being a summerhouse. The idea is to have a table and seats inside and, most important, plenty of climbers growing over the top.

A true summerhouse is even more weather-proof. I suppose you could describe it as a gazebo with walls, or a decorative garden shed, but it has an atmosphere of its own. It, too, can have table and chairs for afternoon tea, but with extra refinements like curtains, pictures and vases of flowers. The great thing about a summerhouse is that it provides somewhere to store upholstered garden furniture when you are not using it.

If you don't want something too large, permanent or expensive, there are lots of other attractive ways of sitting in the garden, without moving garden furniture in and out. Seats made from hardwoods or cast aluminium can be left outside all year round, and if you position them in an arbour, they can make the place you sit in as decorative as the view you enjoy. An arbour is an alcove with sides and a roof formed by trellis and climbing plants. You can make one from a wide, rustic arch with climbers growing over the top and a bench underneath. It is usually placed in front of a hedge, for shelter, or it can be set back into an alcove making a recess in a straight hedge, but this takes a bit of advance planning. You could create extra shelter by planting the back and sides of the arbour with evergreen hedging, leaving only the roof open for climbers.

If you don't want to go to much trouble, all you need to do is make a patch of hardstanding from gravel, paving slabs, concrete or wooden decking and furnish it with permanent outdoor seats and a table. Add pots of small topiary plants, dwarf hedges and lots of scented plants, and all you need to do to get comfy is fetch yourself a cushion and a parasol. It couldn't be easier.

My 'teahouse' is a simple structure built to hide an unsightly shed. BELOW: The problem with garden seats is that someone else gets there first.

DOS AND DON'TS FOR GARDEN FEATURES

✔ Do choose scented plants like herbs, scented-leaved pelargoniums and heliotrope to grow in containers on seating areas. Over arches, pergolas and arbours use honeysuckle or jasmine.

✔ Do mix several different climbers together on the same support to give a changing sequence of colour throughout the season, but check they all need similar pruning, or no pruning at all, otherwise you'll have problems sorting the various stems out.

✗ Don't mix too many different decorative styles together. Keep rustic, stone, timber, trellis or terracotta features in separate areas of the garden. Bricks go with everything.

✗ Don't use prickly climbers on arches and other features near paths as they are likely to snag your clothes as you walk underneath; if you really want to use climbing roses, choose those with very few thorns such as *Rosa* 'Zéphirine Drouhin'.

✔ Do give new terracotta containers an artificially aged look by soaking them in diluted liquid plant food or manure water for a few days before filling and planting them. Alternatively paint them with yoghurt to encourage lichens and algae to grow on the surface. Real old clay flowerpots are sometimes sold in second-hand shops and at older nurseries, but they can be expensive.

Gardeners' vocabulary

Every sport and pastime has its own vocabulary, whether it be sailing or rock climbing, stamp collecting or amateur dramatics. Gardening is no exception. Here are some of the terms most regularly encountered, along with a simple explanation of their meaning.

Acaricide A chemical used to kill spiders and mites. Spiders are the gardener's friend, but red spider mites attack plants and are not.

Acid soil Soil that does not contain an abundance of free lime and in which rhododendrons, heathers, camellias and other lime haters will thrive. On the pH scale, which measures soil acidity from 0 to 14, acid soils have a pH below 7.0 (see page 41).

Aeration The presence of air between soil particles. Spiking a compacted lawn will improve aeration and surface drainage.

Aerial root A root that appears from a stem above ground level.

Air layering The act of encouraging roots to form on a stem by wounding it, encasing it in damp moss and polythene, then severing it once roots have formed. Often used to produce a new plant from the top of a leggy house plant or shrub.

Algae Simple plants which can produce green film on damp surfaces and green, strand-like growths in pools. Chemicals to treat them are called **algicides**.

Alkaline The opposite of 'acid'. Soils that have an abundance of free lime and are generally on chalk or limestone. On the pH scale that measures soil acidity from 0 to 14, alkaline soils have a pH above 7.0. Rhododendrons, camellias and many heathers do not like alkaline soils (see page 41).

Alpine A plant from high mountain areas (see page 204).

Annual A plant that grows from seed, flowers and dies within 12 months. **Hardy annuals** are tough enough to be sown outdoors where they are to flower; **half-hardy annuals** need greater warmth for germination and are usually sown in a greenhouse.

Aphid The posh name for greenfly and blackfly.

Aquatic A plant that grows with at least some part of its anatomy in water (see pages 222–7).

Bacteria Single-celled organisms that may be beneficial, as in many soil bacteria, or harmful, as in some plant diseases.

Bastard trenching An alternative name for 'double digging' (see page 37).

Bedding plant A plant used in temporary displays in the garden – usually for the spring or summer season (see page 166).

Besom A broom made of birch twigs or heather. Useful for sweeping leaves from lawns.

Biennial A plant that flowers in its second year after being grown from seed, and which then dies (see page 171).

Biological control The use of one organism to control another. Many pests, such as whitefly, can now be controlled using predators that feed on them.

Blanching The act of turning stems and leaves of vegetables white by blocking out the light and so preventing photosynthesis. Important in growing celery, seakale and endive to improve crispness and flavour.

Blight A vague term to indicate the presence of almost any pest or disease. Potato blight, however, is a fungal disease causing the foliage of potatoes to turn black and collapse and also affects the tubers.

ABOVE: The border perennial Euphorbia robbiae coupled with a pretty purple hyacinth.

Blind A plant is said to be 'blind' when it has lost its leading shoot or growing point and doesn't flower.

Bolting The act of running prematurely to flower and seed. The condition happens in some vegetables due to unfavourable growing conditions.

Bonemeal A fertilizer made from ground-up bones and which is high in root-promoting phosphates. Gardeners have been nervous about using the substance since the advent of 'mad cow disease' or BSE, but the risk of contracting the human form, CJD, from proprietary bonemeal is said to be extremely low.

Bonsai The Japanese name for artificially dwarfed trees and shrubs.

Bottom heat Heat applied underneath cuttings in a propagator to induce speedy rooting.

Bract A modified leaf, often brightly coloured, as in poinsettia.

Brassica A name given to members of the cabbage family. These include cabbage, cauliflower, Brussels sprout, broccoli, kale, swede and turnip.

Broadcast To scatter seeds over an area rather than sowing them in long, straight 'drills'.

Budding A means of propagation whereby a bud from one plant is inserted into the 'rootstock' of another with the aim of producing a plant of controlled vigour. Used in the commercial production of roses and fruit trees.

Bulb A condensed, underground shoot. Plants such as daffodils, tulips and lilies grow from bulbs (see pages 180–97).

Bulbil A tiny, immature bulb which may form in the leaf axil of, for instance, a lily.

Calcareous A term to describe soils containing chalk or lime.

Calcifuge A plant that hates lime. Examples include rhododendron and camellia.

Callus Wound-protecting tissue that forms where plant tissue has been cut or damaged.

Chitting Encouraging shoots to grow. A process used on potatoes prior to planting them, or to pre-germinate seeds before sowing.

Chlorophyll The green colouring in plants which utilizes sunlight to help them manufacture food, a process known as photosynthesis.

Chlorosis Loss of green colouring due to lack of light or food. Chlorotic leaves become yellow or white.

Cloche Originally applied to glass bell jars, the term 'cloche' is now applied to any small polythene or glass structure used to protect young plants, especially vegetables.

Clone A group of plants produced vegetatively from a single parent.

Coir Coconut fibre used as an ingredient of seed and potting composts but of variable quality. Inferior types are dusty and hard to re-wet when dry.

Compost A term used by gardeners to denote two different things: first, rotted organic matter produced in a compost heap for use as soil enrichment; second, a mixture of such ingredients as loam, sand, peat, coir and vermiculite with fertilizer, to use as a mixture for growing plants in containers (see page 39).

Conifer A tree that bears cones.

Cordon A fruit tree restricted to a single main stem with very short fruiting sideshoots.

Corm An underground storage organ that consists of a condensed stem, as found on a crocus or freesia. Not strictly a bulb.

Crocks Broken clay flowerpots used as drainage material in the base of plant containers.

Crown A term usually used to describe that part of the plant at or around soil level.

Cultivar A variety bred in cultivation, not one that occurs naturally in the wild.

Cutting Part of a plant, usually a stem but in some cases a single leaf or piece of root, which has been removed with the aim of encouraging it to form roots and grow into a new plant.

Damping down The act of wetting the greenhouse floor in summer to produce a humid environment more conducive to plant growth than a hot, dry atmosphere.

Deadheading The removal of faded flowers.

Deciduous A term used to describe plants that lose their leaves in winter.

Die-back Death of a shoot, from the tip, due to damage or disease.

Dibber A tool used to make a planting hole for seedlings and vegetables (see page 32).

Disbudding The removal of flower buds, usually to delay flowering, or to produce fewer, larger flowers.

Division The propagation of clump-forming plants by dividing them up into smaller portions, which are then replanted singly.

Double A flower which has significantly more than the usual complement of petals.

Double digging The cultivation of soil to the depth of two spade blades. Only necessary where soil is tremendously compacted.

Drill A shallow, continuous depression in the soil, usually made against a taut garden line, into which seeds are sown and the soil then pulled back to cover them.

Earthing up The drawing up of soil around plants. In the case of potatoes, this prevents light from reaching the tubers and rendering them green and inedible.

Ericaceous A term used to describe plants that belong to the heather family. It is also used to describe lime-free potting compost (see page 41).

Espalier A trained fruit tree which has symmetrical tiers of horizontal branches.

Evergreen A tree that retains most of its leaves all year round. Many evergreens, such as holly, do shed some of their leaves in summer.

F1 hybrid A first-generation cross that will produce vigorous and uniform plants. However, if seeds are saved from this plant and sown the following year, the offspring will usually be variable.

Fan-trained Trees, especially fruit trees, trained so that their main branches are spaced out on a wall in the form of the spokes of a fan.

Fastigiate Upright, column-shaped e.g. some trees.

Fertilization The union of male and female cells within a flower which will result in the production of seed.

Fertilizer Concentrated plant food in liquid, powder or granular form (see page 40).

Forcing The act of speeding up the growth of plants, usually by applying heat.

Frame A small, shallow, glazed structure in which plants can be grown (see page 250).

Free lime Calcium that is available to plants from the soil, so called because calcium is often locked in insoluble minerals.

Friable A description of soil with the texture of breadcrumbs that can be easily broken up.

Fumigation A method of killing greenhouse pests or diseases by exposing to poisonous smoke.

Fungicide A substance used to kill fungal organisms that cause plant diseases.

Gall An abnormal plant growth, caused by pest or disease.

Gazebo An open type of garden pavilion with a good view.

Germination The first stage in the growth of a seed, when the first root and shoot emerge.

Grafting The system of propagation whereby the shoot of one plant is attached to the roots of another, usually with the aim of controlling vigour.

Group A term used to describe plants that are related to one another.

Hardening off Accustoming plants to lower temperatures than those in which they have been growing, by gradually giving them less heat and more ventilation.

Hardy Capable of being grown outdoors all year and withstanding frost. **Half-hardy** plants can be grown outdoors only when the weather is favourable; frosts will kill them.

Heel A portion of older wood attached to base of a heel cutting.

Heeling in The act of digging a trench and burying the roots of plants temporarily until they can be planted properly.

Herbaceous Non-woody plant that dies to soil level in winter.

Herbicide The posh name for weedkiller.

Humus A vague term applied to the residue of decayed organic matter. Good soil should be rich in humus.

Hybrid A plant that is the result of cross-fertilizing two very different parent plants, often indicated by an '✕' between first and second names.

Inorganic Any chemical compound not containing carbon and therefore not derived from anything living.

Insecticide A substance used to kill insects.

Insectivorous Plants that catch and feed on insects.

John Innes composts A range of seed-sowing and potting composts containing loam, peat, sand and fertilizers.

Lateral A sideshoot growing from the main stem.

Layering A means of propagation whereby a stem is wounded and buried in the soil where it will form roots. The rooted shoot can then be detached and grown separately from the parent.

Leaching The removal of nutrients from the soil by water draining through it.

Leader Main shoot of a branch.

Leaf mould Decayed leaves that are brown and crumbly and which make good soil enrichment.

Lichen Primitive plants that are a combination of fungus and algae. Found on old fruit trees, walls, rocks and roofs. An indicator of clean air.

Lime Usually calcium hydroxide. Used to lower acidity in soils.

Line A garden line is a length of stout twine used as a guide when taking out 'drills' for seeds, or edging lawns (see page 32).

Loam A mixture of clay, sand and humus, which is thought of as the perfect soil.

Maiden A tree (usually a fruit tree) in its first year after budding or grafting before it has any branches.

Manure Farmyard manure often consists of straw or bedding as well as excrement. Stack it for a few months before applying it to the soil (see page 38).

Don't forget the prime reason for having a garden is to rest and relax in. Mind you, I don't do it as often as I should!

Mist propagation A system of encouraging the rooting of cuttings in a propagating frame by automatically spraying them with a fine mist of water at intervals.

Monocarpic Description applied to a plant that dies after flowering.

Mulch A thick covering of material, often organic, applied to the surface of the soil with the aim of suppressing weeds and conserving moisture.

Naturalize To grow plants randomly spaced apart – the term is most frequently used in relation to bulbs being grown permanently in grass.

Nitrogen One of the three main plant foods (the other two being phosphates and potassium, or potash). Encourages leaf and shoot growth.

Node A joint on a stem from where a leaf grows.

Organic Any compound containing carbon. In gardening terms, a system of growing which eschews any chemicals or fertilizers that are not organically derived.

Parterre A level area where plants are grown in elaborate patterns in formally arranged flower beds.

Peat Dead vegetation in an arrested state of decay. Used in seed and potting composts to improve water-holding capacity and texture. Many gardeners are rightly concerned about the conservation of peat bogs and seek alternatives, such as coir and composted bark, not always with great success (see page 39).

Perennial A plant that lives for many years.

Phosphates Vital plant foods which encourage root development.

Photosynthesis The process whereby plants convert water and carbon dioxide into growth-promoting sugars, using the energy of sunlight through chlorophyll in leaves.

Pinching out Removing a leading shoot to encourage the growth of lower shoots and produce a bushier plant.

Piping A cutting of a garden pink or carnation which is simply pulled from the top of the growing shoot.

Pleaching The training out sideways of tree branches to form a flat screen.

Pollarding The act of cutting back severely the top growth of a tree.

Pollination The transference of pollen from the male part of the flower to the female.

Potash One of the three main plant foods, potash, or potassium, is vital for the production of flowers and fruit.

Potting The act of placing a plant in a pot or container. **Potting on** means that the plant is being transferred to a larger container than the one in which it is presently growing. **Re-potting** means that it is being knocked out of its pot, some of the old compost is removed and then the plant is replaced in that same container with fresh compost.

Pricking out or pricking off The transplanting of seedlings from the pot or tray in which they were sown to wider spacings in another tray or pot.

Propagation The art of reproducing plants by seed, cuttings, division, etc.

Pruning The removal of any part of a plant, usually with the intention of regulating growth.

Rhizome An underground stem found on plants such as the bearded iris.

Rootstock A root system on to which fruit trees, for instance, are grafted to control their vigour.

Rotation The practice of varying the position in which vegetable crops are grown each year to prevent the build-up of pests and diseases and to ensure that the best use is made of plant foods.

Runner Also known as a **stolon** (see opposite). A rooting stem produced at soil level on which young plants are formed – strawberries, for example.

Scion A shoot or bud taken from one plant and grafted on to the roots of another.

Scree A type of landscape found at the foot of a mountain and comprising a free-draining mix of finely broken rock. Scree beds are used to raise plants that demand good drainage.

Seed bed Finely cultivated earth in which seeds are sown.

Self-fertile A fruit tree capable of setting fruit with its own pollen.

Shrub A term used to describe a plant with many woody stems arising from ground level (see pages 82–123).

Single A term used to describe flowers with a normal number of petals, as opposed to a 'double' flower, which has more than the usual complement.

Soilless compost Compost that does not contain loam, but which relies on peat, coir or composted bark as its main ingredient.

Spit The depth of one spade blade. A term used in digging.

Sport A freak flower of different colour or shape which arises by chance on one stem of an otherwise normal plant.

Spur a) The long, protruding growth at the back of a flower such as an aquilegia; b) a fruit bud-bearing sideshoot on a fruit tree.

Standard A plant possessing a bushy head of branches at the top of a tall, single stem. A **half-standard** is the same but shorter.

Sterile A term used to describe a plant incapable of producing seed.

Stock See Rootstock.

Stolon Horizontal or trailing stem that produces roots and new shoots at its tip. See also Runner.

Stool The root system of a plant, used for propagation purposes on plants such as chrysanthemums.

Stopping Pinching out the tip of a plant, usually to make plants grow bushy. Also used to delay flowering.

Strain One particular race of plants raised from seed and probably unique to the seedsman who raised it.

Stratification A method of encouraging the germination of certain seeds by placing them in layers (usually with sand) in pots outdoors during the winter and allowing them to be frosted.

Strike To root a cutting of a plant.

Subsoil The layer of soil immediately below the topsoil. Usually lacking in nourishment, but influential in terms of drainage.

Sucker A shoot arising directly from the roots of a plant. In roses and other grafted plants it is removed because the sucker grows into a plant of inferior quality.

Systemic A type of insecticide or herbicide that enters the sap stream of a plant and, as a result, is more effective at doing its job.

Tap root A thick root, as found on dandelions, that goes straight down into the soil.

Tendril A thin, twining outgrowth produced by some plants that will attach to a support to enable them to climb.

Thinning Reducing the number of shoots on a plant or the number of seedlings in a row to improve the growth and quality of those that remain.

Tilth Crumbly soil texture.

Tip layering A similar method of propagation to layering but using the tip of a plant's stem.

Top dressing A layer of organic matter laid on the surface of the soil or the compost in a pot with the aim of improving the growth of a plant.

Top fruit Fruits that grow on trees, as opposed to bushes; for example, apples and pears.

Topiary The art of clipping shrubs and trees into elaborate shapes (see pages 124–7).

Transplant To move a plant from one place to another.

Tuber A thickened underground stem. The dahlia is an example of a root tuber, and the potato is an example of a stem tuber.

Tufa A type of limestone which arises from calcium deposits and which is sometimes used in making rock gardens.

Variegated Having leaves of two or more colours.

Variety A naturally occurring variation produced by a particular plant species.

Virus An organism that can produce diseases in plants in the same way as in humans. Very difficult to eradicate.

Weed A vigorous, invasive or self-seeding plant growing where it is not wanted.

Wilt The collapse of a plant due to restriction of the sap flow.

Winter wash An insecticidal or fungicidal spray that is applied to fruit trees in winter when they are leafless, to kill off overwintering pests and their eggs.

Vital tools

I've seen potting sheds so full of quaint implements that they look like the armoury at the Tower of London. I think I've probably got some myself, simply because I like old gardening tools and because in days of yore there were far more pieces of bespoke hardware in the garden than there are today.

If you are starting from scratch, set yourself up with a few really well-made implements but, at the same time, don't spurn those that have been handed down by your parents and grandparents. Provided they have been cared for over the years, old tools will be silky smooth of handle, sharp of blade and comfortable to use.

Whichever you plump for, remember that the average gardener needs only a handful of essential tools to do most jobs; there is no need to stock up on every minor variation that comes along, unless you happen to have a passion for hardware.

Dibber
A purpose-made tool for making holes in the ground to plant vegetable seedlings and onion sets, and for sowing large seeds such as broad beans. I find an old spade or fork handle works just as well. When pricking out smaller seedlings into trays, you can use the pointed end of a pencil.

Fork
Useful for digging, especially on stony soil, for pricking over compacted soil and moving bulky organic material. Used flat, like a carpet beater, it is great for breaking down rough clods. The smaller border fork, with a head measuring 23 × 14cm (9 × 5½in) instead of 30 × 19cm (12 × 7½in), is the most useful tool in the garden, especially in stainless steel. It can be used in a confined space and does not lift up too much soil at one go.

Garden line
Stout twine, fastened securely to two metal or wooden pegs, is necessary to mark out the line of a seed drill or of a row of plants in a kitchen garden. Make sure the twine is strong – it should not snap easily when pulled tight.

ABOVE: *There are various sorts of dibbers, many of them custom-built, but I often use a pencil when dibbing holes in compost for the insertion of cuttings. A broken spade or fork handle makes a good dibber for plants such as cabbages.*
LEFT: *At the end of the gardening season, clean and oil the blades of all tools and rub all wooden handles with a rag dipped in raw linseed oil. Surface mould might grow on the wood during the winter but will be easy to rub off come spring, and the wood will remain supple and strong as a result.*

Hoe

Hoes come in all shapes and sizes, but the original **Dutch hoe**, skimmed lightly over the surface of the soil, is still one of the best ways of ridding ground of shallow-rooted annual weeds. Don't try to dig with it. The aim is to sever the top growth of the weed from its roots, not to prise the whole plant from the ground. A **draw hoe** is useful for taking out seed drills when pulled along a taut line at an angle of 45 degrees so that the corner of the blade removes the soil. Used flat, it excavates a flat-bottomed drill for peas and also pulls back the soil after sowing.

Knife

Every gardener should have a proper knife (usually known as a budding knife) for taking cuttings and for cutting string. Don't choose one with a shiny, stainless-steel blade – it won't keep its edge for very long. Tempered steel is better and it should be sharpened regularly on a whetstone.

Loppers

Long-handled pruners which are useful for cutting stems too thick to be cut with secateurs.

Rake

The most over-used tool in the garden. It is certainly handy for levelling soil, but should be used sparingly or the surface of the soil will be broken down too finely so that it forms a crust in the first shower of rain. As a general rule, use the fork to break down soil and the rake only to level it. A **rubber-toothed rake** is the best tool for raking up leaves from lawns and gravel paths, though a **garden vacuum cleaner** makes this job even quicker. A **wire-toothed rake** is best for pulling dead grass or 'thatch' from the lawn, but an **electrically powered lawn raker** is gentler on the stomach muscles.

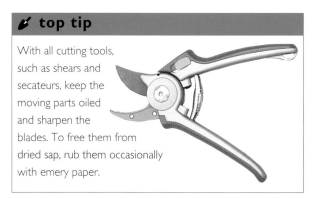

✎ top tip

With all cutting tools, such as shears and secateurs, keep the moving parts oiled and sharpen the blades. To free them from dried sap, rub them occasionally with emery paper.

Secateurs

Some secateurs look very flashy but do not cut cleanly. A scissor action is the most useful, as opposed to the anvil action, where the blade cuts the stem against a flat lower plate. Anvil secateurs can bruise stems if the blade is the slightest bit blunt, and dieback may result. As a general rule, do not use secateurs to cut stems thicker than your finger.

Shears

Where hedges are to be trimmed, shears are vital. Make sure they are not too heavy and that the cutting action is smooth. Cushioned handgrips will minimize the jolting action. If you have a lot of hedges, **powered electrical hedge trimmers** will do the job more quickly.

Spade

Essential for digging, for planting and for shovelling earth. It will also skim off surface weed growth prior to cultivation. The best old spades have comfortable, D-shaped, wooden handles; modern ones have handles of polypropylene. Whichever is the case, check that the shaft, especially where it meets the metal shank, is smooth and free of splinters or rough steel. Don't buy too large or heavy a spade in the belief that you will look more macho. You won't. You will just tire more easily. Sharpen the cutting edge with a file or on a grindstone from time to time to make soil penetration easier.

Trowel

Don't stint yourself when it comes to buying a trowel. Cheaper versions will bend when used on heavy soil, so look for strength, especially where the blade meets the handle. Stainless-steel trowels are especially easy to use, but check that the top of the handle sits comfortably in the palm of your hand. The trowel should be used vertically with a clawing action to take out a hole, not horizontally like a flour scoop. A **hand fork** is an optional extra, useful for cultivating soil between plants.

Wheelbarrow

Some form of transport is essential in every garden, though in small gardens a trug or a willow withy basket may be more manoeuvrable than a wheelbarrow. If you do buy a barrow, make sure that it is well balanced and runs smoothly. Oil the axle regularly and always position the load over the wheel to make it as light as possible.

Preparing the site

The seeds of annual weeds and the thick roots of perennial kinds both lie dormant for a time, then spring into life, throttling new plants and making lots of work. By clearing the ground properly before planting you can save a lot of weeding later.

Spraying

Even if you don't want to use chemicals regularly, the quickest and surest way of clearing a weedy site initially is with weedkiller. All you do is dilute it with water and apply using a sprayer or a watering can fitted with a perforated tube (called a 'dribble bar') instead of a rose. Keep a separate can or sprayer especially for weedkiller – however well you wash it out afterwards, the merest trace of weedkiller can harm plants. Contact weedkillers like paraquat 'scorch' weeds within a few days, but they kill only the green leafy parts, not the roots, so use them for annual weeds which don't re-grow. For perennial weeds use a different family of weedkillers, containing glyphosate. This is taken in through the leaves, but moves down through the plant and kills the roots as well. Treated weeds look perfectly normal for three weeks before they start wilting, and it takes six weeks before they are dead. Very strong clumps of old-established perennial weeds may re-grow, so wait a few weeks and re-treat any new shoots as soon as they appear. Both these types of weedkiller leave the ground quite safe to plant once the weeds are dead, but some products like sodium chlorate and path weedkillers stay in the soil for a long time. For safety's sake, avoid using them.

ABOVE: When digging up a perennial weed, ensure the entire root is removed. BELOW: Herbicides can be more effective if weeds are cut back first and the shoots that begin to grow are sprayed with it.

Burning

A friend's father always used a flame gun to clear ground before planting; it was a vicious brute that ran on paraffin. Nowadays you can get neat little gadgets that work off small gas canisters. They are lightweight and very easy to use. Some models have a small shield that keeps the flame confined to a very small area, so they can be used quite close to plants. They are fine for annual weeds, and a good way to dispose of dead weeds that have been killed by some other means like weedkiller, but are not very effective against perennials – burning just kills the tops, leaving the roots to re-grow.

Smothering

As an alternative to weedkillers, you can kill weeds by covering them with a layer of black plastic, old carpet or even newspaper. This works because keeping the leaves in the dark stops them making food from sunlight and the weed is eventually starved. This method needs plenty of time. Most perennial weeds will need to be kept covered for two years before they die off completely.

OVERGROWN GARDENS

♦ The best time to use weedkiller is in late spring and early summer, as this is when weed growth is young and most affected by weedkiller – once the plants are tough and woody, they are harder to kill.

♦ Before treating notoriously difficult weeds like horsetail and ground elder with weedkiller, beat the plants with a stick to bruise them. The weedkiller is taken in this way, instead of running off.

♦ Cut down areas of tall or tough, old weeds by hand or hire a powered rotary scythe, wait for the new growth to appear, then treat it with a weedkiller containing glyphosate.

♦ Cut large brambles, sycamore seedlings and elder bushes down close to the ground, and when new shoots appear paint them with brushwood killer.

♦ Cut unwanted trees down to a convenient height above the ground, then get a contractor to winch out the stump, roots and all. Where there isn't room for a winch, get a stump grinder in – this turns the lot to sawdust which is easily shovelled out. Fill the hole with fresh topsoil and it's ready to re-plant straight away.

Apply herbicides with a sprayer dedicated to their use. Always spray on a still, dry day.

DOS AND DON'TS FOR IMPROVING YOUR SOIL

✔ Do keep adding organic matter to sandy, chalky, flinty or gravelly soils as they are naturally hungry and added organic matter decomposes to nothing quickly.

✗ Don't add lime to break up clay soil unless you have carried out a soil test first; some clay soil is naturally limy and adding more won't help.

✔ Do save everything that will rot down to put on the compost heap. It is the ideal form of recycling and saves space in landfill sites.

✗ Don't spend a fortune on clay cures. Instead spread 5cm (2in) of gritty sand or fine shingle over the surface and fork it in; or spread grit, then spread a thick organic mulch on top and let the worms mix it in for you.

Eradicating weeds

Digging up some kinds of weeds, like the annual ones, is a good way of getting rid of them (see page 50). But with weeds that spread by underground rhizomes, such as couch grass and bindweed, digging is the worst thing you can do as it actually propagates them. (Rotavating is even more effective at this.) It chops up the roots and every tiny fragment you leave behind acts as a root cutting and grows into a new plant. One thing weeds like this cannot stand is being continually cut down. Think about it, you never see upright-growing weeds in your lawn – they can't take being trimmed to a neat couple of centimetres every Sunday afternoon. So, if you have a big area of problem weeds, cut them back hard, then level and sow the area with grass seed, feed it to make the weeds grow fast and mow often – whether the grass needs it or not – to give them a regular haircut. This is one of the best ways of shifting weeds like horsetail and ground elder that are not easy to get rid of even with weedkiller. But again it takes time – allow about two years.

Spades and other digging tools

However little digging you intend doing, you will need a spade occasionally, even if it is just to make holes for planting trees and shrubs. I like an old-fashioned spade with a T- or D-shaped, wooden handle, though for preparing hard, chalky soil full of flints like I have in my garden, a fork is about the only implement you can lever in between the lumps. You might like to try the continental-style, long-handled spade, which a lot of people claim makes the job much easier. There is also a sort of Third World digging hoe you can use, which is rather like a chop hoe but much bigger and heavier and used a bit like a pickaxe. The idea is that the weight of the head does a lot of the work. It's a very different action from digging, but makes a pretty good job of breaking up the ground.

Rotary cultivation

The idea of just pushing a piece of powerful machinery over the soil, leaving a perfect tilth in its wake, is a very attractive one. Rotary cultivators certainly take a lot of hard work out of soil preparation. Their rotating blades bite into the soil and churn it up to the depth of the blades, which is usually about a spade's depth. However, they have a few drawbacks too. If you have any couch grass or bindweed roots in the soil, a rotavator will chop them into little bits which all take root, so you are actually propagating the weed. If you are on a heavy clay soil, the rotavator blades smear the soil, leaving a hard pan just below the cultivated layer that roots cannot get through. To be most effective, use a big, powerful rotavator and press down hard on the handles so the blades bite down deep, and use it only when the soil is nicely moist. If it's too wet, the machine will bog itself down, and if too dry, it will just bounce along over the top – as it does on stony ground too – without doing much good. My tip is to hire a garden contractor with a big, powerful rotavator, who will know how to use it properly.

Problem soil

There are some soils where you should not even try to dig deeply. If the ground is rocky with lots of

Rotary cultivators are best used on weed-free ground so that they do not chop up and propagate perennial weed roots. You may need to traverse the patch of ground several times to achieve an adequate depth: rotavating to at least 23cm (9in) is essential to allow plant roots to penetrate the soil.

DIGGING OVER VACANT GROUND

Regular digging of cultivated soil is not necessary except on the vegetable plot, where it is useful for working in supplies of organic matter.

♦ On the vegetable patch, or where a new bed or border is to be made, soil needs cultivating to a reasonable depth. Push in the spade, lift up the earth and turn it over, throwing it forward at the same time to create a trench.

♦ Remove thick-rooted perennial weeds, and then spread well-rotted manure, mushroom compost or good garden compost over the sloping side of the freshly turned earth to enrich it.

♦ Dig up the next strip of soil, turning it over and throwing it forward so that it buries the organic enrichment. Continue in this fashion. This is far easier than double digging and, provided the earth is not heavily compacted, suits most plants.

My method of cheat's digging involves throwing forward the soil from a trench, laying well-rotted manure in the bottom, then throwing another strip of soil forward before repeating the process. It avoids moving lots of soil from the first trench to fill in the last.

chalk, pebbles or flints, digging is virtually impossible and not much use. Here it is much better to loosen the topsoil with a fork, and pile as much well-rotted organic matter as you can on top. Make raised beds for growing vegetables and choose ornamental plants which can cope with such conditions. On clay soils you often find that there is a very nasty layer of solid, blue or yellow gunge not too far below the soil's surface. This is the subsoil, and it is very infertile. Digging just brings it up to the surface and mixes it with what is probably not bad topsoil. If this does happen, nothing much will grow for a year or more. Here again, shallow cultivation is the answer – you can fork organic matter into the top spade's depth of soil, but don't go any deeper.

No-dig technique

This is a brilliant idea for people who hate digging, or can't manage it. You just put your organic matter on top of the soil and let the worms do your digging for you. Something seemingly so simple, however, does take a bit of setting up. You do need to dig the soil over reasonably well once, as uncultivated soil is usually a bit compacted. From then on, all you do is mulch. Spread organic matter to a depth of 10cm (4in) over the soil in spring. If you have sandy or stony soil, do this in spring and autumn. Even if you don't have many worms to start with, the numbers will increase as you keep adding organic matter. They'll mix the organic matter with the soil; you'll also do a bit of it yourself each time you do a spot of hoeing.

Soil additives

The best plants are grown in gardens where the soil is not ignored, but regularly improved. Plants are healthier and live longer as a result of additional supplies of compost, manure and fertilizers. Get the soil in good heart before you plant, and your plants will grow faster and establish more quickly.

There are two basic types of soil additives: those that are bulky and which make a difference to the feel and structure of the soil when they are added to it, and those that are in powder, liquid or granular form and which are more concentrated in terms of the nutrients they contain. The bulky types are usually known as soil conditioners and the concentrated plant foods as fertilizers.

All soils benefit from the addition of bulky organic matter. Heavy clay soils will be made less sticky because the organic matter holds their clinging particles further apart and so allows water to escape more easily. As a result, drainage is improved and the soil becomes easier to cultivate.

On sandy soils, where drainage is rapid and moisture retention is poor, organic matter acts as a binding agent, sticking the particles together and as a sponge helping the soil to hold on to water.

Chalky soils tend to be thin and poor, and the organic matter here gives them more body and helps them hold on to plant nutrients.

Even loamy soils need helpings of organic enrichment to keep them 'in good heart'.

You could ask why it is necessary to enrich soil with manure, compost and fertilizer when, in the wild, plants seem to thrive without it. The answer is a simple one: in nature nobody tidies up. Fallen leaves are allowed to rot down and provide the plants with nourishment, thanks to the activity of soil bacteria. Because of the plenitude of organic matter, these bacteria are present in abundance. In addition, the same plants grow in the same spot indefinitely, usually at a comfortably wide spacing,

ABOVE: Organic fertilizers such as pelleted poultry manure encourage bacterial activity in soil – something that inorganic fertilizers cannot do.

and nobody complains if they don't flower profusely or crop heavily. The plants are also native to this country and therefore accustomed to growing in the conditions available.

In a garden, where tidying up removes much of the potential soil enrichment, plants from all over the world are grown cheek by jowl, competing ferociously for water and nourishment. 'Man-made' varieties have been bred to flower over a long period and, in the case of vegetables, to produce a heavy crop. They can do this only if we make sure their roots can grow in earth which provides them with sufficient nourishment.

Farmyard manure

A term used to cover all kinds of animal manure. Stable manure is the most common and is available in town as well as country. This mixture of straw and dung needs to be well rotted before it is dug into the soil. Stack fresh manure for three to six months before digging it in. The reason for this is that fresh manure needs frantic bacterial activity in the soil to rot it down into a form that can be absorbed by plants. Soil bacteria feed on nitrogen, a valuable plant food that is needed to promote growth. If the manure is fresh, the bacteria will use up supplies of nitrogen, making them unavailable for plants, which then become starved.

Mushroom compost

Well-rotted compost in which mushrooms have been grown contains lumps of chalk, so is best not used on chalky soils because it will only make them more alkaline. On the other hand, it is a valuable soil conditioner on acid soils, but avoid using it where lime haters, such as rhododendrons, azaleas, camellias and heathers, are to be grown.

GARDEN COMPOST

Make your own compost: not only is it cheap, it will also use waste products such as lawn clippings, annual weeds, dead flower heads, eggshells and tea leaves. (Do not use food waste or you could attract rodents.)

♦ Make a bin at least 1.25m (4ft) square out of stout posts and wire netting in an out-of-the-way corner of the garden. The front should be removable. Mix up the ingredients as you put them in and keep the heap firm by trampling on it.

♦ Throw a piece of sacking or old carpet on the top to prevent the heap from drying out, and water the heap in dry weather. Powdered compost 'accelerators' are optional, not vital.

♦ The compost will be brown and crumbly in three to six months, depending on the time of year.

A series of compost bins in a corner of the garden ensures that compost is always available – with one heap ready to empty, another rotting down and a third being filled.

Spent hops
A by-product of the brewing industry. Although smelly, this is a good soil conditioner and one which is easy to handle. You might have to live with an 'aromatic' garden for a few days afterwards.

Leaf mould
Autumn leaves can be rotted down in a wire-netting enclosure of their own and then used as soil enrichment. Sweep them up while they are damp, pile them into the wire-netting enclosure and, like compost, keep them firm and moist. In a year's time they will have turned into crumbly leaf mould.

Composted bark
A by-product of the forestry industry, this is usually pine bark which has been pulverized and composted.

Domestic waste
Many local authorities and some water companies are now producing their own soil enrichment, which is based on domestic waste (both household and sewage) and composted straw. It is clean, recycled and perfectly safe to use.

Proprietary soil conditioners
These are usually made from animal manures and are often more concentrated in nutrients, so applied more sparingly. This means that they are not as valuable in improving soil texture and structure simply because their application rates are lower.

Peat
Current concern about our disappearing peat bogs has meant that peat is now frowned upon as a soil conditioner. From the gardener's point of view, as well as the conservationist's, this is a good thing. All the other soil conditioners mentioned here contain a certain amount of plant food, as well as being bulky and therefore improving the soil structure. Peat

contains no food at all – its only value is in its structure. Because of this, its greatest value is as an ingredient of seed and potting composts as a soil conditioner.

Application rates

Generally speaking, one or two bucketfuls of organic matter can be dug or forked into 1 square metre (1 square yard) of soil. Use your discretion – if your ground looks very hungry, go for the heavier application rate. Your plants will grow better as a result. Dig the enrichment into newly cultivated ground during the autumn and winter months or at planting time, or lay it on the surface of the soil between established plants as an 8-cm (3-in) thick mulch in spring when the soil is moist. It will help keep down weeds and seal in moisture.

Fertilizers

Just like us, plants need a balanced diet. They obtain this in part from soil that has been enriched with bulky manures, but such manures do not contain large quantities of food – their value lies more in their soil-conditioning properties. For this reason, fertilizers are used to provide plants with nutrients in concentrated form.

General fertilizers

Plants have a need for three main foods – nitrogen (N), phosphates (P) and potassium (K). I always think of these as the starter, the main course and the pudding. Phosphates are the starter – they promote root growth. Nitrogen is the main course – it fuels the development of leaves and shoots, making the plant grow well and stay green. Potassium, or potash, is the pudding – it encourages flower and fruit development when the other two foods have done their bit. Fertilizers described as general or compound have all three foods or nutrients in balanced quantity. As well as these three main foods, there are others described as trace elements, which are the plant's equivalent of vitamins. Things such as magnesium, boron and molybdenum are all present, to a variable degree, in well-fed soil and in general fertilizers.

Organic or inorganic?

Organic fertilizers are derived from carbon, so at some time have been living material. Inorganic fertilizers are chemically derived. Both can provide plants with the nutrients they need to grow. The difference is that organic fertilizers must be broken down by soil bacteria before they are in a form that can be utilized by plants; inorganic fertilizers can be absorbed as soon as they are dissolved in water. Inorganic fertilizers are thus usually quicker-acting, but organic fertilizers improve bacterial activity in the soil and keep it healthy (see pages 236–7). Use organic fertilizers to keep soil fertile and inorganic fertilizers to give plants a quick boost.

Growmore is an inorganic general fertilizer; pelleted poultry manure is an organic general fertilizer. Application rates for all proprietary fertilizers will be printed clearly on the container.

Sequestered iron

Plants that dislike alkaline or chalky soils – rhododendrons and camellias, for instance – usually do so because they find it difficult to extract iron. This results in a yellowing of the foliage. Sequestered iron is a plant tonic which contains iron and trace elements in a form that they can assimilate rapidly, so it is a useful tonic for lime-hating pot plants being grown in hard-water areas. If you have yellowing lime haters growing in the garden, dig them up and plant them in containers of lime-free (ericaceous) compost.

Liquid feeds

Proprietary liquid feeds, which are diluted in water before being applied to plants, go into action faster than feeds in powder or granular form but they are not so long-lasting. Apply them to container-grown plants once a fortnight in spring and summer.

Foliar feeds

The fastest-acting plant foods are foliar feeds that are diluted in water and sprayed on to the leaves, preferably on a dull day so that they do not evaporate too quickly.

When to feed

As a general rule, garden plants are fed once in spring and once in summer, while they are growing. In winter they do not need feeding, but sulphate of ammonia (high in nitrogen) can be sprinkled around fruit trees to give them an early boost in late winter. Nitrogen is the food most readily leached out of soil by water and this will replace losses due to winter rains. All plants will enjoy a sprinkling of general fertilizer in early spring to give them a good start. Do this if you do nothing else.

ACID OR ALKALINE SOIL?

Knowing the relative acidity or alkalinity of your soil can instantly save you money at the garden centre simply by helping you to avoid buying those plants that will not like your soil.

♦ Soil acidity is governed by the amount of free lime in the soil and is measured on the pH scale which runs from 0 to 14. In the British Isles most soils fall within the pH range of 4.0 to 8.0. Neutral soil is 7.0; soils with a pH below this are said to be acid, while those above are described as alkaline. The ideal soil (which will grow most plants) is slightly acid, with a pH of between 6.0 and 6.5.

♦ Simple soil-testing kits, widely available, will help you to discover the pH of the soil in your own garden. If it is alkaline, you will be unable to grow lime haters, such as rhododendrons and many heathers, except in containers of lime-free compost (see also page 275).

♦ Very acid soil, with a pH below 5.0, will not suit some plants, especially vegetables, so the pH is often raised on the vegetable plot by dusting it with garden lime each winter. The lime should not be applied at the same time as bulky manures with which it will react adversely.

♦ Whatever your existing soil, I would always recommend growing plants that are happy in it rather than trying to change it to suit those that are not. Life is too short to make gardening a constant struggle.

Use a wheeled distributor to apply fertilizer to lawns. It ensures that the correct amount of granules are delivered to each square metre or yard, it avoids uneven application which can lead to scorching, and it also makes the stuff go further, so saving you money.

♦ To boost all flowering plants (not just roses) use a proprietary rose fertilizer, which has added magnesium. It encourages lustrous foliage, especially on soils that are slightly alkaline.

♦ To get trees and shrubs off to a flying start you could use a couple of handfuls of bonemeal around the planting holes. However, most of the phosphates it contains are locked up by the soil and made inaccessible to plants, so I prefer to rely on well-rotted compost or manure to coax out new roots.

♦ To boost plants and lawns that refuse to grow lustily use a light sprinkling of sulphate of ammonia, an inorganic fertilizer high in nitrogen, at the rate of half a clenched fistful to the square metre (square yard). Use in spring and summer. On lawns water it in if no rain is forthcoming within a few hours to prevent scorching.

♦ To promote flower and fruit production sulphate of potash can be used at the rate of a clenched fistful to the square metre (square yard).

Plant pests and problems

Vegetarian insects, arthropods and molluscs can ruin plants in all sorts of ways and are the bane of the gardener's life. Sometimes you need to take urgent action, yet at other times you don't need to bother doing anything at all. This is why it pays to know your enemy.

Identifying absent pests

Plant pests work in lots of different ways. Very often you will never spot what is causing the damage. Many pests are at their most active at night, so unless you venture out with a torch, all you will normally see is the results of their work. In some cases this is enough to identify the culprit and take the necessary action. If leaves have been 'rasped', leaving a skeleton of ribs, with perhaps a few slime trails, you can safely blame it on snails. Nowadays they are

dab hands at climbing – they will even shin up trees and walls, often going to an amazing height to reach something tasty. Brassica seedlings with lacy holes in the leaves have almost certainly been attacked by flea beetle. Rhododendron leaves with scallop-shaped bites out of the edges of the leaves will have been nibbled by vine weevil. If vine weevil adults are around, look out for the larvae that may be attacking susceptible plants, too (see page 44).

Plants with particular pest problems

Some plants attract particular pests. Tomatoes and fuchsias are martyrs to whitefly; cacti are often victims of mealy bug; orchids and citrus trees, in common with many conservatory shrubs, suffer from scale insects. There are also lily beetles, cabbage white caterpillars, and carrot root fly. At least if you know what to expect, you know what to do about it. Alternatively, you might decide not to grow the sort of plants that are susceptible to problems. If you don't grow fuchsias in your greenhouse, for instance, you are likely to keep the rest of the plants relatively clear of whitefly.

Tackling pests

You don't always need to know precisely which creature is responsible for causing damage, as most chemical sprays eradicate most common pests. If aphids are the problem, you can get specific aphicides that kill only aphids and don't harm

ABOVE: *Carrot fly larvae bore into the roots, disfiguring the crop and preventing roots from being stored. Avoid attack by not thinning the crop and releasing the fragrance which attracts the egg-laying flies.* LEFT: *Rose rust is a fungal disease that can be controlled with a fungicidal spray, but act early to prevent serious attacks.*

beneficial insects, so use these wherever possible. Some pests, however, are not easy to get rid of. Large caterpillars and beetles such as the lily beetle are resilient creatures that take so long to absorb a lethal dose of pesticide that, since they continue feeding on your plants in the meantime, it is better to pick them off by hand.

Don't be in too much of a hurry to reach for the pesticide: you do not always need to do anything about pests. If an infestation is small, or likely to disappear on its own, there is no need to do anything at all. Aphids on roses in spring are a good example – there are plenty of baby bluetits and hungry adult birds that should take care of this problem for you. A low level of insect population is actually a good thing in a garden, as it ensures there is always a thriving population of predators ready to increase at a moment's notice if pests start to get out of hand. That is what you call natural balance, and it is well worth having. Keep the pesticide for serious outbreaks of an infestation that really threaten a plant and then use it selectively – there is no need to smother the whole garden with it; just treat the affected plants.

DOS AND DON'TS OF PESTICIDES

✔ Do read, understand and follow the maker's directions. Using the wrong dilution rate or spraying it on to a plant the makers say is sensitive to that product will harm or kill the plant.

✘ Don't spray plants in strong sunlight, if the compost is dry, or if they are wilting or otherwise looking very poorly, as you can scorch them – which causes more trouble than the pest in the first place.

✔ Do take care of beneficial insects like bees, by not spraying open flowers. It is safest to spray plants at dusk when bees have finished work for the day.

✘ Don't mix up large quantities of spray and then save it to use over the next few weeks – it loses its strength once it is made up. If you do use a concentrated product, make it up fresh each time or better still buy ready-to-use sprays, which will save buying a separate sprayer.

✔ Do store pesticides somewhere cool, dark and locked up so that children and pets cannot get hold of them accidentally. Don't leave them in the greenhouse, as extremes of heat and cold as well as strong sunlight make them less effective.

Under the soil

Of all gardening problems, soil pests are the ones you can do least about. Often, you only discover them when it is too late. Plants can look fine one day but collapse the next, and usually you cannot do anything to save them since they have, by then, lost their roots. There are a few early warning signs to look out for and it helps to know your enemy.

Vine weevil larvae

This insect is at the top of most gardeners' hate list. The fat, white, C-shaped grubs lurk under the soil's surface or in pots and eat the roots of plants, which show no symptoms until they suddenly collapse. The vine weevil's favourite plants are cyclamen and primulas, but all sorts of things can be affected. If you spot scallop-shaped notches bitten out of the edges of rhododendrons and other evergreens in the garden, you'll know the adults are about – they are greyish beetles about 1cm (½in) long with elongated snouts at the front end. They are worth squashing whenever you see them. Available on the market now are composts which contain Intercept, a pesticide that will control vine weevils in containers for up to a year. There is also a biological method of control which utilizes a type of nematode that you buy as dry powder, dilute with water and apply to the borders outdoors or in the greenhouse, and to individual pots in late spring and early autumn. It is not cheap, but it is very effective and well worth it if this pernicious pest is a constant problem.

Wireworms, leatherjackets

These unpleasant-looking, tubular grubs are the larvae of click beetle and crane-fly respectively; wireworms are slender and reddish brown, and leatherjackets are fat, soft and a semi-translucent grey-brown. They feed on the roots of vegetables; wireworms prefer root crops, while leatherjackets prefer brassicas. Both are common pests on ground that has been turned over from grass. Use a soil insecticide when digging up old grassland, and use it again before sowing or planting.

Carrot and cabbage root fly

Small, maggoty creatures that are the larvae of tiny flies which are attracted to the growing crops by scent – they often arrive after transplanting

Vine weevil larvae: among the most destructive pests in the garden.

cabbages or thinning carrots. Cabbage root fly tunnels into the base of the stems and roots and can make the plants stunted, or cause them to wilt or collapse completely. Carrot fly tunnels into the roots, making them unpleasant to eat. Use soil insecticide when sowing or after thinning or transplanting as a precaution, or cover the plants with very fine, fly-proof crop-protection mesh to keep the adult flies out. A few varieties of carrot have some natural resistance, such as 'Fly Away' and 'Sytan'.

Fungus gnats (sciarid flies)

These are tiny maggots that you sometimes find living in the compost around pot plants or in containers outdoors. They also inhabit compost heaps, where they don't do any harm. The female flies find peat-based compost specially attractive for laying their eggs in, as it is so much softer and damper than soil. The larvae feed on young roots, but rarely cause much damage unless there is a bad infestation – watering the pots with spray-strength insecticide usually does the trick. Alternatively grow plants in soil-based compost or top dress with grit to deter the adults from egg laying.

OTHER SOIL PESTS

♦ **Ants** These don't harm plants directly, but often undermine the roots of those grown in pots or containers when they excavate nests, and also build up sandy mounds of soil in lawns in summer. Nests are evacuated in late summer after the winged ants fly away. If you can't wait until then, use proprietary ant killer near the nest.

♦ **Keeled slugs** Underground species that ruins potatoes by tunnelling into them and eating out big holes. Common in damp, heavy soil and especially where a lot of organic matter has recently been added to the soil. They are not affected by normal slug pellets as they rarely come to the surface. Use a liquid slug killer or the biological slug remedy which is a different type of nematode from that used against vine weevil.

♦ **Earthworms in lawns** Not harmful but annoying on very highly cultivated, fine lawns due to the wormcasts they make. Don't try to kill them as worms provide valuable surface drainage. Only a few species make casts, and then only at certain times of year, mainly in spring, so bear with them and sweep up dry casts on fine mornings before mowing.

♦ **Moles** All sorts of remedies have been tried and those that make funny noises underground are as good as any. You can buy a sonic device specifically for this purpose which works well for a limited distance, so move it regularly. Some people swear by burying musical birthday cards or transistor radios tuned in to a noisy, all-night pop channel, sealed inside a plastic bag and buried down their runs.

♦ **Millipedes** Black, tubular, multi-segmented creatures with zillions of legs. They feed on plants, but, before you destroy them, check your identification because centipedes, which look similar, are beneficial predators. Centipedes are flatter and chestnut-coloured with fewer and more widely spaced legs. Centipedes run fast, whereas millipedes tend to coil up like a watch spring when disturbed. Both creatures run around in loose litter, so maintain hygiene and cultivate the soil regularly.

Moles can ruin a lawn and wreak havoc in borders, but are especially hard to eradicate if your garden is next to farmland.

Diseases

Plant diseases are caused by microscopic fungi, bacteria or viruses that float around in the air or are carried by insects and develop wherever they find suitable conditions. They are difficult to guard against except by making sure plants are healthy when you buy them, and by keeping them in top condition so they can resist attack. Treat plants at the first sign of any symptoms to avoid a serious outbreak.

Grey mould

Grey mould, also known as botrytis, is responsible for the fluffy, grey, fungal patches that you find on flowers or leaves in damp weather, and on greenhouse plants when conditions have been cool and humid. It can also attack after something else has left an open wound. The same organism can

Botrytis, or grey mould, can affect tomato plants. Guard against attack by ensuring adequate ventilation at all times.

take on different forms in other circumstances. On tomato plants, botrytis causes grey, fluff-filled, horizontal gashes on the stem and also the tiny, round, yellow rings on the fruit known as ghost spot. On peonies, it causes brown spots on the leaves and results in tiny, mummified, black buds which never open into flowers. Remove affected leaves or flowers at the first sign of attack, or spray plants thoroughly with a suitable fungicide.

Powdery mildew

A different type of fungal disease, powdery mildew looks just as though someone has scattered talcum powder over the upper surface of the leaves. Some plants are particularly prone, such as roses and cucumbers, but all sorts of garden plants and weeds are susceptible if they are dry at the roots and the air is warm and humid by day – you commonly see it in late summer, when the nights start getting cooler. Keep plants well watered as a precaution and mulch them well in spring to help keep the soil round them moist. In the case of roses, grow disease-resistant varieties with thick, leathery leaves. The only solution in a bad case is to spray with a suitable fungicide.

Rust

There is no mistaking this disease for anything else; bright rusty orange-coloured spots and streaks on the foliage are the tell-tale signs. Suitable fungicides are available for rust on roses, but other susceptible plants like leeks, pelargoniums, hollyhocks and mint have to take their chance. Cut off affected foliage of perennial plants and burn it, and if the plant continues to get attacked it is best removed and burnt to avoid the trouble spreading. In the case of leeks you can still eat the crop since the outer leaves are thrown away anyway, but don't put them on the compost heap. Fortunately most rusts are specific to one kind of plant, so don't worry about rose rust, for instance, affecting anything else. It won't.

Viruses

Viruses are responsible for the yellow mottles, speckles and streaks you sometimes see on plants. They are often spread between plants by aphids, but you can also spread them on your knife when taking cuttings. There is no treatment for virus diseases – fungicides have no effect on them – and it is advisable to destroy affected plants to make sure they cannot spread.

HONEY FUNGUS

The fruiting bodies of honey fungus, Armillaria mellea.

♦ A series of hot, dry summers has placed trees under stress, which is probably responsible for the big outbreaks of honey fungus. The disease often starts in a dead stump. It sends out black fungal strands, which can infect live trees and cause sudden death, so it is a good idea to not to leave fallen logs or old stumps in the garden. (You can hire a machine that will grind old stumps complete with the biggest roots, leaving a pile of sawdust to shovel away.)

♦ To diagnose affected trees, peel away a section of bark near the base where you may see black boot-lace strands, or a web of white fungal mycelium. Golden-capped toadstools around the tree may not necessarily be honey fungus.

♦ A few plants seem to be fairly resistant to honey fungus and you should grow these in a garden where the disease is widespread. Plant new plants inside a protected area 45cm (1 1/2ft) wide and 60cm (2ft) deep, made from an old-potting compost bag with both ends out. Sink this into the ground and fill it with soil that has not been infected with honey fungus, and make sure the bag extends about 5cm (2in) above the surface of the ground.

Powdery mildew on the leaves of a tuberous begonia, encouraged by a damp atmosphere.

DOS AND DON'TS OF DISEASE CONTROL

✔ Do pick off yellow, brown or damaged leaves and dead flowers to prevent fungal infection taking hold.

✘ Don't spray with fungicide in the evening when plants will stay wet overnight – spray early in the morning on a dry day, but avoid bright sunlight.

✔ Do clean your knife when taking cuttings, by wiping it with methylated spirit to prevent virus and other diseases being spread between plants.

✘ Don't leave badly diseased plants with healthy plants or the trouble will spread. Burn plants that are badly affected with a virus or other disease.

✔ Do grow disease-resistant roses to minimize trouble with blackspot. If you have to spray, you will need to do so every two weeks for most of the growing season to keep plants protected.

✘ Don't bother buying lots of different products where one will do. Special products are available for spraying roses against blackspot, mildew and rust, which often include a greenfly killer too, so you can tackle three or four different problems with one spray. A general-purpose systemic fungicide will deal with most common treatable diseases on other plants.

Disorders

Not all plant problems are caused by pests or diseases. Often it is something as simple as incorrect watering or feeding, or physical damage caused by wind, late frost or other natural conditions. The easiest way to diagnose this type of trouble is by knowing the history of the plant, where it is growing and what the weather has been like. This will help you prevent it happening again, and it is comforting to know that it is not always your fault!

Over- or under-watering

Incorrect watering is probably the main cause of pot plant problems. The trouble is, both over- and under-watering lead to similar symptoms. Plants wilt if they are too dry and also if they are regularly kept too wet so that all the tiny root hairs have rotted away, making it impossible for plants to take up water. Both conditions can cause leaves to turn yellow or brown, or fall off. The solution is to check pot plants every few days, and containers outdoors every day in summer, and water them if the soil feels dry.

Over- or under-feeding

The best way to feed plants is little and often. Large doses of feed all at once can scorch the roots, while lack of feed can cause various sorts of nutritional problems that affect leaf colour, plant vigour, and the ability to flower or fruit. It is very unusual for garden plants to suffer from a shortage of one single nutrient; usually they are short of several at once. The best remedy is to apply a general feed containing trace elements. Foliar feeding with liquid seaweed extract is a good way to replace lost trace elements quickly. In containers, plants need to be fed with liquid feed, or soluble feed diluted in water, as solid fertilizer can scorch. If you find it impractical to feed little and often, opt for a slow-release feed instead. This is mixed into the compost and releases nutrients whenever the compost is moist. In the garden, plants need feeding at the start of the growing season with a general feed, but it is worth topping up heavy feeders like roses, clematis and vegetables every month or six weeks from then until mid-summer with a good general feed such as Growmore. Apply sulphate of potash at 25g (1oz) per square metre (yard) all around spring-flowering shrubs in late summer to encourage them to bloom better.

Strong winds can result in uneven growths of trees and shrubs.

Late frosts

Late frosts affect plants most severely if they are in a situation facing east, since the early morning sun hits flowers or buds while they are still frozen, making them thaw fast, which ruptures the cells and kills the flower. Fruit trees are especially badly affected, and growers will sometimes spray water from a hose over frozen flowers to make them thaw slowly to prevent damage. In a late spring all sorts of normally hardy plants can suffer from frost damage. What happens is that new foliage is hit by frost shortly after it has started to expand and, being very soft and fragile, the leaves are malformed with dead rims or corrugations. Time is the only solution. Eventually new, unaffected growth will appear. Prune off the dead tips of frost-damaged stems, cutting back to live wood just above healthy new shoots.

Wind

Wind scorches plants by making them lose water through their leaves faster than it can be replaced through the roots from the soil. If the roots are in dry soil, the effect of wind scorch will be worse. Wind-burnt plants may have shiny or scorched looking marks, a grazed or bruised appearance, or they may go brown. Plants with thin or fragile leaves or which are naturally woodland species, like *Acer palmatum* cultivars, are the most affected by wind and must be grown in a sheltered spot to do well. Damaged leaves are replaced with normal. healthy-looking ones later, but if wind is a constant problem it is better to move plants to a more sheltered situation or plant other tougher plants around them for protection. See also pages 278–9.

CAUSES OF SOME OTHER PLANT PROBLEMS

♦ **Salt** Put on the roads in winter, salt may be splashed on to front garden plants, making the leaves, especially of evergreens which are in leaf at the time, turn black or black-spotted. Wash plants off with plenty of plain water if you suspect this has happened.

♦ **Weedkiller damage** Tightly twisted, curly or thread-like leaves that suddenly appear on otherwise healthy plants may be due to hormone weedkiller damage (the sort used on lawns); other types of weedkiller will cause leaves to turn brown or spotty. Avoid spraying any weedkiller in breezy weather as spray can carry a long way. If it does happen, wash it off with lots of water, and keep a separate watering can for applying weedkiller to avoid contamination.

♦ **Sun scorch** Shade-loving plants grown in too much sun can turn brown due to scorching. If you find perfect, brown circles of various sizes on leaves of plants growing under glass, it will be caused by sun being magnified by droplets of water on the leaves, so don't spray when the sun is on plants.

♦ **Spray damage** Some products are not suitable for use on plants known to be sensitive to them, and using the wrong product can make leaves go brown or spotted where the chemical has landed; wash off with lots of water if you realize the mistake in time, or remove affected leaves and hope for the best. Always read the instructions carefully when using any chemical product.

♦ **Non-flowering plants** Wisteria, magnolia, tulip tree, davidia and some camellias and other trees or shrubs may not flower for several years after you buy them. This is because they need time to mature, but most should flower within seven to 10 years of planting. Feeding with potash in late summer as they approach this age may help. In the case of wisteria, correct pruning is vital to develop the short spurs arising from the main framework of branches, which carry the flowers. Faulty pruning can also stop plants flowering: a plant can't flower if the shoots that should bloom are removed. This is a common problem in the case of hydrangeas and many large shrubs that are cut back hard to reduce their size.

Frost in winter has a cleansing and often decorative effect; it is in late spring that it can be most damaging.

Weed control

People always tell you weeds are only wildflowers growing in the wrong place. All I can say is there are some pretty notorious wildflowers whose main goal in life is to invade the garden and swamp everything. It is a constant battle, but if you want to win the war, you have to understand the enemy.

Annual weeds

These are the harmless end of the weed spectrum. They include things like groundsel, shepherd's purse, chickweed and fat hen that spread themselves around by seed. They grow, flower, set seed and die all in the same season and are the easiest weeds to control, as once you pull them up or hoe them out they do not re-grow. Provided you don't wait until they have set seed, you can put them on the compost heap quite safely. Alternatively spray annual weeds with a contact weedkiller containing paraquat, which acts like chemical hoeing, but take care not to get it on any nearby plants.

Perennial weeds

These are nettles, thistles, docks and suchlike. This group behaves rather like herbaceous perennials. The tops die down each autumn, leaving dormant roots underground from which a new crown emerges next spring. If you catch them young enough, they are not too bad to deal with. You can just dig them up and that is probably the last you will see of them. However, a big, old clump can be harder to shift, as it will often start spreading out sideways too, so you cannot be sure of getting the lot out. And when perennial weeds grow up through the middle of cultivated plants (which they have a great knack of doing), they are almost impossible to remove unless you dig up the plant and carefully separate out the good and bad roots.

Problem weeds

Some perennial weeds are not just a nuisance, but more of an epidemic in the offing. These are the stranglers and fast spreaders, like bindweed, horsetail, ground elder and couch grass. They are notorious for their thick, white, underground roots which grow to great depths, making it impossible to dig them out. Spot treating with a glyphosate based weedkiller or hoeing thoroughly every time new shoots appear above ground will get rid of them in time.

Eradication by hand

Although it sounds very simple, there is absolutely nothing you cannot kill in time if you keep hoeing it – even nasty perennial weeds cannot survive being constantly chopped off at ground level. The secret of successful hoeing is do it while weeds are small. Choose a sunny day, so that weed seedlings wither straight away, then you don't even need to rake them up and get rid of them.

It is better to weed by hand when the ground is moist as the weeds will come out more easily. Gather them up and compost them afterwards. Do avoid putting thick-rooted weeds on the compost heap, though, as they might survive the rotting process.

Spot treatment

Where perennial weeds are growing in between plants in a border, it is usually possible to spot treat them individually with weedkiller. Choose a glyphosate-based weedkiller, which will be taken in through the leaves to kill the roots as well as the tops. Either buy a gel formulation and paint it carefully on to the weed leaves, or use a ready mixed formulation in its own sprayer bottle. Shield nearby plants you don't get any weedkiller on them.

Very persistent weeds may need several applications. Big, old perennial weeds, whose leaves are tough and fairly resistant to weedkiller, are best treated by cutting the stems down and then treating the soft, new growth that follows, which is much more susceptible. You will probably need to re-treat the same clump several times.

Weed prevention

In some situations you can use special weedkillers that prevent any weeds from growing at all. Use path weedkillers on paths, gravel drives and cracks between paving stones. They kill existing weeds and stop any more coming up for the rest of the season.

Total weedkillers containing sodium chlorate need using very cautiously as they stop anything growing for a long time – often several years. However, unlike path weedkillers, they can often spread sideways in the soil. I prefer not to use sodium chlorate at all.

Weedkiller with the active ingredient dichlobenil stops both annual and perennial weeds growing for a full season, but must be sprinkled over weed-free soil in early spring. It can be used under only established trees and shrubs, not where there are bulbs, perennials or where you will want to plant annuals.

DOS AND DON'TS OF WEEDS

✔ Do tackle problem weeds fast: the older they get, the harder they are to destroy.

✘ Don't try to clear problem perennial weeds growing in a rockery or among a border of choice small perennials by hand. Spot treat them with a glyphosate-based weedkiller. In a particularly bad case it is easier to take out all the plants you want to save and blanket treat the whole area with weedkiller, then start again.

✔ Do break off the flowering heads of weeds if you don't have time to weed properly. This will stop them seeding.

✘ Don't put weeds that have set seed or roots of perennial weeds on your compost heap. It's unlikely the temperature in the heap will get hot enough to kill them, so you will just spread a new crop of weeds along with your compost.

✔ Do learn to recognize the seedlings of most common weeds, so you can leave self-sown seedlings of plants you may want to keep (such as hellebores), to grow safely.

✘ Don't try to dig out problem perennial weeds like horsetail, couch grass and bindweed – every tiny scrap of root that is left in the ground will grow to make a new plant.

SPECIAL SOLUTIONS

◆ If bindweed has grown up into plants, cut it off at the base leaving the stem still twining around the plant. Stems are much easier to unwind after a few days, once they are dead. Treat any new shoots with a glyphosate-based weedkiller before they start climbing.

◆ Cut stems of Japanese knotweed down and paint the soft new growth with a glyphosate-based weedkiller. Repeat every time new shoots appear. It will probably take several years before you kill an established clump.

◆ Cut through the base of the stems of ivy and in time the top growth will die off and lose its grip making it easier to pull off. Clean up brickwork with a wire brush afterwards. Paint the base of the ivy stump with a brushwood killer.

◆ Spray celandines with a weedkiller containing glyphosate in spring when the leaves are unfolded but before the plants start to flower. This kills them before they can form bulbils, which would otherwise remain in the soil ready to emerge the following year.

✎ top tip

If bindweed is a problem in a busy border, push canes into infested areas for the stems to climb up, then spray with a weedkiller containing glyphosate after laying the weed-clad canes down on plastic or protecting nearby plants. If it is growing up into shrubs or flowers, you cannot use weedkiller on the stems as you will kill the plants as well as the bindweed.

Bindweed has the common name of devil's guts. One look at its roots and you will see why.

Watering

Plants simply cannot grow without water. Newly planted ones are especially vulnerable to drying out at the roots and containers rely on the gardener at all times. Established plants should be allowed to find their own water deep in the soil and should be given additional supplies only in severe droughts.

Watering can

The watering can, in plastic or metal, is the most basic way of transporting water to plants. It is especially useful where the plants are growing in containers because it can deliver water at a gentle rate rather than in a powerful jet which can wash the compost out of the pot.

The upright 9-litre (2-gallon) watering can is the most common, but for greenhouse work I find that a 4.5-litre (1-gallon) can with a more extended spout is much more manoeuvrable.

For watering seedlings in pots, trays and nursery rows, a fine sprinkler head or 'rose' should be fitted to the can. Tip the can up to expel the water to one side of the seedlings before moving it over them so that the initial dribble or gush does not damage them.

Hosepipe

The hosepipe is essential where larger numbers of plants are to be watered and for connecting up to sprinklers. Choose a nylon fibre-reinforced hosepipe, which is less likely to kink than one made of plastic, and store it on a reel if possible to reduce the likelihood of kinking even further and make it easier to extend to its full length.

Many connecting devices are now available for fastening lengths of hose together and for attaching spray guns and sprinklers. Try to standardize the type you use or you'll be forever exasperated by their failure to lock together.

When watering plants with an open-ended hosepipe, take care not to use too fast a jet of water which may displace the soil around the roots or wash it out of pots and containers.

Outside taps need to be disconnected or lagged in winter to prevent them from freezing up and bursting, or dripping later.

Sprinklers

Garden sprinklers are especially useful on the lawn and in the vegetable garden, but remember to leave them running for an hour in any one spot so that sufficient water is given to penetrate the earth.

Oscillating sprinklers, which play back and forth, will water a square or rectangular area; rotating sprinklers water in a circular pattern. A jam jar placed underneath the spray will indicate how much water has been applied to the area.

In Britain you might need a licence and/or a meter for a sprinkler, so contact your local water authority.

Water butts

It makes sense to conserve every drop of water that falls from the heavens, and water butts are a great way of doing this. Position them at the foot of downpipes on the house and on outbuildings, and raise them off the ground so that a watering can may be placed underneath a tap at the base to extract the water.

Lime-hating plants, such as rhododendrons and camellias, will appreciate rainwater far more than hard tapwater, which contains lime.

Plastic water butts are more hygienic than those made of timber, and a length of old tights or stocking should be fastened over the end of the downpipe to prevent rubbish from the gutter making its way into the butt. Special connectors are available which bypass the water butt once it is full and divert the supply to the drains. Very large plastic tanks used in the soft drinks industry are often sold off to builders' merchants and these will hold 1360–1820 litres (300–400 gallons) of water.

ABOVE: Laying a mulch around border plants in spring, while the soil is damp, will help conserve moisture.

CONSERVING WATER

As well as providing your plants with additional supplies of water, it pays to conserve water already present in the soil. There are various ways of doing this:

♦ Mulch moist ground with an 8-cm (3-in) layer of organic matter such as chipped bark, manure or compost to seal in the moisture in spring. It will also keep down weeds.

♦ Work in plenty of organic matter in the form of well-rotted manure or garden compost at planting time so that garden soil is better equipped to hold on to available moisture.

♦ Protect the roots of plants such as clematis (which enjoy a cool, moist root run) by laying a few pieces of broken flagstone on the earth above the roots.

♦ Use a gravel or pebble mulch around plants. Apart from being decorative, it is also moisture-retaining.

♦ Use proprietary water-retaining granules in pots and hanging baskets at potting time so that the compost dries out less rapidly.

✎ **top tip**

A 2.5-cm (1-in) layer of water will penetrate the soil to a depth of 23cm (9in).

DOS AND DON'TS OF WATERING

✔ All plants can be watered from above provided the hosepipe or watering can is able to penetrate the rosette of leaves. Only with pot plants such as African violets (saintpaulias), where the leaf rosette is very dense, need the plants be watered from below by filling a saucer with water and giving the plant half an hour to take up what it needs before the remaining water is thrown away.

✔ Water for preference in the morning or evening, but if plants are wilting at midday, give them a drink there and then.

✔ Do water thoroughly, not just wetting the surface of the soil.

✔ Water well any new plant immediately after planting.

✘ Don't wait for fruit and vegetables to wilt before you water them or yields may be adversely affected.

✔ With very few exceptions, pot plants need to be watered when the surface of the compost is dry and not before. Exceptions to this rule include ferns and the Christmas azalea, which should be kept moist at all times.

Downpipes can be fitted with plastic water butts to make full use of rainwater.

Lawns

A lawn is the garden background to everything from starter homes to huge country estates. Depending on the style of the garden, a lawn can be a major element of the design, or a foil to show off glorious borders. But, however you use it, grass needs care to keep the cultivated look.

Classic striped lawn

The traditional idea of a perfect garden lawn is one that is beautifully green, cut very short and striped. This bowling-green finish takes the sort of time and attention that only a professional greenkeeper could afford to spend. To have well-defined stripes you need a fine lawn; the sort you were always told to keep off. This type was once popular for smart front gardens people looked at but never set foot on. You can get a stripy look in a normal, family-type lawn, though the effect won't be quite as pronounced, because this sort of lawn is made up of coarse-textured grass.

The trick is to use a cylinder lawnmower with a roller at the back, and mow the lawn from end to end. The stripes are created by the roller flattening the grass down in opposite directions so that alternate strips appear light and dark.

Contemporary 'designer' lawn

Today's designer garden needs a more modern-looking lawn, so traditional oblong shapes are out in favour of circular, half-moon or overlapping geometric shapes. Although this may sound a bit strange and often look slightly odd when you see them on a garden plan, they actually look very good indeed when they are in place in a garden, surrounded by plants.

A circular shape is very quick to mow, as you just start at the edge and keep going around in circles until you reach the middle. You won't get a striped effect, but the lawn will look nice and velvety if it is well cared for. The thing to avoid at all costs is a lawn with a fussy shape. Lots of tight, fiddly corners and small beds cut out of the grass make it difficult to mow, and edging a lawn like this can be a nightmare.

Neglected lawns

Lawns that have been left to do their own thing for a long time look decidedly run down. The worst are those that were not laid properly in the first place, or have had a lot of hard wear without regular care. Moss and weeds creep in and bald patches appear. The quickest solution is to kill off the old lawn with a glyphosate-based weedkiller, then dig it up and start again with seed or turf. But this is not always necessary. The cheapest and easiest option is to improve the old grass instead. You can do this gradually, by regular feeding and mowing, re-seeding or turfing bald patches and treating problems like weeds or moss.

Play lawns

Lawns that are playgrounds for children and pets get especially heavy wear, but even they can be kept looking good if you give them a bit of extra attention. The smaller the lawn, the more help it needs. Regular feeding is vital to keep grass growing under the pressure of all those feet. Modern lawn feeds that use slow-release fertilizer are the easy answer. A single dose in late spring means that nutrients are released little and often throughout the season. Don't mow too short, especially in dry weather, so the grass is not put under stress. Set the mower blades about 3–4cm (1¼–1½ in), and grass will stay green and stand up to wear very much better. In autumn, treat it to a special care programme (see page 60) designed to rejuvenate both the soil which has been trodden down hard during the summer and the turf which has accumulated all sorts of crushed dead stems. By spring the lawn will be fully recovered.

ABOVE: There is no need to go to extremes with your lawn! RIGHT: I use a rotary mower on all my lawns and still manage to get stripes.

CHOOSING A MOWER

♦ Cylinder mowers with a roller on the back are the best kind for maintaining a top-quality lawn, but the grass must be dry when you cut it.

♦ Rotary mowers will cut long or tough grass and can be used even when the grass is wet.

♦ Ride-on mowers are the most convenient way to tackle large lawns as they have a wide cutting area and move faster than you could walk.

♦ Electric mowers cost less to buy than petrol ones as well as being lighter and quieter, but don't use them on wet grass and plug into an RCD adaptor that will cut out the electricity if you sever a cable.

♦ Hover mowers are ideal for slopes and for small gardens with fiddly beds or tight curves, as they go sideways as well as forwards and the mower will glide over lawn edges. Always use an RCD adaptor.

♦ Petrol mowers need regular servicing, which can be expensive, but they are good for lawns that are too big for electric mowers.

DOS AND DON'TS OF LAWN CARE

✔ Do sink stepping stones or make a proper path in places you need to walk regularly, to avoid wearing out the lawn.

✘ Don't let autumn leaves pile up over the lawn; rake them up, otherwise the grass turns yellow underneath and fungal diseases can set in.

✔ Do mow regularly all the time the lawn is growing – grass keeps growing slowly even in winter if the weather is mild.

✘ Don't walk or push barrows over the lawn when it is muddy as this creates ruts that set solid later, making mowing difficult.

✔ Do lay a patio in a sunny spot where you want to use garden furniture and a barbecue, as intensive entertainment like this on the lawn causes particularly heavy wear.

✘ Don't walk on grass in frosty weather.

✔ top tip

If you can cut the grass regularly, there is no need to use a grass box. The clippings quickly dry up and disappear into the lawn surface as a fine mulch, which recycles nutrients back into the ground. And cutting the grass is much quicker as you don't have to keep stopping to empty the box, or find space to pile up grass clippings while they compost down. However, large clods of cut grass should be removed.

Turf and seed lawns

Making a new lawn takes time. Whether you decide to opt for sowing seed or laying turf, the advance preparation needs to be done thoroughly. You will find it much harder to put things right when grass is covering the ground. But once it is done, a properly laid lawn lasts a lifetime.

Turf

Turf gives you an instant lawn and it can be laid over quite a large part of the year. The usual time for turf laying is from autumn to spring, except when the ground is frozen or muddy. It is risky to lay turf in late spring or summer, because it may not 'take' properly in hot weather and, in any case, will need an awful lot of watering to keep it alive. My advice is to stick to autumn.

Turf is an expensive way to create a lawn. Decent turf costs roughly as much as carpet. And it takes quite a long time to lay. Check what you are actually buying. Cultivated turf is the best buy for a good-quality lawn. Meadow turf is cheaper but is often full of weeds and a job lot may contain a few turves that cannot be used because they have bare patches or are of uneven thickness. Above all, buy the type of turf that suits the type of lawn you need. Extremely expensive turf is a waste of money if it is to be used for non-league football matches.

Seed

People always think growing grass from seed (see page 58) takes too long, as you have to stay off it for months while it grows. That is true, but if you choose to sow in autumn, you will have a perfectly usable lawn by spring. And you probably would not have wanted to use it much in winter anyway.

You can also sow in spring, but it will be three months before you have a real lawn, which is a time when you would have wanted to use the garden. If a spring start is your only option, turf is the best bet.

If you do choose seed, you can select a variety that is perfect for your situation. You can get grass seed that suits dry or shady positions, or which has wildflower seeds already mixed into it. But for family use, choose a hard-wearing mixture containing one of the modern ornamental ryegrasses like 'Hunter'. They look good and don't send up spiky seed-heads.

Soil preparation

Preparation is the foundation of a good lawn and worth taking a bit of time over. Start by getting rid of perennial weeds. Use a glyphosate-based weedkiller six weeks before you plan to begin work on the lawn. Dig the area over well. Avoid using a rotary cultivator as it is difficult to make the machine penetrate deep enough, although sometimes it is the only option if you have a large area and a bad back, or are short of time. Then

---

HOW TO MAKE A NEW LAWN FROM TURF

1 Prepare the ground by forking it over and removing weed growth. Rake the area level then trample it down with your feet before raking it level again. It should be firm and even before the turf is laid.

2 Buy quality turf and lay it as soon after its arrival as possible. Firm it into place by patting it down with your hands, and work forwards, placing a plank over the turves just laid to support your weight.

3 Stagger the joints like those in brickwork and make sure that the turves are butted close together. There should be no cracks between. If dry weather follows, water frequently to encourage the grass to establish.

NEW LAWNS

◆ You should need to water a new lawn only if there is no rain for several days after sowing or turfing; do so thoroughly, then leave it a few days before doing it again. You need to water a new lawn only until the grass is about 2.5cm (1in) tall, and turf no longer lifts up if you try to peel back a corner.

◆ Upright weeds like groundsel will die out naturally as soon as you start mowing a new lawn regularly.

◆ Don't use lawn weedkiller on newly sown lawns until they are over six months old. New turf can be treated as soon as it is properly rooted and starting to grow.

✍ top tip

When you take on a new or neglected garden, sow the whole lot with grass seed while you concentrate on decorating, etc., indoors so the garden is quick and easy to keep tidy. When you start cutting beds out of the lawn, stack the turf you remove upside down in a heap and a year later you will have a pile of free, good-quality topsoil ready to use.

sprinkle fertilizer. You can use a general kind such as blood, fish and bone, but it is better to use a proper pre-seeding lawn fertilizer. Next, rake several times. The first pass is to level out the ruts left by digging. The second is to gather up all the stones, roots and hard lumps. The third raking leaves a smoother, finer surface. You spoil the effect by trampling all over it to firm the ground down well, before raking it once more to get rid of the footprints. By then the surface will be ready for turfing or seeding.

Aftercare
Grass seed grows unevenly to start with and often comes up along with a lot of weeds, but don't

Regular use of pathways across lawns causes bare patches. Reinforce them with stepping stones that are harder wearing.

worry – within a few weeks it will all sort itself out. Give it the first cut when most of the grass is about 5cm (2in) high. Do this by hand with shears if you can. Otherwise choose a day when the grass is completely dry and just cut the top with a lightweight electric or hover mower with the blades at the highest setting. From then on, you can start cutting regularly with the blades set at about an 3cm (1¼ in) high. Turf should start rooting into the soil within a few weeks of laying. Wait until this happens before the first cut, but once it has rooted you can start using the lawn normally.

HOW TO MAKE A NEW LAWN FROM SEED

1 Fork the ground over, trample with the feet and rake level. Decide whether you want a fine lawn (choose a seed mixture without ryegrass) or a hard-wearing one (choose one with dwarf ryegrass).

2 Sprinkle the seed at a rate of 50g per sq m (1oz per sq yd). Weigh the correct amount and mark a plastic cup to act as a measure. Use canes to mark out the metres or yards if unsure.

3 Rake in the seed. Lay twiggy pea sticks or plastic netting over the soil if cats or birds are a problem. Water the soil in dry weather. Cut the grass in two to three weeks when it is 2.5cm (1in) high.

LAWN PROBLEMS

♦ Worm casts are a problem mostly in spring. They don't do any harm except ruin the appearance of the lawn and are simple to get rid of. Brush casts with a stiff brush when they are dry to flatten and spread them before mowing. They are full of nutrients which are good for the grass.

♦ The best mole deterrent is the electronic vibrating device that drives moles away by creating underground sounds. You will need to move it regularly. There is no guaranteed way of banishing moles and if you do find the odd molehill, spread the soil on the borders before mowing.

♦ Rings of fungi, known as fairy rings, appear during the summer and slowly get bigger. If you cannot ignore them, you will have to dig out the soil to a depth of 30cm (1ft), replace it with fresh topsoil and re-seed or re-turf.

With the grass cut, a garden always looks smart, however untidy the beds and borders!

Looking after a lawn

Keeping a lawn in tip-top condition takes a bit more than just routine mowing, but it needn't be hard work. To get the best results from your lawn, feed and tackle occasional problems like weeds or moss. Lawn maintenance does not take long, especially if you do it at the right time.

Mowing
Little and often is the best way to mow. It not only keeps the grass looking tidy, but also eradicates a lot of weeds without using weedkiller. Set the mower blades so that during the growing season the grass is cut at about 2.5cm (1in) high. If the weather turns dry, adjust the mower so it cuts up to 1cm (½in) higher than usual. This helps the grass to stand up to drought and stay green. If you let the grass grow too long, perhaps while you are away on holiday, resist the temptation to cut it down to 2.5cm (1in) high in one go. If you do, you will be left with stubble that looks like a cornfield after the harvest. Instead, cut the grass down to half its height, and keep cutting it a bit closer once a week over the next few weeks until it is back to normal. That way it will stay green and leafy.

Feeding
Feeding takes top priority after mowing, especially for a lawn that gets a lot of use. It helps grass to replace itself faster than it wears out. Start feeding your lawn in late spring, after the worst cold weather is over and the grass is starting to grow faster naturally. Use a spring and summer lawn feed, as this is high in nitrogen and will encourage lots of leafy growth. If you don't want the grass to grow so fast, use an autumn lawn feed instead. If you feed the lawn only once a year, do it at the start of the main growing season, in late spring. But if you want a really good lawn, either use a more expensive, slow-release feed which works all season long, or feed again every six or eight weeks from late spring until mid-summer.

Weeding
Two types of weeds create most of the problems in lawns – the rosette sort like daisies and plantain, and the creeping sort like trefoil and speedwell. Any other weeds that may appear will be killed by regular mowing. Rosette weeds are very easy to get rid of, as they respond beautifully to lawn

Weedy lawns are relatively easy to improve with combined weedkiller and fertilizer dressings that encourage the grass to take over the soil vacated by the weeds.

weedkillers. You can use either granular weedkillers that are sold as combined lawn feed and weedkiller products, or a liquid version that is applied with a watering can. If there are only a few weeds, it is often quicker to use the ready-mixed kinds sold in point-and-squirt applicator bottles. Creeping weeds are more difficult. To get good results on these you need to use the sort of liquid lawn weedkillers that specifically say they are for small-leaved weeds. The alternative, and not a bad one if you have only a few weeds, is to hand weed or use a daisy grubber.

Moss
Moss can crop up in even the best-kept lawns after a wet winter, but if it is a constant problem it may be because the lawn is badly drained or in shade for a lot of the time. If you can identify the cause and improve faulty conditions, this is a big help. But often the only answer for reccurring moss is to leave it alone and try to live with it, or keep treating it. To do this, apply mosskiller every spring, and if necessary, autumn too, and invest in a powered lawn raker, which is used to comb out the dead moss as soon as it turns black, a few weeks after applying moss treatment. You can also feed the grass to encourage it to colonize any bare patches where moss might get in.

The autumn lawn workout

When you stop to think, grass gets a pretty rough time of it. A lawn is made up of thousands of individual grass plants growing very close together. They stay in the same place for many years, where they are trodden on and regularly beheaded, and you cannot get at the soil in between them, as you can between flowers in a bed, to improve things by cultivating and mulching. Trampling feet compress the soil, and old dead grass stems and debris left by the mower accumulate to form a springy underlay below the layer of live, green grass. Both conditions make it increasingly difficult for the grass to grow well, and this is when moss gets in and the lawn starts looking patchy. Small wonder that, eventually, even this most good-natured of plants starts to run out of steam. In time the lawn needs more than just annual feeding and mowing to keep it in good condition. It needs a good overhaul.

The solution is to treat it to a special programme of care in autumn designed to put it back in shape for the start of the next season. Lawns that get only occasional use may go for several years between treatments. But those which are heavily used, such as small lawns that have a family playing on them every weekend throughout summer, need perking up every autumn to keep them dense, green and lush. Enthusiasts who want a perfect lawn will usually give it the full treatment every year to keep it in peak condition. Allocate a full day in early or mid-autumn. Since the complete programme is physically demanding, you could spread the load by tackling a different task each weekend, but do them all straight after mowing as you need short grass to work on.

The basic version

For a healthy lawn there are certain essential jobs you must do. Begin by mowing the grass, picking up the clippings with a grass box if your mower has one. Then mow again, but this time at right angles to the first cut. This lifts up any grasses that usually lie flat, so they get cut off too.

Next rake the lawn. This is not just a superficial raking that scratches over the top of grass as when collecting fallen leaves. You need to rake right down so that the teeth reach the soil under the grass, dragging out all the moss, old, trailing, brown stems and bits of dried-up lawn mowings that have been trodden into the surface. If you are doing the job by hand, the tool to use is a wire rake with a fan-shaped head made up of lots of long, springy teeth or tines. Unless your lawn is quite small or you are into fitness training, the easiest way of doing the job is with a powered lawn raker. Small, electric models are man enough for a medium-sized lawn, but you can get large and powerful lawn rakers from specialist turf equipment suppliers and sometimes from local tool-hire firms. Go over the lawn twice: once up and down and a second time at right angles, to get out as much material as possible. If you have not done the job before, you will be staggered at the amount of rubbish that comes out. Don't worry if it leaves the lawn looking very thin or shaggy afterwards: young, healthy grass will be able to grow to fill in the gaps, which is the object of the exercise.

Now, sprinkle lawn fertilizer evenly over the lawn, using an autumn formulation. This is low in nitrogen so it won't make the grass grow fast, but it is high in phosphates which will benefit the roots and helps to thicken and toughen the grass. Carry out these essential jobs each autumn and you will lay the foundations for a great lawn next season.

The de luxe version

If you really want a prize lawn, there are two more things you can do, after completing the essential jobs. The first is to slash the lawn to aerate it and

Island beds, when well planted, are undeniably spectacular.

DOS AND DON'TS OF LAWN CARE

✔ Do use lawn feeds in showery weather, as they need watering in. In dry conditions, lawn feeds can actually burn the grass, so avoid using them when the soil is dry.

✘ Don't use mosskillers or weedkillers in rainy weather as they need to remain on the moss or weeds for at least 12 hours to be effective: they are taken in through the leaves, not the roots.

✔ Do choose your time very carefully to use combined feed and weed products to get the best of both worlds. Read the instructions. For best results apply when it is not likely to rain for at least 12 hours, and water them in if it does not rain after 48 hours.

✘ Don't put grass clippings on the compost heap for the first four or five cuts after using lawn weedkiller. Compost them separately, then use under a hedge or around shrubs, not where you grow flowers or vegetables, which are more sensitive.

✔ Do wait for liquid lawn products to dry or until granular ones are watered in before allowing pets or children to play on a treated lawn.

loosen up soil that has been squashed down hard over years of use. Lawn aerators have blades that knife down into the ground, letting in air and helping rainwater to drain away. (This is the same sort of treatment that is used on football pitches after matches: sports turf gets even harder wear than domestic lawns and needs even more maintenance for the grass to survive.) Hand aerators are available, but powered ones are much less effort – some mowers can be fitted with special attachments so the grass is aerated at the same time as you mow.

Finally top dress the lawn. You can buy bags of ready-made lawn top dressing, otherwise use bags of

My own lawn is cut once a week in spring and summer and is fed in spring and autumn.

seed compost. Don't use potting compost because it has too much fertilizer for this job. Scatter the top dressing about 0.5cm (¼in) thick all over the lawn spreading it with a rake. Use a besom broom to work it into the surface. It should disappear between the blades of grass, not bury them.

Lawn maintenance is exhausting, but you will notice an enormous difference in the lawn within a few weeks. And by the following spring, it will look as good as new.

Alternative lawns

Grass is not the only plant that makes dense ground cover and can be walked upon: thyme and chamomile are ideal for small areas, providing a delightful aroma whenever they are trampled and a fun alternative to striped greensward.

Chamomile

Of increased popularity, thanks to Mary Wesley's book of the same name, the chamomile lawn releases a wonderfully fruity fragrance when it is walked over. The plant is a member of the daisy family and has fluffy foliage of rich, bright green. Its flowers are small, white, yellow-centred daisies, but *Chamaemelum nobile* 'Treneague' is flowerless and short-growing and therefore a much better bet for a lawn where greenness is the objective.

Chamomile likes sun and soil which is well drained. It is happiest on light, sandy soils, though in such situations watering will be needed during prolonged dry spells. Although the plant is fully hardy, severe winters can kill back much of the growth and make for a rather threadbare lawn.

Obtain plants of the variety 'Treneague' in spring and plant them 15cm (6in) apart to cover the area of the lawn. They will grow to around 10cm (4in) high and individual plants will gradually extend their territory until they meet and knit together. Make sure they do not go short of water in the early stages of establishment.

Before planting make sure that the ground is level, firm and weed-free. To save money, established plants in pots can be divided up into single rosettes of growth and these can be spaced out in seed trays of potting compost and grown on for a few weeks in a greenhouse or frame to establish their roots and

To avoid a wildflower meadow looking too untidy, mown areas of grass can surround it so that it looks more purposeful, and pathways can be mown through it.

FRAGRANT LAWNS

♦ Avoid thymes upright in growth because their stems are more brittle and susceptible to damage if walked on.

♦ Do not use weedkiller on chamomile or thyme lawns. Selective lawn weedkillers leave grasses unharmed and kill off broad-leaved weeds, so cannot be used on chamomile and thyme. Instead, weeds have to be pulled out by hand.

♦ Plants that naturally form cushions can be planted to produce the effect of a lawn, though they are less willing to be walked over. Among those that look good are *Acaena, Ajuga, Armeria, Aubrieta, Calluna, Cerastium, Dianthus, Erica, Helianthemum, Lithospermum, Saxifraga, Vinca* and *Waldsteinia*.

increase their size. These can then be transplanted to the place where they are to grow.

Cut the lawn occasionally during the summer, either with shears or with a mower set high, about 4cm (1½in). Remove the severed shoots. An occasional light rolling will keep the ground even.

Thyme

Creeping thymes make good lawns. Choose species such as *Thymus serpyllum* and *T. polytrichus* and plant them either 30cm (1ft) apart in an expanse of soil, or in crevices between paving stones where their stems can spread across the stonework.

Like chamomile, thymes enjoy well-drained soil, and they prefer it neutral to alkaline rather than acid. Many varieties produce flowers, so as well as being fragrant your lawn will be colourful. Suitable varieties of *Thymus serpyllum* include 'Annie Hall', which has purplish-pink flowers; var. *coccineus*, reddish-pink; 'Minimus', soft pink; 'Pink Chintz', flesh pink; and 'Snowdrift', white.

Wildflower meadows

In spring and early summer, garden meadows look lovely, but expect them to look like a hayfield a little later. On bare earth, special wildflower meadow seed mixtures can be sown in spring or early autumn. Or, give over part of your lawn to a wildflower meadow.

A chamomile lawn is best planted with the flowerless variety 'Treneague' which makes a rich, emerald-green cushion. Planted 15cm (6in) apart the plants soon knit into a dense, aromatic rug.

In early spring, when the grass is short, wildflowers, such as primroses, cowslips, oxlips, lady's smock (best suited to damp ground), field scabious and knapweed, can be planted in divots removed from the grass. Water the plants in and water them again if the weather is dry. Simply sprinkling wildflower seeds over established grass will not produce a wildflower meadow – the grass will offer too much competition.

After planting do not mow again until the spring flowers have shed their seeds. Cut the long grass in mid-summer (after the seeds have fallen) with a rotary mower set high, and then cut it again immediately at a lower setting of 5cm (2in). The cut grass can be removed and composted.

Now let the whole area grow again and you will enjoy a later flush of summer flowers, such as knapweed and field scabious. Mow again in early autumn to tidy up the area in time for winter and allow primroses and cowslips to be visible in spring.

Such areas of garden meadow need no fertilizer; indeed, the grass may well be too strong for the wildflowers if it has been fed on a regular basis. Poor lawns make the best wildflower meadows.

PLANTING
ESSENTIALS

When it comes to choosing the plants for your garden, you will discover a bafflingly wide range of them in nurseries and garden centres. This section makes selection easier by describing those that I have found to be the very best of their kind, with information on where you might want to use them and their season of flowering.

Small garden trees

Trees are the most majestic features of the garden and nearly every garden is better for their presence. They add height and stature, they make brilliant focal points and you can sit under them and admire their blossom, leaves, bark or berries. In fact, there is no greater pleasure to be had.

Many gardeners think they have no room for trees, but there are beautiful, modest-sized trees that can be fitted into even the smallest garden; all you need to do is choose them carefully and plant them wisely. Over the next few pages are suggestions as to which trees you might choose.

The first thing that will worry you is their height. 'How can he suggest planting a tree that grows to 10m (30ft) in a small garden?' I hear you cry. The heights that are given for many of the trees seem to be far from small, but these are ultimate heights, often achieved over 50 years or more by slow-growing trees. In a way, they are misleading. Most gardeners never stay in one place that long, and if they do, they can take remedial action when the tree outgrows its welcome.

I think it is time that gardeners treated their trees as they treat other plants in their garden – enjoying them while they are looking good and growing well, then, when they go over the hill, or take up too much room, replacing them with new ones.

This is a controversial stance, I know, but we are not talking about stately oaks in parkland, towering beeches in the way of a proposed by-pass, or majestic cedars on a spacious lawn. In lots of cases, small garden trees can be pruned to keep them within bounds. If the time does come, many years hence, when they start to worry you, that is the time to replace them.

I do not want to instil a feeling of panic in you. Many gardeners feel threatened as soon as a tree grows taller than they are, but that's silly. Provided a

tree is planted far enough away from a house so that it has enough light and won't threaten the foundations – 6m (20ft) is sufficient with all but the most vigorous of trees – there will be no cause for alarm as it heads skywards. Some trees, such as Japanese maples, have such small root systems that they can be safely planted within 2m (6ft) of the house with no risk at all. Rest assured – all the trees discussed in this section will give little cause for concern for at least 20 years.

When you decide on the type of tree you like, check carefully to see that it will, indeed, have room to grow unfettered for at least the first few years of its life, and that its presence, while not worrying you, will not worry your neighbours either. It is not just rows of Leyland cypress that can cause neighbourly disputes; a tree that blocks out a neighbour's light can become a bone of contention too.

I think I've posed enough of the negative arguments. It is time you read on and discovered the delights of garden trees for yourself, not forgetting that if you feel your garden is simply too small to risk letting any of them loose, you can always grow a tree in a large pot or tub. Any tree will grow in a container, which not only has the advantage of being easily moved, but also causes slower growth because it restricts the roots. You want an oak tree? Plant it in a tub. It will never cause you to lose any sleep, and provided you water it regularly and feed it occasionally, it will last for 20 years or more before you will feel compelled to pass it on to someone who can plant it out in open ground.

That's the one thing about trees as opposed to any other garden plant: they inspire affection, which is why, I suppose, so many people find it hard to cut them down.

LEFT: Laburnum is spectacular when in bloom in spring, its yellow flower trails lighting up the garden. ABOVE: Betula utilis var. jacquemontii is one of the best white-stemmed silver birches, here surrounded by Oriental poppies.

Planting and aftercare

I was once given some useful advice about tree planting: 'Spend as much on the hole as the tree'. Do this and you won't go far wrong. Trees can last literally a lifetime, if not longer, and the better you prepare the soil for them, the better they will do for you. It also avoids a lot of sudden expensive deaths.

The planting hole
Don't skimp. Dig a hole that is at least three times the size of the tree's rootball. Fork a good barrowload (or at least a bucketful) of well-rotted organic matter or special tree and shrub planting compost into the bottom, and mix some more into the soil you dug out to make the hole, along with a handful of fertilizer. If you are planting on clay soil, digging a deep hole just makes a 'sump' that fills up with water; instead prepare the soil well in a wide area all round the tree, to one spade's depth.

Planting
Water the tree then tip it out of its pot. I know it sounds obvious, but you would be surprised how often people don't do it. Part-fill the hole with the improved soil, so when you stand the tree in place, the top of the rootball is flush with the surrounding soil. (It is important to plant trees at the same depth they grew in their pots.) If the tree is a bit pot-bound, gently tease a few of the biggest roots out from the solid mass, but otherwise don't break up the rootball any more than you can help. Then stand the tree in place, check the planting depth and use the rest of the improved soil to fill round the roots and top up the hole. Firm gently, but don't tread the soil down too hard, and water thoroughly. Mulch generously by spreading 5–8cm (2–3in) of compost for 60cm (2ft) all around the tree, to keep the soil moist.

Staking
Until their roots grow out into the ground, all trees need a little support to hold the trunk upright, especially in windy areas. I like to hammer a stake in before I plant the tree, so I can be certain it does not go down through the rootball, but it is easier to support it afterwards if you use the modern technique of staking at an angle of 45 degrees with a stake that sticks out of the ground for 45cm (18in). The tree tie should secure the trunk about

Young trees can be given a rapid start by planting them in staked plastic tree shelters. This tree was planted as a 15-cm (6-in) high sapling only five years ago. The shelter also offers protection from deer and rabbits.

30cm (12in) above ground level. This type of stake lets the trunk bend a little to persuade the tree to make a stronger root system instead of relying solely on the stake. The old way, using a long, upright stake secured at the top and bottom of the trunk, has always worked for me – you just need a more expensive stake. After a few years you should be able to remove the stake anyway, except for trees grown on dwarfing rootstocks as some ornamental crab apples now are.

Routine care
Don't forget about a tree after it has been planted. It will need watering in dry spells, especially if you planted it in summer. Each spring, mulch it by spreading at least 2.5cm (1in) of well-rotted organic matter all around it, then feed it by sprinkling a handful of general fertilizer such as blood, fish and bone in a circle around it, at about the same distance from the trunk as the longest branches reach out to, because this is where the feeding roots are found.

IN SUBSEQUENT YEARS

♦ If the tree is planted in grass, keep a circle of bare soil around it as this prevents the grass competing for water and nutrients, enabling the tree to grow better.

♦ Use proper tree ties when staking trees, and make sure the 'buffer' is placed between the trunk and the stake to stop the bark being rubbed off in windy weather.

♦ Check tree ties regularly and loosen them as the tree grows and the trunk thickens, otherwise they can cut through the tree and make the stem snap.

♦ Take care when using a mower or rotary line trimmer close to newly planted trees. If they are struck, it can damage the bark and a rotary trimmer can kill a young tree by ringing the bark.

♦ Protect tree trunks with special tree guards or wire netting if rabbits are a problem. They nibble the bark in winter, which weakens the tree and can kill it.

🌱 top tip

Plant trees in autumn, when the soil is still warm and there is more rainfall to keep them watered. This way they become established before the next summer brings hot weather and dry conditions. The trees will fare better and you don't need to do so much watering.

DOS AND DON'TS OF TREE PRUNING AND SHAPING

✔ Do check variegated trees and remove plain green shoots when you see them, at any time of year, or they will take over as they grow faster than variegated shoots.

✘ Don't feel obliged to prune a tree just because you think you should. Most ornamental trees can be left pretty much alone if they were a good shape to start with.

✔ Do remove any dead, broken or diseased branches with loppers or a pruning saw as soon as you see them.

✔ Do buy a well-shaped tree in the first place. Look for one with about five main branches spaced evenly around the top of the trunk.

✘ Don't choose a lopsided tree or one with very few branches – it will take a lot of time and effort to improve the shape.

✘ Don't chop and hack here and there. If you need to prune, take off a whole branch back to the junction with a bigger one.

1. Dig a hole which is large enough to accommodate the roots of the tree. Fork well-rotted garden compost or manure into the bottom of the hole and then knock in a short, stout stake.

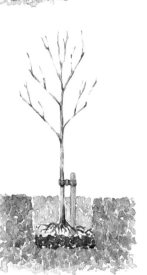

2. Cut off any damaged roots and position the tree. Level the old soil mark with the soil surface. Return the soil, mixing it with more organic matter and firm round the roots.

3. Fasten the tree to the stake with a proprietary tree tie. Water the tree in if the soil is dry and then lay an 8-cm (3-in) thick mulch of organic matter on the surface of the soil.

A–Z trees for foliage

All trees have leaves, but some have leaves of exceptional beauty. I know it is tempting to fill a garden with flowers, but most flowers last for only a few weeks, whereas leaves are present all year round on evergreens, and deciduous leaves last from spring until autumn, often changing colour with the seasons. Some trees have leaves that are brightly variegated. Others produce vivid autumn tints. Use these trees carefully so that their effects are a highlight rather than just a small part of an excessively busy or colourful planting scheme. Green is the most important colour in the garden, and the colour that should be present in largest quantity. A garden filled with coloured foliage can be far from restful, so plant bright-leaved plants with care.

■ *Acer* (Maple)

Apart from the Japanese maples (see pages 72–3), there are other, larger maples with ornamental foliage. One of the most popular is *Acer negundo* 'Variegatum' (the box elder), which grows 6m (20ft) high and 4.5m (15ft) wide after 20 years. This is a vigorous beauty, but

Maples offer amazing variety of leaf colour and shape from spring through to autumn, when they colour up well.

one that can be cut back hard in early spring to keep it within bounds and also to encourage the production of the brightest shoots – the pinnate (rose-like) leaves are pale green variegated with white. The variety 'Flamingo' is a mixture of green, white and pink, and especially well suited to being hard pruned each year.

Cultivation Grow in moist but well-drained soil in sun or partial shade. Occasionally all-green shoots arise and should be cut out completely.

■ *Catalpa* (Indian bean tree)
10m (30ft) high × 10m (30ft) wide

In time the Indian bean tree makes a large, round-headed tree that is boldly spectacular when in leaf between late spring and mid-autumn but it is slow-growing. The golden-leaved form, *Catalpa bignonioides* 'Aurea', is slower-growing than the plain green type and even more showy, with rounded leaves that are more than 20cm (8in) across. They are bronze on unfurling, then rich acid yellow, becoming slightly greener with age.

Cultivation This tree needs a spot sheltered from strong winds in soil that is fertile, moist but well-drained. Protect young plants from frost in cold weather. Try it at the back of a border and prune it hard each spring if space is at a premium.

■ *Chamaecyparis* (Cypress)

There are many varieties of Lawson cypress, *Chamaecyparis lawsoniana*, which have bright foliage and are not nearly so vigorous as Leyland cypress. If you need an elegant, evergreen column in your garden, choose 'Columnaris', which will grow up to 10m (30ft) tall but only 1m (3ft) wide. It has foliage of blue-grey. 'Lane' is wider at the base and its foliage is golden yellow and green, and 'Green Pillar' is rich green. Other varieties have different tones but all offer upright elegance.

Cultivation *Chamaecyparis* is happy in most soils but prefers moist, well-drained neutral to acid soil in full sun.

■ **Eucalyptus** (Gum)

Not all the gum trees are hardy, but many are and will give your garden a sub-tropical feel. Most come from Australia but have adapted well to being grown in British gardens. *Eucalyptus pauciflora* subsp. *niphophila* (snow gum) is one of the toughest, with blue-grey leaves that are disc-shaped in young trees and scimitar-shaped on mature ones. It will grow to around 6m (20ft) high and as much across. But if it's cut back to the ground in the spring the new shoots that arise have the juvenile foliage again. The tree then grows as a bush or multistemmed tree.

Cultivation Grow in full sun in neutral to slightly acid soil that does not dry out.

■ **Gleditsia** (Honey locust)

A good tree for a small garden. *Gleditsia triacanthos* 'Sunburst', will grow to 12m (40ft) high × 10m (30ft) wide, but can be kept smaller by pruning in spring. It has feathery foliage of acid yellow which turns to rich emerald green. I love it.

Cultivation A tree that suits any fertile, well-drained soil in full sun.

■ **Metasequoia** (Dawn redwood)

30m (100ft) high × 4.5m (15ft) wide

Thought to be extinct until seeds were discovered in China in the 1940s, *Metasequoia glyptostroboïdes* is a delicate, deciduous conifer with feathery, green foliage, which turns coppery in autumn. It has an upright, conical habit and is good for large gardens.

Cultivation Plant it in moist, humus-rich, well-drained soil in full sun.

■ **Parrotia persica** (Persian ironwood)

4.5m (15ft) high × 6m (20ft) wide

This tree is a real winner. Tiny, red flowers wreathe its bare branches in winter followed by glossy, green leaves with prominent veins. As early as mid-summer the leaves start colouring up, so that by late summer they are scarlet and crimson, turning to orange and yellow before they fall in autumn. Even the bark is decorative, flaking like a plane tree.

Cultivation Try in any garden, but allow for its sideways spread. Grow in fertile, well-drained soil in sun or partial shade.

■ **Paulownia tomentosa** (Foxglove tree)

12m (40 ft) high × 10m (30ft) wide

Leaves can be 30cm (1ft) or more across and softly downy. Paulownia can be hard pruned each spring to make a smaller tree with stunning foliage. What you will sacrifice, though, are the lilac-pink flowers.

Cultivation Frost damage can occur in exposed gardens, so plant in a sunny, sheltered spot in fertile, well-drained soil.

■ **Pyrus** (Pear)

The weeping, silver-leaved pear, *Pyrus salicifolia* 'Pendula', makes a dome-shaped tree 5m (15ft) high × 4m (12ft) wide with wonderfully bright, silvery-grey leaves from spring to autumn. Cut an opening in its skirt and position a chair beneath its canopy. *Pyrus calleryana* 'Chanticleer' deserves to be more widely planted, for in spite of being deciduous it is always doing something. The white blossom opens ridiculously early – sometimes in winter – and bright green, glossy leaves follow, turning to vivid orange in autumn. It grows to around 8m (25ft) high × 4m (12ft) wide but it is elegant enough to squeeze into even the smallest garden.

The weeping silver-leaved pear, Pyrus salicifolia 'Pendula', seems to glisten in sunlight and is of modest stature.

Cultivation Pear trees are suitable for any fertile, well-drained soil in full sun.

■ **Robinia pseudoacacia 'Frisia'** (False acacia)

6m (20ft) high × 3m (10ft) wide

The rich, acid-yellow leaves of false acacia that unfurl in early summer are most impressive. Although quite a large tree, it is so delicate it could never be described as overpowering.

Cultivation In exposed areas its brittle wood can snap in high winds, so plant it where there is some shelter. Grow in full sun in moist, well-drained soil; it will tolerate poor, dry soils.

■ **Trachycarpus fortunei** (Chusan palm)

4.5m (15ft) high × 2m (6ft) wide

If you want to give your garden a tropical feel, this is the tree for you. It is the hardiest palm tree of all and can be grown outdoors in many regions with impunity. The straight stem is wrapped in fibres and topped by a fountain of fan-shaped palm fronds.

Cultivation Plant it in well-drained fertile soil in sun or dappled shade where it is sheltered from strong or cold winds.

japanese maples *have a rare grace and supreme elegance, and their foliage is not only very delicate and finely cut but is also delightfully coloured in spring, summer and autumn. Added to this, they are of moderate stature and easy to fit into the smallest of gardens. It's not surprising they are so popular.*

There are many maples – some of them making massive trees – but it is the varieties of the smaller and slower-growing *Acer palmatum* we generally refer to as Japanese maples, and also *Acer japonicum* and *Acer shirasawanum*.

Biting northerly and easterly winds can burn their delicate foliage, but, given some shelter, they are easy to grow in any ordinary, well-drained soil that has been enlivened with a helping of well-rotted garden compost. Late frosts can sometimes nip the young shoots, though this is relatively rare.

Plant Japanese maples in full sun (provided the soil is not excessively dry) or dappled shade. They are excellent for growing in the gentle shade of larger trees, as long as the earth in which they are planted is not completely riddled with the roots of the larger specimen.

To grow Japanese maples in pots, choose a container at least 30cm (1ft) in diameter and a compost consisting of equal parts John Innes No. 2 potting compost and a soilless multipurpose compost. Put plenty of drainage material in the base of the container and top dress the compost with gravel. Growth is much slower in a container than in the open garden. Move to a larger pot every two or three years. When the container is as large as you can accommodate, remove some of the compost every other year, re-potting the plant in the same container.

Japanese maples need little pruning. Snip out any dead shoot tips as the buds begin to open in spring.

There are hundreds of different varieties of Japanese maple, but the following are among the most popular. Do not be alarmed by the dimensions, which may seem larger than I have led you to believe; the plants are very slow-growing and will reach the stated size only after many years.

Acer japonicum 'Aconitifolium'
4.5m (15ft) high × 6m (20ft) wide
The downy, green leaves are deeply cut and small, crimson flowers are carried in late spring and early summer. It provides superb autumn colour. Makes a wide-spreading bush.

Acer palmatum atropurpureum
4.5m (15ft) high × 4.5m (15ft) wide
The classic purple-leaved Japanese maple, whose leaves turn from rich plum to fiery red in autumn.

Acer palmatum 'Bloodgood'
4.5m (15ft) high × 4.5m (15ft) wide
A very good form with reddish-purple leaves that turn bright red in autumn. The sycamore-like fruits are also red.

Acer palmatum 'Butterfly'
3m (10ft) high × 3m (10ft) wide
The finely cut, pale green leaves are edged with white and pink – an acquired taste. Delicate but, I think, a bit messy, and the leaves are rather deformed. Don't let me put you off if you like it.

Acer palmatum var. dissectum
2m (6ft) high × 3m (10ft) wide
A dome-shaped bush of very finely cut mid-green leaves which looks wonderful when planted so that it can hang over water. Especially good in containers. The leaves turn golden in autumn. The Dissectum Atropurpureum Group has leaves that are equally finely cut but which are deep plum purple.

Acer palmatum 'Osakazuki'
6m (20ft) high × 6m (20ft) wide
One of the taller varieties, especially noted for its autumn colour when the leaves turn to vibrant red before falling.

Acer palmatum 'Red Pygmy'
1.5m (5ft) high × 1.5m (5ft) wide
Well suited to small gardens, being cup-shaped and of compact habit. The narrow leaves are red in spring and turn golden before they fall in autumn.

Acer palmatum 'Sango-kaku'
6m (20ft) high × 4.5m (15ft) wide
Formerly known as 'Senkaki', this variety has leaves that open orange-yellow in spring, then turn green and finally orange and red in autumn before they fall. It is then that the coral-pink young shoots are revealed. A really good all-rounder.

Acer palmatum 'Seiryû'
4.5m (15ft) high × 3m (10ft) wide
A good choice if you want a strong central trunk and airy, green foliage that is finely cut. Wonderful autumn shades of red, yellow and orange.

Acer shirasawanum 'Aureum'
4.5m (15ft) high × 4.5m (15ft) wide
Formerly known as Acer japonicum 'Aureum', this is a slow-growing Japanese maple of great beauty, especially in spring when its pleated, fan-like leaves open to reveal their rich acid-yellow colouring.

FAR LEFT: Acers produce their most vivid colouring in autumn. BELOW: The acers in my own garden, such as Acer palmatum 'Atropurpureum' (right), burst into life again.

A–Z trees for flowers

'Loveliest of trees, the cherry now is hung with bloom along the bough, and stands about the woodland ride wearing white for Eastertide.' It is not only Houseman's Shropshire lad who is enamoured of the cherry tree; I'm a sucker myself for trees that carry blossom. All right, so blossom may not last very long, but provided there are pleasant leaves to follow, the brief but glorious flowering season is made that much more special by its brevity. If you want to extend the flowering season, there is one way of cheating. Plant a climber such as clematis underneath the extremity of the tree's branches and train the questing stems up bean poles or tall canes into the canopy. If you use a variety of *Clematis viticella* or *C. texensis*, you will be able to cut the clematis down to ground level in winter and leave the tree free of untidy, dead growths. During spring the clematis will put on a couple of metres of growth and in summer it will wreathe the branches of the tree in flowers.

■ **Amelanchier** (Snowy mespilus)
4.5m (15ft) high × 4.5m (15ft) wide
Some gardeners consider the snowy mespilus to be a shrub, but those with tiny gardens will find it a useful tree. Both *Amelanchier lamarckii* and *A. canadensis* are worth growing, and gardeners are often confused as to which one they have. It really doesn't matter, except that the first named is the more vigorous of the two, though both can be kept within bounds by careful pruning in late autumn. Both species have masses of pretty, white blossom in spring and wonderful autumn colours of red and fiery orange. These trees make good supports for clematis.
Cultivation Grow in lime-free, acid soil that is fertile and moist, but well-drained. Choose a spot in sun or partial shade.

■ **Cercis siliquastrum** (Judas tree)
4.5m (15ft) high × 4.5m (15ft) wide
This plant (reputedly the tree on which Judas Iscariot hanged himself) is usually grown as a large bush rather than a tree, but its single main stem allows it to qualify here. A rounded framework of bare branches is smothered, in late spring, with small, bright pink pea flowers. There is also a white form, **C. s. albida,** which is very classy. Attractive, rounded leaves follow the flowers, as do ruddy seed pods in a good summer.
Cultivation Likes sun and a sheltered spot with fertile, moist, well-drained soil. Late frosts can burn the flowers. Older trees resent being transplanted.

■ **Crataegus** (Hawthorn)
10m (30ft) high × 8m (25ft) wide
If you are searching for a tree that seems at home in a country garden, look no further than hawthorn, which is easy to prune and keep within bounds. *Crataegus monogyna* not only provides creamy white blossom in early summer and rich red berries in autumn, but it is also beloved of birds and wildlife – a really good tree for a garden that is also a conservation area. If you want something a bit more spectacular in blossom, choose *C. laevigata* 'Paul's Scarlet', which

Cercis is one of the earliest garden trees to flower, wreathing its bare branches with pink pea flowers in late spring.

has fully double, rich rosy red flowers.
Cultivation It is as tough as old boots
and will grow in all except waterlogged
soils in full sun or partial shade.

■ *Davidia involucrata*
(Pocket handkerchief tree)
10m (30ft) high × 4.5m (15ft) wide
For those of a patient disposition, this is
a rewarding tree. It can take up to
20 years to flower (there, I've lost you
already), but they are worth waiting for.
Its branches are decorated in late spring
with small flowers surrounded by large,
white bracts that hang down like freshly
laundered handkerchiefs. It might flower
after 10 or 15 years if you're lucky!
Cultivation Give it shelter from strong
winds. Plant in sun or partial shade.

■ *Eucryphia*
I am a huge fan of eucryphia, mainly
because it flowers in late summer when
most other trees have long since
blossomed and it looks so attractive.
Some species are slightly tender, but
Eucryphia × *nymansensis* 'Nymansay',
10m (30ft) high × 3m (10ft) wide, is the
best bet for most gardens and one of the
hardiest of the lot. It has dark, evergreen
leaves, and among them in late summer
appear masses of large, white flowers
with fluffy stamens at the centre.
Cultivation Although happiest in lime-
free soil, this tree grows well in my soil,
which overlies chalk. A decent portion of
organic matter at planting time helps. It is
happiest with its head in the sun and its
feet in the shade.

■ *Genista* (Broom)
Although most are usually grown as
shrubs, there is one genista that makes
an elegant, feathery tree – the Mount
Etna broom, *Genista aetnensis*. Here is a
tree that is suitable for a really well-
drained, sun-baked spot. Its slender,
weeping wands of stems are simply
smothered in fragrant, golden-yellow,
pea-like flowers from mid to late
summer, making it wonderfully eye-

catching. It grows to a height of around
6m (20ft) and rather less in spread.
Cultivation Plant it in a warm, sheltered
spot in light, well-drained soil. In cold and
exposed localities it will not be happy.

■ *Laburnum* (Golden rain tree)
In the right place a single specimen of
Laburnum × *watereri* 'Vossii' looks
wonderful in early summer when its
branches drip with long, yellow flower
trails. It is, to be honest, dull for the rest
of the year, but makes up for this in its
weeks of glory. It will reach 8m (25ft)
high × 8m (25ft) wide if left alone, but
some gardeners now plant laburnums in
a row at either side of a pergola and tie
the stems in to the support framework
as they grow. Each spring the trained
trees will combine to make a spectacular
floral tunnel. This variety produces few
seeds, which will pacify those who worry
about children eating them.
Cultivation A hardy tree that will grow
in moderately fertile, well-drained soil.

■ *Magnolia*
The best magnolias are included in the
shrubs section (see pages 88–9) but some
of them, such as **'Heaven Scent'**, also
qualify as trees, especially in small gardens.
This variety has fragrant pink flowers in
spring and will grow 10m (30ft) high and
wide in time. However, the most stunning
of all magnolia trees, as opposed to shrubs,
is *M. campbellii*, a towering beauty up to
15m (50ft) high and 10m (30ft) wide
which produces massive white or pink
flowers, carried in late winter or spring.
Several varieties vary in colour, from
'Charles Raffill', which is purplish pink, to
the white **'Strybing White'**.
Cultivation Magnolias, as a rule, enjoy a
sheltered spot, and soil that is well-
drained and lime-free. Older specimens
resent being moved and almost any
magnolia can be ruined by pruning. Plant
where they have room to grow
unrestricted and then they will become
trees to drool over. Mulch with manure
and leaf mould in early spring.

Magnolia *'Heaven Scent'*, whose pink
goblets are produced from mid-spring to
early summer.

■ *Malus* (Apple)
Crab apples are good fruiting trees for
the garden (see page 80), but there are
others that major on wonderful spring
blossom. The Japanese crab apple, *Malus
floribunda*, which grows 6m (20ft) high ×
10m (30ft) wide, is one such tree. Its
single, pink blossoms open among freshly
unfurling, bright green leaves. If you have
more space, choose *Malus hupehensis*.
Up to 12m (40ft) high and across, it is
positively smothered in fragrant, white
blossom each year.
Cultivation Malus prefers a spot in full
sun although some shade is tolerated. It is
prone to pests and diseases so look out
for any symptoms.

■ *Prunus* (Cherry)
Unbeaten for sheer spectacle, the
cherries can make you gasp with
admiration at the generosity of their
flowering. Garden centres and nurseries
offer a wide range of the larger types,
but for me the daintiest of the lot is
Prunus subhirtella **'Autumnalis Rosea'**,

which opens its double pink flowers (darker pink in the bud) on bare stems through the winter. I love it. At 8m (25ft) high × 4.5m (15ft) wide it is not too big for most gardens and its canopy is especially light and airy.

Of the Japanese flowering cherries, there are numerous varieties, but among the best are: 'Accolade', 8m (25ft) high and wide, semi-double, pale pink, darker in bud; 'Amanogawa', very upright, 6m (20ft) high × 2m (6ft) wide, semi-double, pale pink, good where space is restricted; 'Kanzan', a shuttlecock-shaped tree, often despised, but spectacular in bloom, 8m (25ft) high and wide, rich, double, coconut-ice pink; 'Pink Perfection', 6m (20ft) high and wide, double pink, daintier than 'Kanzan'; 'Shirofugen', 8m (25ft) high × 10m (30ft) wide, double pale pink; 'Spire', 10m (30ft) high × 6m (20ft) wide, single, pale pink, upright-growing; 'Taihaku', the great white cherry, 8m (25ft) high × 10m (30ft) wide, large, single, white flowers; 'Ukon', 8m (25ft) high × 10m (30ft) wide, pale yellowish-green, double; 'Umineko', 8m (25ft) high × 3m (10ft) wide, a wonderful, pure white single.
Cultivation Grow cherry trees in decent soil and choose a spot in full sun and prepare to gasp away.

■ **Sophora**
I've had a specimen of **Sophora microphylla** growing in my garden for 15 years, and it is still barely 3m (10ft) tall and 1.5m (5ft) across. Its stems are angular and orange-barked and its leaves are composed of long ranks of tiny leaflets. It has a dainty habit and a light, feathery canopy. In late spring, dangling, yellow flowers are produced on mature trees. The variety 'Sun King' is bushier and has larger, rich yellow flower clusters.
Cultivation Plant in a sunny, sheltered spot in moderately fertile soil.

Laburnums are at their most spectacular when trained over metal arches to form a tunnel that drips with flowers in late spring.

■ **Stewartia**
A tree that deserves to be more widely grown, **Stewartia pseudocamellia** is a slow-growing beauty at 4.5m (15ft) high and 3m (10ft) wide after 20 years. The leaves are plain green, colouring red and orange in autumn, the bark peels attractively on older specimens. Large, pure white flowers with a central boss of golden stamens appear in mid-summer.
Cultivation This is a tree for lime-free soil that is moist, but well-drained and moderately fertile. It is at home in the dappled shade offered by woodland.

■ **Syringa** (Lilac)
I know that lilac has a reputation for being dreary when it is out of flower, but the spectacle of its blossom, and the heady fragrance, make it an early summer favourite. Strictly speaking, I suppose it is a shrub, but it is so often grown as a tree in small gardens, and is perfectly capable of growing on a single stem to at least waist height, that I include it here. If you can squeeze in only

Cherry blossom may be fleeting but no flowering tree is more spectacular.

one, I'd plump for the graceful **Syringa × josiflexa** 'Bellicent', 4m (12ft) high × 3m (10ft) wide, which has daintier, looser flower clusters than the beefier varieties. They are rich lilac-pink and open, as you would expect, during early summer.

Of the varieties of common lilac, **Syringa vulgaris**, the following are some of my favourites: 'Charles Joly', double, dark purple; 'Congo', single, lilac-purple; 'Katherine Havemeyer', double, lavender-blue; 'Maréchal Foch', single pink; 'Mme Lemoine', double white; 'Mrs Edward Harding', double, purplish-pink; 'Primrose', single, pale yellow; 'Vestale', single white.
Cultivation Lilacs are less keen on acid soils. They like a spot in full sun. Deadhead after flowering and mulch each spring with well-rotted compost or manure to improve flowering. Lilac varieties are often grafted on to a rootstock of common lilac, so pull off any suckers that arise from the roots.

A–Z trees for bark and berries

Trees that earn their keep several times over are especially worth having. These are the trees that, besides bearing good flowers or foliage, also produce coloured or craggy bark or generous crops of fruit. Such specimens have a visual impact and provide a focal point to the landscape and, in the case of berries, a winter food supply for birds – don't begrudge them the rich pickings.

■ **Acer capillipes** (Snakebark maple)
6m (20ft) high x 4.5m (15ft) wide
A very decorative maple with red autumn leaves. Its branches are covered in an extraordinary green bark patterned with white streaks. The youngest twigs are brilliant red. It is a fairly slow-growing tree that has an elegant habit.
■ **Cultivation** Like all the best ornamental maples, this one does best in light woodland conditions with lots of organic matter and some shade from the hottest midday sun. It particularly likes to be grown surrounded by other trees or shrubs in a large garden border, but make sure you plant it where you can get a good view of the branches from fairly close range.

■ **Acer griseum** (Paperbark maple)
4.5m (15ft) high x 4m (12ft) wide
A superb, slow-growing, small to medium-sized tree with typical maple-shaped leaves which in autumn turn brilliant red and orange. It also has craggy, peeling bark in shades of orange-brown and cinnamon that comes away in small, odd-shaped patches, making fascinating patterns. The bark is most outstanding in winter when the tree is bare, but it is very much on show even in the height of summer, since the tree has a fairly high crown.
Cultivation The tree is easy to grow in any fertile soil that contains a fair bit of organic matter and that does not dry out too badly in summer. Grow it in sun or light shade, but it does best in the company of a few other trees. Buy a well-shaped plant to start with and, once it is established, just leave it to grow.

■ **Betula albosinensis var. septentrionalis** (Chinese red birch)
7m (23ft) high x 4.5m (15ft) wide
This spectacular birch makes a neat, upright-domed shape and has wonderful, marble-patterned, pink, cream and orange bark which is eye-catching all year round, but more so in winter when it stands out vividly in a bare garden. It looks especially good grown in front of evergreens. The leaves turn yellow in autumn before falling.
■ **Cultivation** Quite a tough plant like most birches, this one does not mind a windy spot. It does best in a reasonably fertile soil with plenty of organic matter. Keep a new plant watered until it gets going, but from then on there is nothing to do – no pruning, nothing.

■ **Betula utilis var. jacquemontii** (Himalayan birch)
7m (23ft) high x 4.5m (15ft) wide
Dazzling white bark is the first thing that strikes you about this elegant birch, but when you get close it looks as if someone has taken a fine paintbrush and highlighted the trunk with lots of little curved gold lines. The shining white continues right up the tree even into quite small branches.
Cultivation Tough and wind-resistant, this birch will grow even in quite poor soil, but to do it justice give it reasonably fertile soil if possible. Add organic matter before planting unless the ground is naturally rich in humus.

Acer griseum (foreground), Eucalyptus pauciflora subsp. niphophila (background) and Betula utilis var. jacquemontii (right) make a bright-barked trio.

■ **Crataegus persimilis 'Prunifolia'** (Hawthorn)
4.5m (15ft) high x 4m (12ft) wide
A hawthorn with a difference; unlike the usual hedging sort, this one has large leaves like those of cherry (hence the name 'Prunifolia', meaning prunus-like), very long spines and enormous berries three or four times the size of those of a

normal hawthorn. This is a great tree for encouraging birds to the garden, as they feel safe perching in among its armoured stems. The big berries last well on the tree; the blackbirds have to take several gulps to get them down.

Cultivation A good, undemanding tree for difficult sites as it grows happily on heavy clay, as long as it is not totally waterlogged, and is also suitable for windy areas. It makes a good specimen tree in a lawn, at the back of a border or in a wild garden. It is also good planted in a gap in a country hedge and left to grow up above the surrounding shrubs. Fallen berries sometimes grow to provide extra plants for free. Dig them up and transplant them, if necessary.

■ *Eucalyptus pauciflora* subsp. *niphophila* (Snow gum)
6m (20ft) high x 4.5m (15ft) wide
A breath-taking eucalyptus whose pale grey trunk is wildly streaked with white, buff and olive patches where the old bark has peeled away, revealing the young skin below. The tree forms a craggy shape with age, and is usually surrounded by a natural mulch of curling, faintly aromatic bark litter (try a few bits on the barbecue).

Cultivation This is one of the best eucalyptus species to grow as a mature tree because it is reliably hardy and it has the best bark. It will grow in any reasonably good, well-drained soil, but it's not keen on chalk.

ABOVE: *The mottled bark of the snow gum,* Eucalyptus pauciflora *subsp.* niphophila.

The brightly coloured evergreen leaves of Ilex aquifolium 'Argentea Marginata Pendula' grow on a rounded bush no more than 3m (10ft) tall.

■ *Ilex aquifolium* **'Pyramidalis'** (Holly)
3m (10ft) high x 1.25m (4ft) wide

A fairly upright, slow-growing, densely-leaved evergreen tree, that is ideal for a small garden, especially so as this cultivar gives heavy crops of red berries reliably every year even without a male partner nearby. It is self-fertile, and the leaves are not very prickly.

Cultivation It is happy in any reasonable soil and tolerates a fairly windy spot. Does not need any clipping or pruning to keep its shape, and is naturally problem free.

■ *Ilex aquifolium* **'Silver Milkmaid'** (Holly)
4.5m (15ft) high x 3m (10ft) wide

This is a particularly handsome variegated form of holly, with a big lemon and lime splodge in the middle of each deep green, moderately prickly leaf. It is also one of the heaviest-berrying of the variegated hollies, which often substitute leaf colour for berry-power.

Cultivation Grows in any good garden soil, but to bring out the brightest leaf colour plant it in full sun. Like all hollies, it is slow-growing. Tie it to a stake to keep it upright for the first few years. If space is short, keep it smaller by pruning. It can also be grown as a shrub or even a hedge.

■ *Malus* **'John Downie'** (Crab apple)
4.5m (15ft) high x 4m (12ft) wide

The jam makers' favourite. This is one of the very best trees for a small garden, as it puts on a grand show twice a year. In spring it is covered with off-white, fruit tree-like blossom, and in late summer and autumn the branches are weighed down with large, flask-shaped, scarlet-flushed, orange-yellow fruits which make the best clear pink crab apple jelly of all. Great on hot, buttered toast!

Cultivation Very easy to grow and happy in any reasonable garden soil, even the heavier ones. Support overladen branches with props to prevent them breaking. Besides providing decoration, this tree is good to grow in a garden with one or two fruiting apple trees, as it makes a good pollinator for any variety that happens to be in flower at the same time.

■ *Malus pumila* **'Dartmouth'** (Crab apple)
4.25m (14ft) high x 4m (12 ft) wide

An old favourite, but still one of the best flowering crab apples, with white blossom in spring followed by unbelievably huge crops of round, purplish-red fruits like small apples, 5cm (2in) across. It looks like a domestic apple tree run wild, but charming with it.

Cultivation Any good garden soil suits it as long as the drainage is reasonable; improve poor soil with plenty of organic matter before planting. It is best given a stake for the first few years, and prop up some branches if the fruit is too heavy, especially while the tree is young. If the young branches are allowed to be weighed down by the crop, they will stay bent.

Malus 'John Downie' is valued both for its spring blossom and its autumn fruits.

■ *Morus nigra* (Black mulberry)
3m (10ft) high x 3m (10ft) wide
Black mulberry is a much underrated ornamental tree that grows naturally into a gnarled shape. It has shaggy bark that looks wonderful all year round, and even bears the most superb, heart-shaped foliage. It just happens to have edible fruit too. They are one of the most delicious you'll ever taste, but the reason you never find them in the shops is that they are so soft and squashy, they don't travel. In fact, the distance from the tree to the kitchen is often too far for them. The fruits ripen in late summer and drop off the tree. The way to pick them is to put a white cloth under the tree and then shake it – the tree, not the cloth.
■ **Cultivation** Must be grown as a specimen tree in the lawn, so you get the full benefit of the shape. Improve the soil well before planting as it likes a moist, fertile soil that does not get waterlogged. It also likes a sheltered position. The species can take a few years to start fruiting; grow the variety **'Chelsea'** which starts fruiting after three or four years.

■ *Prunus serrula* (Tibetan cherry)
6m (20ft) high x 4.5m (15ft) wide
A medium-sized tree with a trunk the colour of a conker and so shiny it looks as if it has been freshly polished. You won't be able to resist touching it. It looks good all year round, as the crown of branches is held above the trunk so it is always on view.
Cultivation Despite its spectacular, antique-furniture looks, it is an easy tree to grow. Plant in any reasonable garden soil. It will even survive on thin, chalky soil and heavy land. It does not need any attention, but if you feel like buffing up the trunk with a soft cloth, go ahead.

■ *Salix* **'Boyd's Pendulous'**
(American weeping willow)
4m (12ft) high x 4m (12ft) wide
A small, well-behaved version of the popular weeping willow and even better looking in winter, with long, thin, wiry purple branches that are particularly noticeable after the tree sheds its leaves.
Cultivation Enjoys moist soil but is easy to grow almost anywhere. This is a tree that does not mind being hard pruned.

The Tibetan cherry, Prunus serrula, *has wonderful shining bark that is especially spectacular on sunny winter days, when it positively gleams.*

Cut some of the older branches back close to the top of the trunk in early spring to keep a constant supply of young shoots, as these have the best colour. This also helps to keep the tree smaller.

■ *Sorbus* **'Joseph Rock'**
7m (23ft) high x 4m (12ft) wide
A medium-sized tree with stunning autumn tints that bring the mountain ash-like foliage alive with fiery-red and orange shades. The fruit turns a creamy pale yellow some while before the autumn colours appear, but since the birds leave them alone (I always think they are waiting for them to ripen) they remain on the tree quite late into the year and look good against the colourful autumn foliage.
Cultivation Another very easy-going tree, which is happy in most soils but prefers fertile, non-chalky ground. Plant in sun or light shade, and give it a short stake for support in its first few years.

Shrubs

In most gardens shrubs are the big boys – the plants that add stature to the scene and give it body. As focal points or bulky screens, they are of tremendous value, and the fact that they come in so many shapes and sizes, colours and habits makes them the most important plants in the garden.

If you are starting a garden from scratch, it makes sense to have some kind of master plan sketched out on a piece of paper. On this you can mark out not only the major features – a lawn or patio, a pool plus beds and borders – but also some of the larger shrubs that will give the garden a basic framework. Smaller plants can then be infilled around them and, as the shrubs grow in stature, removed to accommodate their larger neighbours.

Bear in mind the overall height and spread of a shrub when you plant it. It is all too easy to fill the garden with young shrubs, allowing them no room to develop: small plants can grow into monsters, and unless these are to be heavily clipped and pruned (which, in the case of plants like magnolias, may ruin their shape and reduce their flowering capabilities), such middle-aged spread must be allowed for. So choose shrubs that you know will look good when they have grown a bit.

In small gardens, shrubs with an upright or columnar habit can be really useful. They add height without taking up too much space and where year-round form is needed, evergreen shrubs, including a few conifers, are invaluable. They also make great focal points at the ends of paths and viewpoints.

Plant evergreens and conifers sparingly. Too many can give a garden a sepulchral feel. Look for dark evergreens as a background for brilliant summer flowers, but remember, too, that there are many variegated evergreens and conifers whose leaves are splashed with silver and gold and which will add light to the garden on the darkest winter day.

Flowering shrubs, such as buddleias, hibiscus, ceanothus and magnolias, attract the most attention, being spectacular when they are in bloom, but flowers are usually fleeting, so it makes sense to plant shrubs with interesting foliage too. It may be

brightly coloured – yellow, purple or crimson – or finely cut, or it may colour brilliantly in autumn. Whatever the case, deciduous shrubs carry their leaves for a good six or seven months of the year, whereas their flowers may last only a few weeks.

As with most things in life, balance is the key to success. Plant some shrubs for their flowers, some for their leaves and some for their evergreen foliage to provide year-round interest in the garden.

Some shrubs flower in the depths of winter, and some are even fragrant. One or two of these, such as sarcococca and winter-flowering honeysuckle, you will come to value as much as their more brilliant summer-blooming relations.

Fruits, too, prolong the season – shrubs such as pyracantha and cotoneaster, which have rather ordinary summer flowers, come into their own in autumn and winter with their huge crops of berries.

Even when there is snow on the ground and the dreary winter days are inhospitable to plant growth, shrubs like the dogwoods and pollarded willows have colourful bark of orange and crimson, yellow and vivid green that sings out in the gloom.

In small gardens it may be tempting to do without shrubs altogether, but that would be a pity. They come in such a range of shapes and sizes that it is possible to fit at least some of them in as meaty backdrops to borders of annuals and herbaceous perennials. Many will also grow in large pots, which can be moved around to change the scene at will.

The right shrubs in the right place provide the garden with a backbone that supports the rest of the planting. Without them it would be flat, formless and far less interesting.

ABOVE: Pieris formosa 'Forrestii' RIGHT: When it comes to spring brilliance, there are few shrubs that surpass the deciduous azaleas.

Planting, pruning and care

Shrubs are a long-term investment, and to reap the best rewards it is worth giving your plants a good start by spending plenty of time on soil preparation. Before you buy it is also worth checking out any potentially nasty habits – like creeping obesity – to make sure that unruly shrubs do not become a nuisance later.

Choosing

Always check the label and ask for advice at the garden centre to make sure the plant's requirements match the soil and situation you have to offer. It is most important to check out its vital statistics. You can't cram a 2m (6ft) shrub into a 1m (3ft) space without problems. If it has to be cut back hard to keep it the right size, the odds are you won't see many flowers. Once you have

Spring-flowering shrubs such as viburnum and spiraea make a cool, white background for variegated hostas.

chosen the right plant, make sure you buy a decent specimen. Look for one with a well-balanced shape and plenty of stems spreading evenly from the base. A skinny, leggy specimen may survive, but it will need a couple of years of restorative pruning before it amounts to anything much. You should also avoid plants with spotty or brown leaves, or those that seem very badly pot-bound – they'll always take time to recover. Weeds, moss or liverwort growing in the pot are not necessarily a bad sign, though they often mean a plant has been standing around for a while, but if it has been well looked after – not pale, stunted or loosing its leaves – it will do fine. Simply scrape the top 2.5cm (1in) of old compost away before planting to avoid introducing weeds along with it, and give it a good feed as it will probably be ready for one.

Planting

If shrubs are dry when you buy them, water well with half-strength liquid feed when you get them home. You should plant your shrubs straight away. The longer you leave it, the greater the chances of plants being neglected or forgotten, and when you do find time to do the job they may have been damaged in the wind, or could even be dead.

   If you are planting in a new border that has previously been well prepared with lots of organic matter, all you need to do is water the plant in its pot, dig a hole big enough for the rootball, tip the plant out of its pot, put it in and fill in with soil (see step by step, page 93). It's a good idea to tease out a few of the biggest roots if your plant happens to be a bit pot-bound, but otherwise it's best left undisturbed. If you are planting into an old border or in grass, then make the planting hole at least two or three times the size of the rootball and loosen the soil at the bottom of the hole with the points of a garden fork. Then mix in lots of organic matter; I recommend at least a bucketful. Always plant shrubs with their best side facing forwards – like film stars, shrubs have their good and bad profiles. Mix lots more organic matter into the topsoil that was removed from the hole and use that to fill the gaps around the roots. Don't go tamping it down as if you were laying foundations for a motorway. Gently firm, then run a trickle of water around the shrub which will settle the soil and water it at the same time. It's a lot kinder.

SHRUBS YOU MUST PRUNE

◆ **Dogwoods** (*Cornus alba* cultivars) grown for their coloured winter stems need to have the oldest stems, which are a darker colour, cut to ground level in late winter to encourage new shoots – as it is these that are the most colourful.

◆ **Ribes, philadelphus and forsythia** become big and untidy unless regularly pruned. Cut the old, flowered shoots off, while you can still see the dead flower heads, just above the next young, unflowered shoot down the stem.

◆ **Hydrangeas** are often wrongly pruned. The best plan is to remove the dead flower heads back to the next healthy, green shoot in spring, after the last frost. Don't cut them back too hard or at other times of year, or they won't flower.

◆ **Variegated shrubs** often develop plain green shoots. Remove these from their base as soon as you see them or they will take over at the expense of the variegated leaves and ruin the plant.

A well-proportioned shrub border containing ceanothus, cistus and Rosa moyesii *'Geranium'.*

Pruning

If you buy decent shrubs in the first place, all the necessary pruning to form a good, basic shape will have been done. Eventually you'll find the odd branch that sticks out and these can be shortened to tidy them up at any time of year. It is also a good idea to cut one or two of the oldest branches down to ground level every winter as the shrubs age. This acts as a sort of continuous, gentle rejuvenation treatment, stopping the centre filling up with unproductive, old wood and encouraging new shoots to develop from the base. If you inherit a garden with shrubs in need of serious restoration, cut out one-third of the oldest stems in winter or spring, feed and mulch well, and continue the process for three years until all the old stems have been replaced. They'll soon be as good as new.

Aftercare

Keep new shrubs well watered, especially if you plant them in summer or when they are in flower. If you are not so keen on doing vital aftercare, autumn is the time to plant, when the weather should take care of them for you. Personally I don't see any point in feeding shrubs when first planted as it takes a while for their roots to settle in – a liquid feed just before planting while they are still in their pot makes more sense. Feed your shrubs at the start of each growing season, in spring, when the soil is naturally moist. Sprinkle a handful of general fertilizer or, better still, a special shrub or rose feed around them. Then mulch well with compost. If you remember, feed them again around mid-summer – use the same amount of rose or shrub fertilizer, and water it well in. But, it's the spring feed that is most important.

A-Z shrubs for spring

Spring-flowering shrubs get the year off to a good start and make a brilliant backdrop to colourful carpets of bulbs. Where there is room, team a small group of bulbs with a deciduous shrub so that the fresh green of the new foliage acts as a halo around the flowers in front. In spring you can take liberties with your colour schemes as everyone is so pleased to see flowers once winter is over.

■ **Camellia × williamsii 'Donation'**
2.25m (8ft) high x 1.25m (4ft) wide
There are hundreds of camellias around, but 'Donation' is a real old favourite with large, clear pink, semi-double flowers that show up well against the oval, deep green, evergreen leaves. It flowers early and reliably every year.
Cultivation Like all camellias, this one needs acid soil, but it does not have to be as acid as for rhododendrons. You can improve neutral soil by forking in sulphur chips every couple of years. Dig in lots of organic matter before planting, and choose a site in light, dappled shade. It loves to be among trees, although it is all right in sun if the soil stays moist and the plant does not get a strong midday baking. The vital thing is not to grow camellias

Camellia x williamsii 'Donation' is one of the most reliable varieties available.

where they are exposed to early morning sun or strong wind, otherwise the buds can fail to open or flowers turn brown. Due to its rather floppy shape, 'Donation' is a particularly good camellia to train on a north-facing wall.

■ **Chaenomeles speciosa**
(Ornamental quince, japonica)
1.25m (4ft) high x 2m (6ft) wide
Ornamental quince has lovely, big flowers rather like pear blossom, but in much brighter colours. Popular cultivars include 'Moerloosei' which has white flowers flushed dark pink, and 'Nivalis' which blooms early and has white flowers with gold stamens in the centres. They are prickly shrubs and, when grown free-standing, can be untidy.
Cultivation Not a fussy plant, as long as the soil is not badly waterlogged. Happy in sun or shade. To stop plants getting straggly, trim lightly every year by shortening the flowered stems back to a sideshoot or strong bud, soon after the flowers are over. They also make good shrubs for training up a wall.

■ **Forsythia × intermedia 'Lynwood'**
2.5m (8ft) high x 2m (6ft) wide
You'll find several different forsythias in the garden centre, but this one has the biggest and yellowest flowers with the widest petals, so it creates the biggest splash of colour in the garden. It is also a particularly free-flowering and reliable variety – you can't go wrong with it.
Cultivation Not fussy about the soil, it grows in sun or very light shade. There is one thing you must do with forsythia and that is prune it, otherwise plants get very leggy and straggle all over the place.

Shortly after flowering, cut the flowered stems back to a good sideshoot, perhaps 60cm (2ft) or more below the tip of the stem. This keeps plants neat, compact and tidy. Forsythia also makes a stunning flowering hedge which, if clipped after flowering, keeps its shape and turns into a wall of flowers every year.

■ **Ceanothus 'Concha'**
(Californian lilac)
2m (6ft) high x 2m (6ft) wide
A compact evergreen shrub with glossy, dark green leaves, this lilac is one of the most reliable. Its late spring flowers are reddish in bud and open indigo blue.
Cultivation Plant in a good soil and full sun. Chalky soil is not enjoyed, and shelter from wind is essential. Trim back flowered shoots as the blooms fade in early summer.

■ **Pieris formosa var. forrestii 'Wakehurst'**
2m (6ft) high x 1.25m (4ft) wide
Bold, acid-loving, evergreen shrub with big bunches of lily of the valley-like flowers that are shortly followed by bright red, new growth that, from a distance, gives the impression that the plant is covered in a second crop of flowers, this time bright red ones.
Cultivation Pieris enjoy similar conditions to rhododendrons: cool, acid soil, with plenty of organic matter, that does not dry out badly in summer, but is not waterlogged in winter. It is happiest in light, dappled shade, but thrives in sun if the soil stays moist enough. Shelter is vital, especially from the east, otherwise pieris flowers and the young, coloured foliage are easily scorched by frost.

The ornamental quince, Chaenomeles speciosa 'Simonii', simply smothers itself in white blossom early in the year.

▥ *Rhododendron yakushimanum*
1m (3ft) high x 1m (3ft) wide

A real, live, baby rhododendron, but without the sleepless nights. Many varieties of this delightful dwarf evergreen are available now that it is getting so popular. **'Percy Wiseman'** is one of my favourites with peachy-pink flowers that slowly fade to apple blossom or cream as they age. There is also a whole series named after Snow White's seven dwarfs.

Cultivation R.Yakushimanum is the perfect rhododendron for small gardens, and tailor-made for tubs. In the garden it wants a very special situation at the front of a sheltered, moist, acid border where you can really enjoy it. In tubs, grow in ericaceous compost, water regularly and feed every spring with a special product for ericaceous plants. Re-pot into fresh compost every third year, soon after flowering, and in other years it will make do with top dressing. Just scrape away the top 5cm (2in) of old compost and replace it with new.

▥ *Viburnum carlesii* **'Aurora'**
2m (6ft) high x 2m (6ft) wide

The powerful scent is the first thing that strikes you about this viburnum, but the flowers look pretty good too. Large, round clusters of pink, star-shaped flowers with deeper pink tubes at the base create a two-tone effect. It provides further interest in autumn when its leaves are burnished red. If I were allowed just half a dozen shrubs in my garden, this viburnum would most certainly be one of them.

Cultivation This is rather an expensive plant as it is not the easiest to propagate, so it's worth taking care over preparing the site. Dig in plenty of well-rotted organic matter, and choose a spot that is sheltered, in full sun or very light shade. This is definitely one to put close to your front door or garden path, to appreciate the scent. Pruning is generally unnecessary, except to cut out any dead wood – a rare occurrence.

Ceanothus 'Concha' is an evergreen Californian lilac with a wonderful display of blue flowers in late spring. It stays relatively compact and so is suitable for small gardens.

magnolias *are shrubs and trees that never fail to draw gasps of admiration. This is partly due to their spectacular, waxy flowers spangling the branches like stars or standing up like goblets, and partly to the fact that many of them flower early in the year, when to produce such fabulous flowers on naked branches is brave and sometimes foolhardy.*

Mild weather will often coax magnolia blooms open in early spring, only to be followed by frosty weather that turns them brown – but not always. The risk is undoubtedly worth taking with a plant that offers great rewards.

The most important thing about magnolias is to plant them where they will have room to grow without being pruned. A pruned magnolia is a butchered magnolia. They will recover from heavy cutting back, but I reckon their graceful shape is never the same again.

Many of them do not enjoy chalky soil, although *Magnolia × loebneri* 'Merrill' has grown well in my garden in Hampshire on shallow soil overlying chalk for the last 10 years or so and flowers freely, but I did enrich the soil generously before planting. Other species worth trying if your soil is alkaline are *M. grandiflora*, *M. stellata*, *M. wilsonii* and *M. sieboldii*.

The roots of magnolias are thick and fleshy, and damage to them at planting time should be avoided at all costs. It can result in their being reluctant to flower for years afterwards. When you plant a container-grown specimen, do so with care, making sure that its root system is not bashed about.

Enrich the soil with plenty of organic matter, such as well-rotted garden compost or manure, and water the plant in before giving the surface of the soil a good mulch with the same stuff. Always choose a site that is sheltered, in sun or dappled shade, and one that is not in a frost pocket where damage to the precocious flowers is more likely than elsewhere.

Background is all important if your magnolia is to look its best. There is nothing better than a forget-me-not blue sky, but that is in the lap of the gods. If you can plant it at some distance from the dark green background of a yew hedge, or where a brick or stone wall will show it off, so much the better.

If the unthinkable happens and you have to move a magnolia, experience shows that it will recover better if it is cut really hard back. This goes against the grain in terms of my pruning advice, but as an emergency measure it is effective.

If you think your garden is too cold to grow a magnolia, but you'd like one nevertheless, try growing *M. grandiflora* or *M. × soulangeana* as a wall-trained specimen.

Few pests and diseases bother magnolias, apart from honey fungus, and coral spot on dead shoots, but scale insects are sometimes a problem.

Propagation is usually by grafting in winter, but most gardeners prefer layering – pegging a suitable branch down to the ground in early spring and removing it a year or so later when it has rooted. Spectacular seed cases sometimes follow the flowers. The seeds can be sown outdoors in autumn but may take up to 30 years to reach flowering age. Or, buy a grafted plant that will flower sooner.

ABOVE: Magnolia 'Leonard Messel' BELOW: Magnolia × soulangeana is everybody's idea of a magnolia, with its waxy, goblet-shaped flowers.

Choosing the best magnolias from the increasing number of varieties on offer is hard, but these are my favourites for garden cultivation.

Magnolia grandiflora
Up to 18m (60ft) high × 15m (50ft) wide
An evergreen with broad, glossy, green leaves that are often felted with foxy-brown hairs on the undersides. Huge, fragrant, creamy-white flowers open from late summer to autumn. Great on south- and west-facing house walls. This magnolia can be kept in bounds by pruning without looking butchered. The variety **'Exmouth'** is hardier than the true species and flowers at an earlier age.

Magnolia liliiflora **'Nigra'**
Up to 2.5m (8ft) high × 2.5m (8ft) wide
For those who like their magnolias dark, this is a reliable choice, producing dark purplish-pink flowers in early summer and then occasionally through until autumn. It is also a compact grower.

Magnolia × loebneri
Up to 8m (25ft) high × 7m (23ft) wide
Especially useful because of its ability to grow on alkaline soils, this magnolia has yielded several excellent varieties. **'Leonard Messel'** has star-shaped, lilac-pink flowers in spring, while those of **'Merrill'** are pure white and start out goblet-shaped before becoming stars.

Magnolia sieboldii
Up to 8m (25ft) high × 12m (40ft) wide
A favourite of mine because it flowers from late spring to late summer and has fragrant, bowl-shaped flowers of pure white, with a boss of crimson stamens.

Magnolia × soulangeana
Up to 6m (20ft) high × 6m (20ft) wide
The archetypal magnolia seen in so many front gardens. Huge, waxy goblets of flowers open on the naked branches of rounded trees in spring. Among the best are **'Lennei alba'**, which is white, and **'Rustica rubra'**, which is dark purplish-red.

The earliest magnolia to flower is Magnolia stellata, whose flowers really do shine like white stars against a dull winter sky.

Magnolia stellata
Up to 3m (10ft) high × 4m (12ft) wide
The earliest, star-shaped, white magnolia, which is so often a martyr to frost. Settle for the true species, or go for **'Water Lily'** or **'Centennial'**, which has up to 32 large petals on each flower. **'Rubra'** has flowers of dark pink.

Magnolia wilsonii
Up to 6m (20ft) high × 6m (20ft) wide
If I could plant only one magnolia, this would be my choice. It is similar to *M. sieboldii*, but here the bowl-shaped flowers hang downwards so that you can look up into their crimson centres. It blooms in late spring and early summer and its leaves have reddish-brown felt on the undersides. Best in dappled shade.

A-Z shrubs for summer

Gardens are so full to bursting with colourful annuals, perennials and roses in summer that you might wonder why you need shrubs to flower at the same time. But without them mixed borders would miss out on one complete tier of flowers. And for anyone trying to cut down the work that is involved with growing lots of annuals and perennials, flowering shrubs provide all the colour with none of the chores. Low-growing species like hebe, potentilla and cistus can even be used as year-round substitutes for bedding plants in both borders and containers.

■ *Abelia chinensis* 'Edward Goucher'
2m (6ft) high × 2m (6ft) wide

An unusual shrub with a very long flowering season covering the whole of summer and early autumn. The greyish-green leaves are the ideal shade to set off the lilac-pink flowers, which come in clusters at the tips of the shoots. The flowers are pleasantly scented.

Cultivation Any good, fertile but well-drained soil suits it; sun and a sheltered spot are essential. It is quite slow-growing and takes a while to reach the maximum size, but doesn't need any regular pruning. If it develops a few long, straggly shoots that spoil the shape, cut them back in late spring after the worst frosts are over.

■ *Buddleja davidii* 'Black Knight' (Butterfly bush)
2.5m (8ft) high × 1.5m (5ft) wide

This shrub is like a mini nature reserve when the flowers are out in late summer. 'Black Knight' is a popular variety, with deep purple, banana-shaped blooms. The plants grow rather upright, and, as well as several species of adult butterflies that are attracted to the flowers, you may find pretty caterpillars of the mullein moth nibbling the leaves – they don't eat much, so don't do the plants any harm.

Cultivation The reason the buddleja is so popular is that, besides looking good, it is very easy to grow. The two essentials are sun and a well-drained soil.

The long, spiky flowers of Buddleja *'Black Knight' are produced in greatest quantity on plants that are pruned hard in spring.*

It doesn't even mind a breezy spot, though the flowers last longer given a bit of shelter. Pruning is vital, otherwise the shrub shoots up to about 4m (12ft) with all the flowers at the top where you can't see them. Trim it back by about half when the flowers are over, then prune properly in spring after the worst of the cold weather has finished, by cutting the stems off just above new shoots about 60cm (2ft) from the ground.

■ *Ceanothus* × *delileanus* 'Gloire de Versailles' (Californian lilac)
2m (6ft) high × 2m (6ft) wide

Looking at this shrub, it is easy to see why it is called Californian lilac; the flowers are exactly the same shape and size as real lilac, except they are a bright powder blue. This is a shade never seen in any lilac, and, in fact, a blue this true is rare among shrubs. The plant makes a large shrub with slightly arching stems. A real summer spectacle.

Cultivation Like all ceanothus this one needs well-drained soil and a warm spot sheltered from the wind really to do its best. Plants can get very big and straggly unless pruned hard every year. Prune this variety in early spring, cutting back to within a few buds of a permanent framework of main stems.

■ *Ceratostigma willmottianum* (Hardy plumbago)
60cm (2ft) high × 60cm (2ft) wide

A real gem that will add a taste of the South of France to any garden. Although small, mound-shaped and compact, this delightful, miniature shrub is covered in plumbago-shaped flowers that are a deep shade of blue. It is good value, with

a long flowering season covering mid-summer to early autumn. After the flowers come to an end, the foliage takes on red and orange autumn tints.

Cultivation Reasonably rich, well-drained soil in a sunny spot and lots of shelter are the keys to success. This plant is normally quite badly browned by the frost in winter, so in mid- or late spring, cut back the stems to a few centimetres above the ground to make way for new shoots. In cold areas it is worth tucking a thick mulch round the plant in winter.

■ *Cistus* **'Silver Pink'** (Sun rose)
60cm (2ft) high × 60cm (2ft) wide

The big, fragile, poppy-like flowers of cistus tell you that summer is really here and you can safely take the sunglasses out of hibernation. It is at its best from early to late summer. This variety has delicate, silvery-pink flowers that are the most beautiful of any cistus I've seen. It is an evergreen plant that remains quite small and neat, unlike some cistus that can get a bit straggly.

Cultivation A handy plant for the front of a border, but invaluable for dry gardens, steep banks and other sunny spots which are its favourite places. It likes rather poor soil, and insists on superb drainage and some shelter from the wind.

Cistus 'Silver Pink' has a fragility about its flowers that belies the toughness of the plant. It is happy in a dry, sunny spot.

■ *Escallonia* **'Apple Blossom'**
2m (6ft) high × 2m (6ft) wide

This big, evergreen shrub is often grown as a flowering hedge around seaside gardens as it is salt- and wind-resistant, but it does well in areas with kinder growing conditions too. 'Apple Blossom' is always popular for its pale pink flowers, which continue from mid-summer well into autumn. There are other varieties with deeper pink white or red flowers.

Cultivation Easily grown in normal garden soil, though it likes good drainage and a sunny situation. Can be affected by hard frosts in colder parts of the country unless given a sheltered spot or trained as a wall shrub.

■ *Eucryphia glutinosa*
10m (30ft) high × 6m (20ft) wide

This is reputedly the hardiest of all the eucryphias (see also page 75) and it is a glossy-leaved deciduous or semi-evergreen beauty that makes an upright shrub with good autumn colour. However, it is the summer flowers that I rate most highly. They open from mid- to late summer and are white and cup-shaped with a central tuft of stamens. A real beauty.

Cultivation This eucryphia requires a rich, lime-free soil and shelter from strong, drying winds. Try to keep its roots cool (rather like a clematis) and its head in the sun. Mulch it with manure or compost each spring.

■ *Fuchsia magellanica* **'Riccartonii'** (Hardy fuchsia)
1m (3ft) high × 1m (3ft) wide

A favourite fuchsia, bearing long, elegant flowers in red and purple with a cluster of long, red, pollen-tipped stamens hanging down from the centre of each bell. It flowers all summer and into autumn, until the first frost.

Cultivation Plants die down to ground level in winter in all but the mildest areas, but in warmer parts of Britain are used as a flowering hedge. Elsewhere, grow individual plants among shrubs or perennials in sun or light shade, and protect the roots by surrounding the plant with a thick mulch in autumn. Cut the dead stems down in spring.

■ *Hebe* **'Great Orme'**
1m (3ft) high × 1m (3ft) wide

One of the taller hebes, with long, narrow leaves and slender, conical-shaped heads of flowers, which are big, fluffy and bright pink. It looks especially good grown with purple foliage. I like it next door to *Weigela florida* 'Foliis Purpureis', which does not grow much bigger.

Cultivation The golden rule with hebes is that the bigger the leaves, the less hardy the plant. By that reckoning this should be pretty tender, but I've never found it to be so. Maybe in colder areas it would be a good idea to root cuttings in summer, to keep in the greenhouse in winter. Like all hebes, this likes a sunny sheltered spot with lots of sunshine.

Fuchsia magellanica 'Riccartonii' makes a great informal hedge. Introduced in 1833, it remains as popular as ever.

■ *Hibiscus syriacus* (Hardy hibiscus)
2m (6ft) high × 1m (3ft) wide
The award for the most exotic flowers imaginable on an outdoor plant must belong to the hardy hibiscus. Its flowers really do look just like those of the popular indoor plant, except that the vivid red of the tropical plant is not one of the many colours on offer in the hardy version. Some of the best varieties are the mauve-pink **'Woodbridge'**, violet-blue **'Oiseau Bleu'**, and white-with-a-red-eye **'Red Heart'**. They flower from mid-summer right into early autumn.
Cultivation Needs a sheltered sunny spot with well-drained soil, but it is no trouble to grow and once established can be left alone. It needs no pruning.

Lavender makes a good low hedge, especially leading up to a front door where it will release its fragrance when brushed past.

■ *Hydrangea aspera*
2m (6ft) high × 2m (6ft) wide
Most people know only the popular hortensia hydrangeas, but some of the species are well worth getting acquainted with too. This one has big, domed heads made up of masses of tiny, fertile, blue flowers surrounded by a loose ring of mauvish-blue, infertile flowers with big bracts that almost look as if they are dangling on short strings. The overall effect is of a large, mound-shaped shrub with big, velvety leaves and lacecap flowers that have run wild. Fascinating.
Cultivation It likes light, dappled shade and cool, moist soil with lots of organic matter and a good mulching each spring. It grows on both acid and alkaline soil. Plants don't need pruning, but you can cut back long shoots that spoil the shape of the plant in early spring.

■ *Lavandula* (Lavender)
60cm (2ft) high × 60cm (2ft) wide
Herb farms offer an enormous range of lavenders, but the best ones to plant in a flower border are the big, smelly ones that are nowadays called the Old English Group. These are like toilet water on the hoof. The plants are a tad undisciplined, with violet flowers at the end of long stalks that wave in the wind, offering a romantic, cottage-garden effect. You can also get more compact lavenders; French lavender, *Lavandula stoechas*, is particularly decorative as the flowers are each adorned by a pair of mauve tufts, **'Helmsdale'** is a particularly good variety, and hardy, too.
Cultivation Well-drained soil and lots of sun are all that lavender needs to do well. Grow it at the front of a border or along the edges of a path to get the full benefit. Old plants can become

Although sometimes short-lived, the tree mallow, Lavatera olbia 'Rosea', makes up for its shortcomings by flowering profusely.

very straggly and often splay open unattractively, but this is easily prevented by clipping them over every year after they have finished flowering to reshape them. Lavenders do not like being cut back into old wood.

■ *Lavatera olbia* (Tree mallow)
2m (6ft) high × 1m (3ft) wide
Imagine a bushy hollyhock and you've got a perfect idea of this plant. Unlike the annual lavateras that are sometimes grown as bedding plants, this kind is hardy and great value in the garden as it flowers non-stop over about three months from mid- to late summer. The most popular varieties are '**Rosea**' which has mauve-pink flowers and '**Barnsley**' which has pale pink flowers each with a deeper pink eye.
Cultivation Lavatera likes lots of sun and well-drained soil; where conditions are not entirely ideal, it lives for only a few years. The plants need to be cut down hard, to within 30cm (1ft) or so of

the ground. Do this annually in spring after the worst of the frosts are past to encourage lots of strong, new, flowering shoots to develop from the base of the plant. It will also clear away all the old, dead stems.

■ *Leycesteria formosa*
(Himalayan honeysuckle)
2m (6ft) high × 60cm (2ft) wide
A very striking shrub throughout the summer, when the tall, upright, cane-like stems are dripping with long, dangly

HOW TO PLANT A CONTAINER-GROWN SHRUB

1 Make sure the rootball of the shrub is sufficiently moist. Soak the compost about an hour before planting to minimize any check to growth. Check that the shrub is suitable for the situation in which it will be planted.

2 Dig a hole that is more than large enough to accommodate the rootball of the plant. Work well-rotted garden compost or proprietary planting mixture into the bottom of the hole and mix it with the soil that has been removed.

3 Plant the shrub so that the top of the rootball is just fractionally below the finished soil level. Firm the earth around the plant with your foot, water the plant in and then spread an organic mulch on top of the soil.

chains of red and purple bracts that have white flowers mixed among them. Later in the season these are replaced by purple berries that last well into autumn.

Cultivation Incredibly easy to grow practically anywhere. It looks best in a large shrubbery or wild garden due to its spreading habit – you may also find occasional self-sown seedlings. Plants need tidying up in spring, so cut any broken or nasty-looking stems down to ground level. In cold areas the whole stem system may be killed off, but plants re-grow from the base without any problems and will flower as usual.

■ *Phlomis fruticosa* (Jerusalem sage)
1m (3ft) high × 1.25m (4ft) wide

A mound-shaped shrub with felty-textured, grey-green leaves shaped like large sage leaves, which will remain on the plant if the winter is mild. Jerusalem sage flowers from early to late summer, producing peculiar clusters of curved, mustard-yellow flowers at the tips of the

shoots. It looks a little unusual, but the flowers complement the foliage, creating a Mediterranean feel.

Cultivation This is a shrub for a hot, dry, sunny spot with rather poor soil. Although it needs watering until it becomes established in very arid conditions, once it gets going you can leave it alone. You don't even need to prune it, but if you cut the whole plant back by about 5cm (2in) in spring, after the worst of the frosts, you will get rid of any frost-damaged shoots and keep the plant shapely. A good plant for a dry garden.

■ *Potentilla fruticosa*
60cm (2ft) high × 60cm (2ft) wide

A reliable garden standby that flowers without problems throughout summer every year, whatever the weather. Lots of different varieties are available, some growing a bit bigger or smaller than average, and with flowers in a huge range of bright colours. Some of my favourites

ABOVE: The grey-green leaves and yellow flower w of Phlomis fruticosa, *have a hot feel to them.*
BELOW: Potentillas are useful in sun or dappled sh

include 'Abbotswood', which is white, 'Tangerine', a warm shade of burnt orange, and 'Princess', which is a really lovely shade of pink.

Cultivation A dwarf shrub that needs a well-drained spot at the front of a border. Most varieties are best in sun but those with red flowers, especially 'Red Ace', last best in very light shade and fade less rapidly.

■ *Spiraea* × *billiardii* 'Triumphans'
2.5m (8ft) high × 2m (6ft) wide

If you can't grow ceanothus, this is the plant for you. It grows to roughly the same size and has leaves similar to deciduous ceanothus, the flowers grow in long, fluffy spikes bigger than the best ceanothus, but instead of being powder blue, they are powder pink. It is an exceptionally striking plant, flowering in mid- and late summer.

Cultivation It is not fussy about its growing conditions. Any good garden soil suits it, and it grows happily in both sun and light shade among other trees and shrubs. Its size makes it more suited to the back of a border. To keep it tidy cut back to within a few buds of a permanent framework of branches, about 60cm (2ft) above ground level in spring each year.

■ *Tamarix ramosissima*
2.5m (8ft) high × 1.5m (5ft) wide

This is the shrub you often see at the seaside making a great, big, feathery bush that flowers throughout the summer holidays. It has rusty-red stems with the top 60cm–1m (2–3ft) tipped with masses of tiny, foamy-pink flowers. But it is also a good plant inland because it flowers very freely and copes well with windy gardens.

Cultivation So long as it gets lots of sun and well-drained soil it is happy. Poor or sandy soil is not a problem. Plants can get a bit shaggy-looking as they grow older, so trim them back a bit every year in early spring to keep them vigorous and shapely.

■ *Weigela florida* 'Variegata'
1.25m (4ft) high × 1.25m (4ft) wide

This is a shrub to get summer off to a good start, and although it flowers only at the start of the season it is such a stunner it is well worth its place in any garden. It is a small, deciduous shrub with pretty, cream-and-green-variegated leaves. In early summer the tips of the shoots are smothered in hundreds of small, pink flowers. Even after the flowers are over, the foliage stays fresh and bright-looking, so the plant makes a good background for surrounding flowers for the rest of the summer. And it stays small enough never to become a nuisance.

Cultivation 'Variegata' grows happily in normal garden conditions, in both sun and light shade. To keep the plant compact and well shaped, long deadhead after the flowers are over by cutting off the dead flowers plus a few centimetres of stem, back to a good pair of buds.

Strikingly architectural, the sword-leafed rosette of Yucca gloriosa *'Variegata' is a good choice for a focal point.*

■ *Yucca gloriosa* 'Variegata'
(Adam's needle)
1.25m (4ft) high × 1.25m (4ft) wide

Every garden needs a spot of architecture, and this chunky evergreen could be just the answer. It has spiky, green-and-cream-striped leaves that grow out in a starburst shape from the base of the plant. A mature plant will also flower, sending up a 2m (6ft) spike strung with lots of big, scented, white bell flowers that look like festoons of light bulbs.

Cultivation A great plant for a container in a special place. Plants need good drainage and plenty of sun. If grown in a pot, give it cactus compost made by mixing about 10 per cent gritty sand into John Innes No. 3. In the garden, give it a warm spot by a wall or on the patio, where it will enjoy the reflected warmth. Although it looks exotic, it is actually quite hardy.

A–Z shrubs for autumn

You don't need a huge garden full of enormous trees to have a good autumn show. By choosing the right shrubs you can enjoy dazzling foliage tints, fragrance and flowers too. Put them together with fruiting and berrying trees, and you will have a garden filled with seasonal colour and interest. Suddenly autumn can become a good finale to the end of the season, rather than a sordid time of brown and rotting vegetation livened only by bouts of leaf raking!

Hebe 'Autumn Glory' waits until late in the season before opening its purple bottle-brush flowers.

■ *Acer japonicum* **'Aconitifolium'**
(Japanese maple)
4m (12ft) high × 3m (10ft) wide

A large shrub that can also be trained as a medium-sized tree. It has typical maple-shaped leaves with a frilly fringe around the edge. The foliage looks good in spring and summer when it is plain green, but in autumn the leaves turn an incredible deep crimson colour. They even look good when they have fallen on to the ground, especially when the plant is surrounded by a carpet of autumn-flowering bulbs.

Cultivation This is a shrub that likes cool, moist roots, so heavy mulching each spring is a good idea, but avoid poorly drained soil. *Acer japonicum* cultivars are not so fussy about their growing

conditions as **A. palmatum**, and are often much easier to accommodate for this reason. They make bigger plants but are very graceful.

■ *Elaeagnus* × *ebbingei*
3m (10ft) high × 3m (10ft) wide

A tough evergreen with a surprise up its sleeve. Although it flowers in late autumn, you'll have to look closely to spot the tiny, green bells dangling beneath the branches. You are far more likely to smell them, and wonder what is causing the delicious perfume that you would expect to come from an altogether more delicate plant. The silvery-bronze-sheened green leaves are remarkably wind- and salt-resistant; on the south coast of Britain this elaeagnus is often planted as a windbreak.

Cultivation Easy to grow, it does well just about anywhere, in sun or light shade. but will establish faster if you dig plenty of organic matter into the soil first. It can be clipped to shape or trimmed as a hedge in late spring, otherwise just prune back long stems to keep it tidy.

■ *Euonymus alatus* (Spindle bush)
2m (6ft) high × 2m (6ft) wide

Most people know euonymus as the small, variegated evergreens used for

Few shrubs can compete with the spindle bush, Euonymus alatus, *when it comes to brilliant-red autumn colour.*

shady foliage gardens and winter hanging baskets, but the relatively little-grown, deciduous spindle bush types are outstanding for their spectacular autumn colour. *Euonymus alatus* is a sensible-sized shrub that will fit into most gardens and still colour up reliably every year, producing a volcanic molten-crimson display. After the leaves have dropped, you can see the peculiar corky flanges that run up and down the stems, which give the plant winter appeal too.

Cultivation Very easy and undemanding, it grows happily in most reasonable soils in sun or light shade. It does not need pruning, though you can tidy it up in early spring by removing any stems that spoil the shape of the plant.

■ *Fatsia japonica*
1.5m (5ft) high × 1.25m (4ft) wide

Whenever anyone mentions a shady spot where nothing else will grow, this is one of the first plants I think of. But what usually gets overlooked is that it also flowers in late autumn. The flowers are rather like those of wild ivy, greenish-white globes that are set off perfectly by the handsome,

glossy, palmate, evergreen leaves. The whole effect is like a giant flower arrangement, except it happens naturally.

Cultivation This plant is virtually indestructable. It thrives in all those dry, shady places where everything else (bar one or two real stalwarts) will turn up its nose. It also grows in better soil, and in dappled shade or even places that get sun for part of the day, but avoid strong sun as this bleaches the leaves and makes the plant look very sick. No pruning is needed: just snip out any dead leaves or shoots to give it a spring clean if necessary early in the year.

■ *Hebe* 'Autumn Glory'
60m (2ft) high × 60cm (2ft) wide

Several hebes, like 'Gauntlettii', 'Midsummer Beauty' and 'Great Orme' flower into the autumn, but this is the one that I find always goes on longest. Good old 'Autumn Glory' can still be flowering almost up to Christmas. It has smaller flowers, rather like purple blobs instead of the long spikes of the other varieties I've mentioned, but they do stand up to increasingly bad weather as autumn goes by, and they look particularly good against the dark green foliage. It begins flowering just as early as other hebes, at the start of summer.

Cultivation Needs a sunny spot and reasonably well-drained soil, but otherwise it's not fussy. Like all hebes, it's very easy to grow. It does not need any pruning.

■ *Nandinia domestica* 'Harbor Dwarf' (Sacred bamboo)
60m (2ft) high × 60cm (2ft) wide

I can never understand why this is called sacred bamboo, as it doesn't look anything like bamboo to me. It is actually a shrubby evergreen plant with spreading upright stems grown mainly for its foliage, which in spring has bold, crimson highlights, but in autumn goes berserk with a flurry of pink, red, apricot, copper, bronze, cream, lime and gold. You will often get red berries as well.

Although it looks tropical in appearance, Fatsia japonica, the false castor oil palm, is tough as old boots.

Cultivation Well-drained soil with plenty of organic matter, so it does not dry out badly in summer, and shelter are essential. A sunny spot is preferred as the most vivid colours develop in this situation, though the plant can be grown in light, dappled shade. Low-growing varieties like this can be planted 60cm (2ft) apart as ground cover. Plants are technically semi-evergreen, so they can drop their leaves if the weather is cold or they are not in a sufficiently sheltered spot.

■ *Spiraea betulifolia* var. *aemiliana*
60m (2ft) high × 60cm (2ft) wide

This small, mound-shaped plant produces the sort of autumn colour you normally see only on giant trees in the gardens of stately homes; few shrubs this small put on anything like this sort of flamboyant display of vivid yellow, orange and red. The leaves have deeper red veins which make them look even more spectacular.

Cultivation Grows in any reasonable soil, but it is best planted in sun as this helps the brightest colours to develop. As it is so small, it's vital not to plant it where it is likely to get swamped by bigger plants as this, too, will stop it colouring up properly.

A–Z shrubs for winter

You'll never make a blaze of colour with winter-flowering shrubs, it's true, but I'm not sure I'd want to. A pale palette of colours looks much more in tune with the season. Real winter wonderland stuff. Those flowers that look so peculiar when you see them on a plant in a pot at the garden centre suddenly look the most natural thing on earth when you see them growing in a winter garden, teamed with evergreen foliage, shining, white birch trunks and bare stems. A sprinkling of winter shrubs really makes the most of the changing seasons and, perhaps more important, gets you on your feet after Christmas dinner for a walk around outdoors.

■ *Chimonanthus praecox* **'Grandiflorus'** (Wintersweet)
2m (6ft) high × 2m (6ft) wide
From a distance the flowers of wintersweet are invisible as they are so translucent. But as you get closer, you can see that the bare branching stems are studded with surprisingly large, fragrant, dainty, nodding, light yellow flowers with purple-stained throats. Young plants take a few years to start flowering, but are well worth the wait. Plant close to a path against a background of evergreens, or on a sunny wall where you'll be able to see and smell the flowers easily.

Just when I think it's all over for another year, the hoar frost rimes the fading leaves and flowers for a late show.

Cultivation Easy to grow in well-drained soil; it's also happy in chalky gardens as long as there is some organic matter. Plant in a sheltered, sunny spot so the new growth can ripen properly at the end of summer, as this encourages better flowering. Does not normally need pruning, but can be cut back immediately after flowering to keep the shape tidier.

■ *Erica carnea*
(Winter-flowering heather)
20cm (8in) high × 45cm (18in) wide
A real winter winner, flowering reliably for months whatever the weather, even in windy gardens. Lots of different named varieties are available with white, pink, red, mauve or purple flowers and some have orange or golden foliage as well. Use them as a colourful carpet in front of shrubs, especially conifers or evergreens, but they are also brilliant for temporary planting in winter containers.

Cultivation Grow in well-drained soil containing plenty of organic matter; the plants hate drying out badly in summer or being waterlogged in winter. Unlike most other heathers, this group will grow in slightly alkaline soil, as well as acid, and put up with very slight shade. In winter containers, grow them in John Innes compost and don't let them dry out.

■ *Hamamelis mollis* **'Pallida'**
(Witch hazel)
2m (6ft) high × 2m (6ft) wide
My favourite of all the witch hazels, this one has big, spidery-shaped, sulphur-yellow flowers all along its bare, spreading branches. It can be in flower continuously

The spidery, fragrant flowers of the witch hazel, Hamamelis × intermedia *'Ruby Glow'.*

from late autumn to spring in a sheltered spot or a mild winter, but the flowers are amazingly weather-proof due to their very narrow petals. Also counts as an autumn shrub because of the bright golden colour of the hazel-like leaves, which lasts for several weeks before leaf-fall.

Cultivation Plant in deep, fertile, well-drained soil with plenty of organic matter; it prefers slightly acid soil but will grow elsewhere if conditions are otherwise good. Grow in sun or light shade. Does not need regular pruning, but take out the odd untidy branch if necessary as soon as it finishes flowering.

■ *Lonicera* × *purpusii*
(Shrubby honeysuckle)
2m (6ft) high × 2m 2m (6ft) wide

Anything less like a conventional honeysuckle would be hard to imagine, though they are close cousins. (If you need convincing, just look at the flowers in close up and think of woodbine.) This isn't a climber, but a neat, rounded bush which in winter is covered with clusters of strongly scented, white flowers – worth growing for the scent alone.

Cultivation Grow in any good garden soil in sun or light shade. It's a good idea to trim the flowered stems back to a handy sideshoot every year as soon as the flowers are over, to keep a good shape. You can also thin out older plants by taking out one or two complete branches.

■ *Mahonia* × *media* '**Charity**'
(Mahonia)
2m (6ft) high × 1m (6ft) wide

An upright sort of plant like a tall rosette of dramatic, tooth-edged, leathery, evergreen leaves, with long spikes of yellow flowers shooting out from the middle in winter. Its theatrical appearance is accompanied by a strong scent of what strikes me as lily of the valley – it's a plant you can smell before you see it. It eventually gets bushier.

Cultivation Plant in any good, fertile garden soil; it prefers light shade and a bit of shelter, so it is a good shrub to grow with others in a big border. Cut it back hard (after flowering) when it gets leggy.

■ *Sarcococca hookeriana*
(Winter box)
1.25m (4ft) high × 1.25m (4ft) wide

This used to be a very unusual plant until garden centres noticed its potential as a winter seller. It makes a medium-sized shrub with clustering, upright stems clad from top to toe with narrow, evergreen leaves and nodding, white-fringed, very fragrant flowers. Not spectacular, maybe, but a great scent – another one that's best seen close to.

Cultivation Ordinary, well-drained soil and a spot in the sun or shade suits it. No pruning is necessary.

■ *Skimmia japonica* '**Rubella**'
60cm (2ft) high × 60cm (2ft) wide

A small, neat, compact, evergreen whose best feature is the bunches of flower buds, looking rather like pink, pint-sized

bunches of grapes, that point upwards all over the plants during winter. They open out into white flowers in spring, but by then there is lots else to look at. Good for a small garden, and brilliant in winter containers. Since this variety has all male flowers, grow it with female skimmias to ensure they give good crops of berries.

Cultivation Plant in a shady spot among other shrubs; it likes well drained soil with plenty of organic matter but doesn't like chalk. In containers, grow it in John Innes compost. No need to prune.

■ *Viburnum tinus* '**Gwenllian**'
(Laurustinus)
3m (10ft) high × 3m (10ft) wide

Everyone knows the winter-flowering vibumum, the big, dense, bushy shrub with small, evergreen leaves and flattish heads of white flowers like mini elders that stay open all winter. This variety is an improvement on it, with deep pink buds. A good grow-anywhere plant.

Cultivation Plant in most good garden soils except acid, including shady spots. No need to prune, though you can tidy up older plants after flowering if necessary – they also put up with quite hard pruning.

The bright flowers and deep evergreen leaves of Vibumum tinus *'Gwellian'.*

Roses

Still the most popular flowers in British gardens, and the ones guaranteed the most star-studded send-off when new varieties are launched at the Chelsea Flower Show each year, roses are exceptionally good, reliable, long-flowering garden plants. No garden should be without some.

If you wanted, you could make an entire garden out of roses – and that is exactly what they have done at the rose growers' Mecca, the Royal National Rose Society's gardens at St Albans. You can have roses in beds, up walls and pillars, over pergolas and arbours, as hedges and ground cover, or in pots.

The great trick is to choose the right rose for the job. Some are tiddlers that would get lost in a normal flower bed, let alone the hurly-burly of the shrubbery, while others, like the giant 'Kiftsgate', are enough to dwarf a small tower block. The true 'rosebed roses' are hybrid teas and floribundas, traditionally grown on their own in formal beds with bare soil, or more likely a thick covering of horse muck, underneath them. Hybrid teas have one large flower at the tip of each stem, while floribundas have a small bunch. Now the plant namers have got at them, so we should correctly call hybrid teas 'modern bush roses', and floribundas 'cluster-flowered roses'. These are the ones to grow if you want flowers all summer.

Climbers and ramblers are the scramblers of the family. Use them to cover walls, pergolas and gazebos, or grow them up through trees for a country-garden effect. Though they are bigger than bush roses, some are only slightly larger while others are gigantic, so it pays to read the fine print before buying. Climbing roses are like bush roses with long legs. Their long stems form a framework that needs tying up to a wall, from which the flowers grow on short stems. Most climbers have two flushes of flower each summer. Rambler roses have a completely different style of growth. Instead of a framework of rigid stems, they make enormous amounts of new growth every year with flowers clustered along the bendy stems. They have only one flush of flowers a year, and some varieties, like

the notorious 'Dorothy Perkins', are terribly prone to mildew. They are good grown through trees where you can forget about them, or along a fence where it's easy to get at them for pruning.

Patio roses are a fairly recent idea: new versions of hybrid teas and floribundas but stepped down in size, suitable for growing in containers. Ground-cover roses are the same sort of thing, but lower and wider; they don't, however, smother out weeds. But they look smashing grown over a bank. Put bark chippings underneath or plant them through a sheet of woven plastic mulch fabric to avoid having to weed round them. Miniature roses are smaller still, around 30cm (12in) high. These look like 'pet' roses, and a lot of people think they are actually indoor pot plants, but they need to be out in the garden. They are a bit fussier than normal bush roses and need good drainage and shelter – a rockery or raised bed suits them fine.

If it's fashion you are after, old-fashioned roses are the last word. Mostly bred in Victorian times, they have unusual-shaped blooms, wonderful perfume (though lots of modern roses are pretty nicely scented too) and olde worlde colours not often found in modern roses, but most flower for only about six weeks at the start of summer. They are part of a large group loosely called shrub roses, as they are all treated like shrubs, and this also includes more recent shrubby varieties such as 'Ballerina' and 'Canary Bird'. Toughest are the species roses, the big, prickly jobs with 'wild rose' flowers and red or orange hips – just the thing for cow- and vandal-proof hedges or a wild garden.

ABOVE: Rosa *'Summer Wine'* RIGHT: *Shrub roses are wonderfully lavish bushes, laden with flower in early summer – and onwards to autumn if you choose the right varieties.*

Planting and care

Roses are high-performance plants that need a generous input before they reward you with a showy output. They are not expensive to buy and they will repay time spent on careful planting, followed by generous feeding and mulching.

Choosing and planting

Roses are one of the few shrubs that are still regularly available in winter as dormant plants sold with bare roots. If you can get them this way, they usually cost less than plants growing in pots, but it is vital to plant them straight away to stop the roots drying out. Pot-grown plants are available all the year round and these can be planted any time the soil is in a suitable state – not too wet and muddy, or parched and bone dry. You can even plant when they are in full bloom, but in this case you need to keep them very well watered as their roots will not have had time to grow out into the soil in search of moisture. Spring and autumn, however, are the best times for planting. When planting roses, it really does pay to dig lots of rich organic matter deeply into the ground first. Old, well-weathered manure is the traditional favourite but garden compost, mushroom compost or the contents of old growing bags will do. Plant roses in exactly the same way as shrubs, but when planting is finished the knobbly graft union (where shoots meet the rootstock) should be just below the soil surface. Roses grow best on rather heavy soil, so on light ground take particular care with the preparation. Choose a sunny spot with some shelter for most types; some rose species such as *R. rugosa* and *R. pimpinellifolia* thrive in a windy spot. When it comes to chalky and limy soils, some roses can tolerate the alkalinity, others cannot. Trial and error is the only answer.

The climbing form of 'Iceberg' might be prone to blackspot but is still a great favourite for anyone looking for a climbing white rose.

HOW TO TAKE HARDWOOD CUTTINGS OF ROSES

1 Take a shoot about 30cm (1ft) at end of year when the wood on the stem ripens. Cut off soft top above a leaf. Trim shoot bottom up to 25cm (10in), ending below a leaf. Remove all but top two leaves; rub off thorns.

2 Insert the cuttings in a slit trench. If the soil is heavy, run sharp sand in the bottom. Bury all but the top 8cm (3in) of stem.

3 In a year's time the cuttings will have rooted and begun to grow. Transplant them in the autumn to their final growing positions. As these roses grow on their own roots, no 'suckers' are produced.

Feeding and mulching

After planting, water new roses in well. Then surround the plants with a thick mulch of well-rotted manure or compost to keep the soil cool and moist. If planting in spring, sprinkle a handful of rose fertilizer around the plants and water this in. Don't bother in autumn or winter, as the feed will get washed away before the plants can make use of it, and in a hot summer wait until the plants are established before feeding them to avoid any risk of scorching the roots. There should be no need to prune roses planted from pots in summer. A good nursery will already have done whatever was necessary. So wait until the usual pruning time.

Routine care

Roses are naturally very heavy feeders. Because they flower prolifically and are pruned hard, they need to have their nutrients topped up regularly so they can really perform at their best. Start when the new foliage starts to unfurl in spring, usually about a month after pruning. Sprinkle rose fertilizer over the surface of rose beds, or around individual plants where they are grown on their own. Hoe or water this in, then follow up with a deep, rich, organic mulch 5–8cm (2–3in) deep. The ground needs to be moist and weed-free when you do this. Besides keeping the roots cool, moist and nourished, a mulch also helps to keep weeds down and saves a lot of work. If you do need to hoe later, the weeds

are a lot easier to remove. Feed again every six to eight weeks, using a liquid feed if the soil is dry. Don't worry about a spring invasion of greenfly – the bluetits should clear them up – but if blackspot, rust or mildew are a problem, the only solution is to spray regularly every two weeks with a rose fungicide, or grow disease-resistant varieties.

I love the soft, salmon-coloured flowers of 'Buff Beauty', a large, repeat-flowering Hybrid Musk with a delicious scent.

Pruning

Bush roses

Bush roses (hybrid teas and floribundas) can be pruned in late winter, but leave it for a few weeks if there are still hard frosts around at the time. The traditional pruning method is to cut out all the weak, spindly or dead stems completely, then cut back all the remaining strong shoots to about 30cm (1ft) above the ground. Nowadays a lot of people prefer to prune less severely and just reduce the main stems to about 60cm (2ft) (see below). There is also the hedge-trimmer method, where you don't prune properly at all, just run shears or clippers over the bush to top and re-shape it. Prune patio roses the same way as other bush roses, but on a smaller scale. Prune standard roses similarly, too, but treat them like rose bushes on stalks and cut the stems back to 20–30cm (8–12in) from the top of the trunk.

Pruning shrub roses

Shrubs roses, which include the species and old-fashioned roses, do not need much pruning. As soon as the flowers are over, treat them to a 'long deadheading' by cutting off the dead flowers plus about 15–20cm (6–8in) of stem, which is enough to keep the shape of the plants fairly tidy. You can also take out the odd ancient or unproductive stem. When shrub roses are grown as a hedge, prune them this way for a natural look or after flowering simply run the hedge-trimmer over the top for a more formal effect. But don't prune or deadhead roses like *Rosa moyesii* 'Geranium' that are grown for their large, colourful hips – or you won't get any.

Climbers

Train a newly planted climber so that its main stems are spaced out evenly, as close to the horizontal as possible to encourage flowers all over the plant instead of just at the tips of the stem. Some varieties flower once in summer, some twice, and others on and off all summer. Prune vigorous varieties as soon as the last flowers are over, cutting back all the current year's shoots that carried the flowers to within 8–10cm (3–4in) of the main framework of the plant. Modest-growing kinds, including those grown on pillars, need only deadheading.

Ramblers

Ramblers vary a lot in vigour. Where they are grown up through trees, don't bother trying to prune them. Elsewhere, strong-growing kinds need to have the flowered stems cut back hard after flowering – cut back to a non-flowered shoot, or if you cannot fight your way through the mass of prickly stems, just cut all the current year's stems back to within 8–10cm (3–4in) of a framework of old stems. Apart from needing deadheading, more modest-growing ramblers can be left alone.

HOW TO PRUNE BUSH ROSES

1 Retain a cup-shaped arrangement of healthy, young wood. Cut out any dead or diseased stems.

2 Remove one or two old stems each year. Cut back the others to just above an outward-facing bud.

3 Space out the branches in a teacup shape and reduce in height to just below your knee.

THE RIGHT ROSE FOR THE JOB

Climbers have stiff stems trained to make a permanent framework covering walls or fences; choose smaller varieties for trellis or pillars and larger-growing ones to cover outbuildings or big walls.

Ramblers are large plants with thin, flexible stems and make a lot of new growth every year; choose giants like 'Rambling Rector' for growing up through large trees; more modest ones are best trained horizontally out along the tops of fences.

Bush roses are hybrid teas, which have a single flower at the tip of each stem, and floribundas, which have a cluster of flowers; these are best for formal rosebeds with a long, continuous flowering season.

Shrub roses include old-fashioned roses and hybrids of the species; these are more like shrubs to grow than roses and usually have a short flowering season. Old-fashioned roses often have blowsy, cabbage-shaped flowers, and many are strongly perfumed.

Species roses are usually large, prickly plants with big hips and 'wild rose' flowers, best for wilder gardens with plenty of space or for hedging.

Patio roses are very compact and free-flowering versions of bush roses and, unlike most roses, are suitable for growing in containers.

Miniature roses are tiny, 30–45cm (12–18in) high, with mini rose flowers, often sold as houseplants, though they are outdoor plants. They need good but well-drained soil, a warm, sunny spot, and only light pruning in late spring to remove frost-damaged shoots. They are less hardy than normal bush roses.

'Maigold' is an orange-yellow climber at its best in late spring.

A-Z shrub roses

Shrub roses have a charm of their own; they flower like roses but behave like shrubs. Modern shrub roses are unpretentious beauties with 'wild rose' flowers on tamed stems. These romantic, old-fashioned roses fill the air with perfume at the start of summer and are perfect for creating the ambience of a traditional cottage garden. New English roses have been bred to match the unique character of old roses, but with a long flowering season. Neither modern shrub roses nor new English roses look right in formal borders, though. They need a natural setting. Use them like any other flowering shrub, in a border with trees and other shrubs, underplanted with perennials. Some shrub roses also make truly outstanding, small trees when trained as standards, perfect for a small garden.

■ 'Ballerina'
1.25m (4ft) high × 1m (3ft) wide

A delightful, small-to-medium-sized compact, modern shrub rose with large, domed heads made up of many small wild rose-type flowers. These are single, with white centres and pink-flushed edges to the petals, and a slight musky perfume. The flowers are produced almost constantly throughout summer.

Cultivation 'Ballerina' is naturally quite disease-resistant and remains healthy without spraying. It makes a good shrub for a border, but also looks superb grown as a low-flowering hedge, or trained as a standard. It does not mind poor soil or a little light shade and is quite happy growing with taller shrubs. Prune lightly to tidy the shape in early spring.

■ 'Belle de Crécy'
1.25m (4ft) high × 1m (3ft) wide

A gallica rose with a profusion of truly old-fashioned flowers of mauve and purple, and a full, frilled rosette shape described as quartered, which looks as if someone has cut the blooms part-way through to form four segments, like an orange. If the flowers look sensational, the perfume is even more so. Though the flowering period is concentrated into a few weeks at the start of summer, this is a magnificent rose.

Cultivation In common with many old roses, this one suffers from rather floppy

'Ballerina' looks good underplanted with the dusky blue Nepeta 'Six Hills Giant'.

stems, so you may need to stake the main stems to hold the plant more upright. You can also surround it with a small cage of rustic poles that blend in with the stems and look reasonably inconspicuous. Prune by long deadheading when the flowers are over, removing each dead head plus about 15cm (6in) of stem, leaving the shape of the plant tidy afterwards.

■ 'Canary Bird'
3m (10ft) high × 2m (6ft) wide

The earliest of the popular shrub roses to flower, blooming in late spring a month before the main rose season. The flowers are of wild rose type, small, single and an intense canary yellow, but the bush is studded with them and they last for weeks despite the weather. 'Canary Bird' makes a large but neat shrub rose. If space is short, grow it as a standard trained tree. Although it flowers only once, in spring, the ferny foliage is an attractive bonus for the rest of the season.

Cultivation Unlike most roses this one grows and flowers best in shade; its ideal situation is in dappled shade among trees. In a more open, sunny spot the flowers fade fast. Little or no pruning is needed. Just shorten any long stems shortly after flowering to keep the bush a good shape.

■ 'Fantin-Latour'
2m (6ft) high × 1.25m (4ft) wide

A real charmer of an old-fashioned rose, with lots of slightly flattened, pale pink flowers that bloom all at once in early summer. It also has a heavenly scent. The plant has strong stems and a naturally rather open branching habit that looks good with campanulas and similar flowers growing up through the stems.

Cultivation 'Fantin-Latour' is fairly disease-free so, it does not usually need spraying. It also has strong stems that do not need staking. However, it benefits from long deadheading after the flowers are over, plus a light tidy-up to keep it a good shape.

■ 'Fru Dagmar Hastrup'
1.25m (4ft) high × 2m (6ft) wide

A very compact rugosa rose, also sold under the name of 'Frau Dagmar Hartopp', with bright pink, single flowers produced throughout summer. These are followed by big, tomato-shaped hips much loved by blackbirds. The foliage is very distinctive, deep green, wrinkled, shiny and naturally disease-resistant.

Cultivation Like most rugosa roses, this one is incredibly rugged and makes a good, low hedge in an exposed spot, and also grows in light shade between other shrubs, though it thrives in better conditions. Do not deadhead, otherwise you will miss out on one of its main attractions, the huge hips. It needs little trimming when grown as an informal hedge; prune it rather than clipping in early spring, just enough to keep it in shape.

■ 'Geoff Hamilton'
1.5m (5ft) high × 1.25m (4ft) wide

A recent new English rose, named to commemorate my old friend and predecessor on *Gardeners' World*. Geoff's rose flowers all summer with delicate-looking, soft pink flowers and an incredibly rich perfume.

Cultivation Like all the new English roses, 'Geoff Hamilton' is good in a mixed border and repays generous

'Geoff Hamilton' is well remembered with the fragrant shrub rose that bears his name.

feeding and mulching. Deadhead as flowers go over. Prune in early spring, cutting stems down by half their length.

■ 'Gertrude Jekyll'
1.25m (4ft) high × 1m (3ft) wide

One of the very best of the new English roses, having all the best characteristics of the old roses such as neatly rolled buds, large, rosette-shaped, clear pink flowers and an outstanding perfume, but it also has strong stems and a neat, compact shape with flowers freely produced all through the summer.

'Gertrude Jekyll' has delightfully shaped flowers of rich pink and a very rich perfume.

Cultivation Plants look good grown in groups of three in a large border, where they make a cushion shape, otherwise grow singly if space is limited. As they are so productive, they do best given a hybrid-tea-type growing regime. Plant in a rich soil, mulched with well-rotted manure and regularly fed with rose food during late spring and summer. Deadhead regularly to encourage more blooms. Prune by cutting back all the stems by about half in early spring.

■ 'Golden Wings'
2m (6ft) high × 1.25m (4ft) wide
Probably the best large, yellow, single-flowered, modern shrub rose, 'Golden Wings' has giant, wild rose-type flowers almost 15cm (6in) across, which it produces almost continuously throughout summer. Although the flower size suggests that the plant should be enormous, it is surprisingly neat and compact with rather arching stems.
Cultivation Grows well even in poor, dry soil, but benefits from a spring feed and mulch. Deadhead during summer. Prune the stems by half in early spring.

The single, yellow shrub rose 'Golden Wings'.

■ 'Graham Thomas'
1.25m (4ft) high × 1.25m (4ft) wide
The most popular of all the new English roses. The flowers are a very good, weather-resistant yellow, which is a colour not often found in genuine old roses, bowl-shaped, with the centres filled with a froth of petals. They have a particularly pleasing perfume. Plants are neat and compact, and look good in any border.
Cultivation This rose is naturally upright-growing, bushy and disease-resistant, so there is no need for support or spraying, but deadhead after flowering to encourage new buds to develop. It needs generous feeding and mulching to support such a free-flowering habit. Prune by cutting the stems back by half in early spring.

■ 'Maiden's Blush'
1.5m (5ft) high × 1.25m (4ft) wide
A lovely old-fashioned rose with pale blue-green leaves that make the perfect background to the neat, shell-pink buds that open to typical old-fashioned flowers with crumpled centres. It has a perfume as fragile as the flowers, though both are more robust than they at first seem. The plant has strong stems and a

'Rosa Mundi' has wonderful candy-striped, compact flowers.

rather more upright habit of growth than many old roses, and the flowers open all together in early summer. One of the more ancient old roses, it can be traced back to the fifteenth century.
Cultivation 'Maiden's Blush' grows well even in poor soil or light shade and makes quite a strong-growing plant that needs pruning shortly after the flowers are over to thin out and tidy the shape; don't leave it until early spring or you will not get such a good crop of flowers.

■ 'Rosa mundi'
1.25m (4ft) high × 1.25m (4ft) wide
A real old favourite that should properly be called *Rosa gallica officinalis* var. 'Versicolor', with loud pink-and-white-streaked red flowers. Unlike many old-fashioned roses, which are often huge, this variety is small enough to fit into even a tiny garden. It is naturally neat and compact, but the flowers all appear over the space of about six weeks in early summer. It is thought to date back to the twelfth century, but it is still the best stripy rose you can get.

Cultivation A very easy-going rose that is tolerant of a wide range of conditions, including poor soil and light shade. It often produces hips, though not the most spectacular ones. It needs little pruning, though if you are not bothered about the hips, deadheading helps to keep the shape neater. It can suffer from mildew. Control it by spraying with a fungicide.

■ 'Schneezwerg'
1.25m (4ft) high × 1.25m (4ft) wide
A very free-flowering rugosa rose with pure white, semi-double flowers like rosettes with masses of yellow stamens in the centre. This is an extremely hardy and weather-resistant variety, with light green, wrinkled foliage and a long and prolific flowering season from late spring well into autumn. The flowers are followed by the big, red, tomato-like hips typical of rugosa roses, and later in the season both flowers and fruits can be seen on the plant at the same time.

Cultivation This makes an informal flowering hedge or free-standing shrub in an exposed garden, but is also good in a more sheltered border. Naturally disease-resistant, it tolerates poor soil and light shade where it is grown between other trees or shrubs. No regular pruning is needed, though plants can be tidied up slightly in early spring if necessary.

RIGHT: The snow-white flowers of the hardy and long-flowering 'Schneezwerg'.
BELOW: Few shrub roses offer flowers quite as dramatic and dark as those of the 'Tuscany Superb'.

■ 'Tuscany Superb'
1m (3ft) high × 1m (3ft) wide
An old gallica rose with flowers a shape and colour that are never seen in modern roses. It is an extraordinary shade of reddish purple somewhere between deep crimson and maroon, and although it has enough petals to qualify as double, you can still see a cluster of yellow stamens poking up though the centre. The effect is unusual but very charming. It makes a nicely shaped, compact plant with a fairly upright habit. The flowers appear all at once in early summer. Being a member of the 'Gallica' group of roses, **'Tuscany Superb'** is compact in habit and so suited to small gardens. It looks especially good when underplanted with grey-foliage plants and hardy geraniums which will carry on flowering when **'Tuscany Superb'** has finished. I love it!

Cultivation Not too fussy about soil, so grow it as a shrub in a sunny spot in a mixed border to compensate for its short flowering season. Long deadheading after flowering is all the pruning it needs plus the removal of any shoots that die back – a rarity with this variety.

A–Z bush roses

They may not always be elegant of habit, but bush roses – be they hybrid teas or floribundas – are the most generous with their flowers, blooming from one end of summer to the other. Contrary to popular rumour, many of them have a strong fragrance, and it is always worth choosing those that are disease-resistant to avoid constant spraying against mildew and blackspot.

■ 'Alexander'
150cm (5ft) high x 60cm (2ft) wide

An incredibly bright colour sets this variety apart from other orange-red hybrid teas; it is a fluorescent vermilion, but warm rather than vulgar, if you know what I mean. The flowers are large, and start out as classic, slender, pointed buds. With its long stems it is another good variety for cutting, though it's not very strongly scented.

Cultivation A very vigorous variety with an upright shape that is suitable for the back of a rose bed. Its strong, upright habit also makes it good for planting as a flowering hedge, either on its own or mixed with other varieties that grow to a similar shape and size.

■ 'Deep Secret'
100cm (3ft) high x 60cm (2ft) wide

This is the one to grow if you have a soft spot for those romantic and incredibly fragrant, velvety-textured, deep black-red roses. The old favourite used to be 'Papa Meilland' but it is such a weak grower and so prone to disease you'll have your work cut out growing him. This variety is much better and it has a fragrance that is second to none. All you need to go with it is a bottle of champagne. If you liked 'Ena Harkness', you'll love this.

Cultivation A strong-growing variety with no bad habits. It forms a fairly upright shape and has a good, natural resistance to disease. A real winner in every respect.

The full-flowered 'Alec's Red' is one of the best red roses for garden cultivation.

■ 'Alec's Red'
100cm (3ft) high x 60cm (2ft) wide

This is one of the best red hybrid tea roses ever, with richly scented, large, deep crimson flowers on rather upright bushes. The flowers have strong stems and necks, which make them good for cutting, and they stand up well to wet weather, which many red roses do not.

Cultivation 'Alec's Red' is a vigorous, medium-sized bush with good, natural disease resistance, so it needs spraying only in wet or humid seasons when fungal diseases are more prevalent. The plant is best used in rose beds or a special cutting bed, if you are a serious flower arranger.

For fragrance, few roses can match 'Margaret Merril'.

'Deep Secret' is the variety to choose if you like your roses dark red and highly scented. It has replaced 'Papa Meilland' as the best deep red.

■ 'Elina'
1m (3ft) high x 60cm (2ft) wide
This best-selling hybrid tea rose has flowers of a truly magnificent primrose-yellow and superb fragrance.
Cultivation A tall, vigorous bush, good for the back of a border or bed of mixed roses. Good, natural disease resistance means it will not need much, if any, spraying – then only in bad disease years.

■ 'English Miss'
75cm (2½ft) high x 60cm (2ft) wide
This beautiful floribunda always strikes me as very aptly named, as it has the perfect English rose colour, shape and scent. The clusters of flowers are the palest pink, heavenly scented, with pointed buds that open to an almost waterlily-like shape.

'Paul Shirville' offers a rich fragrance, too, but with soft-pink flowers.

Cultivation A vigorous, bushy rose that is very good for growing in formal rosebeds – even a small bed of this variety fills the garden with perfume.

■ 'Just Joey'
75cm (2½ft) high x 60cm (2ft) wide
This rose has a very unusual colour, a sort of rich amber that the catalogues describe – rather unexcitingly in my opinion – as coppery orange. The colour is deeper towards the centre of the flower, which gives it hidden depth. Then the petals have very lightly waved edges, which makes **'Just Joey'** look like no other rose. On top of that it is nicely scented and weather-resistant. Although it has been around since the 1970s, there is still nothing else to equal it.
Cultivation A fairly vigorous disease-resistant variety for a rosebed, flowering late into the year.

■ 'Margaret Merril'
100cm (3ft) high x 60cm (2ft) wide
I don't know who 'Margaret Merril' was, but she is one of my favourite roses: a white floribunda with one of the best fragrances you are every likely to sniff. The flowers are pretty good too, a sort of pearlized white with the faintest tinge of pink around the outermost petals which stops them looking cold.
Cultivation A strong, bushy rose with deep green foliage that sets the flowers off brilliantly. However, this is not a particularly disease-resistant variety.

■ 'Paul Shirville'
100cm (3ft) high x 60cm (2ft) wide
To describe this hybrid tea rose as pale pink would be doing it an injustice; if you look at the flowers they are a subtle blend of several different shades of carefully graduated, warm salmon and rose pink. What appeals to me about this rose is its scent, which is exceptionally powerful and truly overwhelming.
Cultivation A fairly vigorous bushy rose for bedding, but not in the first rank of disease resistance, so you will most probably need to spray this one to avoid blackspot. The scent makes it worth the trouble, though.

■ 'Pot o' Gold'

75cm (2½ft) high x 60cm (2ft) wide

Probably the best golden-yellow, fragrant hybrid tea rose around; the flowers stand up to rain well. The plants are bushy with small flowers, but there are lots of them. The stems are thorny, so watch your fingers when pruning or cutting flowers.

Cultivation No trouble to cultivate, this strong-growing variety has glossy, mid green leaves which give it good resistance to disease. For this reason it does not need a lot of spraying.

RIGHT: The miniature rose 'Rise 'n' Shine' is especially useful for planting in containers, where it will flower right through summer. BELOW: 'Pot o' Gold' is a great choice if you are looking for a scented, yellow hybrid tea.

■ 'Rise 'n' Shine'

45cm (1½ft) high x 30cm (1ft) wide

Not all bush roses fall into the rosebed category. This variety is a miniature rose with pale yellow flowers and a perfect hybrid tea shape. Use it in a raised bed, or as an alternative to bedding plants in a container. Like bedding plants miniature roses flower all summer long, but you can leave them in place for years on end without needing to replace them every season.

Cultivation Miniature roses need better growing conditions than normal bush roses; give them well-drained, fertile soil and keep them watered in dry spells. Very little pruning is needed; just snip off frost-damaged stems in late spring and keep them deadheaded during summer. Unfortunately, 'Rise 'n' Shine' is rather prone to disease, so it needs spraying.

■ 'Royal William'

100cm (3ft) high x 60cm (2ft) wide

Yet another good, red hybrid tea rose; this rich cardinal red variety with velvety-textured petals was judged Rose of the Year in 1987, but for some reason, it has never really caught on. It has good-quality flowers which are attractively perfumed and the sort of strong stems that should make it a favourite with flower arrangers.

Cultivation A modest-sized, bushy variety with natural resistance to disease, good for rosebeds.

■ 'Silver Jubilee'

100cm (3ft) high x 60cm (2ft) wide

This deep salmon-pink hybrid tea rose has lighter highlights all covered by a faint, silvery sheen, which gives it a universal appeal. The flowers have the sort of strong scent you somehow always associate with pink roses.

Cultivation This is a vigorous, bushy rose with a string of awards to its name, and deservedly so as it is free-flowering and tolerates sunny and rainy conditions equally well. With a name like that it is always popular for anniversary gifts.

■ 'Tequila Sunrise'

75cm (2¹/₂ft) high x 60cm (2ft) wide

I remember seeing the flamboyant rosegrower Harry Wheatcroft at Chelsea many years ago. When he named a rose after himself, I was not surprised to discover it was a vivid combination of red and yellow stripes – not in the least bit subtle. This is a modem-day equivalent. An amazingly coloured hybrid tea rose with blooms that are yellow, edged with bright scarlet – it really is a striking mixture. It is not a rose for the faint-hearted, but for those who like the unusual it is irresistible. The fragrance is slight, but then the flower colouring makes up for this deficiency.

Cultivation A vigorous and bushy plant with dark, glossy green foliage which has good resistance to disease. The flowers are carried clear of the leaves on sturdy stalks.

ABOVE: 'Royal William' is a red hybrid tea that deserves to be more popular.
RIGHT: I once overheard the Queen Mother describing 'Silver Jubilee' as 'a confection of pinks'; nicely summed up, I think.

■ 'Sue Lawley'

60cm (2ft) high x 60cm (2ft) wide

Now, as they say, for something completely different. **'Sue Lawley'** does not immediately strike everyone as a rose at first glance. Her flowers look as if someone has taken a white floribunda rose and used a paintbrush to highlight the blooms with carmine red. This is not far from the truth as it is what is called a 'painted rose' in rose-breeding circles. The pattern of solid red is augmented by white spots, which creates an impressionistic effect. The flowers open out so wide they are almost flat and they have a hollow centre filled with golden stamens, thus adding to the unusual appearance.

Cultivation Not a big plant at all, **'Sue Lawley'** is not especially vigorous and is not very disease-resistant either; but you will seldom find flowers like this, so it's worth making that little effort to accommodate her. Use her rather like a shrub rose to get the best effect.

A-Z climbing and rambler roses

Roses aren't just for beds; there are larger varieties suitable for growing on pillars, up walls and fences, over outbuildings and through large trees. Climbing and rambler roses have a relatively short flowering period compared to bush roses, but they make a spectacular show at the peak of their display. Use ramblers trained horizontally to turn post-and-wire or chain link fences into fortified boundaries.

■ 'Albéric Barbier'

A medium-sized rambler rose with old-fashioned flowers the colour of rich clotted cream, which appear in one flush during mid-summer.

Cultivation This is a very good variety to train up a pillar to add height to the back of a border. Prune in autumn: cut the stems that carried this year's flowers back to just above a strong, new shoot – these will take over and flower next year.

■ 'Albertine'

This classic, medium-sized rambler rose is very popular. It has pale coppery-pink flowers and a sensational, heady perfume. It has a single flush of flowers each season, towards the start of summer.

Cultivation Although it is an old favourite, it suffers from mildew and often needs spraying, but devotees agree it is worth the effort. Grow it on a sheltered wall to protect the blossom from weather damage. It needs pruning in autumn to remove all the flowered stems: cut them off just above a strong, healthy, non-flowered shoot.

■ 'Altissimo'

A very unusual-looking, medium-sized climbing rose with large, single, vermilion-red flowers. It resembles a much improved form of wild rose, but keeps flowering all summer. Very little perfume, but to be frank it does not look like the sort of rose that would have a scent: somehow it's too earthy.

This is 'Albéric Barbier' at his best, welcoming visitors with one spectacular summer flush of creamy white flowers.

'Bobbie James' is a great rambler to send up into an old fruit tree, where the branches can act as a support system.

Cultivation Apart from the usual mulching, feeding and deadheading you don't need to do anything. No pruning – nothing. Well, if you spot any stems that have died off, do cut them out, but that is about all. Roses don't come much easier than this.

■ 'Bobbie James'

Ideal for training into a big, old tree. This rose has large clusters of fragrant, semi-double, creamy-white flowers with golden stamens, similar to the varieties 'Kiftsgate' and 'Rambling Rector', but without making such outrageously enormous plants. This variety also looks spectacular trained out along the top rung of a ranch-style fence or horizontally over chain-link fencing.

Cultivation Grow it into a tree or through the wilder sort of hedge and don't attempt to prune it is my advice. It will be fine. This is a variety that will cope with poor soil, in much the same way as many of the species roses.

■ 'Climbing Cécile Brunner'

If you are familar with the normal bushy version of 'Cécile Brunner' – the old-fashioned china rose with slender buds and lots of small, fragile-looking, shell-pink flowers – this climber is almost the same, just a lot bigger. Trained up a framework of rustic poles, it makes a good standard tree, but otherwise it is best grown into an old apple tree as it needs plenty of support. It has one main flush of flowers in early summer, followed by occasional blooms throughout the summer when it feels like it. One of its characteristics is its shortage of foliage, but this just shows off the flowers better.

Cultivation Take a lot of trouble preparing the ground well before planting, but from then on, apart from spring feeding and mulching, there is virtually nothing to do. It does not need any proper pruning; you hardly even need to tidy straggly shoots as it keeps its shape without much help. It does not mind a tiny bit of shade for part of the day.

■ 'Compassion'

This is probably the most popular climber of them all: a medium-sized variety good for growing on walls or fences, with lots of large, pale-peach-and-apricot-shaded, slightly muddled-looking, blooms with a very strong scent. Expect two flushes per year.

Cultivation It is easily grown, too, as you don't need to do anything beyond normal routine cultivation. No pruning is needed. Just train the stems out evenly in the first place and leave it alone.

■ 'Crimson Shower'

The perfect rose for people who like ramblers, but don't like their bad habits, 'Crimson Shower' has lots of crimson, semi-double flowers, as the name suggests, whose hollow centres are tightly packed with golden stamens. It flowers from mid-summer well into autumn, unlike your average rambler, which has a pretty short flowering season. Unlike some other ramblers, this one does not get smothered in mildew. Its only drawback it that it has hardly any scent.

Cultivation A good variety for growing over an arch or arbour, or on trellis. Prune it in autumn, cutting back all the stems that have flowered as far as the first strong, unflowered shoot.

'Compassion' is a deservedly popular climber, having two flushes of flower each summer.

■ 'Danse du Feu'

A very free-flowering, medium-sized, scarlet climbing rose which has a couple of flushes of blooms every season and one enormous asset – it will perform just as happily on a north-facing wall. This makes it invaluable for anyone wanting something colourful for this notoriously difficult situation, where very few roses will grow well and bloom freely.

Cultivation Improve the soil well before planting as the ground at the foot of any wall is often very poor and filled with rubble. Train the stems out over the area, keeping them as close to the horizontal as possible as this improves their flowering potential. No routine pruning is needed: just deadhead and remove any dead stems as you spot them. Where it is grown on a north wall, avoid surrounding it with tall plants that will decrease the light even more.

One of the greatest features about 'Danse du Feu' is that it will do well on a north-facing wall.

■ 'Golden Showers'

The brightest and goldest of the yellow climbing roses, 'Golden Showers' also has a very long continuous season of flowering, from early summer until autumn – as good as any bush rose. Not surprisingly, it is very popular. Add to that its medium size and comparative lack of thorns, which makes it a good choice for an arch where you might snag your clothes on a thornier rose, and you have a real winner.

Cultivation Take trouble over planting it, then train the stems out to cover the area evenly, but from then it does not need any proper pruning. Just cut out dead stems and remove dead flower heads regularly. It is also worth keeping it well fed to fuel the exceptionally prolific flowering season.

■ 'Mme Grégoire Staechelin'

A very impressive, large, modern climbing rose which, at the height of its flowering season, is covered in heavily perfumed, large, pink, frilly flowers. Its greatest fault is that the season is too

The small flowers may look demure, but 'Kiftsgate' is the most rampant garden rose of all.

short – it flowers for only a few weeks at the start of summer. Like a lot of good things, it is worth waiting for.

Cultivation It repays a rich diet and good general care, but beyond that is very easy to look after. Prune it after flowering by shortening the sideshoots on the flowering stems back to spurs about three or four leaves from their base.

■ 'Mermaid'

A real giant of a climber, with great, prickly stems and flowers in keeping with the scale of the plant – huge single, golden-yellow blooms with a central nest of amber stamens that are produced all summer. It is also surprisingly well perfumed. Seen at its best on a south-facing wall or trained along a sunny pergola, it needs room to develop, so don't think you can keep it pruned back to size.

Cultivation It is not the hardiest of roses and needs a reasonably mild location and a hot, sunny spot to do well; nonetheless, it does very well in a lot of places that are too hot and sunny for most 'tamer' roses. Train the stems out

over the wall, keeping them as horizontal as possible. Prune in autumn after the flowers come to an end: just shorten the sideshoots of the flowered stems back to 15cm (6in) or so from their bases.

‘Kiftsgate’

This is the giant of giants, not to be trifled with. A positively mega rambler for growing up into a large tree – I've seen it reach the top of a 12-m (40-ft) high beech tree. Just take a look at the specimen at Kiftsgate Court, if you want proof of its enormity. The giant clusters of single, white flowers with a bunch of short, golden stamens in the centre of each look like prolific fruit blossom. If you have the right spot, then give it a go. It may take a couple of years to start flowering as it needs to build up some bulk first. Don't try to shoe-horn it into a small garden or you may start the neighbours complaining.

Cultivation Prepare a planting hole a good distance away from the base of the tree, somewhere close to the drip line under the tips of the branches in the case of a large beech or similar. Dig in lots of rich organic matter, plant the rose and lead the stems up into the tree on ropes or rustic poles. Then just sit back and wait. Once the stems grow up through the branches and get a good support, they'll head for the light and flowers will appear around the outside of the canopy. Give it time.

‘Schoolgirl’

What is special about this modern climbing rose is its colour – a subtle, warm, coppery apricot orange. It is not a colour you find much in climbing roses, in fact I can't think of anything remotely similar to it. They are scented too, which automatically moves it up a few notches on my list. It makes a good, medium-sized plant.

Cultivation Plant, train and forget; this is one of those handy climbers that is happiest left unpruned. There is one small fault you might like to do

something about, though – the stems at the base of the plant tend to be a bit bare of both flowers and foliage, so plant a few bushy annuals in front of them or grow annual climbers up the stems where the prickles will provide a good grip. Choose something with a suitably complementary colour, or else be bold and go for a complete contrast.

‘Zéphirine Drouhin’

Agatha Christie fans will recall that this plant provided the solution to the crime in *Sad Cypress*. I've not been able to look at the plant since without thinking of bodies in libraries. Its great asset is its lack of thorns, though it does, in fact, have a few. I'd have taken issue with Ms

Christie's plot, which revolved around that fact. The flowers are something between cerise and magenta – not easy to place but having the advantage of flowering all summer. It is brilliant for growing over an arch or in a garden with children, as nobody will get scratched unless they go looking for trouble.

Cultivation The only drawback with this rose is that it tends to get blackspot, so in a bad year you will need to spray. Deadhead regularly to encourage new flowers, but otherwise there is no need to prune. Train the main framework of stems evenly to cover the space well.

The thornless ‘Zéphirine Drouhin’ lends itself well to being trained over a colonnade.

Hedges

Hedges are the most natural form of garden boundary and have been used for centuries to keep out intruders or animals and to create shelter and privacy. They are also a key part of the garden landscape, acting as a living, green backdrop to colourful borders.

Fences are fine if you are in a hurry. You can have a bare site today and a sheltered, private garden tomorrow, but hedges are worth waiting for. Hedges improve with time and, what's more, are continuously regenerating, whereas fences have a limited life span, especially in windy areas.

If security or livestock-proofing are your main requirements, choose a prickly hedge of something like hawthorn, holly or berberis. For a belt-and-braces approach you could plant a double row of plants with a wire-netting fence in between them.

If you want a low conifer hedge that won't need a lot of clipping, choose *Thuja plicata*, but avoid the dreaded Leyland cypress which, unless it is regularly cut back, is capable of reaching 30m (100ft) tall. For a dwarf hedge to grow around a formal flower bed or herb garden, there is plenty to choose from, such as *Buxus sempervirens* 'Suffruticosa', a neatly clipped row of upright rosemary, or a dwarf lavender like *Lavandula angustifolia* 'Munstead' or *L.* 'Hidcote'.

The plants you choose determines the style of hedge. You can have close-clipped formal hedges, or more ebullient flowering hedges created from suitable shrubs or roses. In some situations a screen may make a better alternative. In a wild garden or to shelter a windy, rural site, grow a row of native trees and shrubs such as bird cherry, elder and dog rose, or even miscanthus, a tall, bamboo-like grass, which does not need cutting at all.

Planting

The secret of a good hedge lies in its roots. Since a hedge will probably stay put for 50 years or more, good soil preparation is terribly important. If your soil is reasonably good, just mark out the row and dig in lots of organic matter. On soil like heavy clay, stony chalk or light sand which is particularly impoverished, dig out a trench and fill it with a mixture of good topsoil and organic matter. Yes, I know it takes ages, but it's worth it in the end. Some kinds of hedge are fine planted as a single row: flowering shrubs, low evergreen or conifer hedges, and the really dwarf hedges sometimes used around flower beds. With shelter belts a single row is also enough. But formal hedges of beech, hornbeam and yew, and any hedge that you want to grow up tall, need to be planted as a double row. Stagger the plants so they interlock.

As a general rule most hedging plants should be spaced about 45cm (18in) apart, but it varies according to the variety and its ultimate height and vigour, so check with the nurseryman when you buy your plants. The cheapest way to grow a new hedge is to plant bare-root plants in autumn. This is the way beech, hawthorn and hornbeam seedlings are sold. Evergreens like yew, box and conifers are mostly sold as pot-grown plants. So too are ornamental shrubs suitable for hedging, such as many roses, forsythia and escallonia. These are much more expensive to buy, as you will probably be buying normal garden centre plants. If you want to cut costs, take a look in gardening magazines for firms that specialize in hedging, since they often sell young, pot-grown plants in bulk at a reasonable price. Alternatively, buy a few big plants, take cuttings and grow your own.

Once you have established a hedge, look after it. Each spring, give it a good feed using any general fertilizer, such as blood, fish and bone or even rose food. If possible, mulch underneath it, and keep the base weeded.

ABOVE: *A neatly trimmed hedge smartens up any garden.*
RIGHT: *Use gaps and arches in hedges to frame garden views and tempt the visitor to explore.*

Informal hedges

Informal hedges are the bohemians of the boundary world. Not for them the conventions of clipping and trimming: they are free spirits. And like human free spirits they need lots of space. A flowering hedge of forsythia, weigela or flowering currant will occupy the same width as a single plant grown as a free-standing shrub in the garden, only in this case you have a whole row of them. They look absolutely magnificent when in flower, and when they are not, they make a good foliage backdrop to a flower border.

If you decide on a rose hedge, do go for shrub or species roses which don't need hard pruning. Hybrid tea roses need cutting back hard every year, so your hedge would only be about 30cm (12in) high in early spring. *Rosa rugosa* makes a particularly good flowering hedge for windy gardens or where there is poor clay soil, as it tolerates the worst of conditions. It has huge hips that keep it looking colourful after the flowers are finished and also provide a tasty snack for blackbirds. This rose is prickly too, and a whole hedge of it acts like living barbed wire. Many shrub roses such as 'Buff Beauty'

and species like *R. glauca*, which has purplish-pewter foliage and single, pink flowers, make spectacular informal hedges with quite a long flowering season.

You could have an informal hedge of large-leaved, evergreen foliage shrubs such as *Elaeagnus* x *ebbingei* or laurel – either the spotted laurel, *Aucuba japonica*, or the cherry laurel, *Prunus laurocerasus*. I can especially recommend *Elaeagnus* x *ebbingei*, which despite its rather plain looks is enlivened by almost invisible, greenish bell flowers in late autumn. It has a remarkably strong and pleasant perfume that always comes as a great surprise. It makes a good seaside hedge too.

Left to do their own thing, these large-leafed hedges can grow truly enormous. Clip with shears or hedge trimmers immediately before the main flush of growth in spring, so halved leaves, which turn brown leaving a mangy-looking hedge, vanish under the new growth quickly. As a general rule, cut back flowering hedges like forsythia that flower before mid-summer immediately after flowering. Just clip enough to tidy the shape and remove most

A light clipping over after flowering will keep lavender like this in trim for four or five years, after which it is best replaced.

Escallonia makes a perfect informal hedge in coastal localities due to its ability to withstand a certain amount of salt spray.

of the dead heads. Prune later-flowering hedges like hydrangea and roses in early spring. Hardy fuchsias are a bit of an exception as a hedge. In most parts of the country they are hardly worth growing as the plants are killed down to ground level by the frost every winter. But in a mild region the old stems remain living throughout the winter and new sideshoots grow from them in spring. So just give them a quick tidy in late spring after the worst of the frosts are over.

You can make life easier for yourself. If you fancy an informal hedge with a difference, plant a row of shrubs with a naturally compact shape that need virtually no trimming or pruning. Choose compact ornamental conifers, like the foxy red-gold *Thuja occidentalis* 'Rheingold' or blue *Chamaecyparis pisifera* 'Boulevard', and leave them to grow into their own characteristic shape – they make a marvellous, undulating hedge that looks as if it is sculpted by the wind without any trimming. You could plant a row of compact berberis such as *Berberis thunbergii* 'Bagatelle', which grows only about 60cm (2ft) high and naturally makes a neat, rounded shape, or choose *B. thunbergii* 'Helmond Pillar' for a more normal sort of hedge shape – it is a bolt upright berberis which grows to about 1m (3ft) high. Both berberis varieties are deciduous with mauvish-coloured foliage. You can go lower still, by planting a row of cotton lavender, *Santolina chamaecyparissus*, or lavender. True, you can clip

these to give a formal dwarf hedge, but if you just run a pair of shears over the top to deadhead them after flowering, you can have an informal but reasonably tidy mini hedge that keeps its shape and is full of flowers in summer. They are also headily aromatic and are ideal for planting along the edge of a garden path where their scent will be released as you brush past.

Informal hedges are more like a row of shrubs than a normal hedge, so you need to treat them as such. Mulching and feeding in spring are essential, especially for those kinds of plants that grow prolifically, like forsythia, and for heavy feeders like roses. A second feed in mid-summer is a good idea if you can manage it too. Use a high-potash feed like sulphate of potash at 25g per square metre (1oz per square yard) and water it well if the soil is dry. This encourages spring-flowering shrubs to initiate more buds for an even better display the following year and helps later-flowering shrubs like hebes to ripen their wood, which is vital for those that are a tad tender and need a good summer to flower well.

If you really put your mind to it, you can be quite creative with informal hedges. One of my favourite hedges is owned by two sisters, who live in adjacent houses. They removed their dividing fence and planted a great mixture of flowering shrubs along the boundary. The result looks wonderful. It flowers in different places throughout the year, and there is a seat nestling in a gap so they can meet half-way down and sit and chat in comfort.

Formal hedges

Any plants that tolerate close clipping can be trained into a formal hedge which is the green equivalent of a wall. Beech and hornbean give a very traditional look and, although they are both technically deciduous, they hold their brown leaves in winter so you still have a solid-looking hedge. For a more unusual hedge plant alternate green and copper beech plants, which gives a stripy effect. Conifer hedges are very popular, but yew is the traditional favourite. Yew has the advantage of letting you have a tall hedge that is also quite narrow – you can clip 1.25–1.5m (4–5ft) high yews to little more than 30cm (12in) wide, without harming the plants.

There are all sorts of other species suitable for a formal hedge, including several kinds of chamaecyparis such as *Chamaecyparis lawsoniana* 'Green Hedger'. Privet is a particularly good hedge for suburban gardens, as it withstands poor conditions and will tolerate a lot of maltreatment. A good thick hedge of privet actually helps to filter out the dust, litter and other debris normally thrown up by passing traffic into gardens. If you don't like the look of the old, green privet, go for one of the variegated or golden forms, which also make a very good hedge. Another point in favour of privet is that it grows easily from cuttings, so if you need spare plants to fill a gap, these are very easy to produce. Its biggest drawback is that it needs cutting quite often. Holly and hawthorn both make good, dense, wind- and livestock-proof, formal boundaries. For a more interesting look you can let the occasional plant grow up through the line of the hedge to make a tree and, if you are really feeling adventurous, this can be trimmed to a lollipop or mushroom shape. Box is the best choice for a shady garden as it can grow happily even if it receives only an hour of sunlight per day. It is also slow-growing, so can be kept small.

The more traditional sort of hedging plants like beech, hornbeam and privet are the ones you are most likely to find sold in autumn as bare-root seedlings. With these, small plants are undoubtedly the best buy, since the first thing you need to do after planting bare-root plants is to cut them down. This may sound wasteful, but it is the only way to make the plants branch right from the bottom. As the new growth appears, trim the hedge just enough to take the very tips off the new shoots each time they reach about 5cm (2in) long. This way the hedge grows up while also thickening out, so you don't end up with lots of gaps along the bottom. (Gaps are almost impossible to rectify later, short of planting ivy to fill any holes, or making a border along the front to hide them.)

With conifers and evergreens you will probably have to buy pot-grown plants which are expensive, but do have the advantage of being grown in a fashion that encourages them to branch naturally from the base, so they should not need cutting back after planting. With pot-grown plants you begin shaping the hedge right from the start.

Any formal hedge needs to be clipped so that its base is slightly wider than the top, with the sides sloping very gently inwards. This helps to shrug off snow and wind and avoids the splayed specimens you sometimes see among older hedges. You will do more clipping than usual while the hedge grows up but, once they reach the required height, most types of formal hedge need cutting only twice a year, in late spring and late summer. If you grow privet, expect to cut it at least five times a year as it grows so fast. And if you choose a flowering formal hedge like escallonia, clip it immediately after flowering, not before, to avoid snipping off the shoots that should flower.

Yew is about the most accommodating hedge. You can get away with cutting it only once a year, in late summer, then it will remain neat and trim through the winter.

Since hedge clipping is a regular and lengthy chore, it pays to invest in a power tool. Electric hedge-clippers are the answer. Petrol clippers may be the only option if you have a long hedge miles from a power point, but they are tremendously heavy to use. Whether you use old-fashioned shears or a powered tool, the big problem with hedge clipping is keeping the top straight. It is much harder than you think to judge it by eye as you are too close to the job, so put up a couple of posts and run a level line along the top to act as a guide.

Because you determine the shape and size of a formal hedge, there is the potential to do all sorts of interesting things with it if the mood takes you. Cut peepholes through it or clip a castellated top and give yourself delusions of grandeur. However, if you like an easy life, take my advice and keep it simple.

This yew arch took me 12 years to grow, but it was worth the wait. It is linked to kerbs of dwarf box that surround the kitchen garden.

Topiary

You do not need a stately home to cultivate topiary; anyone can clip plants into interesting shapes and indulge in a few horticultural whimsies. With a little time, the right plant and some bent wire, you can create anything from a teapot to a complete set of chessmen (with gold *versus* green pieces).

Traditional shapes

Traditional topiary, the sort you often see at stately homes, is living architecture and comes in many forms. It can be a background shape, such as a scallop-shaped niche cut out of a hedge to house a classical statue; a fancy wreath of foliage outlining a gateway; or sculpted holly trees growing up above a neatly clipped formal hedge like a row of umbrellas. But the best-known topiaries are free-standing shapes set against a backdrop of manicured lawns and raked gravel paths. Individual evergreens are clipped into formal, geometric shapes like domes, pyramids and squares, often topped by knobs. You also find the occasional owner with a vivid imagination, and room to play with, who has something slightly more eccentric, such as a complete steam engine or a large peacock, which is great fun, but the larger specimen you have in mind the longer it will take to grow.

Potted projects

Mini topiary planted in pots is quicker to grow and a more practical option for most gardens. If you are a novice, classic pyramids and spheres are the easiest to train and can often be adapted from fairly mature plants for a head start. A pair of pyramid box trees in classy containers makes a grand entrance, even if your front door opens straight on to the street. They also look good decorating formal herb gardens, a potager or a gravel garden, and you can move potted topiaries around the garden wherever you need instant architecture. A few potted spheres are worth keeping in stock. They can be dropped into a flower border at any time of year to fill gaps, which is a good way to cover up a disaster. More elaborate shapes like potted peacocks make temporary patio plants, ideal for the winter when there is not much in flower. In summer they can be put out to grass. Why not have a whole family of them pecking around?

Cheat's topiary

The quickest way of growing topiary is to use pre-formed frames and plant them with climbers. Ivy is the usual choice as it provides a reasonably formal effect, but there is no reason why you should not use annual flowering climbers like morning glory or, if you have a big enough frame, perennials like trachelospermum or even clematis. Topiary frames can be used in pots or in garden borders and are available in formal shapes such as spires and balls or novelty designs like teddy bears, cats and rabbits. If you want to be really creative, make your own shapes such as dinosaurs or motor bikes from stiff wire bent with pliers or scrunched-up chicken wire.

Creating topiary

Box and yew are probably the best subjects for topiary. I know they are slow-growing, but not as slow as you might think. Don't be tempted to speed things up by using privet or *Lonicera nitida*, which is an evergreen shrub, as they grow so fast you'll have your work cut out keeping them clipped and in my experience they always look shaggy. The quickest way of making a start is by choosing quite large box or yew plants that are dense and fairly symmetrical. Opt for one that already has the makings of a good topiary-type shape such as a dome, sphere or spire, so that all you need to do is accentuate it. Pot it up or plant it out and do all the usual things like watering, feeding and mulching to get it growing well.

ABOVE: *A duck clipped out of box grows in a pot, along with more traditional shapes such as this spiral (*RIGHT*).*

SUITABLE TOPIARY PLANTS

Traditional topiary plants are slow-growing evergreens, but use climbers to cover wire frames for a fast result.

Buxus sempervirens (Common box)
A slow-growing evergreen which is good for shady places as long as it gets a little sunlight every day. Suitable for small topiary shapes in the ground, but best in pots trained as spheres and similar simple shapes. Don't use the miniature box, though, as it is too small.

Taxus baccata (Yew)
The classic plant for traditional topiary. Where it is used for large shapes, plants need a fairly heavy-duty internal support structure. The Victorians used iron bars in a 'cage' construction, but now large pre-formed frames are available. Small, complicated shapes like crowns on top of pillars need a framework of scrunched-up wire netting for support.

Ilex aquifolium (Common holly)
The holly needs pruning rather than clipping and it is fairly slow-growing. Use it for simple mushroom or sphere shapes on straight, bare stems or grow variegated varieties for a slightly different effect.

Conifers
Many dwarf to medium-sized conifers are ideal for creating simple topiary because of their naturally symmetrical shapes; upright, spire-shaped conifers are perfect for training into spirals or obelisks, and dome-shaped trees make good pillars or spheres. Use golden, blue, grey or green plants for greater variety.

Hedera (Ivy)
A slow-growing, evergreen climber which can be trained over wire frames to make small, potted topiary shapes.

BEGINNERS' TIPS

♦ Start with a simple box ball or bay pyramid that has already been trained to shape and keep it in shape by trimming it twice-yearly, in early summer and early autumn.

♦ Use sheep shears or other single-handed clippers to trim small-leaved plants like box, but prune large-leaved plants like holly with secateurs as the leaves turn brown if cut in half by shears.

♦ Water potted topiary well in summer and protect the roots from freezing in winter to keep the plants healthy and foliage in good condition.

♦ When training free-standing shapes from box or yew, don't be over-ambitious to start with. Simple shapes like domes and obelisks are the easiest to train and trim. Complicated shapes can come later!

To grow variegated box cones to this height (1m/3ft) can take about eight years.

before. The wire gradually vanishes into the growing shape, providing a strong framework that will hold the plant together. Once the shape reaches the size you want, you no longer need to clip quite so often. Twice a year, in early and late summer, should be enough. Cut it back to the required size, leaving a close-shaven finish. Electric hedge-trimmers are the easiest way to trim simple shapes, especially those with straight sides, but for anything more elaborate hand shears are the only real answer.

When you have been successful with a few simple pillars, pyramids and spires, you may feel ready to move on to more advanced shapes. If you have a good shape established, you may feel it is just asking for a knob on top. To form this, let a single strong stem grow up to provide a length of bare stalk, then 'stop' it by pinching out the growing tip, rather as you might a standard fuchsia to make it branch out. This is how I produced the peacocks on top of my yew orbs. But if you lack confidence, you can hammer a stake carefully down through the centre of your basic shape and attach a chicken wire

As your topiary grows, clip it very lightly every couple of months. The idea is to take off the very tips of the shoots each time they grow 2.5–5cm (1–2in). This way you keep the natural shape of the plant while it grows steadily bigger, at the same time encouraging it to branch freely; the resulting sideshoots will help to thicken up the shape. To adjust the shape, you can clip the sides tighter than the top to encourage it to grow into a pillar shape to start forming an obelisk, or clip the top tighter than the sides to make it more rounded. As the shape grows, you may like to alter it more, perhaps by letting the base grow wider to make a plinth. Avoid having overhangs towards the top of the plant as this just makes it splay out. If you keep to a reasonably blocky shape that is wider at the base than the top, and you don't want it too big, box and yew are quite capable of holding their shape without any internal supports.

If you want something bigger and fancier, hammer a few upright metal rods, such as lengths cut from concrete reinforcing bars, around the plant before it gets too big and use them to support a cage of heavy-duty wire netting. Allow the stems to grow through the netting and continue clipping as

shape to it. Now it is a simple matter of training the sideshoots around the shape as they grow. Tie them in place and, as the shape develops, begin clipping. A sphere is the easiest finial to start with, but you use exactly the same technique whether you want a griffin rampant or a pineapple. If you want a ground-level peacock, construct a shape from wire netting (add metal bars for extra support if the end result is to be more than about 1m (3ft) high) and train a bushy plant around it in the same way as for the finial. Use strong upright shoots splayed out to form the fan for the tail and within a couple of years you'll have saved yourself a considerable amount of money that it would cost for a ready-grown mini peacock.

The hardest part is constructing your wire frame in the first place, but you may find a suitable frame you can buy ready made. I found it easier just to train emerging shoots to left and right to make head and tail, tying them to bamboo canes as they grew and removing these when the shoots had thickened up. Don't feel that topiary only has a place in a formal garden. An occasional piece can also look good in a cottage garden, a herbaceous border or a garden 'room'. It makes great statues and sculptures to provide focal points all around the garden. Next time you fancy a giant terracotta amphora, bust of Napoleon or armless nymph – you can just grow your own.

Ivy topiary
The quickest-growing topiary specimens can be made from ivy – plain-leaved or variegated – and they can be created in pots and containers or planted direct in garden soil. Erect a wire-netting framework of the required shape and cultivate the soil around it. Plant ivy around the framework and train the stems over it, tying them in as they grow. Alternatively, secure the framework to a container filled with John Innes potting compost. You'll need to clip and train ivy topiary almost monthly in summer, it grows so fast.

I started growing my peacocks 14 years ago from small tufts of yew and now they're fully fledged!

Climbers and wall plants

Trained up pillars and obelisks or over arches and pergolas, climbers can create the impression of a rolling landscape in miniature. They can also be used as outdoor throws, draped artistically over hard surfaces, such as walls and fences, to make them blend in with surrounding plants.

I can't think of many upright surfaces around the garden that wouldn't be improved with something green climbing up them. Climbers are the easy way to enhance features like rustic arches that just want a bit of window dressing. They are also the perfect solution for hiding eyesores fast, like the old outhouse you meant to knock down but didn't because it is such a good place to park the garden seats in winter. But from a down-to-earth, gardening point of view, there are several very good reasons for growing climbers.

If you have only a small garden, it makes sense to grow things that go upwards instead of outwards because you can fit a lot more plants in the space. Wall-training, for instance, converts a shrub that would normally grow a couple of metres in all directions into something which, grown flat, fits a narrower border than a row of daffodils. You can grow several climbers in the same space so they mingle together. This is now almost compulsory over arches, where a mixture of climbing roses and clematis or two or three different varieties of honeysuckle will, between them, keep it in flower all summer long. Or you can grow climbers up through trees, creating the illusion of a plant that seems to flower several times over; each time with someone else's flowers.

If you have a passion for plants that are slightly too tender for your garden, walls are the way to house them. By providing shelter and storing heat, a wall creates a mild microclimate that acts as a winter life-support system for tender plants. This is the place to grow ceanothus and fremontodendron, campsis, pineapple broom or the giant, evergreen *Magnolia grandiflora* 'Goliath' (but be warned: the one at Chartwell in Kent did reach the fourth floor before it was pruned to a more manageable size).

Even if you don't have walls or fences, you can grow climbers over a framework of posts and netting to make a fast screen, with the potential to turn your new patio into an enclosed suntrap or mask an unsightly view. Garden structures offer even more opportunities to be creative with climbing plants. Gazebos and arbours with their open-plan construction virtually cry out for climbers to complete the missing parts. Metal pagodas and basketweave pyramids are the garden decorator's alternative to pillars for growing climbers up in flower beds. If space is limited, you could even use smaller versions of the same sort of structure to give a vertical dimension to large tubs.

On the whole, climbers and wall plants are a gift to gardeners, but they are not without the occasional problem. Wisteria probably causes more consternation than any other climber I could name. I've heard of people planting three on an arch, which collapsed under the weight within two years. And we all know the odd overgrown wisteria that dwarfs the house it grows on with tendrils but with hardly any flowers. The first is a classic case of the right plant in the wrong place. Climbers come in all sorts of different sizes, and the first rule of gardening with climbers is to match the spread to the space. The second is a classic case of faulty research. While some climbers need little or no pruning, others, like wisteria, have to be handled just right or they go wrong. So, more so than with almost any other plants in the garden, the golden rule is to do your homework first.

ABOVE: Clematis 'H.F. Young' RIGHT: Roses and clematis can be trained together over a pergola to make a walkway that is brightly coloured and exquisitely fragrant.

Planting and training climbers

Climbers add an extra tier of colour and life to a garden. They are the ideal way to merge walls and fences into the garden and can completely hide an eyesore. Use them more unconventionally too, scrambling over a wire-netting structure to make a fast screen, or growing up through trees and large shrubs to give them a second season of flowering. Most need proper planting, support and training.

Parthenocissus quinquefolia is a rampant climber, which will quickly cover eyesores and offer autumn colour.

Self-clingers

Plants like ivy and Virginia creeper cling to walls and fences without needing any help. Some self-clingers use aerial roots that creep into crevices, then expand, so the stems hold tight; others use a sort of suction-cup system to hold on. This type of climber is easy to grow since you don't have to put up any trellis or wires for it, or spend time tying in new growth. However, it can damage crumbly mortar, so is best grown on sound surfaces.

Twiners

Plants like honeysuckle grow in the wild through trees and shrubs, winding themselves around the trunks and branches for support. In the garden, this useful habit means that once you have threaded the stems of a young plant through a support such as trellis or the branches of a tree, the plant will keep going from there without further help. You may need to tie the stems loosely to the support while the plants become established.

Scramblers

Most climbers grow by scrambling up through shrubs, allowing the twiggy branches to support their rather weak, floppy stems. Roses use their thorns to help them get a grip and clematis cling on using their leaf stems which curl around the nearest branch, but even so scramblers need more help to climb than most. Provide them with trellis, netting, a rustic framework or a large, twiggy tree or shrub to grow into. Where they are grown on a wall you will probably need to tie in some of the stems.

Wall shrubs

These may be shrubs with naturally floppy stems, such as winter jasmine, that make an untidy heap when grown in the open. They are grown against a wall because it is the easiest way to hold them up and see them at their best. Some wall shrubs are slightly tender, like fremontodendron and pineapple broom, and need the protection of the wall to thrive. Others, like pyracantha, may get too big for the garden when grown as free-standing shrubs – wall training keeps them flat so they take up less room. Wall shrubs have no means of supporting themselves, so will need help. Train them out over the wall on horizontal wires held out at least 15cm (6in) from the wall with special nails, or put up trellis and tie all the main stems and new growth securely in place.

PLANTING CLIMBERS

♦ The soil at the foot of a wall or under trees is often poor and dry. Before planting improve the whole area by digging in lots of organic matter, and prepare a larger-than-usual planting hole especially well. Keep new climbers very well watered, as walls and fences act as umbrellas, sheltering the soil from the rain.

♦ Plant climbers 45cm (1½ft) away from the foot of a wall and 60cm (2ft) or more from the base of a small tree or large shrub. Lean the climber over towards its support, allowing it to climb on to the support via a cane.

♦ If planting climbers to grow into a large tree, plant them at the drip line below the ends of the branches, and let them grow into the lower branches via a rope – if you plant them too close to the trunk, they will not thrive because the soil is too dry soil and the shade too deep.

Cotoneaster horizontalis *will snake its way upwards when planted against a wall.*

TRAINING CLIMBERS

♦ After planting, untie a new climber from the cane that holds it, unravel the stems and spread them out well, then tie them into a fan shape so they spread out to cover the fence or wall they are to grow on.

♦ When planting a climber up through a tree or shrub, lead it up into the canopy, then, as it grows, divide the stems so that a few grow up each main stem. Loosely tie them in place to start with – if you don't do this, all the stems will grow over to one side of the tree instead of covering it evenly.

♦ Tie the shoots of self-clinging or twining climbers into place at first; once they are established, the new shoots will hang on for themselves. Self-clingers should be clipped over every couple of years to reduce their weight.

♦ Tie the main stems of wall shrubs out into a fan shape over the wall or fence, and tie in new stems to fill in any gaps in the framework. Prune shoots that grow outwards from the wall close to the main framework to stop the plants looking untidy.

A-Z climbers for north walls

With good, indirect light, north walls are not the inhospitable places for plants you might think. They remain cool and moist in summer when the rest of the garden gets baked and some very interesting, unusual or even colourful plants grow best in this situation, safe from the direct glare of the sun that would scorch their leaves and bring flowers to an early end. There are many plants worth growing that will transform what is often regarded as one of the garden's problem places into a special habitat.

■ *Clematis* '**Nelly Moser**'
3m (10ft) high × 1m (3ft) wide

A real old favourite and one of the earliest hybrid clematis to flower. It has mauve, barred-pink flowers appearing in late spring with a longer second flush during summer. Team it with **Clematis alpina** varieties, which also like the conditions.

Cultivation Plant deeply so that plants can regrow if affected by clematis wilt. Mulch generously in spring and liquid feed occasionally during the summer. The first flowers often have a greenish tinge if the weather is cold, but feeding with extra potash (such as tomato fertilizer) helps. Don't prune – or you'll miss out on the spring flush of flowers.

The tassels of Garrya elliptica liven up a wall in winter, especially if they can be floodlit at night.

■ *Crinodendron hookerianum*
(Lantern tree)
2.5m (8ft) high × 1.5m (5ft) wide

This unusual, evergreen shrub is hung with flowers that look just like a crop of miniature, bright red lanterns in early summer; it sometimes has another flush later in the year if the weather stays mild. Its rather upright stems take readily to wall training, and by spreading them out fan-style it is easy to achieve a good result without much effort. Not always easy to find, but well worth the search.

Cultivation A slightly tender shrub that in all but the south of Britain is safest grown against a wall. Both flowers and foliage suffer badly if exposed to strong sun or wind, so a shady, sheltered spot is essential to see it at its best. It needs lime-free, neutral to acid soil. No pruning is needed.

■ *Garrya elliptica* (Silk-tassel bush)
3m (10ft) high × 2m (6ft) wide

Best known as a big, evergreen shrub with long, dangly, lime-green catkins in winter, *Garrya elliptica* can suffer in a cold or windy part of the country where wall training is advisable just to give it some protection. But it also does well on a north-facing wall elsewhere and it deserves to be much more widely used for this purpose. Looks even better teamed with variegated ivy.

Cultivation It grows in most soils, but is slow-growing, especially to start with. Train a main framework of stems out over the area to be covered and fix them in place by tying them to horizontal wires. The closer to the horizontal the main branches are, the more densely they will be clothed with sideshoots. This is also a good way to display the dangling catkins. No pruning is needed.

■ *Hedera colchica* '**Sulphur Heart**'
(Ivy)
3m (10ft) high × 2m (6ft) wide

A self-clinging ivy that grips on to surfaces such as brickwork by pushing aerial roots into cracks; the roots expand till they jam themselves in place, so don't plant it on a wall with crumbly mortar. But on sound walls this is one of the more spectacular ivies with huge, sulphur-and-lime-variegated leaves that create a thick, well-upholstered effect.

Cultivation Plant in good soil and keep well watered to start with. Ivies often take a while to start clinging. The long stems they already have when you buy them never seem to want to grip. I find the best way to get them started is to lay

The ivy 'Sulphur Heart' is a reliable plant for a north wall and is especially handsome when its top growth becomes woody or 'arborescent'.

the stems out horizontally in the soil along the base of the wall so they root along their length, then the sideshoots that grow up from them seem to get the idea straight away. Clip over the plant annually in early spring.

■ *Hydrangea anomala* subsp. *petiolaris* (Climbing hydrangea)
4.5m (15ft) high × 2m (6ft) wide; potentially as much as 20m (66ft) in time
This plant doesn't look anything like a hydrangea until you see the flowers, which are like white lacecap hydrangeas almost 30cm (1ft) across. Each one has a ring of petal-like bracts with smaller flowers clustered in the centre looking like

tight buds that never open. The foliage turns a nice, golden yellow in autumn, then falls, revealing coppery stems.
Cultivation A self-clinging climber, which holds tight using aerial roots. It doesn't need any regular pruning, though you can trim it to fit the space available after it finishes flowering. Patience is needed; this plant takes several years before it is established and starts climbing freely, and another few before it begins flowering.

■ *Jasminum nudiflorum* (Winter jasmine)
3m (10ft) high × 2m (6ft) wide
A popular plant that has masses of small, yellow flowers on bare, green stems throughout winter in all but the very worst weather. A naturally very floppy shrub, it is almost always grown against a wall to keep it tidy and it does best on a north wall as it does not really like sun.

Cultivation Grows in most soil and enjoys a cool, shady root run. Clip it back with shears and snip out a few older stems as soon as the flowers are over.

■ *Rosa* 'Souvenir du Docteur Jamain' (Rose)
2m (6ft) high × 1.5m (5ft) wide
Very few roses really do well on a north-facing wall, so this one is especially worthwhile as it is rarely seen at its best anywhere else. The flowers are a rich claret colour, whereas in sun they fade to weak cherryade almost immediately. There is a main flush of blooms in early summer with smaller flushes all through the rest of the season. It makes a small, well-behaved climber.
Cultivation This rose even grows in poor soil. Tie the main stems out to horizontal wires and prune the flowered stems back to within a few buds of this permanent framework as soon as flowering finishes for the year. Mulch well in spring but avoid overfeeding as in a shady situation it can encourage over-vigorous shoots to grow and produce few flowers.

You'll need patience when growing the climbing hydrangea, but when it does start to flower it is suitably impressive.

A–Z climbers for south walls

These are the sort of walls you can never have enough of. They collect all the sunshine that is going and, though conditions at the base of the wall can be pretty dry, this is the ideal position for all those plants that need plenty of sun to ripen their stems or initiate flower buds. If you have set your heart on growing slightly tender plants or want to create a Riviera effect, a south-facing wall is the place to do it. And if you live in one of the warmer parts of the country, this is also the situation to have a gamble on something that needs a good summer to reach perfection.

■ *Abutilon vitifolium* var. *album* (Flowering maple)
3m (10ft) high × 2m (6ft) wide
A spectacular, slightly tender, deciduous shrub that appreciates the shelter of a sunny wall. The leaves look like sycamore leaves and are about the same size but, instead of being dark green and shiny, they are grey-green and downy. The flowers are white, nearly 8cm (3in) across and slightly bowl-shaped. It will sometimes produce large seed capsules after the flowers are over.
Cultivation A well-drained soil is needed for this plant which, once established, does not mind it a bit dry. Train the main stems out over the wall and tie to wall nails. No regular pruning is needed, but tidy the shape and, if necessary, cut back to keep it within its allotted space in early spring.

■ *Campsis* × *tagliabuana* 'Madame Galen' (Trumpet vine)
10m (30ft) high × 3m (10ft) wide
A real South of France special, with great bunches of orange-red trumpet flowers sprouting out all over a big, exuberant vine in late summer. Though the plant itself is fairly hardy, it flowers well only on a south wall in a mild area and does best after a hot summer. But if you live in the right spot, it's well worth a try. Every time I see it I am reminded of summer holidays.

Cultivation Well-drained but fairly rich soil suits this plant perfectly, and once established it does not mind summer drought. It needs a reasonable space to grow in, but you can cut it back a bit in early spring to stop it getting too big and to keep the plant tidy if you need to. Do not be dispirited if a few dull summers prevent it from flowering; in bloom it is stunning.

■ *Fremontodendron californicum* (Flannel bush)
3m (10ft) high × 2m (6ft) wide
Another real cracker that does well only on a south wall. When grown naturally it makes a small, slightly tender tree, but takes well to wall training. It has three-lobed, evergreen leaves which are slightly felty, as are the stems. (Some people are sensitive to the hairs, so take care when handling it.) It is simply smothered in large, waxy, yellow flowers that look like giant buttercups right through the summer months.
Cultivation Train the stems out over the wall and fix to wall nails. This plant needs well-drained soil and, because it has a small root system and can just about flower itself to death, it is best given some water and occasional liquid feeds during dry spells. No pruning is needed. Plants are slow-growing and can be short-lived, but you can grow your own replacements by collecting and sowing the seed that will be produced after a hot summer.

The trumpet vine, or campsis, brings a real South-of-France feel to a sunny wall. It does best in very good summers.

■ *Humulus lupulus* 'Aureus'
(Golden hop)

6m (20ft) high × 2m (6ft) wide

If you don't happen to live in a place where you can grow slightly tender plants, you can still grow this. The golden hop has bright golden, five-lobed leaves, which get even brighter when grown in full sun. It can also produce spikes of hop flowers, the sort you see twined around fireplaces in Kentish pubs.

Cultivation This plant needs a fertile soil that holds water, so it likes lots of organic matter. Plant it against trellis or similar supports and the twining stems will hold on by themselves. Although it's not wild about dry summers, a well-established plant should be able to cope without watering. It does not need pruning, but you can cut it back in early spring to stop it getting too big.

■ *Rosa banksiae*

6m (20ft) high × 3m (10ft) wide; potentially larger in time

A big climbing rose with bunches of small, yellow flowers in early summer. The double variety '**Lutea**' is best known, but single-flowered '**Lutescens**' has more scent. Either one will add an exotic touch to the wall. Team with later, flowering clematis to extend the floral display or, on a very big wall, another sun-loving climbing rose like the white *R. laevigata* 'Cooperi'.

Cultivation Needs deep, rich rosebed conditions, a mulch of manure and rose feed during the summer, and a sunny sheltered wall. Train a framework of stems out over the wall, and do not prune except to take out the old stems that no longer flower well. This is one reason it takes up so much room.

■ *Vitis vinifera* 'Purpurea'
(Purple grape vine)

4m (12ft) high × 1m (3ft) wide

This grape vine has pewterish-mauve leaves and small bunches of sweet, edible grapes in late summer. The foliage colour deepens to purple in autumn just before the leaves fall off. It looks superb swirling

around classical columns, but if you can't stretch to that, it is equally at home on trellis.

Cultivation Rich, deep soil and plenty of organic matter is best. It doesn't necessarily need regular pruning, but if you tidy the shape in mid-winter and shorten over-long shoots, you will concentrate the display right where you want it.

■ *Wisteria floribunda*
(Japanese wisteria)

8m (25ft) high × 8m (25ft) wide

A potentially big climber that is popular for the front of large houses. It has dangling spikes of fragrant pea flowers in early summer that are shaped like bunches of grapes. The mauve sort is best known, but

The yellow, open-faced flowers of fremontodendron look superb against mellow brickwork. Here lilies in pots add to the opulent feel.

you can get named varieties in white, purple and pink. Plants take a few years to start flowering, so you need to be patient.

Cultivation Prepare the soil well before planting because wisteria is a heavy feeder. Dig out a large trench and fill it with a mixture of topsoil and garden compost. Keep plants well fed, and water in dry spells at least for the first few years. Tie in growths that are needed to extend the plant's territory, but cut back any others to 30cm (1ft) in summer, and then to finger length in winter.

clematis *are incredibly versatile climbers, available in a huge range of varieties from the familiar, wide-open star shapes of the large-flowered types to those with nodding bell flowers and wispy seed-heads. If you grew enough different kinds, you could have a clematis in flower every day of the year. Clematis lend themselves to all sorts of creative growing possibilities right around the garden and are firm favourites for growing up a trellis.*

Clematis are also ideal for growing up through trees and shrubs, and look great scrambling along the arms of espalier-trained fruit trees or up the thorny stems of roses climbing over arches or pergolas. Far from being unnatural, this is the way clematis grow in the wild, with their roots in the shade of other plants, their flimsy stems supported by somebody else's branches and their flowers growing out into the sun.

Clematis make good plants for containers, and you can grow them in a flower border if you give them an obelisk or a rustic willow framework to climb up.

Plant clematis deeply, so that the rootball is buried by about 15cm (6in) of soil. Then, if the stems are affected by clematis wilt, the plants can grow back from new shoots that start out from underground growth buds. They are hungry plants and like good soil; feed them in spring and add a generous moisture-holding mulch. A couple of pieces of broken flagstone laid on the soil around the stem will keep the roots cool.

Once established, clematis don't need tying up as they use the 'elbows' in their leaf stalks to hold on with. Although youngsters may need a bit of encouragement at first, they soon get the hang of it. There is often some confusion about when to prune a clematis. Basically, the instructions vary from plant to plant, but as a general rule if it starts flowering before mid-summer, don't prune. If it flowers after mid-summer, prune hard in late winter. And if it is one of the evergreen species, such as *Clematis armandii*, you don't *need* to prune it, but you can if you like.

ABOVE: The evergreen Clematis armandii *has masses of small, vanilla-scented flowers.*

There are hundreds of clematis; garden centres stock a good range, but specialist nurseries have an even bigger choice. These are a few favourites:

Clematis alpina 'Frances Rivis'
Up to 2.5m (8ft) high

A relatively small mid- to late spring-flowering clematis with nodding, blue and white flowers shaped rather like lanterns. Fluffy, white seedheads follow the flowers and there is sometimes a later flush of blooms. It likes a cool situation and grows well on a north-facing wall. It does not need pruning.

Clematis armandii
6m (20ft) or more high

An evergreen clematis with distinctly handsome foliage and clusters of small, white, vanilla-scented flowers in early spring. It needs a sunny, sheltered spot to do well, but isn't as tender as people make out. No need to prune. Makes a fast-growing plant, but is great trained out along a wall or pergola.

Clematis cirrhosa 'Freckles'
6m (20ft) or more high

An evergreen species with red-speckled, nodding, white bell flowers throughout winter. It needs a sheltered spot so the flowers are not ruined by bad weather; in a cold area it is best grown in a cold conservatory. Does not need pruning.

Clematis 'Perle d'Azur'
3m (10ft) high

Hybrid clematis with masses of single, violet-blue flowers from late summer to early autumn on a generous-sized plant. Cut all stems hard back to a pair of buds as low down as possible in late winter.

Clematis 'Duchess of Edinburgh'
3m (10ft) high

A modest-growing hybrid clematis with big, double, white flowers in late spring, then, after a brief mid-summer pause, single, white flowers until early autumn. No pruning needed.

Clematis montana rubens
Up to 10m (30ft) high

Terribly well-known species with small pale pink flowers in early summer and faintly sun-bronzed foliage. The very similar-looking **'Elizabeth'** has slightly paler flowers which are scented. Makes a big plant unless pruned, though it doesn't normally need it.

Clematis tangutica
Up to 6m (20ft) high

Large species with yellow, lantern-like flowers in late summer and autumn followed by spectacular, feathery seed-heads that are good for drying. Prune or not as you wish.

Clematis viticella 'Purpurea Plena Elegans'
Up to 6m (20ft) high

Stunning, double Parma violet flowers in the shape of tight little rosettes from mid-summer to early autumn. Like all viticella varieties, it is reputedly immune to clematis wilt. Can be pruned but best left to grow up into trees and shrubs.

Two clematises frame a doorway: the yellow lanterns of Clematis tangutica, *and the blue flowers of 'Perle d'Azur'.*

A-Z climbers for east walls

East-facing walls get the early morning sun, so plants wake up bright and cheerful ready to show off their flowers, leaves and possibly even an overnight crop of spiders' webs neatly outlined in dewdrops. If you are up early on a frosty morning, you can enjoy the sight of stems and evergreen leaves with their rime of frost haloed in sunlight. But since sun on frosty flowers spells scorched petals, which in the case of fruiting plants also means no fruit, choose east walls for plants that flower after the worst of the frost is over. This situation is perfect for plants that like a cool root run, as they get plenty of sunlight for up to half the day, but are shaded from summer sun during the hottest parts of the day.

■ *Chaenomeles japonica*
(Flowering quince, japonica)
2m (6ft) high × 2m (6ft) wide
Flowering in late spring, japonica will remind you of pear blossom but in more colours – deep pink, peach and red as well as the usual fruit-tree shades of pink and white. As a shrub it is always straggly, but it looks good grown on a wall. The flowers open at about the same time as the leaves unfurl, and later in summer you can watch knobbly, green fruits developing. These ripen to a golden yellow and hang on the plant late into autumn.

Cultivation Japonica is happy in any garden soil. It can be formally trained into a fan or something like an espalier by training a framework of main stems out over the wall and tying them in place, then pruning back forward-growing stems to about 8cm (3in) from these soon after flowering. Or just grow it very informally, with the main stems tied up to the wall and the rest growing bushily. Again, cut out any forward-growing branches after flowering to keep it fairly flat.

■ *Clematis*
2.5–4m (8–12ft) high × 1.25m (4ft) wide
An east wall is an ideal situation for virtually all clematis, both the species and large, flowered hybrids, as they all grow best where they have a cool root run. Even the early flowering kinds like **Clematis alpina** will be happy here. Make the most

Clematis 'Comtesse de Bouchaud' lends herself to being planted with her feet in the shade and her head in the sun.

of an east wall by growing several varieties through each other. Choose a mixture of early species like **C. macropetala** and **C. alpina**, large-flowered hybrids and late **C. viticella** cultivars, and you can keep the wall flowering for six months or more and still enjoy late seed-heads of species like **C. tangutica**.

Cultivation Plant deeply so that plants can recover, should they suffer from wilt. Mulch heavily in spring and feed generously in late spring and summer. Prune cultivars that do not start flowering until mid-summer or later in the year to about 15cm (6in) high in early spring to keep plants more compact. Not all clematis need pruning, so check the pruning instructions on the label when you buy the plant.

■ *Cotoneaster horizontalis*
(Fishbone cotoneaster)
1m (3ft) high × 2m (6ft) wide
I always think this is a very precise sort of plant, with all those flat, fishbone-shaped branches that overlap to make geometrical shapes. It looks best in the later part of the year when the rows of stems are picked out with red, bead-like berries. When grown against a wall, it hangs on to its leaves better than when grown in the open as a shrub. It is one of those plants that is semi-evergreen, sometimes keeping its leaves in winter but dropping them if it is cold or windy.
Cultivation A very easy-going plant that grows in any reasonable soil. Train the main stems out over the space to be covered and tie them to wall nails. The rest will be stiff enough to support themselves. Not a fast grower, so it does not need regular pruning, but if it starts to climb down off the wall just snip off the sticking-out stems in mid-spring.

■ *Lathyrus odoratus* (Sweet pea)
2m (6ft) high × 30cm (1ft) wide
This much-loved, traditional, hardy annual climber, with scented flowers in a host of colours, is superb for cutting. In fact, the more you cut, the more you get. This is

Sweet peas seldom disappoint – provided they are cut regularly they will flower right through the summer.

because cutting acts as early deadheading, without which the plant sets seed and stops growing any more flowers.
Cultivation For the earliest flowers and for show, sow in narrow sweet-pea tubes in a cold frame in autumn. For normal use it is much easier to sow in spring. Sow either in pots in a cold greenhouse, or, if you don't have mice, straight into the ground where you want the plants to flower. Pinch out the growing point when seedlings are about 5cm (2in) high to make them grow bushy. Let them scramble up netting, or train single stems up canes for the longest, straight-stemmed flowers, ideal for cutting or village flower shows.

■ *Parthenocissus tricuspidata*
(Boston ivy)
15m (50ft) high × 3m (10ft) wide
A most spectacular plant with three-lobed leaves up to 20cm (8in) across that are green in spring and summer but turn violent red and purple in autumn when the nights start to get cold.
Cultivation It will grow happily in most gardens, though it is, potentially, a very large, self-clinging climber. Do not unleash it unless there is plenty of room, though

it does not have to be allowed to grow to full size. If wall space is short, it looks outstanding grown over a pergola leaning against the wall. Although it does not need to be pruned regularly, you can cut it back to keep it within its allocated space in mid-winter and, if necessary, hack it back a bit in summer too.

■ *Pyracantha* (Firethorn)
2.5m (8ft) × 2.5m (8ft) wide
If you think this sounds a bit ordinary, just take a look at a good, wall-trained specimen. You cannot see anything of the brickwork, just a solid wall of evergreen foliage with bunches of orange, red or yellow fruit dotted evenly over it. The berries last much longer here than out in the open garden, so the show goes on longer, from late summer until well into winter.
Cultivation Train the main stems of the plant out evenly over the wall in a rough fan or espalier shape and fix to the wall with nails. Around flowering time in early summer, clip the plant over lightly to remove all the new growth back to just beyond the flower clusters; this way the fruit will be more visible instead of half-hidden by foliage. Give it a second clip a bit later to keep it tidy, but again cut just above the developing berries. This treatment also helps to thicken the plant up and fill in any gaps.

A-Z climbers for west walls

A wall that benefits from afternoon and evening sun has the perfect aspect for plants that flower early in the year. They receive warmth to ripen their growth, while delicate flowers are protected from any risk of early morning sun scorching frosted petals. A sheltered west wall is also good for growing slightly tender plants, especially those that prefer gentle warmth rather than the fierce heat of a south wall. This is the wall you will be sitting by to sip a well-earned drink at the end of a day's work, so take the opportunity to spend your time surrounded by some of your favourite plants.

The spectacular Carpenteria californica *is a rewarding plant for a sunny, west-facing wall.*

■ *Abeliophyllum distichum*
(White forsythia)
2m (6ft) high × 2m (6ft) wide
An unusual wall shrub, with clusters of small, pink flowers for six or eight weeks in early spring. You know immediately it is in flower by the scent of almonds on the breeze. Wonderful trained informally round a gateway, where you can appreciate the aroma each time you go through.
Cultivation Give it well-drained soil and it is entirely trouble-free. The only pruning you need to do is to tidy it up and keep it within bounds soon after flowering.

■ *Actinidia kolomikta*
3m (10ft) high × 3m (10ft) wide
This plant always looks as though a painter has been splashing a couple of pots of paint about as the young leaves are tipped with pink and white, giving the plant a distinctly dappled look from a distance. Although it does produce fragrant, white flowers in summer, it is grown for its foliage.
Cultivation Prefers fertile garden soil; spend a bit of time preparing the ground if the soil is poor as this is going to be quite a big plant. Stems self-twine and will need something to grip on, but no tying in is needed. The only slight drawback is that it takes a few years for the leaves to start colouring up. Until then they are plain green.

■ *Carpenteria californica*
2m (6ft) high × 2m (6ft) wide
A real stunner of a wall shrub that has a bit of everything. It makes a neat, compact shape and has evergreen leaves. In mid-summer it is covered with big, fragile, white, poppy-like flowers, almost 8cm (3in) across, with bunches of yellow stamens in the middle of each. It is very slightly tender, but should be quite safe on a west wall. If the shoots do get hit by frost, new ones grow from below ground.
Cultivation Needs a well-drained soil, but otherwise it's not fussy. It does not need pruning, but look the plant over in spring and cut out any frost-damaged shoots and tidy the shape if necessary.

■ *Clematis* 'Etoile Rose'
3m (10ft) high × 1m (3ft) wide
Not your usual clematis flowers by any means, the pink, dangling bells of this variety have silvery edges. By growing it on a wall, you can look up into the flowers which are out from mid-summer until autumn.
Cultivation Plant deeply as a precaution against clematis wilt. Mulch generously in spring and feed in early summer. Keep new plants watered until they settle in. This is a clematis that benefits from hard pruning each year, so cut it down to about 15cm (6in) above ground level in early spring.

■ *Hoheria lyallii*
6m (20ft) high × 6m (20ft) wide
A slightly tender tree from New Zealand, needs the protection of a west wall when grown in Britain. It has large, pointed leaves about 10cm (4in) long which are so serrated they almost look as if they have a fringe around the edge. In summer it has clusters of bowl-shaped, white flowers which are nicely scented and attract lots of butterflies.
Cultivation Needs a neutral or alkaline soil, but other than that it is not fussy as long as drainage is good. You will

ABOVE: Clematis viticella *'Etoile Rose'* with Cotinus coggygria *'Royal Purple'*

probably have to train your own plant, so start with a small one and gradually train and prune in spring to get a flat shape with evenly spaced branches spread out over the wall. Once it covers the area, just prune lightly in spring to keep the growth flat to the wall, and train in any new shoots you need to fill in gaps.

■ **Magnolia grandiflora** (Bull bay)
4.5m (15ft) high × 3m (10ft) wide; potentially larger in time
This plant has large, shiny, evergreen leaves that put you in mind of a rhododendron, but it flowers in late summer with big, white, chalice-shaped blooms that could only belong to a magnolia. I've seen it growing in the Channel Islands as a tree, but in mainland Britain it needs the protection of a wall if it is to flower reliably. Plants can take up to 10 years to begin flowering but the cultivar **'Exmouth'** should flower within about five years.
Cultivation Unlike many magnolias, this one will tolerate most soils, even chalky soil, but is easiest to get going in the first place if the ground is good with plenty of organic matter. Train it against a wall so that the plant has a central leader with branches off to either side. Train and prune to size as necessary in spring.

■ **Solanum crispum 'Glasnevin'**
(Chilean potato tree)
6m (20ft) high × 6m (20ft) wide
When you visit a garden and overhear people talking about the potato climbing on the wall, this will be what they mean. The bunches of blue and yellow flowers this plant sports for most of the summer look just like potato flowers, and the two are indeed distantly related. The variety 'Glasnevin' is the hardiest; other potato vines are for mild locations only.
Cultivation Grows in any well-drained soil. Prune lightly in late spring to tidy the plant and stop it getting too big. Cut out any shoots growing too far out from the wall that you cannot train in to fill gaps.

BELOW: *Few flowers have the mouth-watering qualities of* Magnolia grandiflora, *the evergreen magnolia with massive, fragrant, waxy blooms.*

Border perennials

Perennials provide the splashes of colour that really bring a garden to life. Use them to add fresh crops of flowers to a permanent back-drop of trees and shrubs, or let them star in beds of their own. There is a perennial for every garden position and for every situation from sunny to deep shade.

Ever since we realized that we do not have to grow them the traditional way, in herbaceous borders, perennials have been gaining in popularity. Don't get me wrong. There are few better sights than a really well-stocked and carefully maintained herbaceous border. The trouble is, to make a good show you need a junior stately home, with lots of room for the obligatory yew hedge along the back and enough plants to keep the colour coming from spring until late autumn. A bevy of gardeners is also a good idea to keep up with the staking, weeding and snail-evicting, much of which is due to the yew hedge – which also needs to be clipped.

Of course, in a smaller garden you can still have a herbaceous border, but instead of trying to pack in enough plants for all seasons, it is a good idea to concentrate on making a fine mid- and late summer show. Alternatively, you can team spring and early summer perennials with spring bulbs, then rely on roses to provide colour for the rest of the season. And instead of a yew hedge, try backing the border with fencing panels: woven willow hurdles or the sort made from dried heather look especially stylish. They take up much less room, and don't harbour weeds and pests like a hedge.

You can opt for a different way of using perennials entirely. A mixed border is one alternative. The idea here is to use perennials to fill the gaps between your year-round framework of trees and shrubs. Island beds get my vote, because they stand out in the open with nothing behind them, which means less weeding and snail control, and also cuts down on staking since plants receive more light and don't grow weak and leggy. You can also reach the plants from all round, so if there is any work to be done, like the occasional hoeing, it is much quicker and easier.

To get the best from perennials, choose the right plant for the place. It pays to assess the situation before buying your plants, to make sure the two match up. Most of the classic herbaceous border perennials like phlox, campanula and lupins grow happily in both sun and the sort of light, dappled shade you find in between other plants. Some plants must have full sun to do well, such as delphiniums and red hot pokers. These are tall enough to get plenty of sun, even when grown in a border, if you take care to surround them only with low-growing neighbours. Short sun lovers like nepeta and *Stachys byzantina* are suited to the front of a border on account of their low-spreading shape. They also make very good, flowering ground cover for a sunny bed under roses.

Although plants like Solomon's seal, astilbe and hosta are well known as shade lovers, they can be grown in sunnier situations too, as long as the soil stays moist enough for them in summer. In very deep shade you can't go far wrong with *Iris foetidissima*, *Arum italicum* subsp. *italicum* 'Marmoratum' and *Euphorbia amygdaloides* var. *robbiae*. Choose drought tolerant ground covering perennials such as *Alchemilla mollis* for tricky situations like dry banks, where they make an alternative to grass and don't need to be mowed. Ultra sun-loving perennials such as *Euphorbia characias* subsp. *wulfenii*, *Rhodanthemum hosmariense* and sedums are extremely well suited to a drought-tolerant garden and low-growing subjects such as thymes are suitable for growing in chinks among paving.

ABOVE: *Oriental poppy*, Papaver *'Curlilocks', brilliant in early summer.* RIGHT: *When a mixed border is planned well, its success is obvious: a wonderful display of colour, with each plant best positioned to show off its flowers and foliage.*

The latest trend in perennial cultivation is for growing them in containers. Choose the right plants, and the results can be as good as using bedding plants but without the twice-yearly replanting. The same perennials can stay in their pots for three years or more before they need tipping out and dividing. How do you know which are the right plants? I like to use naturally compact plants which either have a long flowering season or very good foliage. For a sunny spot, pinks like *Dianthus* 'Doris', dwarfer penstemons and anything with silver foliage, such as *Artemesia* 'Powis Castle', look good. Also, they all enjoy similar growing conditions, so you could team them together in one large tub. For a shady area, hostas are brilliant. In fact, they are my first choice for container growing – and grown like this they are so much easier to protect from snails.

Cultivation and care

Perennials do not make a lot of work, but they do need the right care at the right time to do their best for you. It is not difficult to fit perennial chores into your schedule since they mostly happen all at the same time, regardless of which plants you grow.

The very best time to plant perennials is in spring. This gives you the rest of the season to enjoy them. Virtually all kinds will produce a few flowers even in their first year, though they will be much more prolific in year two when they have had a chance to spread and fill the space better. By not buying until you can see a few fat shoots emerging from the pot, you can be sure you have chosen a pot containing a live plant. If you buy in autumn, this is not always possible, since a lot of perennials have died down by then and you can later find you have bought a pot with compost but nothing else in it. If you do not mind watering them for the rest of the season, there is no reason why you should not buy perennials in summer, even when they are in flower, to fill a gap in the border and add instant colour.

Prepare the soil very well before planting perennials and dig in lots of well-rotted organic matter to hold moisture. If you are making a new border from scratch, do the groundwork the previous summer if you can (see pages 34–5). This gives you time to exterminate any perennial weeds that appear after you have dug the border and forked in compost – do this by spraying them with a glyphosate-based weedkiller. You will also have time to repeat the treatment if a second crop of shoots comes up, which indicates an old, established problem.

Most border perennnials can be planted about 30–45cm (12–18in) apart. After planting, water new perennials in well and mulch round them with a layer of compost or old manure up to 5cm (2in) thick. Each spring, just as the new growth starts to appear, clear away any weeds and plant debris to tidy the border, then sprinkle a general-purpose fertilizer like pelleted poultry manure carefully between the plants. If a handful ends up in the crown of an emerging plant, wash it off with plenty of water to stop it 'burning' the soft, young shoots.

HOW TO STAKE BORDER PERENNIALS

1 Taller border plants that tend to flop need to be supported. The most inconspicuous supports are twiggy pea sticks which can be pushed in among the emerging shoots.

2 Prevent clump-formers such as peonies from taking a nose dive by placing circular wire supports above them. Position the supports when the plants are about 30cm (1ft) tall.

3 Plants such as delphiniums, which produce tall spikes, need their stems supporting individually. Use a 2m (6ft) bamboo cane and loop the stem to the cane with soft green twine.

Then mulch the whole area with 5cm (2in) of garden compost or old manure. You can also use bark chippings, which last longer and only need topping up annually, or cocoa shell, which seems to ward off snails. (Take care to prevent dogs from eating the stuff when it is dry – it can lead to poisoning if ingested in quantity.)

Make sure your plant labels are still visible if you like to know what your plants are – there is nothing like mulching for losing names.

Mulching is the best operation gardening ever invented. Not only does it help to improve the soil, since worms gradually pull the organic matter down into the ground, doing the digging for you, but the layer of material over the soil reduces water loss (which is why you must mulch only when the soil is already moist) and smothers weed seedlings. You may find a new crop of weed seeds blown in from surrounding gardens starts to germinate later in the season, but by then the perennial plants have grown up and will smother them out, keeping weeding to an absolute minimum. In fact, the only other real job, apart from a bit of light deadheading to keep plants flowering during summer, is the end-of-season clear-up.

Keeping things neat

Clearing up used to be done in autumn when the last of the flowers came to a natural end. Now the idea is only to do a partial tidy-up and leave anything with interesting stems or seed-heads to

Few plants are more stately than delphiniums (provided you can control the slugs and snails that also admire them!). This is 'Blue Dawn'.

feed birds or provide a 'frost garden' for the winter. Old foliage and stems also house beneficial insects like money spiders, black beetles and centipedes over winter, leaving them poised to attack garden pests in spring. The rubbish gets cleared up in spring, when you do your pre-mulch tidy-up. Apart from looking a little untidy, the garden will come to no harm if you leave the whole job until then if you prefer.

Perennials spread slowly to make quite large clumps in time. Eventually the middle dies out, leaving the original plants looking a bit scruffy. This is the time to divide them. Some plants, like hostas, which are quite slow to get established, can go happily for five years or more without dividing. Others, like the fast-growing Michaelmas daisy and golden rod, may need dividing every two or three years. So play it by ear. Spring is the best time to divide perennials because open wounds may cause the plant to rot in damp soil in winter, but autumn is all right for tough customers or if you garden on fast-draining soil. The only plants that need dividing at different times are bearded iris, which are best tackled about six weeks after they finish flowering, in the middle of summer. Chop them up with a spade and throw away the old bits from the middle of the plant. Refresh the soil with some compost and fertilizer before replanting the young, healthy bits from around the edge, as if they were new plants.

A-Z border perennials for spring

Whatever else you do without in the garden, you should not pass up the opportunity to grow lots of spring-flowering perennials. They are the first sign of the new growing season and are the perfect partners for carpets of spring bulbs. They provide the missing link that teams the ground level of the border with taller spring shrubs. If you want an antidote to a flower-deprived winter, I strongly recommend spring perennials for a riotous, over-the-top display.

■ **Bergenia × schmidtii** (Elephant's ears)
30cm (1ft) high × 60cm (2ft) wide
A particularly good form of the old favourite bergenia, this version has dark, bronzy-green leaves shaped like elephant's ears, which make a good background for the big clusters of raspberry-pink flowers. In a mild year they can begin flowering as early as late winter and continue virtually throughout the whole of spring.
Cultivation A really reliable evergreen perennial that slowly builds up into broad clumps, and does well in just about any soil and situation all round the garden, in sun or shade. I specially like it as ground cover under shrubs.

For growing under trees, such as this silver birch, the perennial forget-me-not, Brunnera, is very useful.

■ **Brunnera macrophylla**
(Perennial forget-me-not)
45cm (1½ft) high × 60cm (2ft) wide
Big, kidney-shaped leaves and masses of tiny, frothy, blue forget-me-not flowers at the end of long, wiry stems make this a superb accessory for spring bulbs like Spanish bluebells and narcissi; plant the lot together under an early-flowering tree like amelanchier for a lovely spring island in the lawn. The variegated *Brunnera macrophylla* 'Hadspen Cream' is even prettier.
Cultivation Happy in just about any soil, even the heavier ones, so long as it is in light shade and does not get waterlogged in winter. Plants do not need any attention, but clear the old foliage when it starts to die down naturally towards the end of the season. Until then, the leaves make a good background carpet for later summer flowers.

■ **Convallaria majalis** (Lily of the valley)
20cm (8in) high × 45cm (1½ft) wide
The catalogues never seem able to make up their minds whether this is a bulb or a perennial. You may find it listed under both headings. It certainly isn't a bulb as it has spreading rhizome-like roots that enable the plant to creep about in the bottom storey of the border, popping up its small and scented, white bell flowers and neat pairs of upright leaves in spring. The gold-striped form 'Albostriata' is particularly attractive but is quite expensive.
Cultivation People always think lily of the valley is difficult to grow, but it isn't. It just needs time to settle down, then likes to be left alone. Give it a shady spot with soil containing plenty of organic matter that does not dry out too much in summer or become waterlogged in winter and it will be quite happy.

The roots run quite close to the surface, so take care when hoeing around it, especially in summer after the leaves have died down and you can't see where it is.

■ **Dicentra spectabilis** (Bleeding heart, Dutchman's breeches)
75cm (2½ft) high × 75cm (2½ft) wide
A pretty plant with pink-and-white, heart-shaped flowers that last for six or eight weeks in late spring. Long after they are over the foliage continues to make a nice, ferny frieze under trees or around shrubs.
Cultivation No trouble to grow, the plant enjoys a spot with humus-rich soil in light shade. It prefers woodland conditions, but is perfectly happy in a sunnier border so long as the soil does not dry out in summer.

ABOVE: Euphorbia robbiae *makes great spring-flowering ground cover, even in a shady spot, though it can be a touch invasive.* RIGHT: *Look closely at the flowers of* Dicentra spectabilis *and it is easy to see why the plant has the common name of 'bleeding heart'.*

■ *Doronicum* (Leopard's bane)
60cm (2ft) high × 60cm (2ft) wide

The big, yellow blooms of leopard's bane are the first daisies to appear in the border each year, on surprisingly neat and tidy plants. There are several different varieties available, with single or double flowers. There's not a lot to choose between the singles, but *Doronicum* 'Frühlingspracht' is by far the best double.

Cultivation A very easy-going daisy that likes sun or light shade. It just keeps coming up and doing its stuff every year without needing a lot of fuss.

■ *Euphorbia amygdaloïdes* var. robbiae
45cm (1½ft) high × 45cm (1½ft) wide

A very useful plant to use as a carpet in a shady spot, where the dark, evergreen leaf rosettes give rise to lime green shepherd's crook flower spikes in spring. Don't plant it where its invasiveness could be a problem; instead, establish it where nothing else will grow.

Cultivation Easy to grow in any soil and situation and needing little care and attention other than the removal of faded growths in spring..

■ *Geum* 'Dolly North' (Avens)
45cm (1½ft) high × 45cm (1½ft) wide

This is one of those incredibly useful plants that forms good-sized clumps and can always be relied on to make an attractive show in spring and early summer. The best-known varieties of geum are both double; the paprika-red 'Mrs J. Bradshaw', and the yellow 'Lady Stratheden'. But for anyone who fancies a change. 'Dolly North' has light orange, semi-double flowers with a rather curiously shaped inner row of petals that give it more character.

Cultivation Happy in any border, in sun or light shade, between shrubs or other flowers. It does not need staking and can go for years without needing to be divided.

■ *Helleborus orientalis* hybrids (Lenten rose)
60cm (2ft) high × 60cm (2ft) wide

Hellebores are going though a fashionable phase, and nicely coloured hybrids of the Lenten rose, which has large, single flowers, are particularly collectable. Heavily pink, spotted-white flowers, misty mauves and purple-blacks

are the most sought-after shades. Plants flower from around late winter and early spring and have semi-evergreen leaves.

Cultivation Since hellebores hybridize and self-seed freely, just buy two or three good plants, plant in moisture-retaining soil in light shade and leave them to set seed after flowering. The seeds germinate best if you let them come up where they fall, so take care when hoeing around hellebores. Pot the seedlings or move them to a new spot while they are small and you'll get lots of new plants, each with slightly different flowers. Older plants do not transplant well.

■ *Iris,* **bearded**
1m (3ft) high × 60 cm (2ft) wide
Unmistakable flowers with three petals curving up and three curving down to make the characteristic fleur-de-lis shape, and sword-shaped leaves growing from thick rhizomes. They look good at the front of formal rosebeds to get the flowering season off to an early start. You can get dwarf, intermediate and tall bearded iris, which flower in order of size, with the smallest first.

Cultivation Unlike most herbaceous plants, bearded iris do not like the close company of other plants. They must have sun on their rhizomes or they will not flower. For the same reason they must be planted very shallowly, so the top half of each horizontal rhizome is exposed above ground. The plants need dividing every three to five years: do this about six weeks after flowering and replant only the young bits of rhizome from the outside of the clump. A very well-drained, sunny spot is essential for their success.

ABOVE: *The classy, nodding flowers of* Helleborus orientalis *are stalwarts of the spring garden.* BELOW: *Pulmonarias carpet the ground among shrubs in a shady spot.*

Wood anemones (Anemone nemorosa) and spring star flowers (Ipheion uniflorum) carpet the ground at the foot of a tree.

■ *Omphalodes cappadocica*
20cm (8in) high × 30cm (1ft) wide

Delightful, slightly unusual, ground-covering plants with small, true-blue, star-shaped flowers to grow under shrubs or with spring bulbs. The variety 'Cherry Ingram' has azure flowers, and 'Starry Eyes' has blue-and-white-striped flowers which show up best of all.

Cultivation Omphalodes needs moist but not waterlogged soil containing plenty of humus; it enjoys light, woodland conditions and grows particularly well under shrubs. Plant groups of three or five if you have a large gap to fill or want to make more of a splash.

■ *Polygonatum multiflorum* (Solomon's seal)
1m (3ft) high × 60cm (2ft) wide

The long, arching, wand-like stems of Solomon's seal with rows of neat, white bell flowers dangling down underneath are so precisely arranged they look as if they were designed by a mathematician. Flower arrangers remove the leaves and use the stems of flowers alone.

Cultivation Grows best in a moist spot in dappled shade and is an ideal plant for light, woodland conditions under trees or among shrubs in a border. It spreads slowly and you can divide large clumps in early spring if they get too big, but it prefers to be left alone as it takes a while to re-establish itself after a move. Clumps are occasionally attacked, and completely defoliated by the larvae of Solomon's seal sawfly. Spray with a contact insecticide at the first sign of attack.

■ *Primula* 'Harlow Carr hybrids'
60cm (2ft) high × 30cm (1ft) wide

A particularly good strain of candelabra hybrid primulas developed at Harlow Carr gardens in Yorkshire, my old stamping ground. The flowers form in tiers up the upright stems in late spring. Very pretty, and perfect near a pond where you can see their reflections in the water.

Cultivation Grow them like other candelabra primulas, in moist soil among other waterside plants round a pond, or in a moist border. They enjoy the light, dappled shade cast by neighbouring plants; in fact, in strong sun they wilt unhappily.

■ *Pulmonaria* (Lungwort)
30cm (1ft) high × 30cm (1ft) wide

Pink and blue spring flowers are only part of the charm of this old-fashioned plant; the spotty foliage makes a good background carpet for summer flowers long after its own have finished. Choose *Pulmonaria saccharata* cultivars for the spottiest leaves; or **Argentea Group** for leaves that are almost pure silver with just a hint of sage green. Varieties are available with white flowers, such as 'Sissinghurst White'; 'Mawson's Blue' is a deep gention blue, and *P. rubra* 'Redstart' is a good coral red. There are many shades in between and I find them all tremendously useful for shady spots. They look very pretty under roses.

Cultivation Does well just about anywhere in light shade. If the soil dries out in summer, the foliage can turn a bit mildewy, but cut the leaves back almost to ground level and a new, healthy crop will soon replace them. In full sun the plants wilt rapidly, even if there is moisture at the roots.

■ *Veronica gentianoides* (Speedwell)
45cm (1½ft) high × 30cm (1ft) wide

Don't let the name speedwell put you off. This is no lawn weed, but a truly lovely perennial with upright spikes of palest sky-blue flowers in late spring and early summer. It spreads gently, and has a rather ethereal, wildflower quality about it that puts you in mind of the sort of thing fairies would like to live in at the bottom of your garden.

Cultivation Give it any normal border soil and let it make small clumps between shrubs or other flowers for a natural look. It is happy in sun or light shade. Individual rosettes can be prised up and re-planted at a wider spacing for easy propagation.

A-Z border perennials for summer

In summer you are completely spoilt for choice. Whether you like your perennials big, loud and bold, fashionably natural or cosily cottage, there are heaps to choose from. Grow them in beds and borders or in flowering meadows. Forget traditional advice about planting them in threes or fives, especially if yours is a small garden. Go for the biggest range you can squeeze in, for an over-the-top effect that makes the most of everything the height of the season has to offer.

■ **Achillea** (Yarrow)
60cm (2ft) high × 60cm (2ft) wide
Old border favourite with flat, plate-shaped flower heads, which are traditionally yellow but have now been joined by cultivars with other colours too. The variety **'Fanal'** has startling, brick-red flowers that fade to terracotta-pink and A. *filipendulina* **'Gold Plate'** is still the biggest and boldest, with stems up to 1.5m (5ft) topped by 20-cm (8-in) wide golden, yellow flowers.
Cultivation Very easy-going and happy in any well-prepared border so long as the plants can grow in plenty of sun. Tall varieties need their stems supported, but the more compact ones can stand up for themselves.

■ **Alstroemeria 'Ligtu Hybrids'**
(Peruvian lily)
60cm (2ft) high × 60cm (2ft) wide
The bright, sunny colours of these lily-like flowers make them firm summertime favourites. *Alstroemeria* **'Ligtu Hybrids'** are reliable, long-stemmed varieties that are best for borders; they are good for flower arranging too. There is also a range of more compact, modern alstroemeria varieties, useful for large containers on the patio, producing flowers for most of the summer.
Cultivation A warm, sunny spot and very well-drained, even sandy or gravelly soil, are essential for alstroemeria. On heavy soil their thick, fleshy roots just rot away. They are good plants for the foot of a south-facing wall, or along either side of a garden path, as they enjoy the reflected heat. After planting,

it takes a year or more to settle down, so do not expect a sensational display in the first year. Avoid moving them once they are established, as plants will have to go through the whole settling-in process again.

■ **Aquilegia vulgaris 'Nora Barlow'**
(Columbine)
75cm (2¹/₂ft) high × 30cm (12in) wide
This improved form of the old-fashioned grannies' bonnets, which seeds itself around cottage gardens and hybridizes with gusto, is a great favourite with flower arrangers. It has a more cultivated appearance too, with double, pink and white flowers that look rather like helichrysum. It flowers in early summer.
Cultivation Plants are short-lived perennials, lasting perhaps three to five years. It's no good relying on this aquilegia to replace itself by self-seeding, as the resulting seedlings do not always look like the parent plant. Nor does it seed itself around as freely as normal *Aquilegia vulgaris*. The only way to be sure of having more of the same is to buy seed, raise plants and plant them where you want them.

ABOVE: Aquilegia 'Nora Barlow' is a bright, pink and white double-flowered beauty that hybridizes freely. BELOW: Alstroemeria 'Ligtu Hybrids' are reliable plants that are excellent for well-drained soil and a sunny spot in borders.

■ Astilbe

75cm (2¹/₂ft) high × 45cm (1¹/₂ft) wide

Big, feathery plumes of flowers are the most striking feature of this popular plant, which seems to have coloured pampas grass heads growing out of a neat perennial with ferny foliage. Pinks and reds are the favourite colours, though there are also lilac-, white- and purple-flowered varieties. The plants make great partners for hostas.

Cultivation Astilbe enjoys the same sort of situation as hostas – moist soil with plenty of organic matter in light shade, though like hostas it grows in sun if the ground stays damp enough. It is brilliant for pondside planting and is even suitable for a bog garden.

■ Campanula lactiflora (Bellflower)

1m (3ft) high × 60cm (2ft) wide

Campanulas have an old-fashioned English countryside air about them that makes them suited to cottage gardens, though they also look good grown in flower beds and between shrubs in big borders, or even in wilder gardens. This species has tall stems topped with sprays of star-shaped flowers. The flowers are usually white to pale blue, but several named varieties are available in darker shades of blue such as 'Prichard's Variety' and 'Loddon Anna'. There is also a compact form called 'Pouffe' which grows about 30cm (12in) high with very pale blue flowers.

Cultivation A good border plant that grows happily almost anywhere in sun or light shade between other plants. It spreads slowly, but makes quite big clumps in time, so be prepared to dig it up and divide it in early spring every few years when it grows too big.

■ Delphinium hybrids

2m (6ft) high × 60cm (2ft) wide

The backbone of a traditional herbaceous border is its tall, upright stems of blue delphiniums in all shades from lightest sky blue to deepest violet. The variety 'Black Knight' is such a dark

purple-blue it looks almost black from a distance. There are some modern delphiniums that are pink and even red, and short varieties that are so compact you don't need to stake them, but you still can't beat the old favourites like the 'Pacific Giants' strain.

Cultivation Delphiniums need rich herbaceous border soil with plenty of manure dug in during the autumn before planting. Stake the stems of tall varieties individually with canes, but the more compact kinds are best with a plant frame stood over them in spring, so the stems can grow up through it. You must protect delphiniums from slugs and snails, otherwise the young shoots will be eaten as fast as they try to come through.

■ Dianthus (Pinks)

20cm (8in) high × 60cm (2ft) wide

Pinks are like 'buttonhole' carnations but smaller and much easier to grow. They have perfectly circular flowers in all shades of pink, mauve, red, maroon and white, which grow from mats of grassy, blue-grey, evergreen foliage. Some varieties are heavily scented, smelling of cloves and other spices. Modern varieties will flower from early to late summer, but old-fashioned pinks have a short flowering season at the start of summer. A favourite variety is 'Doris', which has double, pink flowers all summer.

Cultivation A sunny, sheltered spot with very well-drained soil containing little or no organic matter is the magic formula for pinks. They grow best in alkaline or even chalky soil; add a sprinkling of lime to neutral soil if it is otherwise suitable, but don't bother trying to grow pinks if the ground stays wet in winter or is acidic. Plants are rather short-lived, so propagate new ones every three years. Take cuttings called 'pipings', which are made by pulling the stems out from a leaf joint rather than using a knife, soon after flowering.

Eremurus robustus (Foxtail lily)
3m (10ft) high × 1m (3ft) wide

A real border giant, with tall, shooting spires of pink flowers. It is not often seen because the foxtail lily is incredibly fussy about its growing conditions. If you have the right situation, go for it.

Cultivation A sunny border with very well-drained soil is essential. If the ground holds too much moisture, the thick roots just rot away. Plants are often sold as dormant roots in early spring; these look rather like the spokes of a wheel and need to be planted carefully without breaking,

The tall spires of the foxtail lily, Eremurus robustus, *add elegant height to sunny, well-drained beds and borders.*

just below the surface of the soil. When sold in containers, big pots are inevitable, so the price tends to be steep. Mulch well and take great care when hoeing as the plant sulks or may even die if the roots get damaged. Plant with well-disciplined neighbours that are not going to smother the foliage (which is much shorter than the flower spikes) and which won't get in a tangle with the eremurus roots.

Eryngium alpinum (Sea holly)
60cm (2ft) high × 45cm (1½ft) wide

Sea holly flowers are often mistaken as artificial when seen for the first time. The plants have spiky, silver-green leaves and flowers like a big, metallic-blue thistle head surrounded by a frilly, silver-blue ruff. Though they look stiff, the flowers of this species are surprisingly soft.

Cultivation Very well-drained, even sandy, neutral to alkaline soil and lots of sun are essential for eryngium. Once it's planted, leave it alone to form a nice clump; these plants hate to be disturbed. The flowers are good for cutting, if you can bring yourself to do it.

Euphorbia characias subsp. wulfenii (Spurge)
1m (3ft) high × 1m (3ft) wide

Probably the most architectural perennial available. This bushy evergreen plant is covered in big, dome-shaped, greenish-yellow heads of flowers in early summer. The blue-grey foliage remains quite a feature even after the flowers are over. This euphorbia teams well with red hot pokers.

Cultivation A sun-loving euphorbia that enjoys well-drained soil and is also a good candidate for a drought garden. When the flowers are completely over in mid-summer, cut the flowered stems off close to the base of the plant, taking care to avoid the thick white sap that can squirt out: it will irritate skin or eyes. Plants self-seed, but the offspring are inferior to the parent plant.

Geranium × oxonianum 'Claridge Druce' (Cranesbill)
75cm (2½ft) high × 75cm (2½ft) wide

A hardy cranesbill which is unusual because it keeps its leaves all year round, when most of its relatives lose theirs. This useful habit, together with its broad, spreading shape make it very useful for ground cover under shrubs or roses, and it looks especially good grown with a mixture of other herbaceous plants in a border. The deep pink, purple-veined flowers are large and shaped like wide funnels. The same plants keep flowering throughout summer. If I were only going to grow one hardy cranesbill, this would be my first choice.

Cultivation Easy to grow in any reasonable border soil, in sun or light shade, between other plants. Old clumps can be divided up if they get too big, but it is not usually necessary for years. If you grow several different hardy cranesbills, watch out for occasional self-sown seedlings – though these will not usually be the same as either parent, there are often some good plants among them. Wait until they flower, usually the following year, before deciding their fate.

▨ *Hemerocallis* (Day lily)
1m (3ft) high × 1m (3ft) wide

Day lilies are available in a range of colours, including some very good pinks and strong reds. The flowers look like lilies and do last only a day, but the name is rather misleading since the plants produce so many of them that you would never know. They flower throughout mid- and late summer, so you can't complain of a short season. Anyway, I rather like the arching, strap-shaped,

evergreen leaves, which form an attractive clump. Compact varieties such as **'Stella de Oro'** are good for smaller spaces; or for a pretty pink grow **'Catherine Woodbery'** which, unusually for hemerocallis, has scented flowers.

Cultivation The day lily enjoys a sunny spot in a fertile well-prepared border with plenty of organic matter and reasonably good drainage, but is not too fussy. There is no need to stake or split, as it will grow happily for years once established.

▨ *Hosta* **'Frances Williams'**
45cm (1½ft) high × 45cm (1½ft) wide

One of the more cabbage-shaped hostas, this has big, thick, waxy leaves which are blue-green in the centre with an irregular, lime-green, splodgy margin around the edge. When it is grown in a brighter-than-usual situation, the edge can turn quite a light gold. Unlike some hostas, whose flowers are rather insignificant, this one has pretty spikes of white bells in early summer.

Cultivation Moist, fertile soil and light shade is the usual formula for a hosta, but the kinds with thick leaves, like **'Frances Williams'**, also do very well in a sunnier spot, as long as the soil stays damp enough.

This is a good variety to grow by a pond and is also an exceptional plant for a container, grown in John Innes potting compost. Hostas are adored by slugs and snails, but the thickness of the leaves on this variety make it one of the most mollusc-resistant.

▨ *Iris sibirica* (Siberian iris)
1m (3ft) high × 60cm (2ft wide)

This plant flowers just after the tall bearded irises, and is a good way to keep the continuity of these distinctive flowers in the garden. Although the flowers are the same basic iris shape, *Iris sibirica* does not have rhizomes but instead forms clumps. A limited range of varieties is available, mainly in white, mauve and different shades of blue, often with what looks like gold or purple pencilling on the petals. One of the most popular is **'Flight of Butterflies'** which has violet-blue and white flowers. Another good one is **'Butter and Sugar'** which has yellow and white flowers the colour of raw cake mixture. Delicious!

The Siberian iris is one of my favourite plants and, I think, one of the easiest irises to grow.

The Himalayan blue poppy has a unique colour of flower – a zingy, electric blue.

Cultivation This species likes very different conditions from the bearded irises: sun is still essential, but give it a damp border or boggy soil around the edge of a pond to keep it happy. In a normal border it needs mulching heavily and keeping well watered in dry spells.

◼ *Kniphofia* **'Atlanta'** (Red hot poker)
1.2m (4ft) high × 60cm (2ft wide)
This cultivar has the tall, red-tipped, yellow flowers that I call a real red hot poker, unlike the tamer kniphofias you sometimes see with small, discreet, greeny-yellow or cream flowers that look as if their fire has gone out. 'Atlanta' makes a clump of rather sharp-edged narrow, evergreen leaves. A good dramatic plant in flower or not.
Cultivation This sort of red hot poker needs a sunny situation with well-drained soil. Once established it withstands a fair degree of drought. Tidy the dead spikes: cut them close to the base after flowering.

◼ *Lupinus polyphyllus* (Lupin)
1m (3ft) high × 60cm (2ft) wide
These stately flowers with tall, upright spikes made up of rows of small flowers always manage to remind me of coloured corn on the cob. You can get plain or multicoloured varieties. The leaves are equally fascinating, like the spokes of a wheel radiating out from the tip of the stalk.
Cultivation Lupins like good, rich border soil. The plants live longest on slightly acid soil, curling up their toes in a short time in chalky soil. Watch out for lupin aphids, a giant species that sucks so much sap from the plants they have problems growing – pick the brutes off by hand as they seem immune to pesticides. Lupins flower at the start of summer, but if you cut off the dead flower stems complete with the stalks as soon as the flowers are over, you can often persuade the plants to produce a second flush towards the end of the season.

◼ *Meconopsis betonicifolia* (Himalayan blue poppy)
1m (3ft) high × 45cm (1½ft) wide
Not the easiest plant to please, but worth the effort. This stunner has fragile, 8-cm (3-in) diameter blue poppy flowers that each last for only a couple of days and a short flowering season lasting a few weeks in mid-summer.
Cultivation The Himalayan poppy does best in light woodland, as it needs well-drained, lime-free soil containing plenty of humus (leaf mould is ideal) so it never dries out badly. Under these conditions it will self-seed, and the best way to establish a colony is to plant out a few pot-grown plants and let them do just that, leaving the seedlings to grow where they come up naturally. Adult plants don't like being moved and even seedlings do not transplant very well. You can also grow it in a shrubbery if the soil is suitable and the shrubs are big enough to create light, dappled shade. When planting out pot-grown plants, it is

advisable to remove any flower buds that appear in the first year, otherwise plants may die after flowering. There is no need to bother doing this to self-sown seedlings as they have an altogether stronger constitution.

◼ *Monarda* **'Cambridge Scarlet'** (Bergamot)
75cm (2½ft) high × 75cm (2½ft) wide
Nothing else looks quite like bergamot and 'Cambridge Scarlet' is the loudest of the lot. The flowers grow in bright red, shaggy whorls at the top of stems that curve out from the middle of the plant like an exploding firework. There are pink, lavender, purple and white varieties, all smelling of Earl Grey tea, but frankly they are not a patch on this one. It is a real extrovert of a plant, flowering all summer long.
Cultivation What bergamot must have is plenty of water and a moist, fertile border with lots of organic matter. It just struggles anywhere else. A sunny place suits it best, but it does not mind a little light shade cast by neighbouring plants for part of the day. Mulch in spring and cut out the dead flower stems. When the clumps get too big, split them up in early spring and re-plant a few of the youngest pieces from around the edge.

◼ *Nepeta* × *faassenii* (Catmint)
60cm (2ft) high × 60cm (2ft) wide
This old cottage-garden favourite makes a loose mound of grey-green, wrinkled leaves which are dotted with short spikes of small, lavender flowers all summer. The foliage is aromatic, so it is a good plant for the edge of a path, where the unique fragrance is released each time you crush a stem underfoot. The popular variety, 'Six Hills Giant', grows slightly bigger. Cats differ in their opinions of catmint: some go mad rolling in it and others are not bothered.
Cultivation Plenty of sun and well-drained soil are the winning formula for catmint. Cut off the dead flower heads regularly to keep the plant flowering

continuously for the whole season, and delay cutting the plant down to tidy away the dead stems until the middle of spring, to protect the tender, young shoots.

■ *Paeonia* (Peony)
60cm (2ft) high × 60cm (2ft) wide
Paeonia officinalis varieties are the old cottage-garden type of peonies that flower first, in late spring. *Paeonia officinalis* '**China Rose**' has big, bowl-shaped, single, pink flowers, though a few double varieties are available. The biggest choice is in *Paeonia lactiflora* varieties that flower a few weeks later. As in the case of all peonies, the flowers are rather short-lived, but are glorious while at their best.

Cultivation Plant peonies shallowly, with their crowns no more than 2.5cm (1in) under ground, or they will not flower. Do not mulch closely around the plants or you risk burying them too deeply, which can cause the same problem. Peonies need a sunny spot with fertile garden soil. Stake the stems to keep the heavy flowers upright, which is especially important if the weather turns rainy at flowering time.

■ *Papaver orientale* (Oriental poppy)
75cm (1½ft) high × 75cm (1½ft) wide
You just can't ignore this immensely spectacular ladybird-red poppy; even the jagged foliage is eye-catching. If only it flowered all summer, instead of for a few weeks at the start of the season. Plant it next to something that flowers later in the summer to fill the gap it leaves in the border when it is over, and don't let the short flowering season put you off. Pink, and black and white varieties are also available – all staggeringly lovely.

Cultivation Any good border soil suits the Oriental poppy, though it must have a sunny spot. Push pea sticks in among the crowns when the shoots start appearing above ground in spring to support the big, heavy flowers, and mulch well.

■ *Penstemon*
75cm (2½ft) × 30cm (12in) wide
Despite a reputation for not being entirely hardy, penstemons have become favourite border plants. Nurseries list pages of different cultivars in a good range of colours: '**Apple Blossom**' is pale pink, '**Alice Hindley**' has blue-purple

ABOVE: Penstemons are becoming increasingly hardy and are reliable members of my beds and borders, flowering over a long season.
LEFT: The Oriental poppy 'Curlilocks' has petals that are frilly at the edges.

flowers, '**Andenken an Friedrich Hahn**' is ruby red and '**Stapleford Gem**' a lovely lilac and mauve. The plants are bushy, with upright flower stems laden with big, tubular bell flowers, and are incredibly free-flowering. They are in flower continuously from early summer right up to the first frosts.

Cultivation One of the best plants I've found for hot, dry summers, penstemon just keeps on flowering, even if it does not get watered. It actually prefers a warm, sunny site with well-drained soil. As each flower stem goes over, cut it off about 8cm (3in) below the lowest of the old flowers and just above a nice bunch of sideshoots – that way it will bloom again in no time. Take a few cuttings in late summer to keep in the greenhouse just in case of a bad winter. It is very easy to root.

Black-eyed Susan, or rudbeckia, is a summer stalwart of the border – cheerful and reliable.

■ Phlox
1m (3ft) high × 60cm (2ft) wide

In any border there comes a time when the early summer flowers are over and the late ones have not started. This is where phloxes are invaluable to fill the gap. They are also the most attractive plants with neat bunches of tall-stemmed flowers in a wide range of colours, from mid-summer until autumn. Add to that a heavenly scent and you have the perfect border flower. Some of the most popular cultivars include **Phlox paniculata** 'Balmoral', which is pink, and the bright carmine red 'Starfire'. There is also a very good variegated-leaved phlox with deep purple flowers called 'Harlequin' that is worth looking out for.

Cultivation Good border soil with plenty of organic matter is best; phlox also likes a deep mulch every spring to retain moisture. There is no need to support the stems, especially where it is growing in a busy border with other plants around to hold it up. Plants grow easily from cuttings taken while the

stems are still fairly short in early summer. There is no need to divide the clumps until they grow too big and start to die out in the middle, which does not happen for quite a few years.

■ Rudbeckia fulgida var. sullivantii 'Goldsturm' (Black-eyed Susan)
75cm (2¹/₂ft) high × 75cm (2¹/₂ft) wide

The common name for rudbeckia is black-eyed Susan, due to the big, black cone in the centre of the huge yellow daisy flowers. Old-fashioned rudbeckias grew tall and lanky and took a lot of keeping upright, but compact modern cultivars like 'Goldsturm' are quite different. They are naturally bushy and self-supporting, with a very long flowering season from the middle of summer well into autumn, and look great with autumn foliage colours.

Cultivation An easy-going plant that is happy in any well-prepared border given a reasonably sunny spot. It is one of those plants that flowers better if regularly deadheaded, but the flowers are also good for cutting, so the more you cut, the more you get. You will probably need to divide the clumps every three years or so, when they start spreading sideways.

■ Salvia argentea
45cm (1¹/₂ft) high × 45cm (1¹/₂ft) wide

Think of a grey, furry dinner plate. Better still, think of half a dozen grey, furry plates arranged in a circle so they overlap slightly. That is **Salvia argentea**. There is nothing else like it. It starts out as a foliage plant with incredible, silky-textured leaves you just have to stroke, then in summer it sends up a grey, furry spike which turns into a branching, sage-green candelabra studded with white flowers. Quite a curiosity, but a superb foil for hot, bright flowers like vivid half-hardy perennials. I especially like it with other flowering sage species, like the deep blue **S. cacaliifolia**.

Cultivation A very well-drained, even dry, sunny border is essential. Even so plants are quite short-lived, lasting only two or three years. Raise more from seed from time to time. When it flowers, the leaves become coarser and lose their silky texture; to keep it as a foliage plant, remove the flower spikes when they first appear.

■ Sisyrinchium striatum
45cm (1¹/₂ft) high × 20cm (8in) wide

The neat clumps of narrow, upright, evergreen leaves look like those of an iris, though when you see the flowers the difference is obvious. *Sisyrinchium striatum* has upright spikes of small, cream flowers that grow in a lazy spiral around the stem, as if they were stuck on by someone with a rather unsteady hand. The effect is very natural and charming. It flowers all summer.

Cultivation A plant that likes sunny, well-drained or dry soil, it will self-seed gently around so that seedlings pop up in the most unlikely places – by a pond, in cracks in paving, or in between stones in a wall or rockery. It grows in borders too. The one thing it does not like is disturbance.

■ *Verbascum olympicum* (Mullein)
2m (6ft) high × 1m (3ft) wide

This plant always reminds me of a triffid. In its first year it forms a huge, silver cabbage shape which, being evergreen, sits there throughout winter. Then the following year it sends up a tall, branching, silvery flower spike which is dotted with yellow flowers growing from cotton-wool-like tufts. The year after it may do the same thing again, but more so. The trouble is that like all the best triffids it wants to move on, and tends to die off after a year or two. However, it leaves behind a legacy of baby triffids to keep up the good work.

Cultivation A short-lived perennial that needs infertile, well-drained to sandy soil and lots of sun; it is also a very good architectural plant for a gravel garden. Self-sown seedlings are produced in enough quantity to replace the parent plants, and look good 'wandering' through the garden. They are effortless to grow if you leave them where they appear naturally, though they can be transplanted while small. The surplus, potted up, make good stock for summer charity gardening stalls.

■ *Viola* (Perennial pansy)
15cm (6in) high × 15cm (6in) wide

Although you can get so many good pansies from seed, they won't have the distinct characteristics of perennial, named varieties. There are dozens of old-fashioned varieties such as 'Jackanapes' which has yellow and maroon petals. There are also strange colours that don't really exist in modern bedding pansies, like the greeny-gold 'Irish Molly' and purple-black 'Molly Sanderson'. Specialist nurseries also stock varieties with scented flowers.

Cultivation Rich, fertile borders where they won't get swamped by bigger and bouncier plants are essential, and protection from slugs and snails even more so. Plants can be rather short-lived, so root cuttings from non-flowering shoots in the summer. Most do not come true from seed, and seedlings can look very different from the parent plant. They will hybridize with other pansies and violas nearby to produce lots of (what are often very attractive) mongrels.

The white-horned pansy, Viola cornuta *'Alba', has masses of spurred flowers on dense hummocks of foliage in summer.*

A–Z border perennials for autumn

Plenty of late summer perennials continue flowering long into autumn, but the start of this new season deserves a new set of plants to complement the spectacular colour changes taking place in the rest of the garden. For an interesting autumn display grow a mixture of old favourites as well as some novelties which, although they may take a bit of finding, are well worth the effort.

■ *Anemone × hybrida* **'Géante des Blanches'** (Japanese anemone)
1.25m (4ft) high × 60cm (2ft) wide
For me, an autumn border would not be complete without Japanese anemones. This giant, white variety has single flowers 5cm (2in) across, looking rather like thickset poppies, on stiff, upright stems with good foliage. I also like to see them in big drifts either on their own, or wandering through a shrub or woodland border.
Cultivation This plant is happy in sun or light shade and most soil types. Clumps tend to spread once they have been established a few years. If you do divide them, they take a year to grow and flower again, so, ideally, plant them where they can be left undisturbed.

■ *Aster novae-angliae* **'Andenken an Alma Pötschke'** (New England aster)
1.25m (4ft) high × 60cm (2ft) wide
The New England asters, as well as being attractive, seem to be immune to mildew, which often attacks other types of aster. 'Andenken an Alma Pötschke' is a particularly pretty, deep cerise pink.
Cultivation Good border soil and plenty of sun are all it asks. The taller varieties, like this one, stay tidiest if you slip one of those plant support 'cages' over them in late spring when the shoots are about 15cm (6in) high. The leaves soon hide the framework, but it is just enough to keep them tidy without looking too stiff and starchy. Dig up and

Far brighter than the old Michaelmas daisies, the New England aster 'Andenken Alma Pötschke' is a really bright, cerise pink.

divide large clumps in early spring every few years, and feed and mulch generously in spring.

■ *Chrysanthemum* **'Emperor of China'** (Hardy chrysanthemum)
60cm (2ft) high × 60cm (2ft) wide
The plant looks like a compact chrysanthemum, but its flowers look more like a giant double lawn daisy, in two shades of pink. It is a very old variety and is a real charmer. Like many chrysanthemums it is good for cutting, but for my money is best left in the garden where it will flower throughout most of autumn.
Cultivation The old-fashioned cottage type are still some of the most reliably hardy garden chrysanthemums you can grow. Just treat them as you would any

fairly rugged perennial. Plant in a well-prepared border, in plenty of sun. Unlike 'normal' cut-flower chrysanthemums, there is no need to lift it in autumn. This is a shorter variety, but its flowers may need support due to their weight, especially when wet.

■ *Cimicifuga simplex* **'White Pearl'**
1.5–2m (5–6ft) high × 60cm (2ft) wide
This is not a plant that is very well known in Britain; it is much more commonly grown in America. From a distance it looks almost like a tall, white delphinium, but with much smaller flowers massed together along long, wiry, upright flower spikes. It flowers only in autumn, long after the delphinium season is over.
Cultivation Don't let its size put you off: this is a wonderful plant for the back

Sneezeweed seems rather an unkind name for Helenium *'Moerheim Beauty', but the plants were once used to make snuff.*

of a border or, better still, grown among trees. It enjoys soil with plenty of organic matter that does not dry out rapidly and prefers light dappled shade.

■ *Cortaderia selloana* '**Pumila**'
(Dwarf pampas grass)
1.5m (5ft) high × 1.25m (4ft) wide
It is some dwarf that stands 1.5m (5ft) tall, but compared to what the full-sized pampas grass is capable of, it is properly named. Dwarf pampas grass looks just like its larger relation, but its smaller size makes it a good plant to use as a large ornamental grass in a perennial border. Being evergreen, it is also a very good plant for a large container if you do not want to keep replacing annuals twice a year. The seed-heads are at their best in autumn, and look good in winter outlined by frost.
Cultivation Grow it in any well-drained border with good, fertile soil. Cut away any brown leaves and the old seed-heads as close as possible to the base of the plant in spring.

■ *Helenium* '**Moerheim Beauty**'
(Helen's flower, Sneezeweed)
1m (3ft) high × 60cm (2ft) wide
The rich warm orange, daisy-like flowers, with their distinctive brown centre, have all the classic colours of autumn leaves, making this the perfect plant for anyone who would like the hues of Sheffield Park or Westonbirt Arboretum on their doorstep but is short of the necessary acres. It looks good with all the yellow, late summer and early autumn flowers like rudbeckia and helianthus, and keeps flowering into autumn.
Cultivation Grows happily in most reasonable borders and, although it will put up with a bit of light shade, the plant's rich colour scheme looks best in sun.

■ *Kniphofia* '**Samuel's Sensation**'
(Red hot poker)
1.5m (5ft) high × 1.25m (4ft) high
This is what you might call the late giant of the red hot poker world. Unlike most kniphofias, which are over by early autumn, 'Samuel's Sensation' does not start flowering until the end of summer and builds up to a climax of

tall, scarlet poker-flowers that last right through autumn.
Cultivation Like all red hot pokers, it enjoys a hot, sunny spot and good drainage and will not mind slightly poor soil. It is evergreen, but cut out any blackened, old foliage from the clumps in spring and remove the dead flower stems at the same time.

■ *Liriope muscari* (Lilyturf)
30cm (12in) high × 30cm (12in) wide
Autumn's best-kept secret. An evergreen plant with short, grassy leaves which, from early to late autumn, are packed tight with upright, lavender spikes of what look remarkably like out-of-season grape hyacinths. You hardly ever see plants in garden centres, but this is one to hunt out at specialist nurseries, plant fairs and flower shows.
Cultivation No trouble, lilyturf grows in poor, dry soils and shade as well as better border conditions. The only things lilyturf cannot abide are chalky soil and waterlogging. Tidy the plants up in spring by trimming off dead leaves and old flower stems close to the ground.

■ *Phygelius* × *rectus* **'Salmon Leap'**
1.25m (4ft) high × 1m (3ft) wide

This phygelius looks like a particularly good hardy fuchsia with an exceptionally heavy crop of long, tubular, crimson-red flowers that hang in great, chandelier-like bunches at the top of the stems in late summer and most of autumn. According to reference books, this plant is a shrub, but since in Britain it usually dies down to ground level in winter, that makes it herbaceous by my reckoning.

Cultivation Give it the same conditions a hardy fuchsia would enjoy – a warm, sheltered, sunny border with plenty of humus, so it does not dry out, but which is not waterlogged in winter. In cold areas protect the roots with ashes or a thick mulch to help it survive a hard winter. Otherwise plant it against a south-facing wall, where it will grow up to twice the usual height because the stems are not killed off completely in winter.

■ **Physalis alkekengi**
(Chinese lanterns)
75cm (2½ft) high × 75cm (2½ft) wide

You could grow this plant for years without noticing the flowers, which open in summer and are small, white and insignificant. What you will never miss

are the rows of 5-cm (2-in) long, bright orange lanterns dangling down the stems in autumn. They remain on the plant for some time, slowly changing to a faded rustic terracotta shade if you don't cut them: the lanterns dry out on the stems and make natural winter decorations.

Cultivation Physalis spreads by underground 'runners' so it is a good plant to let loose in a shrub border where it cannot swamp delicate neighbours. It grows in any border soil, in sun or light, dappled shade between other plants. Tidy it up in late winter or early spring by cutting all the old stems down to ground level.

■ **Schizostylis coccinea** (Kaffir lily)
45cm (1½ft) high × 30cm (12in) wide

This unusual autumn plant looks a bit like a miniature gladiolus in appearance, but the large, reddish pink freesia flowers are bright enough to belong to an exotic indoor bulb. The flowers just go on and on until late autumn. Pink varieties like 'Mrs Hegarty' are also exceptional.

Cultivation Although it looks like a plant for a hot, dry, sunny situation, it does not do well there. What it actually needs is moist soil with plenty of organic matter in a sunny spot. It will survive the

The flowers of the Kaffir lily are produced most abundantly in rich, moist soil.

occasional waterlogging, but prefers well-drained soil. Large clumps can be divided up in spring, but this is a plant that looks best when there is plenty of it.

■ **Sedum spectabile** (Ice plant)
45cm (1½ft) high × 60cm (2ft) wide

This is the butterflies' favourite, with domed heads of pink flowers that look like dyed cauliflower florets. Even before the flowers open the waxy, green buds, set against thick, fat, succulent leaves, have a rather architectural look that is very appealing. In Holland they use the green stems of immature buds as cut flowers. The variety **'Brilliant'** is vivid pink and **'Iceberg'** is white.

Cultivation Lots of sun and well-drained or dry soil are all ice plants need. Avoid rich, fertile soil, or the plants will grow too lush and out of character, like overfed cacti. Plants can stay put for years without needing to be divided. Cut the dead stems down close to the ground in spring after the new growth is safe from late frosts.

Physalis alkekengi – *the Chinese lantern flower.*

■ *Solidago* (Golden rod)
1m (3ft) high × 60cm (2ft) wide

An old border stalwart, with upright
stems topped by feathery, golden plumes
of flowers from late summer well into
autumn. Although the older varieties
were very tall and spread atrociously,
new kinds are more compact. Try
'Queenie' which is only about 30cm
(12in) high, **'Goldenmosa'**, for its
mimosa-like blooms and **'Crown of Rays'**
which has strange, horizontal flowers
much fancied by flower arrangers.

Cultivation Solidago grows anywhere,
but don't risk growing the bigger and
more aggressive varieties near your best
plants. Let it spread freely in a wild
garden or big shrubbery, but grow only
the smaller and prettier varieties in a
border. Cut back the old stems close to
ground level after it has finished
flowering and divide big clumps at the
same time or in spring every year or two,
whenever necessary.

■ *Tricyrtis formosana* (Toad lily)
60cm (2ft) high × 30cm (12in) wide

If ever a plant got lumbered with a rotten
common name, this is it. The flowers look
nothing like toads, more like exotic
miniature lilies with white flowers
smothered in mauve spots. Even the leaves
and stems are lily-like. An unusual plant that
flowers from early on in autumn to late in
the season.

Cultivation A rich, moist soil with
plenty of organic matter and light,
dappled shade are needed for tricyrtis to
succeed. It does best when it is
naturalized between shrubs and likes to
be mulched well each spring. Try not to
move it after it has been planted, as it
takes time to settle. Clumps spread
slowly, so it is likely to be a long time
before it needs dividing. Slugs and snails
are a huge problem – this plant is one of
their favourite snacks.

*The ice plants, or sedums, are a reliable
bet for autumn; this is 'Autumn Joy', whose
dusky pink flowers last for weeks.*

A–Z border perennials for winter

You might think winter would be a dead time for perennials, but far from it. All those choice, small, early or evergreen kinds come to the fore at this time of year. Positioned strategically, perennials with winter interest create pools of colour under shrubs and stand out from a distance, or provide intriguing detail in beds close to the house where you can enjoy them every time you pass. You can also group them together to make very striking winter arrangements.

■ ***Acorus gramineus* 'Ogon'**
(Japanese rush)
20cm (8in) high × 30cm (12in) wide
Fan-shaped sprays of brilliant gold-and-lime-green-striped foliage are the main characteristic of this dwarf sedge, which is at its very brightest in winter. The clumps make good-textured ground cover if you plant them 30cm (12in) apart, but they look best planted with clumps of purple-leaved bergenia. This is also a good plant for winter containers.
Cultivation Moist to wet soil is ideal for this plant; in a container grow it in John Innes potting compost but plant it out in the garden after one season.

The ferny foliage and anemone-like flowers of Adonis amurensis *'Fukujukai'.*

■ ***Adonis amurensis* 'Fukujukai'**
30cm (12in) high × 30cm (12in) wide
An unusual little perennial that makes an appearance extremely early and has lacy leaves and flowers like big, upmarket buttercups. You will probably need to find it at a specialist nursery, but like all good things it is worth the effort.
■ ***Cultivation*** Quite precise in its requirements, this choice plant likes light woodland conditions or a shady shrubbery where the soil contains plenty of well-rotted organic matter but drains quickly after rain. An acid soil is best.

■ ***Arum italicum* 'Marmoratum'**
(Lords and ladies)
30cm (12in) high × 30cm (12in) wide
This striking, winter foliage plant has large,

This wonderfully variegated arum, 'Marmoratum', has glossy leaves that really stand out in the winter garden.

arrowhead-shaped leaves in shiny green, decorated with cream dots and dashes that create a neatly marbled pattern. The effect looks slightly unreal, almost as if it were artificial. The leaves appear only in late autumn and form a dense, ground-covering carpet all winter and through early spring, until they die down, leaving the tubers to rest during summer.
Cultivation This arum is easy to grow and enjoys a wide range of conditions in sun or shade including dry or damp soil, even clay. Buy plants in pots when they start to come into leaf in autumn, so you know you are not just buying a pot of empty soil. Plants can take a while to get going when they are first planted, but can eventually spread and self-seed, and even become slightly invasive. The tubers dig themselves in deep and are not easy to get out if you want to move them.

Bergenia 'Abendglut'
(Elephant's ears)
30cm (12in) high × 30cm (12in) wide
Bergenias are known for having flowers
in early spring, but if you want one for
really good winter effect choose
'Abendglut' which has bright reddish-
purple foliage in mid-winter and also
looks good in spring when its red flowers
come out. Another attractive form is
'Bressingham Ruby' with deep mauve-
pink flowers.
Cultivation The plants grow in any
reasonably good border soil in sun or
shade, but for the best winter colour
grow them where they get plenty of
sunlight and not too rich a soil.

Carex testacea (Sedge)
45cm (1½ft) high × 45cm (1½ft) wide
A semi-evergreen sedge, with very fine,
grassy leaves that form a mound rather like
a tiny haystack with metallic bronze,
mahogany, gold and coppery highlights. It is
the perfect complement for purple
bergenias or gold-leaved evergreen shrubs,
and looks at home by a wintery pond.
Cultivation It likes moist soil with
plenty of organic matter, but can run
into problems in ground that is too
wet. It grows slowly, and looks best
given a haircut in spring to remove all
the old foliage close to ground level
and make way for the freshly coloured,
new growth.

Helleborus niger (Christmas rose)
45cm (1½ft) high × 30cm (12in) wide
If I had £1 for every time someone had
asked me how you persuade Christmas
roses to actually flower at Christmas, I'd
have enough money to stock a complete
border with **'Potter's Wheel'**, which is
the form with the biggest and best
flowers. Whether they flower on
Christmas day or a little bit later, the
huge, white flowers are a treat, and the
bold, evergreen foliage keeps in good
shape for the rest of the year.
Cultivation The Christmas rose wants
a sheltered spot in light shade with

humus-rich soil. Protection from slugs
and snails is essential; plants will not
flower if the buds are nibbled off. As for
flowering on schedule, you could buy
plants that are in bud just before
Christmas, then grow them in pots in
your greenhouse so that they open early.

Iris foetidissima (Stinking gladwyn)
45cm (1½ft) high × 45cm (1½ft) wide
Another good plant handicapped by a
revolting common name. The stinking
gladwyn stinks only if it is badly handled
and the leaves are crushed. Since it is
evergreen, this is not something you
want to do anyway as it spoils the look
of the plant. It flowers in early summer,
but the display is really nothing special,
although *I. foetidissima* var. *citrina* has
prettier flowers that are pale yellow
marked with darker veins. The big selling
point is the seed pods which split open
in late autumn, showing off rows of
bright orange seeds that look like peas
on the half-pod.

ABOVE: Helleborus niger *has one or two forms
that really will bloom at Christmas.* BELOW:
Bold leaves and bright flowers of bergenias.

Cultivation These plants will grow in poor, dry soil and deep shade without a problem. Once they have shed a few seeds, you will find self-sown seedlings popping up all over the place, in gravel paths, in bright sun and even under big trees where nothing else grows. Make the most of them as plants for problem spots.

◾ *Iris unguicularis* (Algerian iris)
30cm (12in) high × 20cm (8in) wide
It is difficult to believe that a flower this big and this fragile could possibly survive out in the open in the middle of winter, yet it does. The wide-open, purple flowers, that are 5cm (2in) across, are typical iris-shaped and sit on short stems which appear from among sparse sprays of wiry, evergreen foliage in late winter.
Cultivation This iris needs to be grown in exactly the right place. Poor, dry soil at the foot of a south-facing wall is perfect. The plants like to be left undisturbed and do not appreciate having something else planted around

The Algerian iris prefers poor, dry earth by the house wall and thrives on neglect after planting.

them in summer. They also need a good summer baking, so do not feel tempted to water them. If they are to have neighbours, choose nerines or *Amaryllis belladonna*, both of which flower in autumn and like the same inhospitable set of conditions.

◾ *Ophiopogon planiscapus* 'Nigrescens'
15cm (6in) high × 30cm (12in) wide
It is not every day you come across a black plant, but this is one of the very few. The plant spreads very slowly to make clumps of blunt-ended, grassy leaves that look their most striking in winter when nothing much else is around them. Black may sound dull, but the leaves are really a very dark purple and look stunning grown with bright gold foliage plants or shocking-pink flowers.
Cultivation The plants need good drainage to grow happily and a sunny position is necessary for the leaves to develop their maximum colour.

For shady spots, lungworts are without equal. This is Pulmonaria rubra *– like all the others it is a generous bloomer.*

◾ *Primula rosea*
15cm (6in) high × 15cm (6in) wide
This is one of the very earliest primulas to flower, and you might think that a plant so small and apparently frail would be suitable only for a rockery. Actually it needs moist soil and looks good in a damp border grown in clumps between shrubs, or next to a pond. The bright pink flowers appear just ahead of the leaves.
Cultivation As long as the soil holds plenty of moisture, this primula will grow in good garden soil, improved clay or a woodland-style mixture with lots of leaf mould. It likes very light shade.

◾ *Primula vulgaris* subsp. *sibthorpii* (Primrose)
15cm (6in) high × 20cm (8in) wide
Common primroses are among the first wild flowers to come out in spring, but this pink version is one of the first to

open in the garden, well ahead of most cultivated hybrid strains. The flowers are slightly larger than those of the common yellow primrose and are an unusual shade of light mauvy pink, each with a distinctive yellow eye.

Cultivation If you can provide similar conditions to those you find on the wild woodland floor, you will have no trouble keeping this plant happy – moist, leafy soil, humus and dappled shade. It also takes to short grass in a shady spot.

■ *Pulmonaria rubra* (Lungwort)
20cm (8in) high × 30cm (12in) wide
Not all lungworts have the characteristic spotty foliage you always expect. This evergreen, the earliest one to flower, has completely plain, light green leaves that are accompanied by clusters of small bell flowers of a most unusual, pale terracotta colour. Although small, a few clumps of these among early-flowering bulbs really bring the garden to life for spring. They are a favourite with bees too.

Cultivation Moist border soil in dappled shade suits it best, though it is also happy in a position where it gets sun for part of the day, avoiding the midday period. Don't let it get swamped by more boisterous plants later in the season.

■ *Ranunculus ficaria* 'Brazen Hussy' (Lesser celandine)
15cm (6in) high × 15cm (6in) wide
I regularly hear from people who want to rid their gardens of celandines, but this is one enthusiasts queue up to buy. 'Brazen Hussy' has dark purple-black leaves which form a carpet under the mass of large, single, yellow buttercup flowers. Plants soon form a neat mound that looks very effective in early spring. Unlike wild celandines, which certainly can become a problem, this one hardly spreads at all, even in ideal conditions.

Cultivation This plant needs moist soil with plenty of humus and light shade. It does very well under trees and shrubs and looks wonderful grown with early spring bulbs. The plants die down in early summer, making it difficult to know quite where they are. To avoid them when hoeing mark the spot carefully. Watch out for the occasional self-sown seedlings, which mostly come true to type, and hoe around them or pot them up.

■ *Salvia officinalis* 'Icterina' (Gold variegated sage)
45cm (1½ft) high × 60cm (2ft) wide
Several ornamental sages are commonly grown in gardens, but most appear positively depressing in winter, when the foliage fades, turns brown or just sits there looking withered and wrinkled. This one, however, keeps its fresh-looking lime-and-chartreuse-variegated foliage all year round, particularly when it is grown in a sheltered spot. It makes an especially good background for early bulbs with yellow flowers, such as winter aconites.

Cultivation Badly drained soil will make the roots rot, so choose a sandy or gravelly spot where the plant receives lots of winter sun. Prune the plant lightly in spring to keep it a good shape; if this is not done annually, plants tend to become woody and can splay open. If you need to replace the old plants, take cuttings in summer when they will root easily.

ABOVE: *It may have a mouthful of a name, but* Primula vulgaris *subsp.* sibthorpii *is well worth growing for its early primrose flowers.* BELOW: *The lesser celandine,* Ranunculus ficaria, *in its bronze-leaved form 'Brazen Hussy'.*

Seasonal colour

Not all plants live in the garden permanently; some are only temporary visitors to provide a seasonal splash of colour. Though they can all loosely be called bedding plants, what this means to most people is the half-hardy annuals, which include all the popular petunias, lobelia and French marigolds.

Half-hardy annuals

These are the sort of flowers you buy in trays at the garden centre in late spring and plant out after the last frost. They flower themselves silly all summer until they are killed by the first autumn frost, when they can be pulled out and replaced with spring flowering bedding or bulbs.

Nowadays, the most popular way to use bedding plants is in containers on the patio, in hanging baskets, tubs and troughs. The colour schemes and containers may change from year to year, but the general idea stays much the same.

Apart from containers, bedding has other uses too. Few people these days plant up entire beds with formal bedding in the tradition of parks department schemes, with rows of salvias and

ageratum and a neat edging of lobelia along the front. Yet we still turn to bedding plants the moment there is a bare patch in a mixed border that needs filling in a hurry, or if we want to spruce the garden up quickly for a special occasion. They are also a good way to fill a new bed or even a whole, new, small garden in a hurry while you decide what you want in the long term. As bedding plants are all about instant colour, you can buy them in flower and plant them to make a splash of colour where, a few hours before, there was nothing. You can plant bedding in different combinations to create a natural, random cottage-garden effect or a sophisticated colour scheme.

Correct care is vital to keep bedding blooming. First make sure it is properly hardened off before you plant it out. (Bedding plants can take a terrible check if planted out into cold conditions straight after being grown in a warm greenhouse.) So, unless you buy plants that were standing outside at the nursery, put them outdoors on fine days and bring them under cover at night for a week or ten days before planting them out.

Choose a spell of fair weather for planting your bedding and prepare the ground well beforehand (see pages 34–7). Get rid of the weeds and fork in a little well-rotted organic matter and a sprinkling of general fertilizer like blood, fish and bone. Water the plants in well and keep them watered whenever there is a dry spell, since they have very shallow roots and are not in the ground long enough to become established. Keep them well fed, especially in containers where weekly feeding is the secret of success. Plants with

ABOVE: The orange daisies of Rudbeckia *'Marmalade'.*
LEFT: Traditional summer bedding edged with blue and white lobelia. RIGHT: A purple-leaved cordyline set among busy lizzies.

large flowers, like petunias and French marigolds, should be deadheaded regularly to stop them setting seed and encourage them to flower for longer.

Most people buy half-hardy bedding plants in early summer all ready to plant. But you can raise your own from seed if you have the right facilities. They need warmth, so either sow them in a propagator in a heated greenhouse or on a warm, bright windowsill indoors in spring. You'll need enough room to prick them out into seed trays to grow, when they still need to be kept heated until they are big enough to plant out. Alternatively, you can buy 'plug plants', which are simply small plants in tiny pots like the cells of a honeycomb, all ready for potting up, and save yourself the early work.

Hardy annuals

Hardy annuals are different as they are not killed by cold. These are old-fashioned, cottage-garden flowers like clarkia, sweet pea, larkspur, cornflower, calendula, nasturtium and godetia and they are the easiest to raise as they do not need any heat and you can sow them straight out into the garden in spring. Or, if your garden soil is full of weed seeds and the seedlings risk being swamped, sow a row in the vegetable garden and transplant seedlings when they are big enough. They start flowering sooner than half-hardies, but stop before the end of summer, which can leave an awkward gap in your borders unless you combine them with something else – such as summer-flowering biennals, for instance.

A mixture of hardy annuals: love-in-a-mist or nigella (blue) and catchfly or silene (pink).

In mild areas people often sow hardy annuals in autumn so the plants are bigger and start flowering earlier the following spring. Sweet peas are in fact traditionally sown in a cold frame (see page 250) in autumn to get plants off to an earlier start the following year. But you could also risk other kinds this way – I often sow a few trays in a cold greenhouse. Compact varieties of calendulas and nasturtium actually make good spring-flowering pot plants for a cold greenhouse.

Tender perennials

In the last few years, tender perennials have shot to the top of the popularity stakes. These are the same plants we used to call half-hardy perennials, but the

---

HOW TO SOW GERANIUM SEEDS

1 The sooner the seeds of geraniums (pelargoniums) are sown, the sooner they will flower. Space the seeds out evenly on the surface of a pot of soil-less seed-sowing compost.

2 Lightly cover the seeds with compost. If you haven't got a 3mm (⅛in) sieve, put some compost in a plastic flowerpot and shake the compost through the holes in the base.

3 Label each pot, and stand it in a saucer of water for an hour to let it soak up moisture. Put it in a warm place – a propagator on a windowsill is ideal. Prick out the seedlings later.

marketing men have no doubt decided that tender perennials sounds better. It seems to have worked, because we are buying lots more of them – especially when they are called by their ultimate 'marketing name': patio plants. Tender perennials include old favourites such as pelargoniums and fuchsias, which are more popular than ever. But they have now been joined by a huge range of fiendishly fashionable plants like argyranthemums, gazanias and osteospermums, the kingfisher daisy (*Felicia amelloides*) and shrubby salvia species. Some summer-flowering tuberous plants like canna and dahlia also qualify as tender perennials, and you'll find compact versions of these included under the term patio plants.

One common trait they all share is that they do not stand frost. Because of this, tender perennials are temporary summer visitors to gardens. They are planted out in early summer, after the last frost, and have to be taken in and given winter protection if you want to keep the same plants for another year.

In practice, tender perennials are really just a type of bedding plant, albeit with the option of keeping the same plants instead of having to buy new ones each year. They like the same growing conditions as bedding plants: a sunny, sheltered position with well-cultivated soil that contains a reasonable amount of organic matter and a sprinkling of fertilizer raked in just before planting. Like bedding plants, they need regular watering while they get going and in dry spells later in summer. Regular liquid feeding and deadheading are also important to keep the plants flowering throughout the season.

As tender perennials are mostly flamboyant plants with bright colours, large flowers or striking foliage, they are best used in conspicuous displays round the garden. They are the perfect choice for containers on the patio and by front and back doors, but are also excellent for making loud, subtropical-style displays in a sunny bed. Plants like canna combine well with shrubby salvias such as *Salvia cacaliifolia* (tall, blue spikes) or *Salvia fulgens* (which has bushy stems of red, fluffy, helmet-shaped flowers) plus the bronze-red foliage of castor oil plant (*Ricinus communis* 'Carmencita'). Add some compact patio dahlias and you could almost be in the south of France.

You can also use tender perennials exactly as you would do bedding plants: to fill odd gaps in borders during the summer. Here's a good tip that a head gardener once gave me: after peonies or Oriental poppies have finished flowering and you have cut the foliage down, stand a pot of large and exotic tender perennials in their place to fill the gaping hole they leave behind. Their bold shapes and strong colours have much the same effect on the border as the glamorous, early summer flowers that went before them, but last much longer.

Getting hold of tender perennials is easy. Now that they are fashionable, you can find a good selection at most garden centres. But it is more fun to visit specialist patio plant nurseries, plant fairs and nursery stands at flower shows, where you will find an even bigger selection – including the very newest varieties – right through summer. If you plan ahead, you can save money by buying small plants cheaply in spring. Look in the patio plant areas of garden centres for tender perennials sold as 'plug plants' (tiny plants in small pots or multiple 'cell' packs like egg boxes). These need potting up straight away. Some nurseries also sell rooted cuttings of plants like fuchsias very cheaply for you to continue growing at home.

If you are going to buy early, while there is still a risk of frost in the garden, you will need somewhere warm to keep the plants in the meantime. A heated greenhouse or conservatory is ideal, but otherwise

Spring colour provided by mixed wallflowers interplanted with the tulip 'Apeldoorn's Elite'.

Many foxgloves are biennial and die after flowering, but Digitalis purpurea *'Sutton's Apricot' is perennial and comes up every year.*

you can usually fit quite a few plants on to windowsills indoors. Don't buy them if you don't have suitable 'storage' facilities. Wait until after the last frost and buy bigger plants that are coming into flower and can go straight outside.

Like bedding plants, tender perennials need careful hardening off first. If you buy plants that were standing out in the open at the garden centre, the odds are this will already have been done for you. But if they were in a greenhouse, you'll need to spend a few days standing them outside during the day and bringing them under cover at night before planting them out.

As the summer progresses, you need to think what you are going to do with the plants in winter. If they are left out, they will be killed by frost for certain. Stemmy perennials like pelargoniums, fuchsias and argyranthemums can be stored 'whole' if you like. Dig them up just before the first frost, cut the stems off to 10–15cm (4–6in) above the base of the plant, pot them and keep them on a bench in a frost-free greenhouse for the winter. They do take up a lot of room this way and don't

do as well as new young plants second time round. The way I prefer to overwinter tender perennials is to take cuttings in late summer. Most of them root very easily. Just take cuttings about 10cm (4in) long from the tips of the shoots, non-flowering if possible, otherwise remove all the flowers and buds. I root mine into small individual pots filled with seed compost, but you could put up to thirty cuttings into a standard seed tray. When they have rooted, which takes only a few weeks, nip the tips out of the cuttings to make them start branching, feed and water them lightly, but do not pot them up yet. Keep them on the dry side through the winter, removing any dead leaves or flower buds if they appear. They will not take up much room, either in the greenhouse or on a sunny windowsill indoors. Then in spring, they will be ready to pot up, space out, and, after the last frost, plant out.

Biennials

It is not only annuals that are used for temporary colour around the garden. Biennials, which are old-fashioned flowers that are raised from seed one year to flower the next, also provide a seasonal display. Years ago, gardens relied on biennials like sweet Williams and Canterbury bells for colour in the 'gap' between the last of the spring bulbs and the first of the summer annuals. Wallflowers and polyanthus – both also biennals – made up spring bedding schemes on their own or were planted with spring bulbs. It was almost a gardening tradition to sow your biennials in the vegetable garden in summer, thin them, then plant them out as soon as your summer annuals were coming to an end. You looked after them all winter, protecting them from snails and bad weather, and hoped for a decent show in spring. If the weather was dreadful, a lot of them probably died. Nowadays few people go to all the bother. You might buy the odd bundle of wallflowers to put in during the autumn, but that is about it. And in any case, the word 'biennals' sounds dreadfully old-fashioned.

Fortunately plant producers have caught up with the desire for instant gardening. Those same spring-flowering biennials are available in garden centres in spring, only we call them spring bedding instead. You buy them in exactly the same way as summer bedding, just as they are coming into flower, in pots or trays, but earlier. So now, instead of having to nurse polyanthus and double primroses and even spring bulbs through the winter and protect them

Some fuchsias are hardy, but the larger-flowered kinds are generally tender: this is one of them – 'Love's Reward'.

from slugs, you can simply plonk them in wherever you want a fast flash of colour. They are especially good in containers or round the edge of a border. Plants like stocks and forget-me-nots, which flower slightly later and are not so rugged, have traditionally been planted in spring anyway.

The only time spring bedding does not work well is in particularly bad weather. If the ground is frozen hard and the garden is lashed by storms and gales, the plants take umbrage at being moved from a cosy greenhouse or cold frame into arctic conditions, and vote with their feet. In a year like that, it is probably worth giving spring bedding a miss altogether. If you were to wait for the weather to improve, in a late spring, you would hardly have time to plant instant spring bedding before it was time to take it out in favour of summer bedding.

The only spring bedding worth planting in autumn these days are wallflowers, which you almost never see grown in pots and sold in flower in spring. If you want winter colour, you can plant winter-flowering pansies and coloured ornamental cabbages and kales as winter bedding. Teamed with a few ivies or small euonymus or dwarf evergreens for foliage, you can create superb, colourful, winter container gardens.

Summer flowering biennials

Not all biennials flower in spring. There are summer flowering kinds, too. It is just that you do not hear so much about them.

The term 'summer biennials' covers quite a few different plants. First there are the old-fashioned cottage-garden kinds that flower in early summer, like Canterbury bells, sweet Williams and foxgloves. You can buy plants in a garden centre or raise your own from seed and plant them in late summer or early autumn. But there are also less well-known summer-flowering biennials you would probably have trouble finding unless you grew your own from seed; plant them in late summer or early autumn. They include variegated honesty (*Lunaria*), chimney bellflower (*Campanula pyramidalis*), Miss Willmott's ghost (*Eryngium giganteum*), evening primrose (*Oenothera biennis*) and *Verbascum bombyciferum* and are becoming quite sought after by fashion-conscious gardeners. Left to their own devices these flowers will gently self-seed, automatically providing their own replacements without any help. All you need do is to plant a few out in the first place and leave them to it, simply pulling out any seedlings that come up where you don't want them.

At Tresco, on the Scillies, Echium pininana *is hardy, but on the mainland it is difficult to get through all but the mildest of winters. It survived for me in the winter of 1997–8 and flowered spectacularly.*

dahlias *are back in vogue. Grow them country-house-style in formal double borders, either side of a path, or in rows to screen your vegetable patch for a cottage-garden effect. The latest way is to grow modern, compact forms in pots on the patio. Old, named varieties of dahlia are also proving very collectable and are ideal for tender perennial borders.*

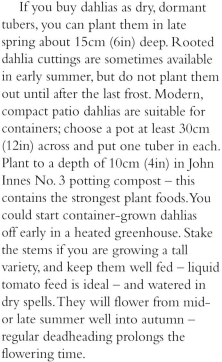

The key to producing good dahlias is rich soil. They are known in the trade as 'heavy feeders'. Choose a sunny spot and prepare the soil well in autumn or early spring. Dig in lots of organic matter deeply and sprinkle a double dose of general fertilizer, like blood, fish and bone, a few days before planting.

If you buy dahlias as dry, dormant tubers, you can plant them in late spring about 15cm (6in) deep. Rooted dahlia cuttings are sometimes available in early summer, but do not plant them out until after the last frost. Modern, compact patio dahlias are suitable for containers; choose a pot at least 30cm (12in) across and put one tuber in each. Plant to a depth of 10cm (4in) in John Innes No. 3 potting compost – this contains the strongest plant foods. You could start container-grown dahlias off early in a heated greenhouse. Stake the stems if you are growing a tall variety, and keep them well fed – liquid tomato feed is ideal – and watered in dry spells. They will flower from mid- or late summer well into autumn – regular deadheading prolongs the flowering time.

After the first frost blackens the leaves, get the tubers ready to store over winter to use again next year. Dig them up, cut the stems off 5cm (2in) above their base and wash the soil off the roots. Allow the tubers to dry off, then store them in a frost-free shed or greenhouse for the winter, protected from mice and damp.

'Alva's Supreme'
1.25m (4ft) high
This is the sort of dahlia technically known as a giant decorative: at 20cm (8in) across, the flowers are big enough to be bordering on the vulgar (they look like shaggy blonde wigs on stalks); however, its classic cream colouring is a redeeming feature.

'Bishop of Llandaff'
1m (3ft) high
An old favourite with 5-cm (2-in) wide single, red, anemone-like flowers and beetroot foliage on neat, compact plants. The foliage alone warrants its inclusion in a perennial border. It looks especially good planted with brightly coloured, tender perennials.

OPPOSITE, TOP TO BOTTOM: 'Bishop of Llandaff', 'Lavender Athalie', 'Arabian Night' BELOW: 'David Howard' (orange) and 'Harvest Amanda'

Dahlia merckii
1m (3ft) high

A dahlia species with large, single, lilac or white flowers that seem to hover over the plants on their long, wiry stems. It is a good plant for a cottage-style border or planted with unusual tender perennials, growing 60cm (2ft) wide. This species is almost hardy, so in mild regions leave the tubers in well-drained soil with bark chippings for winter protection.

'Doris Day'
1.25m (4ft) high

Called a cactus dahlia, this one is a ball of long-quilled, crimson-red spikes. The long stems make this a good dahlia for cutting.

'Ellen Houston'
45cm (18in) high

A dwarf dahlia with beetroot-red foliage that makes a striking contrast to the large, double, orange flowers which appear from mid-summer onwards. A scarce classic for a collector.

'Giraffe'
75cm (30in) high

'Giraffe' has small, nice-but-weird, artificial-looking, red and yellow flowers on long stems. It also makes an eye-catching flower arrangement. It can be found at specialist dahlia nurseries.

'Jescot Julie'
1m (3ft) high

If you did not know it was a dahlia, you would take this for a particularly exotic, tender perennial. The flowers are something like daisies but lacking an obvious centre, with long petals which are orange-yellow on the front and red on the back. They curve slightly inwards so you can see both sides at once, which gives the flowers an unusual two-tone look that is incredibly striking.

'Harvest Tiny Tot'
45cm (18in) high

A compact patio dahlia, growing about 45cm (18in) across. Plants have lots of double, orange-red flowers freely produced over four months. They can be grown in pots or borders, where they are best teamed with bedding plants or tender perennials.

'Willow Surprise'
1m (3ft) high

Really tiny, tight pompons, like Victorian sofa buttons, are the hallmark of the miniature pompon dahlias. There is nothing blowsy about them at all. This variety has red flowers, which are weather-resistant in the garden and are superb for cutting.

'Zorro'
Up to 1.25m (4ft) high

A real monster dahlia with big 20-cm (8-in) wide, deep red flowers that are almost black in the centre. Wide petals give the blooms a very chunky, solid look. The big flowers become very heavy as they fill up with water after rain, so the stems need to be supported.

A-Z plants for bedding

Bedding plants come in various types. The spring-flowering sort need to be sown the previous year, and the summer sort in early spring. Of these, hardy annuals are the ones that stand a spot of cold, so they can be sown straight into the garden. Half-hardies are the traditional summer bedding plants, which cannot be planted until after the frosts have finished but they will keep flowering longer than most hardy annuals. Biennals are raised from seed one year to flower in the next, while tender perennials, such as pelargoniums and fuchsias, are the sort you can keep under cover over winter for next year.

■ **Agrostemma githago 'Milas'** (Corn cockle)
1m (3ft) high × 30cm (12in) wide
A pale, silvery lilac-pink version of the wild corn cockle, 'Milas' is a summer-flowering hardy annual with large, five-petalled flowers that open out flat. It withstands wind and rain and, with its wildish looks, is seen at its best in a cottage garden border or wild garden.
Cultivation Sow seeds where you want them to flower in spring, or grow in trays to transplant later. Plants self-seed gently if you leave a few seed-heads to mature in late summer; just pull up any plants that grow where you do not want them. Agrostemma needs a sunny situation.

■ **Antirrhinum** (Snapdragon)
Up to 45cm (1½ft) high × 30cm (12in) wide depending on variety
The old-fashioned snapdragon has had a revamp lately and now you can obtain azalea-flowered varieties, which have frilly, semi-double flowers, tall varieties with strong, upright stems for cut flowers, and very compact dwarf varieties for edging beds or containers. There is also an incredible colour range including almost-black varieties and some with wildly spotted or streaked flowers. Irresistible!
Cultivation Antirrhinums are half-hardy annuals; sow them in early spring in a heated propagator and prick out seedlings spaced 2.5cm (1in) apart in seed trays. The old-fashioned kinds can be pricked out as small clumps of seedlings, which gives bushier plants for less effort. Plant out after the last frost. Grow in a reasonably sunny spot in good garden soil.

■ **Bellis perennis** (Double daisy)
15cm (6in) high × 15cm (6in) wide
Not the dreaded lawn daisy of the same name, but cultivated versions with big, shaggy or double pompon flowers in pink or red, sold in spring for spring bedding. They flower from early spring to early summer and, though treated as spring bedding, are actually short-lived perennials.
Cultivation To raise your own plants, sow seeds in late spring to flower the following year, or divide up clumps of existing plants in spring – if the new clumps are a good size, they should flower the same year. The plants thrive in most soils including quite heavy clay, in sun or light shade. Most people buy plants from nurseries for an instant display in containers or to fill gaps in the spring border, then throw them away to make room for summer bedding.

■ **Calendula officinalis** (Pot marigold)
30cm (12in) high × 30cm (12in) wide
This hardy annual marigold is not to be confused with the frost-tender French and African marigolds. Pot marigolds have large, double daisy flowers in all shades of yellow, orange and rust on robust, bushy plants. This is the marigold to plant in your potager with the leeks and brassicas for a decorative effect, or to let loose in your cottage garden border where it will self-seed gently around. It is also brilliant sown in the greenhouse in late summer or early autumn, or used as an early-flowering pot plant – compact varieties are best.
Cultivation Sow in early spring where plants are to flower, or in a spare row in the vegetable garden to transplant later. Alternatively sow a tiny pinch of seed into small pots. No heat is needed for germination.

■ **Cleome spinosa** (Spider flower)
1.25m (4ft) high × 38cm (15in) wide
Arachnophobes will be relieved to know that spider flowers look nothing like spiders – it's the long stamens growing out like whiskers between the pink

Old favourites such as antirrhinums (snapdragons) are still worth growing and flower over a long period in summer.

The spider flower, Cleome spinosa, *has whiskery flowers of white, pale or dark pink carried on tall, bushy plants.*

flowers that suggested the common name, and even then they look more like daddy-long-legs to me. These strange flowers make a leggy halo round the top 15–20cm (6–8in) of the tall, upright stems. It is a striking plant which is not very well known, so if you grow it, expect to be asked what it is.

Cultivation A half-hardy annual, which does not flower until mid-summer, so group it with other flowers that start sooner. It looks good grown in clumps among shrubs, or with other tall bedding like cosmos; it's no good teaming it with compact species. It needs a sunny spot with good, well-drained soil.

▓ *Dimorphotheca* (African daisy)
23cm (9in) high × 30cm (12in) wide

A sort of annual osteospermum, African daisy has the same sort of big, wide-open daisy flowers and bright colours that range from tawny orange or salmon shades to pale gold and glistening white. The plants are bushy and compact.

Cultivation Raise as for half-hardy annuals and plant them out after the last frost in a very warm, sunny spot – the flowers close in shade or when the sun

goes in. African daisies are good for containers and also for places that are too hot and bright for most normal bedding to thrive.

▓ *Echium pininana* (Tree echium)
4m (12ft) high × 1m (3ft) wide

A real giant, this is a stunning half-hardy biennial that self-seeds in a very mild location. In Britain this includes areas such as the Scilly Isles and Cornwall; it is a native of the Canary Islands. From a giant rosette of slightly bristly, silvery leaves an immense, rocket-shaped flower spire shoots up, packed with short, strappy leaves and small, blue, bell-shaped flowers.

Cultivation The fact that this plant does not survive winter outside in most of Britain presents a slight problem, but it can be overcome. Sow in late spring to flower the following year. Grow the plants singly in large pots and them keep under cover for the first winter, while they are still only large rosettes of leaves; the flower spikes will appear the following summer. Plant out in a warm, sunny spot after the last frost, and stand well back.

▓ *Limnanthes douglasii*
(Poached egg flower)
15cm (6in) high × 8cm (3in) wide

A low-growing plant with attractive, light green, ferny foliage that is topped with a

mass of white-edged, yellow flowers. Even with a huge stretch of the imagination, I feel they look only the tiniest bit like poached eggs – and frilly ones at that. What is special about this flower is that it attracts bees and hoverflies by the thousand, very much the organic gardeners' friend. A hardy annual, the plant flowers continuously from early to late summer.

Cultivation Sow where it is to flower, or grow it in trays to transplant later. Once you have a few plants growing happily, they will self-seed gently, so you should always be able to find a few seedlings coming up in roughly the same spot. Just pull out the ones you don't want.

▓ *Myosotis* (Forget-me-not)
Up to 20cm (8in) high × 15cm (6in)
wide depending on variety

The ultimate go-anywhere spring bedding, forget-me-nots look brilliant teamed with tulips, late daffodils, double daisies or ranunculus, in borders and containers. The new strains, like 'Blue Ball', are very neat and compact and vivid blue: ideal for edging. Look out for pink-flowered strains like 'Victoria Rose' and 'Pompadour' for a change.

Cultivation Sow seeds in summer, and treat them as biennials. Plant them out in spring.

Forget-me-nots seed themselves freely; here they are growing round an ornamental snail shell in my garden.

■ *Nicotiana × sanderae* **Domino Series** (Tobacco plant)

30cm (12in) high × 15cm (6in) wide

A short, compact, bushy tobacco plant, this strain is available as a mixture of colours, or as a particularly good, pale salmon-pink, Domino Series **'Salmon Pink'**. Besides being compact, this and other newer strains of nicotiana have flowers that stay open during the day – the old-fashioned ones folded up until evening. However, the new ones don't have so much perfume.

Cultivation Sow in warmth in spring, prick out into trays and plant out after the last frost. Nicotiana likes a reasonable soil with plenty of moisture and, unlike a lot of bedding plants, will thrive in light shade. In a hot summer, the plants look a lot happier grown this way.

■ *Papaver nudicaule* **Oregon Rainbow Group** (Iceland poppy)

38cm (15in) high × 15cm (6in) wide

As a race, Iceland poppies are about the closest you'll come to perpetual motion in the garden. Once you have grown some, they cannot help self-seeding, and you'll have more flowering in the same spot for years to come. This is fine by me, as they are quite lovely. The large,

attractive poppy flowers look fragile with crumpled petals in a wide range of colours, supported by wiry stems with delicate, ferny foliage.

Cultivation Like any poppies they do not take kindly to being transplanted,

so sow where you want them to flower if you have reliably weed-free soil, or else sow a pinch of seed into small pots, thin to leave only one or two seedlings and plant when the pot is full of roots without breaking up the rootball. Plants will flower the same summer, and the seedlings that come up from self-sown seed will flower the next year. Iceland poppies like plenty of sun and a soil that is well-drained and not too rich.

■ *Rudbeckia hirta* **'Marmalade'** (Cone flower)

60cm (2ft) high × 20cm (8in) wide

An annual version of a perennial favourite, **'Marmalade'** has large, tawny-orange daisy flowers each with a black cone in the middle. This variety is a particular favourite with flower arrangers because it has tall, straight stems and

produces an incredible number of flowers. Cutting them acts like major deadheading and, as with sweet peas, the more you cut, the more you get.

Cultivation Annual rudbeckias are half-hardy annuals, so sow them in warmth in spring, prick them out into trays and plant them out after the last frost. As this is such as popular variety, you can usually buy ready-grown plants at the garden centre in late spring. Grow in a sunny spot with good, fertile soil and keep watered in dry spells. Feed generously if you are growing for cutting.

■ *Salpiglossis sinuata*
75cm (2¹/₂ft) high × 20cm (8in) wide
With its brightly coloured flowers, salpiglossis adds an exotic touch to a garden. The plants have tall, upright stems topped with big, velvety-textured, trumpet-shaped flowers. '*Bolero Hybrids*'

is a good mixture with a wide range of veined and highlighted flowers. Two very good single-colour strains are '**Chocolate Pot**', which has luscious, deep purple-brown flowers with a golden eye, but only 30cm (12in) high, and '**Kew Blue**', which has true midnight blue and indigo flowers, again with the golden eye.

Cultivation Salpiglossis is a half-hardy annual; sow it in early spring in warmth, prick out and plant after the last frost in good, rich soil with plenty of organic matter. Water in dry spells and protect from slugs and snails. Deadhead regularly to keep the plants flowering. They should flower continuously from mid-summer until autumn. Grow in large containers or in clumps in a border.

■ *Salvia involucrata* '**Bethellii**'
(Shrubby sage)
1m (3ft) high × 45cm (1¹/₂ft) wide
Nothing could be more unlike the traditional bedding salvia than this. A shrubby tender perennial, this plant makes quite a large, bushy shape. Throughout summer, each of the upright stems is topped by a cluster of bright, mauve-pink, single-lipped flowers that almost put you in mind of a snapdragon, and at the very top is a large, round, pink 'bud' rather like a Christmas tree ornament, which never opens. A very unusual and spectacular plant.

Cultivation In cold parts of Britain this could be grown as a conservatory plant, but in warmer areas plant it out or grow it in a container on the patio for the summer. Plants grow quite large and woody in time, so prune them down by two thirds before moving them back under cover before the first frost, or take cuttings in late summer and root them in small, individual pots to save space, in the same way as you would for pelargoniums.

Iceland poppies 'Oregon Rainbows' are brilliant of colour and supremely delicate in petal formation.

Brilliant in a border or hanging basket as a stunning show of soothing colours, Verbena 'Peaches and Cream' is a new variety assured of a long life.

■ *Verbena* '**Peaches and Cream**'
20cm (8in) high × 15cm (6in) wide
One of the best hanging-basket and container plants ever, the semi-trailing forms of bedding verbena have really come to the fore lately. This is my favourite variety – each domed head of flowers contains a mixture of peach, apricot and warm cream shades which change as the florets mature. Plants stay in flower from mid-summer until the start of the cold weather in autumn; if you sow early, you can persuade them to flower a few weeks earlier.

Cultivation This type of verbena is a half-hardy annual, so sow it in warmth in spring, prick it out into trays and plant out after the last risk of frost. Plants benefit from regular deadheading, which keeps them flowering better and for longer. Frequent watering and feeding also help them produce a top-quality display.

pelargoniums

are the perfect plants for problem places; they thrive in hot, dry, sunny spots where other flowers just fry up, and in containers they won't turn up their toes if they happen to dry out occasionally. They are also very reliable free-flowering plants with an exceptionally long flowering season. Pelargoniums keep going from early summer until you dare not risk leaving them outside any longer in autumn.

Visit a specialist pelargonium nursery and you will be amazed at just how many different kinds exist. There are the familiar zonals, with geranium-type flowers and kidney-shaped leaves that have a distinctive dark 'zone' banding the middle. There are variegated versions with coloured leaves, and ivy-leaved pelargoniums which are the sort usually sold for hanging baskets as they have trailing or scrambling stems. Swiss balcony geraniums are just a very free-flowering type of ivy-leaved pelargonium with narrow petals that make stunning displays, especially when seen from a distance. There are also miniature pelargoniums which bring out the collector in most people. They are so small and addictive that you just have to complete the set.

Scented-leaved pelargoniums are different again. They look quite distinct from normal pelargoniums, with sparse and often uninteresting flowers. Their main attraction is the foliage which is amazingly variable in shape and which, when bruised, emits a powerful fragrance. Depending which kind you choose, you could have a whole pharmacy of scents, from lemon and orange to rose, cinnamon and peppermint to balsam. I like to grow scented pelargoniums in a large, mixed container with more colourful tender perennials – this way you get the best of both worlds: scented leaves and pretty flowers.

Pelargoniums are among the easiest plants to grow. Give them sun, superb drainage and rather poor soil and they'll flower their hearts out. On an over-rich diet they are likely to go all leafy on you. I saw one overfed plant, with leaves the size of dinner plates, which had not flowered for years.

In containers, use John Innes compost and let plants virtually dry out between waterings. Although they do best in poor soil, a few drops of liquid tomato feed does no harm to plants in containers. Do remove dead leaves and flowers straight away. If you grow scented pelargoniums, plant them somewhere you can run your fingers through them, or brush against them as you walk past, to release the fragrance.

Pelargoniums of all sorts do best if you grow new plants from cuttings every year, so instead of trying to overwinter old plants, root half a dozen cuttings round the edge of a plastic pot filled with cuttings compost and pot them up to provide replacements the following year.

Specialist nurseries keep the biggest range of pelargoniums and most sell plants through the post. However, your local garden centre should stock a reasonable selection. Spring and early summer are the best times to buy. Choose strong, healthy plants with plenty of branching stems to avoid the seaside landlady syndrome: tall, lanky pelargoniums with bare, twiggy stems.

ABOVE: Ivy-leaved pelargoniums are well suited to hanging baskets.
LEFT: 'Caroline Schmidt' has cream-edged leaves and double flowers of bright, magenta pink.

'Apple Blossom Rosebud'

A most intriguing plant with clusters of tight, pink and white buds that look just like tiny rosebuds and which open out like fruit-tree blossom. The plants are neat and compact and, despite being an old variety, do not become leggy.

Pelargonium crispum 'Variegatum'

One of the prettiest and most compact of the scented-leaved pelargoniums, this one has upright stems lined with neat, frilly-edged, cream and pale green leaves and occasional, tiny, pink flowers. Squeeze the foliage gently to release the lemon scent.

'Fragrans'

Another very compact, scented-leaved pelargonium; it has pale silvery-green, rounded leaves on a neat, dome-shaped plant. It is like a living air freshener with a perfume that is a combination of pine needles and spice – the ideal scent for a gardener's aftershave.

'Happy Thought'

Spinach-green leaves each with a gold butterfly-shape in the centre make this unusual variegated zonal pelargonium easy to recognize. The flowers are small, single and orange-red. This old variety is not easily found outside specialist nurseries, but it's well worth looking for.

'Irene'

Large clusters of semi-double flowers in an unusual shade, something like the peachy-red of an over-ripe nectarine, make this an outstanding zonal pelargonium. A very prolific bloomer on good, naturally bushy plants.

'Mrs Henry Cox'

A classic variegated pelargonium that remains popular. It has bright red-, yellow-, purple-black- and green-marked leaves, and small, single, pink flowers that complete a bold but curiously well co-ordinated colour scheme. Occasional plain green shoots sometimes appear, as happens with most variegated pelargoniums, which must be cut out quickly to prevent the whole plant reverting to green.

'Rouletta'

A striking ivy-leaved pelargonium with large clusters of bold, red-edged white, semi-double flowers. Like all ivy-leaved pelargoniums this can have rather long joints between the leaves and hence easily becomes a bit straggly, so when growing plants from cuttings, 'stop' them two or three times by pinching out the growing tip to make them bushy from the base.

'Splendide'

A miniature pelargonium which is closer in character to a regal than a zonal. It has silvery, sage-green leaves and two-tone flowers shaped like butterflies with one wing cerise and the other pale pink – an extremely pretty combination.

This wooden 'theatre' in my own garden supports auriculas in pots in spring, and through the summer is filled with a mixture of pelargoniums. Windows in the roof allow in the light they love.

Bulbs

Bulbs bring a special seasonal bonus to any garden. Use them as flowery ground cover, tall accents for a border or intriguing curiosities. Although spring bulbs are best known, different species flower at other times and you could have a bulb in bloom most of the year.

The term 'bulb' is used by gardeners to refer to many plants that botanists tend to be much more precise about, like corms, tubers and rhizomes, as well as true bulbs. As far as most gardeners are concerned, if it grows from an underground storage organ and it features in bulb catalogues, bulb is as good a name for it as any.

In addition to old favourites, like spring daffodils and tulips, summer lilies and gladioli, a huge range of not-so-ordinary bulbs is available, too. You can naturalize clumps of snake's head fritillary in long, damp grass; grow foxy-scented crown imperials in your border; plant a carpet of hardy cyclamen under shrubs or dot autumn-flowering nerines at the foot of a south-facing wall. Or, if you want something to turn heads, try the tall, rocket-like spires of foxtail lilies (*Eremurus*) or the jewel-like, three-cornered peacock flowers (*Tigridia*). They are two of the best garden conversation-starters I know.

Buying bulbs

Bulbs are normally sold when they are dormant, to make it easier to send them through the post or pre-pack in boxes or bags. You can also buy loose bulbs from display stands in garden centres, which is often more economical. They are sold at their natural planting time, so look for spring-flowering bulbs in late summer and autumn, and summer-flowering bulbs in spring. If shopping in a garden centre, buy your bulbs at the start of the selling season, to have the pick of the crop. Choose plump, healthy-looking bulbs and reject any that are battered, bruised or have cut marks on them, as they stand a good chance of rotting after they are planted. By shopping early you can also pick the biggest bulbs which will produce the most flowers and you can avoid buying bulbs that have already started to sprout.

If you want bulbs after their normal planting time, it is quite difficult to avoid buying sprouted bulbs, as they naturally want to start growing. The odds are they will be perfectly all right, but it's much better that they sprout leaves after they have had the chance to grow roots in the ground, which is why it is usually advisable to plant bulbs as soon as possible after buying them. Daffodils, for instance, start growing roots in late summer, so the sooner you get them into the ground, the stronger the plants will be. Hyacinths and tulips don't root until late autumn, so it is much safer to leave these in an open paper bag in a cool room indoors until late autumn before planting them. If they are planted into cold, wet soil in early autumn, they may rot instead of rooting.

Some bulbs are actually best not bought when they are dormant. Snowdrops and hardy cyclamen have a very short dormant season and bulbs may fail if they have been kept dry for too long, so these are best bought when they are visibly growing. Buy snowdrops 'in the green', as grassy tufts of foliage dug up out of the ground just after flowering. Both snowdrops and hardy cyclamen can be bought growing in pots, which is the best way to establish them.

You need to be quick if you want to buy autumn flowering crocus and colchicums. They are available only for a few weeks in late summer and they start flowering almost immediately.

Summer-flowering bulbs don't appear on sale until spring. Lilies do not like to be kept dry for long, so they should be planted straight away, and some summer bulbs are not hardy and should not be planted out until after the last frost – tuberous

ABOVE: The early spring flowers of Iris reticulata *'George' RIGHT: Snowdrops erupt through the lawn by the 'teahouse' in my garden.*

Narcissus cyclamineus is a dwarf narcissus that flowers best when naturalized in damp meadows.

begonias, tigridia, canna and eucomis fall into this category. These less hardy bulbs can be started in pots in a heated greenhouse and planted out later if you want to make an early start.

Increasingly, bulbs of all sorts are being sold in pots, just as they are coming into flower, so if you miss the sale season for dormant bulbs, you can have a second bite at the cherry. Just treat these as you would bedding plants: carefully slide the roots out of the pot and plant for instant effect. You can even plunge the pot to its rim in the soil to avoid disturbing the roots, which bulbous plants hate.

How to plant bulbs

Bulbs are generally quite trouble-free, but you must choose the right bulb for the right spot. Most bulbs need well-drained soil, so don't waste your time trying to grow things like tulips and hyacinths in heavy, wet or clay soil, unless you improve it well first, as they'll just rot. If the soil is a bit heavy, dig in plenty of well-rotted organic matter and about a bucketful of grit into 1 square metre (1 square yard). You can improve things even more by putting 5cm (2in) of sand into the bottom of the hole when planting damp-hating bulbs, and if you are planting crown imperials, lay the bulbs on their sides on a bed of sand, so that water cannot collect in their hollow centre. In damp conditions, it is safest to plant the

smaller bulbs that need especially good drainage, like *Iris histrioïdes*, species tulips and dwarf fritillaries, on a raised bed or rock garden. Some bulbs, though, enjoy slightly wetter soil, such as daffodils, bluebells, snake's head fritillaries (*Fritillaria meleagris*) and camassia, but even these don't like boggy conditions. Lilies and most other summer bulbs need soil containing plenty of organic matter to hold moisture in dry weather, but it must also be well-drained so that in a wet summer they are not left sitting in water. This is not as difficult to achieve as it sounds. Just start with good, deep border soil and dig in lots of well-rotted manure or garden compost.

The right planting depth is very important with bulbs. If they are planted too shallowly, which is a common mistake, they will probably flower the year after planting but they may take several years to do so again after they have hauled themselves down to the right depth. (Yes, they can really do that.) As a general rule, plant bulbs so they are buried three times their own depth. This means that a bulb measuring 5cm (2in) from tip to base wants a hole 20cm (8in) deep, so the tip of the bulb is covered by 15cm (6in) of soil. It seems deep, but if you have ever tried to dig up daffodil bulbs that have been left in the ground five or six years, you'll find they are way below a spade's depth down.

A proper bulb-planting tool is the easiest way to plant bulbs. This punches out a core of soil, leaving a perfect hole for one bulb. You could also use a trowel, but if planting several bulbs in a group it is often just as easy to use a spade to make a flat-bottomed planting hole. When planting, allow plenty of space between each bulb: approximately one-third the height of their flowers. Always make sure they are the right way up (except for things like *Anemone blanda* corms which look the same from all angles and do not mind) and 'screw' them down so the blunt end of the bulb makes firm contact with the soil. If they are left suspended halfway down a too-narrow planting hole, for instance, they won't take root.

A natural look

Naturalizing is the way to grow bulbs to look as if they really belong, and so that you don't have to keep digging them up and replanting them. You can naturalize bulbs in a border, as spring-flowering ground cover under trees and shrubs, and in 'drifts' in the lawn. A well-cultivated border should not need any extra preparation before planting bulbs, but, in the case of grass, you will need to strip off the turf and fork over the soil to loosen it and add some fertilizer. If you are planting only a few bulbs in grass, you can use a bulb planter to 'bore' holes in the turf, then replace the plug of turf over each bulb when it is in position. For a natural, random look, scatter the bulbs by hand, dropping them from about waist height, then plant them where they fall. Since naturalized bulbs stay in the same place for many years, you need to feed them by sprinkling a special bulb fertilizer or any general-purpose feed over the ground in autumn, and again in late spring just as the flowers go over. If bulbs are growing in grass, just feed the grass with lawn feed. When the clumps eventually get overcrowded, dig them up, divide them, then replant. The best time to do this is about six weeks after flowering, as you can still see where they are by the dying foliage. You can also do the job in late summer, just before the bulbs start back into growth, if you mark the clumps carefully.

A mixture of narcissi naturalized in grass. They are fed with general fertilizer at flowering time to promote the following year's blooms.

Bulb bedding

The other way of growing bulbs is to plant them as temporary 'bedding'. This is mostly done with the spring-flowering sort, especially tulips and hyacinths, though it can be done with frost-tender summer bulbs too. Plant the bulbs in straight rows as an edging around a formal bed – spring bulbs are popular for planting in autumn with wallflowers, polyanthus or other spring bedding. Alternatively, you can plant them in informal clumps, in the gaps where you will want to plant summer bedding plants later, to add splashes of early colour.

The essence of using bulbs for bedding is that once the flowers are over, the plants are taken out to make room for the next lot of plants. The old bulbs can be kept to use again in future years. Dig them up while still in leaf and replant them in a spare bit of ground, perhaps in your vegetable garden, while they complete their annual growth cycle. Give them a spot of liquid feed at this stage to help build up the bulbs. When the leaves have died down naturally, dig the bulbs up, dry them off and store them in open trays in a cool, shady shed for the summer. Then just replant them as usual in autumn.

Bulbs in pots

Spring bulbs signal the start of a new growing season, but they are much too valuable a resource to limit to beds in the garden. Grow them in pots to bring instant splashes of seasonal colour to patio planters, window boxes and balconies. They can also be used indoors and to decorate greenhouses and containers, too.

The best varieties
The best bulbs for growing in pots are the more naturally compact kinds. Hyacinths are a real favourite due to their strong scent. Place them next to your front door in spring or, better still, just inside the porch so that you carry the fragrance in with you each time you go indoors. Dwarf narcissi like 'Hawera' and ' February Gold' are perfectly proportioned for pots, as are the sort of tulips we used to call waterlily tulips. These are the ones that flower in early spring which bulb catalogues refer to as *Tulipa fosteriana* and *T. kaufmanniana* hybrids. Avoid tall, large-flowered tulips and daffodils. They look top-heavy if they are grown in pots, and they are prone to being broken by strong winds. Although daffodils, tulips and hyacinths are probably the most popular bulbs for containers, you can also grow grape hyacinths, anemones and other small spring bulbs in this way. If you have a large container you can make it into an attractive spring display with a few striking bulbs like lily-flowered tulips (the elegant ones with nipped-in 'waists') or parrot tulips (the big, blowsy ones that look like a flower painting by one of the Dutch Masters).

Large container displays
You can plant spring bulbs straight into outdoor containers and leave them on the patio, or where they are to flower, until spring. If you grow them in this way, you can get a lot of bulbs into a single tub. Plant them only a few centimetres apart and plant in two or three layers – each layer 8cm (3in) above the one below. The bottom layer of bulbs will have 15cm (6in) or more of compost over them, and the top layer will have be just below the surface of the compost. Plant larger bulbs such as tulips and narcissi lower down and smaller ones such as crocuses and dwarf irises nearer the top. A container planted up in this way will produce flowers in several successive waves throughout spring.

Perfect pots
If you plant all your bulbs in big containers and the winter is wet, some bulbs can rot, leaving you with gaps. Also, bulbs grow at slightly different rates, even those of the same type, so you end up with some plants in full flower while others are hardly in bud. To be sure of a specially good show in my best containers, I often cheat. I plant each bulb separately in an 8-cm (3-in) pot, which I keep in the cold frame for the winter. Then, when the

HOW TO POT UP TULIP BULBS

1 Choose a flowerpot of 20–30cm (10–12in) diameter. Place some pebbles in the bottom so that the drainage hole does not become blocked with soil.

2 Fill two-thirds of the pot with multipurpose compost and arrange the bulbs, spacing them evenly. Use fat and firm bulbs with no sign of fungal disease.

3 Add more multipurpose compost and then a top dressing of sharp grit to discourage slugs. Water well and then stand by the house wall. Water when dry.

flowers start to appear, I choose plants that are all at the same stage of development and plunge the pots to their rims in the final container. This makes a great show, and when the flowers are dead you can lift out the pots and stand a second crop in the same holes. You can replenish the same container several times during spring and have people wondering how you manage to keep your containers colourful over such a long season.

ABOVE: Bring hyacinths indoors as soon as the flower spikes start to show colour, but keep them cool. BELOW: One of my favourite dwarf narcissi is 'Jetfire' – wonderful in pots.

Aftercare

Once they are planted, stand containers somewhere cool and sheltered to allow the bulbs to take root. Apart from giving them a drop of water to keep the compost damp when you first plant them, they don't need much water until the leaves are growing well. Overwatering is a common mistake; it doesn't make the bulbs come up faster, it makes them rot instead. The same thing can happen if you leave tubs of bulbs on the patio. If there is heavy rain, the compost goes soggy and you end up with bulb soup. While they are emerging, bulbs are happier with compost very slightly on the dry side, so you might need to cover the top of the container in wet weather. (Bulbs also need protecting from mice and snails, as they provide a tasty snack in winter.) Only start watering more when you can see flower buds. While your bulbs are in flower, if the weather is fairly mild, give them a weak liquid feed. Keep feeding after the flowers die, then you can plant the clumps of bulbs out in the garden where they will flower the following year. If you do this, remember to plant extra deeply, not so the bulbs are just below the surface.

A–Z bulbs for spring flowers

At the end of a long winter, the things you really look forward to are flowers, and lots of them. Spring bulbs provide that surge of bright, sunny colour that leaves you in no doubt that the serious cold weather is behind us and a new season has arrived. Plant spring bulbs all over the place in autumn to bring your garden to life and offer the brightest possible start.

■ *Anemone blanda* (Windflower)
10cm (4in) high × 8cm (3in) wide
One of the best bulbs to grow as a carpet, which looks like a mass of large, single, coloured daisy heads lying over a mat of ferny foliage. You can buy mixed colours of white, red, pink, blue and violet shades, or each one separately. These anemones flower in early spring and the foliage dies down by late spring without ever looking untidy.
Cultivation Soak the odd-shaped corms in water overnight before planting them 5cm (2in) deep. Naturalize them in big drifts under trees and shrubs in a border or light woodland for best effect. They do well in light, dappled shade in ground with plenty of organic matter, where they will spread slowly.

■ *Erythronium* 'Pagoda'
(Dog's tooth violet)
25cm (10in) high × 25cm (10in) wide
This robust version of dog's tooth violet makes a clump of strong, large, light bronze-green leaves, with stems of sulphur-yellow flowers growing up through the centre in mid-spring. The flowers are initially bell-shaped, then as they mature they open wider and the petals curl back and open out almost flat to reveal a mass of yellow stamens clustered in the middle.
Cultivation These rather choice plants need woodland conditions to do well; naturalize them by planting three or five tubers in a group 8cm (3in) deep in light, dappled shade. They enjoy well-drained soil with lots of moisture-retentive humus, such as leaf mould. Leave them undisturbed. Plant the tubers as soon as you get them in autumn, as they don't like to dry out completely, even when they are dormant.

■ *Fritillaria imperialis* (Crown imperial)
1m (3ft) high × 30cm (1ft) wide
These used to be grown in neat rows in cottage gardens, but now they are not seen so often. They are incredibly striking plants with tall, upright stems topped by what looks like a pineapple from a distance – a ring of nodding, bell-shaped flowers with a tuft of spiky, green foliage standing up from the top. The common crown imperial has orange flowers, but you can get yellow and even double-flowered varieties and there is a scarce one with variegated foliage.
Cultivation Crown imperials have very large bulbs with a hollow centre, so unless the soil is extremely well-drained, plant them tipped over on to their sides on a 5cm (2in) bed of sand to stop them rotting. Planted like this the bulbs will still grow and flower perfectly well. Plant them 20cm (8in) deep in sun or light, dappled shade and well-drained but fertile soil. They are also suitable for containers.

■ *Fritillaria meleagris*
(Snake's head fritillary)
30cm (12in) high × 5cm (2in) wide
Seen in close up, the nodding, bell flowers of snakeshead fritillary look nothing like a snake or even snakeskin;

Hyacinths always look best mixed with other plants. Here they are accompanied by the spurge Euphorbia robbiae.

they have a delicate, chequered pattern. The normal species has flowers chequered with light and dark mauve, but there is also a white form, *F. meleagris* var. *unicolor* subvar. *alba*, which has its pattern outlined in palest green. If you have only a few plants, they need to be grown in containers filled with moisture-retentive soil where they can be seen easily, but they are best naturalized in grass under trees and allowed to form drifts.

Cultivation Plant 10cm (4in) deep during autumn in moisture-retentive, but not waterlogged, soil, in sun or light, dappled shade.

▪ *Hyacinthus* (Hyacinths)
20cm (8in) high × 10cm (4in) wide
Though they have large, showy flowers in an amazing range of colours, the most outstanding thing about hyacinths is their scent. Half a dozen in a pot will fill a room with fragrance, and odd 'pockets' dotted around outdoors on bends in the path bring added pleasure to a spring stroll in the garden. The flowers are also very good for cutting, if you can bear to.

Cultivation Don't plant hyacinths until late autumn as they do not start rooting until then. Plant them in a sunny, well-drained border 15cm (6in) deep, and dig the bulbs up to store dry during the dormant season in summer. If left in the ground, they are often attacked by soil pests that bore into them to leave an open wound which encourages the bulbs to rot.

▪ *Iris reticulata* (Dwarf iris)
12cm (5in) high × 5cm (2in) wide
Real charmers with fragrant, delicately marked flowers in early spring, that look positively outsized compared to the height of the plants. The leaves continue growing for some time after the flowers are over and eventually reach about 30cm (12in) tall, but they are so thin you hardly notice them.

Cultivation Dwarf irises make delightful spring flowers for a rock garden and in containers or anywhere the soil is very well drained. A sunny situation is essential, but it's a good idea to grow them in a sheltered position to protect the fragile petals from wind damage. Plant them 8cm (3in) deep.

▪ *Leucojum vernum* (Snowflake)
20cm (8in) high × 10cm (4in) wide
If you see what looks like a giant, bell-shaped snowdrop with green spotted petals, it will almost certainly be a snowflake. There are several different sorts that flower in spring; *L. vernum* flowers first, at about the same time as crocus, but the rather larger *L. aestivum* flowers in late spring and early summer. Both spread slowly to form clumps.

Cultivation An easy-going plant that grows well anywhere the soil stays moist, in sun or light shade. It is best naturalized and left undisturbed, to spread slowly and make bushy clumps. Plant 8cm (3in) deep.

▪ *Muscari* (Grape hyacinth)
15cm (6in) high × 7cm (3in) wide
You have only to look closely at a grape hyacinth flower to see how it got its name – each flower head is like a perfect, miniature bunch of tightly packed, bright blue grapes. The plants flower at the same time as early daffodils, and, with their contrasting colours, the two look wonderful growing together.

Few bulbs offer flowers of a truer blue than the grape hyacinth, or muscari.

Cultivation Plant grape hyacinth in autumn 8cm (3in) deep. Any reasonable garden soil suits them and they thrive in sun or light, dappled shade. They also do well in containers. In Holland I've seen them planted to make a 'stream' of flowers running through woodland, which is quite an amazing sight.

▪ *Narcissus* (Dwarf narcissi)
30cm (12in) high × 10cm (4in) wide
Dwarf narcissi are neat, small-scale versions of normal daffodils and are available in a huge selection of named varieties. As a group they tend to flower slightly earlier than most large-flowered hybrid daffodils. Especially good varieties include 'Jetfire', which has bold orange and yellow flowers in early spring and quickly forms good, solid clumps, and 'Pipit', which has unusual lemon and white flowers in mid-spring.

Cultivation Naturalize dwarf narcissi in moist soil in sun or light, dappled shade under trees and shrubs, or in grass. Plant the bulbs 10cm (4in) deep and leave them to spread into carpets. Since dwarf narcissi also have smaller foliage than daffodils, you are not left with the usual mess of straggly daffodil

I love narcissi naturalized in grass, and these, in my own garden, are welcome heralds of spring.

leaves to contend with for weeks after the flowers have died. With dwarf narcissi, the foliage can be lost among a sea of herbaceous plants growing up around them.

Cultivation All but the most choice and expensive varieties grow happily in quite damp soil and even tolerate clay. They enjoy light shade or full sun and should be planted 15cm (6in) deep. Provide better growing conditions for any expensive bulbs as they are a bit fussier. 'Blind' bulbs, that don't produce flowers, can be caused by overcrowding or underfeeding, and by planting too shallowly. To avoid this, plant deeply enough (to 20cm/8in on dry soils), feed well after flowering while the old foliage is dying down, and dig up and divide overcrowded clumps when they no longer flower well. Deadhead large daffodils after flowering, as this helps to build up bigger bulbs, saving the energy spent in producing unwanted seeds.

■ ***Scilla sibirica*** (Siberian squill)
15cm (6in) high × 5cm (2in) wide
The Siberian squill has short spikes of small, widely spaced, nodding, blue bells with an uncultivated air about it that suggests a wildflower rather than a garden plant. It is related to the better-known bluebell. It looks best naturalized in clumps at the foot of tree trunks or in a carpet under shrubs and is ideal for a wild garden or in light woodland.
Cultivation Plant the bulbs 8cm (3in) deep in well-drained soil containing plenty of organic matter so that it does not dry out badly while the bulbs are growing and flowering. Squills are happy in full sun or dappled shade. Unlike bluebells they do not spread vigorously.

■ ***Narcissus***
(Large-flowered hybrid daffodils)
45cm (1½ft) high × 15cm (6in) wide
Daffodils are firm favourites whether you prefer the sort with long trumpets or those with short cups in the centre. Plant breeders have even produced daffodils with pink flowers, which are pretty, and some with frilly, double 'butterfly' flowers.

■ ***Trillium grandiflorum*** (Wake robin)
45cm (1½ft) high × 30cm (12in) wide
The wake robin does not look like a bulb, but more like a herbaceous plant, and since it actually grows from a rhizome you could say it is about halfway between the two. The plant makes a clump of stems topped by three leaves, forming what looks like a big clover leaf, in the middle of which sits a single, three-petalled, white flower. It is very striking.

The quaint, tripartite flowers of the wake robin, Trillium grandiflorum.

Cultivation Most trilliums are tricky to grow, but this is the easiest as well as the showiest. Plant the rhizomes 8cm (3in) deep in autumn in woodland conditions – very humus-rich soil that stays moist but never gets waterlogged and dappled shade are essential. This is not one of those plants that will 'make do' in a border. Once it is planted, leave it alone and let it grow into a good-sized clump.

■ *Tulipa* (Dwarf rockery tulips)
15cm (6in) high × 8cm (3in) wide
Dwarf tulips are small species tulips, which are real charmers for rockeries and raised beds. Compared to the big bedding tulips, they have small, sophisticated flowers, and finer foliage, and most bloom much earlier. Two of my favourites are *T. humilis* (Violacea Group), which has small mauve flowers with yellow centres, and *T. saxatilis*, which has pale lilac-pink flowers with a yellow centre.
Cultivation Plant 8–10cm (3–4in) deep in late autumn in very well-drained soil in a rock garden or raised bed. After flowering the bulbs can be lifted and dried to store for replanting again later, but if conditions are hot, dry and sunny, and pests are not a problem, they are best left in the ground all year round. Mark the spot to avoid damaging the bulbs when hoeing or planting nearby.

■ *Tulipa* 'Apeldoorn'
60cm (2ft) high × 20cm (8in) wide
'Apeldoorn' is one of the best-known tulips in the world because of its popularity as a cut flower: it is available from most florists' shops in spring, but you can also grow it at home. It is one of the Darwin Hybrid tulips, flowering in mid-spring slightly ahead of the main bedding tulips. It has wineglass-shaped flowers with red petals and a yellow base. There are several reliable 'Apeldoorn' variants, such as 'Beauty of Apeldoorn', which has red-streaked yellow flowers, and 'Apeldoorn's Elite', which has yellow-flared orange flowers.
Cultivation Plant the bulbs 15cm (6in) deep in late autumn, as they are late to start rooting. Choose a sunny spot with very well-drained soil. After flowering let the foliage die down, then lift the bulbs and store them in a dry place for the summer. This is much safer than leaving them in the garden, as they often rot in a wet summer. Before replanting, peel away the dead, brown outer skin, as this helps tulip bulbs to root more easily.

The Greigii tulips are useful, self-supporting dwarf kinds. This is the variety 'Mary Ann'.

A–Z bulbs for summer flowers

Summer bulbs make outstanding partners for shrubs in your garden and are an excellent way of adding instant colour to those shrubs that are at their peak in spring or autumn.

The more exotic species make fine patio pot plants, and are ideal placed next to giant-leaved ones, loud half-hardy flowers and coloured foliage to create a tropical effect.

■ *Allium* (Ornamental onion)
60cm (2ft) high × 15cm (6in) wide
Alliums include some of the most spectacular summer bulbs of all. Garden centres stock the popular kinds like *A. sphaerocephalon*, which has 2.5-cm (1-in) wide, mauve 'knobbles' at the top of tall wiry stems. Look in a specialist mail order bulb catalogue for more unusual kinds. ***A. cristophii*** has 20-cm (8-in) heads of lilac flowers on 60cm (2ft) stalks, and

Allium 'Purple Sensation' growing in twin narrow borders in my garden, alongside a path that has become known as 'allium alley'.

A. schubertii has enormous, loose, spiky, globes of flowers held close to the ground.
Cultivation Alliums need well-drained soil and a sunny spot. They are hardy bulbs which should be planted in autumn at a depth equal to three times the depth of the bulb.

■ *Cardiocrinum giganteum*
(Giant Himalayan lily)
3m (10ft) high × 60cm (2ft) wide
Probably the biggest plant you will ever grow from a bulb, this one really lives up to its name. It's a whopper. A very architectural plant, it has strong, upright

stems furnished with big, heart-shaped leaves. The large, white, trumpet-shaped flowers, which are streaked with mauve, are concentrated at the top of the stem. It flowers in mid-summer.
Cultivation You need a woodland garden or a very big border, as this lily likes to grow in the dappled shade cast by trees or large shrubs. It also enjoys woodland-type soil that is well-drained but with lots of humus, such as leaf mould, so it does not dry out in summer or get waterlogged in winter. Bulbs will not flower for several years, as they need to be very big to produce such a large flower stem, and

usually die after flowering. If growing in ideal conditions, they will set seed to provide another crop a few years later.

■ *Crocosmia masonorum* (Montbretia)
1.25m (4ft) high × 30cm (12in) wide

These are clump-forming plants with upright, iris-like leaves which in mid- and late summer have elegant, corsage-shaped sprays of orange-red flowers. They look as if they would be at home in the bride's mother's buttonhole.

Cultivation Being hardy, vigorous and robust, crocosmia is usually treated as a herbaceous plant, although it actually grows from underground corms. If you buy dry corms, plant them 8cm (3in) deep in late spring, otherwise buy plants growing in pots and position them in a reasonably well-drained, sunny border. In cold areas, cover the roots with bark chippings for protection after the leaves have died down for winter.

■ *Dracunculus vulgaris* (Dragon arum)
1m (3ft) high × 60cm (2ft) wide

This slightly sinister-looking plant lets you know it's around by its smell. Its flowers, which appear in early summer, have a distinctive scent that makes you think something has gone off. If you can forgive it that one indiscretion, it is an amazing-looking plant with big, dramatic leaves and huge flowers like those of an arum lily but dull red, frilly edged and about four times the size, in early summer.

Cultivation Plants enjoy light, dappled shade and a rich border soil with plenty of organic matter that holds moisture in summer, but is not waterlogged in winter. The tubers can often be bought from bulb catalogues, but seeds are also dropped by birds. They grow fast, but die down soon after flowering and are dormant for most of the year.

■ *Eremurus* (Foxtail lily)
2m (6ft) high × 60cm (2ft) wide

Not often seen, but a plant with very striking flowers like pale orange or yellow rockets shooting up from the back of a border in early to mid-summer. The flowers don't last long, but the seed-heads are quite dramatic.

Cultivation Foxtail lilies grow from very big tubers which need to be planted in autumn or early spring. Plant them 8cm (3in) deep in very well-drained soil, somewhere you are not going to damage them by hoeing or forking the soil; mulch well to avoid needing to weed around them. Well-drained soil is essential otherwise the tubers rot in winter. Plant where the flowers can grow up into sunlight for all or most of the day, though it does not matter if the bottom of the plant is partly shaded.

■ *Eucomis bicolor* (Pineapple flower)
60cm (2ft) high × 30cm (1ft) wide

Although it is not hardy, the pineapple flower is a good, tropical-effect plant for a sunny border or containers. The leaves form a wide, funnel shape. In mid-summer, a spike of greenish flowers

The darkest of the montbretias is the bright red Crocosmia *'Lucifer' – stunning when grown alongside the purple-leaved smoke bush,* Cotinus *'Royal Purple'.*

topped by a spray of green leaves pops up through the middle of the funnel, looking just like an under-ripe pineapple on a stem. Grow it with pineapple sage (*Salvia elegans* 'Scarlet Pineapple') which will supply the pineapple scent.

Cultivation Plant in late spring a few weeks before the last expected frost in a sunny, well-drained border or, better still, start in pots of John Innes compost in the greenhouse or indoors. This bulb does not want planting deeply, so plant it with the tip of the bulb just about level with the surface. After the flowers are over and the leaves are dying down, but before the first real frost, dig the bulbs up and plant them in a pot. Keep them almost dry and safe from frost for the winter.

■ *Galtonia candicans* (Summer hyacinth)
1m (3ft) high × 60cm (2ft) wide

The common name is misleading as this plant does not look much like a hyacinth.

The wonderfully elegant flowers of galtonia make it a good choice for a sunny border.

It makes a big clump of strap-shaped leaves, which are more like a soft yucca, and has tall stems of well-spaced, white, bell-shaped flowers in late summer.
Cultivation This is a bulb that is best planted in a group and left undisturbed to form a big clump, more like a perennial plant. Plant dry bulbs 15cm (6in) deep in spring, or plant pot-grown plants during late spring or early summer. Choose a sunny border with well-drained, fertile soil and do not let surrounding plants smother it as it needs plenty of light.

◼ *Gladiolus communis* **subsp. byzantinus**
75cm (2¹/₂ft) high × 45cm (1¹/₂ft) wide
This isn't the usual sort of gladiolus, which has to be dug up each autumn and replanted in spring, but a hardy perennial kind with magenta flowers. It grows in profusion from Cornish hedge bottoms and looks lovely in cottage gardens. The flowers are slightly smaller than the flower arranger's gladiolus, but there are lots of them in early summer, growing from a clump of elegant, narrow, upright foliage.
Cultivation Choose a fairly sunny spot and plant corms 8cm (3in) deep in

autumn or early spring in a fertile, well-drained border and then just forget about them. The plants spread slowly and form clumps without becoming too much of a good thing. Clear the dead foliage in autumn and mulch with a layer of bark chippings in a cold area to protect from frost.

◼ *Gladiolus callianthus*
60cm (2ft) high × 20cm (8in) wide
A very sophisticated, late summer, flowering bulb with iris-like leaves and a starburst-effect spray of large, white flowers that droop from the ends of long tubes at the top of the stalks. Each flower has a deep maroon star in the centre around a white eye.
Cultivation This gladiolus, which was previously known as *Acidanthera*, is not hardy. Plant 10cm (4in) deep in late spring about two or three weeks before the last frost in your area; the shoots take several weeks to reach the surface, so they will be safe. Choose a warm, sunny, sheltered spot. After the flowers are over, allow a few weeks for the foliage to start dying down, then dig the corms up before frost kills the plants. After drying them off, store the corms in a frost-free place for the winter. This is also a good specimen for containers.

◼ *Iris xiphium*
60cm (2ft) high × 15cm (6in) wide
The Xiphium Group of irises are all very similar to look at and are favourites with flower arrangers. They include Dutch iris like 'Wedgwood', English iris and Spanish iris, which flower in that order from early until mid-summer. They have upright flower stems with narrow foliage, and flowers in various shades of blue, yellow and white.
Cultivation This type of iris is not 100 per cent hardy and needs a fairly mild climate. Plant it 10cm (4in) deep in autumn in a sunny, fertile border with plenty of organic matter to hold moisture in summer, but which is also well-drained so the bulbs are not sitting in water in winter. If you are growing it for cut flowers, plant a few Dutch iris bulbs in the greenhouse for early flowers and a row of all the different types in the vegetable garden so you can cut them without spoiling your borders. Dig the bulbs up when the flowers are over and the leaves die down naturally, separate the tiny bulblets, which won't flower for several years, and replant the biggest bulbs where you want them to flower in autumn.

Spectacular in an unusual sort of way, that's nectaroscordum, an onion relative with nodding, bell-shaped flowers.

My favourite lily has to be Lilium longiflorum: *pure white and deliciously scented.*

■ *Lilium longiflorum*
1m (3ft) high × 45cm (1½ft) wide

One of the lily species that you often see in florists as a cut flower – it has very long, white, trumpet-shaped flowers and a strong, heady, perfume, with narrow, deep green, glossy leaves. It flowers naturally in mid-summer, but when it is grown commercially it is 'forced' to provide out-of-season cut flowers.

Cultivation Unlike most garden lilies, this one is not entirely hardy and is best grown in large pots (38–45cm/15–18in) of John Innes compost. Plant 2.5cm (1in) above the base of the pot in autumn or early spring and overwinter the pots in a frost-free greenhouse or conservatory or by a sheltered house wall where they will survive all but the hardiest of winters. Keep the compost barely moist, but not bone dry as lily bulbs die if they are allowed to dry out completely. Those overwintered under glass can be left in the greenhouse or conservatory or located outside in sun or light shade in spring. Don't place outside until after the last frost, and harden them off by putting them out only during the day for a while. While they are growing in summer, water well and feed regularly with liquid tomato feed.

■ *Lilium tigrinum* (Tiger lily)
1.25m (4ft) high × 30cm (12in) wide

A very well-known and striking-looking flower, with large, bright orange, spotted flowers with incurving petals that make a ball shape and long, curving stamens like tiger's whiskers. It is one of the easiest lilies to grow.

Cultivation Plant the big bulbs 15–20cm (6–8in) deep in autumn or early spring, whenever they are available. They need lime-free soil which is deep, fertile and well-drained but rich in humus. Plant so the base of the plants will be shaded by neighbouring plants, but the flowers can grow up into sunlight. Mulch generously and feed well – lilies seem to enjoy a couple of handfuls of concentrated manure spread around them in spring. Leave the plants alone for several years until the clumps are overcrowded, then dig them up in autumn or early spring and replant them straight away, after improving the soil.

■ *Nectaroscordum siculum*
1.25m (4ft) high × 30cm (12in) high

This slightly unusual bulb looks perfect growing among shrubs in a border, where its umbrella-shaped heads of nodding, greenish, allium-like flowers make subtle little patches of detail against leaves in mid-summer. The subspecies *bulgaricum*, once called *Allium bulgaricum*, is especially good as the petals each have narrow, mauve pencil-lines. Plants take up virtually no room as the foliage is narrow and minimal and the stems are wiry – so all you see are the flowers.

Cultivation Plant the bulbs 5–8cm (2–3in) deep in autumn, choosing reasonably well-drained border soil, and leave the bulbs undisturbed. Plants may self-seed gently; leave the seedlings where they appear for a natural look.

■ *Tigridia pavonia* (Peacock flower)
30cm (12in) × 5cm (2in) wide

A real stunner, this is the one to plant in your front garden if you like chatting to passers-by. Everyone will want to know what those big, fluorescent pink, orange and yellow, three-cornered flowers with the spots in the middle are. Otherwise grow it in containers, or in a tropical-looking bed where its vibrant, hot colours will be most appreciated. It flowers in late summer.

Cultivation Plant the bulbs 10cm (4in) deep in late spring. They are not hardy, so dig up the bulbs shortly after the flowers are over, when the leaves start to die down naturally, but before the first frost. Store them in a frost-free place for winter and replant again next year.

Tiger lily Lilium tigrinum *'Splendens' has flowers shaped like a Turk's cap.*

A-Z bulbs for autumn flowers

It is easy to forget that there are bulbs that brighten up dull autumn days, but the gardener who does so misses out on some real treats. These unseasonal flowers are especially welcome because they give their all during a part of the year when most plants choose to die down and colour in the garden can be scarce. Plant them where they can be best appreciated, bearing in mind the state of the plants around them at that time of year. Many of them look good pushing up through bark- or leaf-mould-covered earth which shows off their bold flowers to perfection. Those that are naturalized in grass must be allowed to keep their foliage until it dies down in spring.

Naked ladies – the elegant flowers of Colchicum speciosum 'Album' – push up through the soil in autumn.

■ *Amaryllis* (Jersey lily, belladonna lily)
60cm (2ft) high × 10cm (4in) wide
One of the most spectacular autumn-flowering bulbs with pink, trumpet-shaped flowers carried on stout stalks. The strap-shaped leaves appear after the flowers. There are several good varieties of **A. belladonna**, many of them reflecting the plant's South African origin: '**Cape Town**' has flowers of rich rosy red; '**Hathor**' has white flowers that are soft pink in the bud; '**Johannesburg**' has pale pink flowers; and '**Kimberley**' has deep pink flowers with a white centre.
Cultivation Plant just below the surface of the soil in late summer or spring in well-drained but humus-rich earth and a very sunny spot. Protect in winter with straw or bracken.

■ *Colchicum*
8–15cm (3–6in) high × 8–15cm (3–6in) wide
Real heralds of autumn, with spectacular, crocus-like flowers that may be white, pink and even chequered. The leaves are large and leek-like and follow the flowers, which push up first. **C. agrippinum** has chequered pink flowers; **C. autumnale** is the meadow saffron, which has small, pink or white flowers carried in profusion; **C. speciosum** has large, goblet-shaped flowers of pink which are white in the throat, and its variety '**Album**' is pure white; **C.** '**Waterlily**' has fully double flowers that have difficulty standing up. There are many other varieties, all worth trying.
Cultivation All those mentioned enjoy well-drained, fertile soil in full sun. Plant 10cm (4in) deep and 15cm (6in) apart in late summer. Can be naturalized in grass. Divide in summer when overcrowded.

■ *Crocus* (Autumn-flowering crocus)
5–10cm (2–4in) high × 5–10cm (2–4in) wide
Most people think of crocuses as spring flowers, but there are some that flower in autumn, of which these two are the most reliable performers in the garden: **C. laevigatus** '**Fontenayi**' has lilac flowers that are veined with purple and have a delightful fragrance; **C. speciosus** is violet blue with darker veins and is especially good in its deep blue variety '**Conqueror**'. It also has a white form. Other species flower more reliably in a bulb frame (a cold frame set up specially for bulbs) rather than the garden.

Cultivation Plant 8cm (3in) deep and as much apart in late summer in really well-drained soil in a sunny spot on a rock garden or at the front of a border. Both the above species can be naturalized in grass. They are happiest left undisturbed so that they can spread.

■ *Cyclamen* (Sowbread)
10cm (4in) high × 15cm (6in) wide
There are several autumn-flowering cyclamen, but only one that is reliably hardy in gardens. Not to worry – it is a real cracker, very reliable and no garden should be without it. **C. hederifolium** (syn. **C. neapolitanum**) has dainty, reflex-petalled, pink flowers marked with a darker shade at the base. The form **albiflorum** has white flowers. The flowers are produced from the flat tubers before the marbled leaves appear and are sometimes scented.
Cultivation Plant 5cm (2in) deep in summer in well-drained soil which has been enriched with well-rotted leaf mould. They are happiest in dappled shade under trees and shrubs. Mulch with leaf mould when the foliage fades. Self-seeds freely.

■ *Leucojum* (Snowflake)
15cm (6in) high × 5cm (2in) wide
One of the daintiest bulbous flowers, **L. autumnale** produces reed-like leaves and nodding, white, bell-shaped flowers in autumn. Sometimes the flowers precede the leaves, sometimes they push up at the same time, and each white bell is delicately tinged with pink.

Cultivation Plant 8cm (3in) deep and 10cm (4in) apart in spring. Enjoys a moist but well-drained soil in full sun. Good on the rock garden.

▧ *Nerine* (Autumn lily)
60cm (2ft) high × 10cm (4in) wide
Wonderful bulbs for the foot of a sunny wall or fence. *N. bowdenii* is the hardiest species and produces clustered heads of up to eight bright pink flowers with wavy-edged petals in early autumn. The leaves that follow are fresh green and strap-shaped. There are named varieties which vary in tone, and a white form, *alba*. All of them will take your breath away once they settle into flowering.
Cultivation Plant the bulbs in spring with their tips just below the surface of the soil. A winter mulch of bark or

No garden should be without a carpet of Cyclamen hederifolium, *which look absolutely stunning in autumn and are tough as old boots.*

leaves is a good idea in cold areas. The bulbs need well-drained soil and a sun-baked spot. Can be divided, but are happiest undisturbed, when they will make large clumps in time.

▧ *Schizostylis* (Kaffir lily)
60cm (2ft) high × 30cm (1ft) high
Graceful South African plants with clumps of narrow, sword-shaped leaves and dainty flowers that look individually like those of a crocus, but which are carried in clusters on a stalk like those of the freesia. All are good for cutting.
S. coccinea has scarlet flowers, and there are several varieties which vary in colour. The form *alba* is white; '**Jennifer**' is soft pink and has larger flowers than the older '**Mrs Hegarty**', which flowers slightly later. '**Major**' is the best red variety; '**Sunrise**' is salmon pink and '**Viscountess Byng**' has pale pink flowers that are later and may suffer from frost damage.
Cultivation Plant from containers at any time of year. Enjoys a sunny, sheltered spot in well-drained soil that

never fully dries out. Mulch with organic matter in winter to offer protection from frost. Not suitable for really cold gardens. Divide in spring when overcrowded.

▧ *Sternbergia lutea*
12cm (5in) high × 8cm (3in) high
Resembling giant golden crocuses, sternbergia are choice bulbs with price tags to match. Plant a small clump where they will stand out well, leave them alone and if happy they will slowly increase. They flower best after a hot summer. It's essential they have a summer rest when the bulbs are dry.
Cultivation Buy bulbs in late summer and plant in a sunny, sheltered, well-drained spot at the base of a south-facing wall with 8cm (3in) of soil over them. The leaves start to appear at the same time as the flowers in early autumn, and persist through the winter; don't cut them back. Leave the plants undisturbed until overcrowded before digging them up to divide them.

A-Z bulbs for winter flowers

The few bulbs that flower in late winter are invaluable as harbingers of spring, when we are all desperate to see living colour in the garden again. Collect them all, and plant them in decent quantities to make a good splash – or use them in containers close to the house.

■ Crocus tommasinianus
10cm (4in) high × 2.5cm (1in) wide

This beautiful species is one of the earliest crocuses to bloom. It has narrow, upright, pencil-shaped buds which are palest lilac on the outside, opening out in the sun to reveal deeper lilac centres. The whole flower has a slight silvery sheen that makes it stand out well in a still, wintery garden.

Cultivation Plant the corms 8cm (3in) deep in autumn, in any reasonable garden soil in sun or light shade. Plants are a bit smaller than the better-known Dutch crocus and have neater foliage. They are particularly good for naturalizing in carpets in the lawn or under shrubs. When planted in grass, delay mowing that area until the crocus foliage has died down after flowering. The plants will spread slowly and do not need to be divided until clumps are badly overcrowded. Tubers bought in packets may be reluctant to flower for a few years after planting if they have become at all dry.

■ Cyclamen coum (Hardy cyclamen)
5cm (2in) high × 5cm (2in) wide

This miniature species of cyclamen has tiny, pinkish-mauve flowers with reflexed petals and neat, dark green, kidney-shaped leaves. Leaves may be attractively silvered.

Cultivation A single plant hardly shows up in the winter garden; the trick with this species is to get a colony established. Dry corms rarely do well, so buy growing plants in pots and place them so the top of the compost is level with the surface of the soil after planting. This way the top of the corm will rest at ground level – it should not be buried. Choose a place with humus-rich, well-drained soil in dappled shade. Plant a group of three

or five – odd numbers always look best for some reason – and leave them. In time they will set seed and produce a very pretty, spring-flowering carpet without breaking the bank.

■ Eranthis hyemalis (Winter aconite)
10cm (4in) high × 5cm (2in) wide

If you spot what look like mini buttercups in early spring, they'll be winter aconites. The 2.5-cm (1-in) wide, yellow, single flowers have a frill of green, rather like an Elizabethan ruff, around them. The plants are in flower at the same time as snowdrops and the two look very good growing together.

Cultivation Plant the tubers in autumn 5cm (2in) deep and 8cm–10cm (3–4in) apart in good-sized groups and leave them to spread and form carpets. Winter aconites are not fussy about soil and grow in sun or shade. Lift and divide clumps soon after flowering if they become overcrowded. If you have only a few tubers, plant them in containers where they will make much more of a show than out in the garden.

■ Galanthus elwesii (Snowdrop)
25cm (10in) high × 10cm (4in) wide

To most people a snowdrop is a snowdrop, but to a collector each of the hundreds of named varieties is very slightly different. This snowdrop is obviously different, even to a non-expert. It is a different species that is taller-growing than the common snowdrop (*G. nivalis*) with larger flowers, though they both bloom at the same time in late winter.

Cultivation Grow in any reasonable garden soil in sun or dappled shade. Snowdrops are especially good naturalized in carpets under trees, though this species is big enough to look impressive planted in clumps under shrubs. Plant the bulbs 10cm (4in) deep and about the same distance apart as soon as you get them as they will not succeed if allowed to dry out. Better still, buy snowdrops 'in the green' – as clumps of leafy plants – shortly after flowering and plant straight away. This is also the best time to move or divide established clumps.

Crocus tommasinianus is one of the easiest crocuses to naturalize in grass, where it will make a sheet of amethyst stars.

■ *Iris danfordiae*

10cm (4in) high × 5cm (2in) wide

This is the earliest of the miniature rockery irises to flower. It has lovely, bright yellow, three-petalled flowers dappled with a light sprinkling of tiny, brownish spots, like freckles. The narrow leaves follow on shortly after the flowers and grow slightly taller.

Cultivation This species needs good drainage and a sunny, sheltered situation. A rock garden or raised bed is best, though it also does well in containers and it is particularly good in pans in a cold greenhouse where the early flowers are protected from bad weather. Plant the bulbs 8cm (3in) deep in autumn. Plants normally flower best in their first year after planting, so, for the best display, it is better to buy new bulbs every year, but there is no harm in leaving them in the rockery to see what sort of show they put on the following year.

■ *Narcissus* 'February Gold'

(Dwarf narcissus)

20cm (8in) high × 8cm (3in) wide

'February Gold' is an elegant yellow trumpet daffodil, but about half the usual size. It also flowers almost two months earlier and is one of the first daffodils to open. It looks lovely naturalized in grass or under trees, planted with snowdrops, winter aconites and *Cyclamen coum*.

Cultivation Plant the bulbs 10cm (4in) deep in late summer or early autumn, as soon as you can get hold of them, since they root early. They need to be planted early to give them enough time to become established before flowering. Like most daffodils, they do best if naturalized and left to form clumps. Where they are grown in grass, wait at least six weeks after the flowers are over before mowing to give bulbs a chance to absorb food.

■ *Scilla mischtschenkoana*

8cm (3in) high × 5cm (2in) wide

A very early-flowering scilla with very pale blue flowers, with a tiny, deeper blue stripe down each petal. The flowers are single and wide open, almost like clusters of daisies, set against miniature bluebell-like foliage.

Cultivation Scillas are happy in sun or dappled shade under deciduous trees or shrubs, since they complete their annual growth cycle before the trees have come into leaf. They like soil containing plenty of humus so that it does not dry out in summer, but is well-drained; they don't like sitting in puddles of water in winter. Plant the bulbs 5cm (2in) deep in autumn and leave them undisturbed to form good-sized clumps, which show up better than single bulbs. They are also good subjects for planting in containers to decorate patios and terraces in spring. They are cheap, too!

Patio gardening

One of life's greatest pleasures must be relaxing in a comfy seat on the patio, surrounded by your favourite plants all growing happily in pretty pots. Patio gardening not only scores top marks for looks, it lets you have time off to enjoy the results in nice surroundings too.

Having paving immediately outside the house is an attractive design feature that is also very practical. You don't want to step straight into a sea of mud when you go out of your back door, nor do you want that same mud trampled back indoors. But it wasn't until the great craze for sunbathing that patios took off. Now they are like multi-functional entertainment facilities, full of elaborate recliners, complicated barbecues and hammocks that don't need a tree. You can even have a bubbling spa bath plumbed in. It is great fun to relax in comfort with instant leisure laid on, but whatever else you put on a patio, it does need plants.

From a plant's point of view, a patio provides a superb place to put down roots. It is warm, sunny and sheltered: all the things that make it attractive to us for relaxing in and perfect for species that enjoy sunbathing, too. Cannas, pelargoniums, gazanias and other sun-loving tender perennials really look the part. If you are not so bothered about sunbathing and prefer to relax in cool shade, a pergola clad with a selection of climbers makes an elegant retreat.

Make the most of a patio that has to be positioned in a spot that is naturally shady by creating a foliage garden with a fountain. This can look wonderful. The secret is to choose strong foliage shapes and lots of textures: bamboos, Japanese maples and variegated ivies or euonymus, with trained box shapes. Friends and neighbours with sunnier sites will envy your sophistication.

You can keep the regular maintenance of a patio garden down to a minimum by creating planting pockets instead of using pots everywhere. Take up a row of paving stones and improve the soil to make a bed. Or build a wall along one edge of the patio using a double row of bricks with a gap for soil in between, to make a narrow raised bed. And if you need to put up a screen wall to give the patio privacy or shelter (which is always a good idea, if you have a rather open garden), leave a bed along the foot of it, for climbers. Remember that if you make a bed along the wall of a house, it will need enriching because of the amount of rubble underground and the soil is always bone dry because the house and patio deflect most of the rainwater. But it can be a great spot for sun-loving bulbs such as nerines and winter-flowering irises.

A patio also needs containers. A good collection of tubs, troughs and planters is a must for any patio gardener, and because they can re-used year after year, it pays to buy good ones. Choose terracotta or ceramics, but make sure they are frost-proof (these are usually more expensive, but worth it). You can change the whole look of a patio simply by investing in a new set of pots.

A patio garden needs to be kept clean and tidy. I know it sounds daft to suggest using a vacuum cleaner out of doors, but the sort made especially for gardens is a great way of clearing up dead leaves and other patio debris. Before putting out the bedding plants I always like to spring clean the patio to set it up for summer. Use an old dinner knife to lift out any weeds or moss growing in the crevices between slabs, or treat the cracks with path weedkiller. Sweep (or vacuum) up any soil, leaves or other debris. If the slabs still look dirty, clean them with a pressure washer. If you have containers still standing outside from previous years, empty them out, refill them with fresh potting compost and there you are: all ready to go.

ABOVE: Lilium longiflorum (white) and Lilium 'Omega' RIGHT: Even when the weather is showery I can persuade myself that summer is still here, thanks to a linen parasol and some all-weather garden furniture.

Containers on the patio

A new patio is a big, empty expanse of paving just crying out for a few plants to decorate it, but it is amazing how quickly it fills up. An afternoon at a garden centre or a bit of self-indulgence at a plant fair, and before you know it your big, empty space is looking positively cluttered. The buy-whatever-takes-your-fancy technique has a lot to recommend it for spontaneity, but a bit of co-ordination creates a much better-looking result.

Grouping plants together instead of dotting them about helps to add structure. A few good-sized plants in large, matching pots arranged together looks like a thought-out display. Positioning two or three groups like that around a patio not only looks better, but they are also a lot quicker to water than lots of tiny pots. What's more you don't have to keep picking them up after a windy night.

If you do want to grow lots of small plants in pots, find a way of giving them the designer touch. I've

seen patio gardens with rustic shelf units on the walls housing collections of bonsai plants or cacti that are summering outside. You can also group them together on a table, or line them up along the edge of a row of steps.

A theme will also add a sense of style. It could be a colour scheme or a planting style – tropical or Mediterranean, for instance. You might fancy a scented garden using plants like pinks, scented-leaved pelargoniums, lavender or herbs, which all grow well in containers.

Seasonal patio displays

Most people want lots of colour on their patio. For summer displays, bedding plants and tender perennials are the answer. You cannot beat pelargoniums, fuchsias and petunias as they have the longest season and most prolific flowering of just about any patio plants. With so many wonderful summer flowers you are spoiled for choice.

Containers provide an easy way of changing the patio display with the seasons. Here lilies and fuchsias provide summer colour.

During winter, pansies such as *Viola × wittrockiana* 'Universal Series' are the most reliable plants for flowers, and ornamental kales and cabbages make a first-class foil for them. Try standing the two together next time you are at a garden centre and you'll see what I mean. Otherwise go for weather-resistant arrangements of evergreens like winter-flowering heathers, or santolina, ivies and lamium. For an even more seasonal look, plant Christmas box (sarcococca), skimmia and *Gaultheria procumbens*. These are all evergreens which make good, temporary, winter patio plants that you can plant out in the garden afterwards.

By the time spring comes round, the garden centres are full of spring bedding and pot-grown bulbs that you can use to make a new potted display. Plant a mixture of daffodils and polyanthus, tulips and forget-me-nots, or ranunculus and violas. It doesn't matter if their flowering season is not terribly long, as you need them only for a seasonal splash of colour to take you up to the start of the summer bedding season. If your early spring flowers are over too quickly, you can often fit in a second display in the same pots. Don't bother changing the compost, just whip out the old plants and put the new batch in.

Cultivating containers

Caring for patio containers is not difficult, but it does mean spending a bit of time almost every day and allocating a session two or three times each year for replanting. I like to start the container year by cleaning my containers and refilling them with fresh compost just before the summer bedding goes in. Keep the same compost for the winter and spring displays, but add a top up after you've pulled out all the old roots between batches.

Containers can be washed or scrubbed to clean off algae outside, but don't forget to clean the inside too. Clay pots often look nicest left with a patina of limescale or watermarks, as it lends them an air of antiquity. When planting up containers with big drainage holes, put a few bits of broken flowerpot or a handful of clean gravel into the bottom: this will stop the compost washing out each time you water. There is no need to bother if you use plastic pots with small holes. Then fill the containers with potting compost to about 5–8cm (2–3in) from the top. Don't use garden soil because it never grows such good plants in containers. I often mix water-retaining gel crystals

Hanging baskets, if they are to do well, need to be watered daily and fed once a week. This way the display will be long lasting.

plus some slow-release fertilizer into the compost as it makes a tremendous difference to the way they grow for the rest of the season.

When adding the plants, try to avoid breaking the roots more than you must. Tip plants out of their pots carefully, holding them securely between two fingers while you turn the pot upside down, then tap the rim down sharply on something hard to loosen the rootball. If you get it right, it should drop into your hand intact. Take care with the sort of plants you buy in 'strips' as their roots grow all tangled together. These need prising gently apart with your fingers. Put plants in the containers so their stems are at the same depth as they were in their pots or trays, then water them well.

For the first few weeks patio plants don't need a lot of water because, at the start of summer, the weather is not normally too drying and the plants have only small roots. But don't let them dry out. As summer moves on the combination of hot, dry weather and containers that are filled with roots means that daily watering is essential. Remember to nip off the dead flower heads and feed regularly with a tomato feed (even if you added slow-release fertilizer to the compost), so that any patio plant worth its salt has no excuse for not flowering itself silly right up to the end of the season.

Planting a hanging basket

If you choose a traditional wire basket, place a coir liner inside. This is much easier than lining it with moss, and watering is less bother later. Alternatively, buy a solid-sided basket with a drip tray fitted underneath, although you won't be able to plant the sides as you can with a wire basket. Meanwhile, stir some water-retaining gel crystals into water, following the manufacturer's instructions. When the granules have swollen up to make a lumpy jelly mix, put this into a bucket of potting compost. Half-fill a lined wire basket with the mixture, and tuck trailing plants in through the slots in the sides of the liner. Place a mixture of plants evenly all the way round. Fill with more compost to 8cm (3in) of the rim. Go straight to this stage if you use a solid basket. Then plant the top of the basket, using a taller plant like a trailing fuchsia in the middle and surrounding it with shorter, bushier plants. Finish with trailing plants round the edge. Pack in as many plants as you can for maximum flower-power. Water well and hang up.

All-year-round containers

Not everyone has the time or inclination to keep planting a new batch of bedding in their patio containers every few months. However, there is an alternative, at least for large tubs or planters, which can be planted permanently. (It is a waste of time trying to plant hanging baskets and small pots permanently, as the plants quickly outgrow them.)

The best sort of plants to use for a permanent display are evergreens with striking architectural foliage, as they give you something to look at all year round. *Fatsia japonica*, ivies, *Euonymus fortunei* and phormiums are all suitable patio pot plants. A large trough planted with bamboo provides a 'patio divider' almost like a portable hedge that gives you instant privacy when you want to enjoy a quiet afternoon in the sun. Evergreens that have good flowers and attractive foliage are best of all. Try the variegated *Hebe × franciscana* 'Variegata' and *Yucca gloriosa* 'Variegata'.

You can also use containers to grow plants that are not suitable for your garden soil. Camellias, rhododendrons and pieris make good plants for large tubs – simply plant them in ericaceous (lime-free) compost.

If you have a heated greenhouse, you can grow all sorts of tender shrubs and small trees in tubs which can be placed on the patio in summer. There's nothing quite like plucking your own personal supply of oranges or lemons for an evening gin and tonic! You might fancy sitting in the shade of a palm tree while you do so. Choose *Trachycarpus fortunei*: it is the best one to risk outdoors in our climate but looks very South of France. You could dabble with plants like the bottle-brush and pomegranate. Although they are not hardy, they can be wheeled out of a greenhouse or conservatory to provide summer colour.

Climbers are very under-rated as container plants. Clematis (see pages 136–7), in particular, will brighten up a patio. Plant one per large container with a smart, metal obelisk or a rustic plant frame for support. It doesn't matter if you can't plant clematis the regulation 15cm (6in) deep as, in a container, they should be safe from wilt disease. But they do need cool, shady roots, so cover the compost with large pebbles after planting and surround the tub with other containers. You can also grow clematis in tubs alongside a wall where there is no soil border; just let them scramble up trellis as usual.

If smaller plants take your fancy, you can make all sorts of delightful arrangements of herbaceous perennials in large tubs, but you need to choose

Instant sunshine can be brought to a summer patio with a tub filled with coreopsis.

Diascias are among the best plants for summer containers, flowering right up until the frosts of autumn.

them carefully. The trouble with a lot of compact garden perennials is that they do not flower for long enough to make good patio plants. Dwarf grasses and grassy plants like sedges offer something a bit different. *Festuca glauca, Carex oshimensis* 'Evergold', *Acorus gramineus* 'Ogon' and the strange, black-leaved *Ophiopogon planiscapus* 'Nigrescens' are all suitable. Evergreen herbs like rosemary, French lavender and variegated or purple sage also make a solid, year-round tubful.

A large tub without any drainage holes in the bottom is ideal for making a bog garden. Fill it with a peat-based compost, plant a mixture of creeping Jenny (*Lysimachia nummularia* 'Aurea'), variegated iris, *Houttuynia cordata* 'Chameleon' and hostas, and top up with water until it is nice and boggy. Hostas are enormously good plants for tubs, and growing them in pots without drainage holes solves the usual problem of keeping them moist enough. (You still have to worry about slugs and snails, but they can be discouraged by top dressing the pots with sharp grit.)

All-year-round growing techniques

Growing all-year-round containers is obviously a big time saver, as the same plants can be left in the same tubs year after year. However, after a while, the compost deteriorates and plant foods diminish to the point where liquid feeding no longer makes up

the difference. Even permanently planted pots need some attention. I repot plants completely every three or four years, and the best time to do it is in spring or just after plants like rhododendrons and camellias have flowered. Use John Innes No. 3 for everything except lime-hating plants, which must have ericaceous compost. To repot, lift the plant out of the tub and scrape away all the loose compost from the roots. If you tease away enough of the old compost, it can go back into the same container with some fresh compost, otherwise tease away as much of it as you can and repot into a slightly bigger container. If a plant becomes too big, plant it in the garden and replace it with a smaller plant. Perennials will need dividing by the time the tub needs replanting, so this is a convenient time to do both jobs at once.

In the years when you don't repot, you can top dress instead. Scrape away the top 2.5–5cm (1–2in) of the old compost, replace it with new and add a sprinkling of slow-release fertilizer.

Regular feeding is even more essential for permanent plants than for temporary bedding, so start feeding in spring, using a tomato feed or, if you grow lime-hating plants, a liquid or soluble feed especially for ericaceous plants. Continue feeding until mid-summer, then stop for the winter. You may need to keep watering all through the winter, especially if the tubs are standing in places where rainwater can't get to them, or if evergreen plants make a natural umbrella over the container.

You will need to plan for serious cold snaps. If the compost in containers left outside in winter freezes solid, the roots of even normally very hardy plants will die. Overnight frost is not usually enough to do any harm, but several days when the temperature stays below freezing may well be. In this case, you need to provide some extra protection. You can move your containers into a greenhouse or shed – even evergreens won't mind being in the dark for up to three weeks in a winter emergency, so long as they are truly dormant. Alternatively, group all the pots close together and lag them by spreading straw, bark chippings or even newspapers around them. Cover the tops of the pots with about 8cm (3in) of material, pack more around the edge of the group and drape the plants themselves with horticultural fleece.

Don't be tempted to surround plants outdoors with polythene. It prevents air circulation and encourages rotting.

Rock and alpine plants

There is something appealing about tiny plants. Perhaps this is what makes rock plants so collectable. There are alpine or compact versions of most plants you would find in a full-size garden – all perfect for creating a landscape in miniature.

I'm often asked what, exactly, a rock plant is and if it is the same as an alpine. If you want to be technically accurate, an alpine is any plant that grows above the tree-line on mountains. But what most gardeners, and particularly garden centres, mean when they refer to alpines are any dwarf plants that are suitable for growing in rock gardens. The difference between alpines and rock plants is very woolly, but alpines tend to be the posher end of the market – the more difficult to grow, expensive, collector's kind – while rock plants are commoner plants like aubrieta, arabis and sedums. What most alpines have in common is that they need the same growing conditions – an open, sunny site that is well-drained and has lots of shingle in the soil. If you give them too much fertilizer or rich humus, they blow up like cabbages instead of being small and compact and looking like they are battling against the elements on a craggy, windswept mountainside. But don't assume *all* alpines want the same thing. There are a few that need shadier places; some need to be grown in lime-free soil, while others prefer growing in pockets of moist, peaty soil. Always read the instructions on the label.

Contrary to popular belief, you don't have to have a rock garden to grow rock plants. A proper rock garden needs a lot of space, as it consists of giant rockfaces with rocks traditionally 'planted' like icebergs with two-thirds below the surface, and relatively few plants. This sort of thing is better viewed at a botanical garden. The idea is to duplicate real rock strata and show rock plants growing as they do in the wild, clinging to crevices – it is not to stuff in as many plants as possible, which is what you really want to do at home. In the past domestic rockeries earned themselves a bad name when people used to pile up old rubble, half-bricks and sacks of cement over a heap of unwanted soil. This is not a rock garden, and doesn't even look nice.

You can make a small-scale rock garden using a few pieces of weathered stone, and a mixture of good topsoil and gravel. Instead of piling it in a mound, set it into a bank or slope so that it looks as natural as possible. Place the stones in a row, flat sides together, to look like a continuous rockface rising out of the ground, and plant your alpines in between them.

Nowadays there is much concern about people taking real rock from the wild, so as an alternative to newly cut or quarried rock, you can use reconstituted or second-hand stone, or make your own rocks by pouring hypertufa mixture (equal parts of coarse sand, rough peat and cement mixed to a sloppy paste with water) into 'moulds' made by digging irregular-shaped holes in the ground. When they harden enough to handle, which takes several weeks, lift them out and stand them somewhere to continue drying for a few weeks more. Yes, it seems quite a bit of effort, but it can be fun designing your own tailor-made rocks. Don't worry about a bit of soil sticking to them as this adds an instantly weathered look. To continue the weathering process, water your homegrown chunks with diluted liquid plant feed when you set them out for their final drying, or spray them with the same mixture after they are in position, to encourage lichens and mosses to start colonizing.

There are lots of other ways to grow rock plants that are easier to set up and maintain than a traditional rock garden.

ABOVE: *Helianthemums have visual impact in a rock garden or border from early summer onwards.* RIGHT: *An established rock garden on a slope, where it always looks more natural, with the round pink flowerheads of* Phuopsis stylosa *making a bright carpet.*

Scree gardens

In the wild, a scree is the result of lots of tiny pieces of rock rolling down a mountain and ending up as a sloping pile of shale at the bottom. At home, a scree garden is a very good way of growing alpines in a reasonably realistic setting without the bother of making a rock garden. If you have naturally well-drained soil or a sloping site from which water freely runs away downhill, you can make a scree garden just by digging lots of gravel into the area. To make it look natural, cut it into a contour of your slope as if it were a feature of the land. A scree also looks good as a more formal feature in a garden. You can make a round bed edged with granite sets, or try two overlapping shaped beds of different sizes. Circles, octagons and squares work well.

Raised beds

If your garden soil is not well-drained enough to make a scree at ground level, the remedy is to make one in a raised bed. This will need to be at least 30cm (12in) above normal ground level, surrounded by a retaining wall of stone walling blocks or those chunks of prefabricated dry stone walling that you glue together. (It looks incredibly realistic, but it is made from reconstituted stone so you are not responsible for ripping up areas of natural beauty.) This is enough to provide sufficient depth of well-drained soil for most rock plants, though you can

Tender echeverias growing in a Cretan dish. They are moved under glass in winter to protect them from frost.

make it higher if you like – you will simply need more materials. It is not a bad idea to make your wall about 60cm (2ft) high, as the edge makes a nice place to sit while you are weeding, and I'm all in favour of making gardening as comfortable as possible.

These auriculas in a stone sink in my garden flower reliably every spring and have been growing here for several years now with no more than an occasional liquid feed.

Once the wall is built, fill the bottom of the bed with a layer of large stones. This is where you can put your old half-bricks and spare rubble, if you have some to hide – it will all help to provide sharp drainage. Fill the rest of the bed with a mixture made of half and half good topsoil and gravel. The sort of gravel sold for making a gravel path or drive is perfectly all right if you want an economical result. Do make sure it does not come from under the sea, or it will be very salty, and check with the supplier that it is does not contain lime. Make sure, too, that the topsoil you use is neither wet and sticky nor filled with the roots of perennial weeds. If these start growing up through your plants once the bed is established, they will be the very devil to remove, and the whole thing may have to be dismantled and replanted to get rid of them. A top dressing of sharp grit will make the plants look good.

Sink gardens

It's odd that alpines are grown in sinks. Water plants I could understand, but not plants that need very good drainage. Surely you should be growing them on the draining board? But then alpines do look exceptionally at home in sink gardens. The ideal sink is an old-fashioned butler's sort, which is big and shallow and made of real stone. They are second-mortgage jobs these days, so don't turn down the offer of a deep ceramic sink if you get it – try junk shops, a salvage yard or car boot sales. You can give it a realistic stone-effect finish by coating the outside with the same hypertufa mix used to make fake rocks. Used on its own, it would just slide off the slippery sink surface, so dab bonding adhesive over the sides first, and allow it to become tacky before slapping the hypertufa roughly over the bottom, the sides and the rim.

You can also make your own sink using stout cardboard boxes as a mould. Take two cardboard boxes, one a bit bigger than the other, and fit the smaller box inside the larger one. Cut pieces of wire netting to fit in between the two as reinforcing. Fit these in place, then pour hypertufa in between the two boxes so that it fills the base and sides. Leave it for a few weeks to set, peel away the cardboard, drill a few drainage holes in the base, and you have a pretty passable impression of a real sink. Fill it with a mixture of topsoil and grit and it is ready to plant up.

Planting and cultivating

Whatever else you do, ensure you have killed off any perennial weeds (see page 36) before planting alpines. I make no apologies for repeating myself in the interests of saving you prolonged heartache. Alpines just cannot stand up to bindweed, thistles and the like.

The best time to plant alpines is in spring. This way you will see the full flowering of your new rock feature in its first year, but you can still add more plants during summer. In fact, it is not a bad idea to do so as this way you make sure of a good sprinkling of summer-flowering plants too. Since the main flush of rock plants flowers in spring it is very easy to have a brilliant splash of colour then, followed by nothing much later on. So make a special point of looking out for some summer and autumn flowerers and include plenty of evergreen plants for winter interest.

After planting, spread a 2.5-cm (1-in) deep layer of granite chippings, grit or rounded pebbles over the entire surface of the feature. This not only gives rock plants a nice, natural, rocky-looking background, it also helps improve the surface drainage. Tuck it underneath rosette-shaped plants, as they often begin to rot around their 'necks' if water gets trapped there. A deep top dressing of grit also acts as a mulch, which will keep the soil cool and moist and suppress weeds. Weeding is probably the most important job to do in a rock garden. If you let weeds take over, even the annual ones, they very quickly smother small plants.

Houseleeks, or sempervivums, are quite hardy and can be left outdoors in their containers all the year round.

A–Z alpines

Alpines can be anything from choice collectable treasures to sturdy fillers for difficult places, including hot, dry or windy spots, but they all have a charm and grace that is hard to match among bigger plants. With their beauty and versatile nature, they will always find a place in my garden.

■ ***Aethionema 'Warley Rose'***
15cm (6in) high x 25cm (10in) wide
A good, sturdy evergreen, with rounded, mauve-pink heads of flowers at the top of slightly rumpled-looking stems that sprawl over each other to make a loose mat of grey-green leaves. It flowers from late spring until the end of summer. It looks like the sort of plant that might spread, but it doesn't, and remains a modest if rather relaxed clump.
Cultivation Most sunny situations with well-drained soil suit it nicely. It is happiest on slightly chalky ground, but will tolerate most conditions except seriously acid soil.

■ ***Armeria maritima*** (Seapink thrift)
15cm (6in) high x 30cm (12in) wide
A native seaside plant that grows wild on windy cliffs, this is a brilliant plant for a windy rock garden or a hollow-topped wall that is very dry during summer. In kinder conditions the plant may grow a bit bigger with taller stems of lilac-pink flowers and a looser mound of foliage; when grown in harsh circumstances, it becomes very hard and compact, making tight mounds studded with pink tufts of flowers on wiry, chive-like stalks. It flowers for a couple of months in early summer.
Cultivation It must have lots of sun and very good drainage, and will grow in very inhospitable conditions where little else survives. It is tremendously tough and self-sown seedlings can colonize cracks in walls or paving where there is hardly any soil. A natural choice for coastal gardens.

The alpine pink comes in a variety of colours; this is Dianthus alpinus 'Fusilier'.

■ ***Artemesia schmidtiana 'Nana'*** (Sagebrush)
15cm (6in) high x 25cm (10in) wide
This lovely, lacy-looking plant is about as silver as they come. It grows into a loose mound that makes a superb foliar background for fragile-looking plants such as alpine phloxes, and looks especially good teamed with pink, blue, purple and mauve flowers. This is a plant grown for its foliage; it does have flowers but they are greyish-coloured, inconspicuous and you really have to hunt for them. This semi-evergreen looks its best in late spring and summer.
Cultivation Tougher than it looks, this is a plant for a very sunny spot with well-drained, gritty soil. New plants are fairly easily rooted from cuttings in late spring. Older plants are not keen to be disturbed, so grow it where you won't need to move it again.

■ ***Campanula carpatica*** (Bellflower)
This bellflower is trim and well-behaved enough for a rock garden. It is covered with cup-shaped, sky-blue flowers with deeply scalloped edges which bloom throughout the middle of summer. The plants are perennial but die down in winter.
Cultivation A plant for a pocket of reasonably humus-rich but fairly well-drained soil in a rock garden. It also makes a good outdoor pot plant grown in a 15–20cm (6–8in) pan filled with a mixture of John Innes and grit. Stand it on top of a low wall, on one side of a garden step or even in the middle of a table on the patio to view it at its best. New plants are easy to grow from cuttings in late spring or late summer.

■ ***Dianthus alpinus*** (Rockery pink)
10cm (4in) high x 20cm (8in) wide
These compact charmers are drought-

resistant, evergreen plants that form neat cushions of silvery foliage. From late spring to the end of summer they are studded with what seem like outsize flowers for their height: these, which are 2.5cm (1in) across, look as if they should belong to an altogether bigger species of pink. You can obtain rockery pinks with white, pink or mauvish flowers, which usually have a deeper-coloured centre. There are also some very good hybrids such as **'Little Jock'** which is bright pink with a magenta ring around the eye.

Cultivation Rockery pinks need full sun and very well-drained soil, and are happy in coastal or windy gardens and poor soil including the sandy and chalky kind. Once they are established, they won't mind if this dries out, so long as they are watered when newly planted. They are not keen on soil with a lot of organic matter in it.

■ **Gentiana sino-ornata** (Gentian)
10cm (4in) high x 20cm (8in) wide
Gentians are generally considered to be tricky to grow, and some certainly are hard to persuade into flower, but this is a pretty reliable one. It flowers in autumn with the typical large, blue trumpets associated with gentians, growing from a reasonably compact rosette of foliage which sometimes keeps its leaves in a mild winter. The flowers have a faint, greenish stripe down the outside.

Cultivation This is a plant for a pocket of moist, peaty soil in otherwise well-drained surroundings; somewhere that it will get a bit of shade from nearby plants or rocks during the hottest part of the day. In the wrong spot, it won't do well.

■ **Helianthemum** (Rock rose)
20cm (8in) high x 45cm (1½ft) wide
Often sold for the front of a sunny border, helianthemum is a bit bigger than a lot of rockery plants, but there are times when you need something on a larger scale for sheer impact. The plants are covered in a mass of small, fragile-looking, poppy-like flowers for a couple of months or more from early summer onwards.

There is a good range of varieties in colours including yellow, orange and red.

Cultivation Lots of sun and good drainage are the main requirements; helianthemum is also happiest in fairly poor soil. The plants can get rather straggly over a few years – prevent this by clipping them with sheep shears after flowering. This deadheads them and keeps them compact and tidy.

■ **Lithodora diffusa 'Grace Ward'** (Lithospermum)
10cm (4in) high x 45cm (1½ft) wide
A rock garden classic, lithodora, which used to be called lithospermum, makes a low, spreading mat of foliage studded

Helianthemums tumble attractively around paving stones to make a flowery path.

with blue, star-shaped flowers throughout summer and into early autumn.

Cultivation This variety of lithodora needs lime-free or acid soil with plenty of humus, but cannot stand shade or wet feet, so a peaty pocket in a well-drained but sunny part of the rock garden suits it perfectly. Clip the plants lightly in early spring to keep them tidy.

■ **Phlox 'Chattahoochee'**
15cm (6in) high x 30cm (12in) wide
This is one of those plants that you must have when you see it in flower at a

nursery. It makes a low mat of semi-evergreen leaves with large, single, five-petalled, lilac flowers, each with a mauve eye, and it's very pretty indeed. It flowers in summer and early autumn, and its only real fault is that it is rather short-lived, so take cuttings from the new shoots in summer and root them in a pot somewhere shady.

Cultivation This is another of those plants with rather precise requirements. 'Chattahoochee' needs moist soil with plenty of humus, and light shade for most of the day, so plant it in between taller plants or behind a rock to keep it happy. Propagate it every two years so you always have a replacement on hand.

■ *Rhodanthemum hosmariense*
30cm (12in) high x 60cm (2ft) wide
An alpine with a bit of everything – a mound of finely cut, evergreen, silvery foliage and masses of large, robust but

Mossy saxifrages are among the easiest of alpine plants to grow. Their feathery rosettes are studded with bright flowers in spring.

neat, yellow and white daisy flowers, which keep on coming right through the summer for five months or more. It keeps its shape without trimming and does not spread or have any bad habits. You really can't go wrong.

Cultivation A sun lover, it needs very well-drained, gritty soil and all the sun it can get. It even thrives in the sort of baking, drought-prone spots that sempervivums enjoy.

■ *Saxifraga exarata* subsp. *moschata* 'Cloth of Gold'
2.5cm (1in) high x 23cm (9in) wide
The name describes it perfectly: the plant makes hundreds of tiny, tufty, golden rosettes that spread out to form a mat that covers the soil like a bright yellow, lacy tablecloth. Although it is mostly grown for its foliage, it has tiny, white, star-shaped flowers through the summer. A mature plant looks almost like lichen growing among rocks and it is useful as a background for other alpine flowers. Plants are virtually evergreen, but look best in spring and summer when the new growth is brightly coloured.

Cultivation This is one of the mossy saxifrages and needs well-drained, gritty soil containing enough organic matter so that it does not dry out badly in summer, which makes it turn brown. Grow it in

The encrusted saxifrage 'Tumbling Waters' has a handsome rosette of leaves before the flowers appear.

light shade: it needs fairly good light but tends to scorch in bright sunlight. If grown in too much shade, it turns lime green. When you want a few more plants, just tease out a few of the rosettes along with their roots and put them into a pot until they make a clump about 5cm (2in) across, then they are ready for planting. Late spring is the best time to plant or propagate 'Cloth of Gold'.

■ *Saxifraga* 'Tumbling Waters'
(Encrusted saxifrage)
5cm (2in) high x 20cm (8in) wide
The encrusted saxifrages have rosettes of hard, dark green leaves covered with a crusty, silver pattern which is made up of lime secreted by the plant through its leaves. 'Tumbling Waters' is one of the biggest and most spectacular, reaching the size of a saucer. It will be several years before it flowers, but when it does, it produces a 60-cm (2-ft) long spray of tiny, white flowers that looks, as the name suggests, rather like a waterfall.

Cultivation Very well-drained soil containing limestone, and lots of sun, is the recipe for success. If they are at all damp in winter, the plants will rot easily. Plants of this variety often die after flowering and do not produce offsets so can be propagated only from seed.

▨ *Sedum spathulifolium* 'Purpureum' (Stonecrop)
5cm (2in) high x 23cm (9in) wide
Delightful, little evergreen succulent, with fat, pink and red leaves that grow in flat rosettes all over the top of low-growing bushy plants. Its cousin **S. spathulifolium** 'Cape Blanca' looks the same but with grey, white and mauve leaves. The two look brilliant grown together, or with sempervivums, which like similar growing conditions.

Cultivation A great ground-cover plant for hot spots, as it does not mind how hot and dry it gets. Being compact, it is especially good for alpine sink gardens and pots. Give it rather impoverished, well-drained, gritty compost as its biggest enemy is damp, which can cause the stems to rot, as can rich conditions.

▨ *Sempervivum* (Houseleek)
5cm (2in) high x 5cm (2in) wide
Fascinating and very collectable, little, rosette-shaped plants that form clusters. As soon as you think you have a full set, you find a new and different variety. Houseleeks come in green, red, purple; some have red-tipped leaves; they may be covered with hairs, or be bald and shiny. The cobwebbed houseleek, **S. arachnoïdeum**, is the best known, but the purplish-red **'Commander Hay'** is a real stunner. But perhaps the most amazing thing about houseleeks is the flowers, which look like fat turrets 30cm (12in) tall, that suddenly push up through the middle of a mature rosette. Being evergreen, they look good even in winter, when rock gardens are often pretty lifeless.

Cultivation Lots of sun and dry soil are what they like best; they make ideal plants for the front of a hot, sunny rockery, but are also perfect for sink gardens and pots and will even grow on a roof, given the tiniest scrap of clay to root into. New plants grow very easily from offsets that appear all around the mother plant. Detach them and grow them on.

A dry stone wall retains a sunny bank, where, in well-drained soil, sempervivums and silver-foliage plants are happy.

Water in the garden

Once you have fallen under its spell, you'll wonder how you ever lived without a water feature. As well as providing an ideal environment for moisture-loving plants and a habitat for wildlife, it offers movement, soothing sounds and relaxed surroundings in which to enjoy brilliant reflections.

Although ponds are the most popular, there are all sorts of water features and it is important to choose one that fits both the style and scale of its surroundings. For instance, at a grand stately home, a lake, complete with boathouse, is what's called for. Most of us have room for only a small pond but this is open to just as many possibilities. You can dress it up with garden lighting to add ambience to your evening barbecues in summer, or landscape it. Some people like to combine a pond and a rock garden, for a two-storey effect with water cascading between boulders into the pool. You can blend a pond into a bog garden, or even surround it with bright perennials for a subtropical effect. There is also the natural look, consisting of a wild pond surrounded by native waterside wildflowers, designed especially for wildlife. While children are small it is unwise to have standing water, however shallow, in the garden. Instead you can have water features like wall masks, pebble pools and free-standing fountains where the water disappears for recycling as soon as it appears.

The type of water feature you go for determines the amount of work it will take to maintain. Water plants need dividing just like perennials, and ponds need weeding just like a border – you can even have problems with snails. But you shouldn't be put off.

The simplest type of water feature to maintain is one that does not have any fish or plants at all, such as a fountain or pebble pool. To keep the stones clear of algae, which grows on any wet surface after a while, simply put an algicide into the water. Various types, both chemical and those based on friendly bacteria, are available from water-garden centres. In a proper pond, plants are vital to create and maintain the ecological balance that keeps the water clear and everything in it happy.

The water-gardening year traditionally starts in spring with planting time. However, since young plants are now available all summer, too, you can actually plant at any time of year except late autumn or winter. Always grow water plants in special pond plant baskets filled with aquatic compost to keep potentially invasive species within bounds, and also make it much easier to remove them from the water when they need dividing. It's a good idea to wash new plants well, ideally repotting them into clean baskets with fresh compost, to avoid introducing unwelcome nasties like duckweed or water pests that may prove impossible to eradicate.

Stand marginal plants on shallow planting shelves around the edge of the pond, and deep-water aquatics, such as waterlilies, on the floor near the centre of the pool. In a large pond you will need an extra pair of hands to help lower them into position. Thread string through the sides of the basket and, with one person each side of the pool, lower the plants into place, then just let go of one end of the string and pull the other end out.

Spring is also the time to spring clean an existing pond. Lift out baskets of overgrown plants, divide them just like splitting a clump of hostas on dry land, then replant the best bit back into the same container with new aquatic compost, which is specially formulated with little nitrogen to stop it turning the water green. Spread 2.5cm (1in) of gravel over the surface of the compost to stop it floating out, and lower it slowly back into the pond.

ABOVE: The waterlily Nymphaea 'Masaniello' RIGHT: Moisture-loving irises and lady's mantle enjoy the damp fringes of a pool.

Water features

The basic ingredients of a conventional pond include a pond liner, either a flexible one cut to fit the shape of a hole dug in the ground or a pre-formed fibreglass shape; something to hide the edge of the liner (usually paving or plants); marginal and floating plants; and of course water. Tap water is fine as any chlorine disperses once the water has been standing for a few weeks. Optional extras include fish, fountains and landscaping. What you choose depends on the style you are aiming for; some of the ingredients are not suitable for certain styles of pond. The aim is to create a pond in which an ecological balance is maintained, so it looks after itself and does not develop problems like algae or weeds.

A formal pond has a geometric shape, usually round or square, often with a raised edge surrounded by paving. Traditional formal ponds contained waterlilies and fish, but no wildlife, such as frogs, and few marginal plants as these spoiled the symmetry. At stately homes, formal water gardens are on a much bigger scale – perhaps a canal flanked by fountains and parterres running into the distance, or a series of pools containing Versailles-style waterworks. Plants and fish rarely figure in this sort of spectacular scene as they are far too untidy, and likely to block something vital.

Family fish ponds

A fish pond is a fairly casual affair, with something for every member of the family. Marginal and floating plants satisfy the gardener, while fish appeal to the pet lovers, and the paving that inevitably surrounds a pond makes a good place to put the garden furniture so everyone can enjoy a waterside picnic. A family pond should be about 75cm (2½ft) deep in the middle to make it deep enough not to freeze solid in winter, so that fish and submerged plants can survive. Include planting shelves around the sides to house marginal plants that grow in shallow water: these normally need 2.5–5cm (1–2in) of water over the top of their planting baskets. Allow at least one section of the pond to have a gently shelving edge where birds can bathe and hedgehogs drink, but where they can also get out again – otherwise float one end of a small log on to the water to make a bridge. Landscaping can include a bog garden or rock feature with a cascade of water or a fountain; but don't mix waterlilies with fountains or cascades as they quickly fail if their leaves are subjected to splashing water. If you opt for landscaped bog gardens or soil borders

BELOW: A formal pool surrounded by paving stones and planted up with waterlilies and marginal aquatic plants. RIGHT: A more informal, natural-looking pond.

DOS AND DON'TS OF FISH PONDS

✔ Do put Canadian pondweed into the water if you keep fish. This evergreen keeps oxygenating the water all year round even when the pond is covered by ice. There is no need to plant it. Bunches are sold weighted down at one end and will root into the debris that slowly builds up in the bottom of a pond. Because it grows fast and is invasive, you will need to thin out Canadian pondweed several times during the summer to stop it taking over.

✘ Don't be in too much of a hurry to put fish into a new pond. Let it settle down for at least six months, so the water plants can grow to provide a spot of shade and a few hiding places, and oxygenators can establish themselves.

✔ Do let fish acclimatize to the pond water gradually – float them in a plastic bag on the surface for an hour while the water adjusts to pond temperature, then open the bag and let them swim out in their own time rather than tipping them out.

✘ Feeding fish during spring and summer will encourage them to grow tame and come to the surface where you can see them: they appear regularly if you feed them at the same time every day. If you don't feed them, they will find plenty of natural insects like daphnia and mosquito larvae. If you do feed, stop in autumn and winter and don't overfeed at any time as unused food can foul the water.

✔ Do make a hole in the ice if the pond freezes over in winter, but don't break it with a hammer as the shock waves can harm the fish. Instead stand a pan of hot water on the surface to melt a hole.

MAKING THE MOST OF YOUR WATER FEATURE

◆ Site a pond in a sheltered, sunny spot well away from deciduous trees whose fallen leaves will pollute the water in autumn.

◆ Choose a feature with no standing water while children are small.

◆ Make sure the edges of the pond are completely level – check by laying a board over the top and rest a spirit level on it, fore and aft and side to side – otherwise the water will all slop down to one end.

◆ The bigger the pond, the easier it will be to keep the water clear. Pools under 2 × 3m (10 × 6ft) are most likely to be susceptible to green water.

◆ Choose low-wattage submersible pumps to power fountains and cascades.

◆ Get an electrician to install proper outdoor powerpoints and use the correct waterproof fittings to provide power to pumps and lighting.

◆ Where possible use solar-powered fountains, garden lights, etc. – they cost more to buy, but are free to run and avoid the cost of laying underground armoured cable.

◆ Be patient when stocking a pond. Leave the water to settle for a few weeks before putting in plants, and wait six months before putting in fish.

around the pond, keep the two separated by a sunken wall of bricks or a polythene membrane. If soil gets into the water, apart from making the water look murky, the nitrogen it contains will encourage algae and blanket weed to grow, turning the pond green.

Wildlife ponds

If frogs, newts and other pondlife are your main interest, opt for a proper wildlife pond instead. This is a 45cm- (18in-) deep depression lined with flexible pond liner, with marginal and water plants growing in mud in the base of the pond and edges that are gently shelving so that wildlife can get in and out easily. Marginal plants are encouraged to form dense clumps and scramble out of the pond into adjoining boggy soil to blend the pond into its surroundings. Moisture-loving wildflowers like *Eupatorium cannabinum* (hemp agrimony), *Caltha palustris* (marsh marigold), and *Geum rivale* (water avens) can colonize the surrounding area freely to complete the wild and watery environment. A pond like this will attract huge numbers of waterside insects. Use plenty of reedy-stemmed plants around the margins as these encourage dragonflies to lay their eggs, and allow the nymphs to climb out of the water. Don't make the mistake of putting fish into a wildlife pond, as they will not be able to withstand the competition, and it will be almost impossible to protect them from predators like herons.

Moving water

A stream feature with slowly moving water makes the best possible form of water garden for the waterside plant enthusiast. It provides a much bigger area to grow irises and similar marginal plants, and offers greater landscaping possibilities as you can incorporate whole drifts of moisture-loving plants, such as primulas, into its banks. Though you cannot grow waterlilies in a stream, as they hate moving water, you could grow *Aponogeton distachyos* (water hawthorn) which has oval, floating leaves and scented, white, waxy flowers all summer. You can also include architectural features like a beach of smooth pebbles, or a bridge made from something very simple like two parallel railway sleepers with wire netting tacked over the top to stop them becoming slippery in wet weather. If you are a little more adventurous, build a rustic bridge with a wisteria-clad handrail. The stream could even incorporate low rapids cascading into a fish pond, from where the water is recirculated via a pump back to the start of the stream.

Fountains

To avoid any risk where small children are concerned, opt for a water feature that does not involve standing water. Fountains are ideal as they are fun but safe. A good water centre or specialist firm will be able to supply a large range including formal fountains with a vertical spray pattern, and bell fountains in which the water forms a dome shape. But the water does not have to form a vertical jet; you can get informal features where water runs out of a jug carried by a stone figurine or runs from the spout of an old-fashioned water pump. There are also fountains incorporated into decorative sculptures: for instance, those where water trickles down a row of bronze plant leaves. In each case the water runs into an underground reservoir from where it is recycled via a pump hidden beneath the structure.

Pebble pools

Provide the sound and movement of water without posing a threat to small children. Here, water gurgles up through an ornament such as a large terracotta oil jar filled with water, or out of a hole in the middle of a mill-stone, and runs away into a carpet of smooth cobblestones that surround the central feature. Under the stones is a tank housing a pump which recycles the water. A vital feature of

This wall-mounted fountain recycles water from the half barrel with the aid of a pump, pushing water through a pipe that runs up against the surface of the wall. The pipe is hidden from view by slats on the wall.

This wall-mounted lion's head squirting water into a half barrel makes an eye-catching feature without taking up much space.

this type of pool is that the pump must be adjusted so all the water falls within the catchment area so it is recycled back into the reservoir. If the feature is in a windy site and adjusted too high, water can be blown out over the side of the feature and eventually the reservoir is emptied and the pump will take in air instead of water. This is not good for the pump and also spoils the effect.

Wall water features
All sorts of running water features can be built into a wall; the best-known is the lion's head mask which spouts water into a small container from where it is recycled (see illustration). But many different ideas can be used. You can even make up your own such as a trickling tap filling a watering can, which is filling a plant pot containing a water plant. Choose a plant like cyperus, that is happy standing in water and won't mind being splashed. Wall water features are tricky to install but no more trouble than any other once they are in place.

Dry stream features
A dry stream makes a good water feature with no water at all. Mark out a narrow, winding bed, excavate it to 30cm (12in) deep and line with pond liner. Then refill with a mixture of good topsoil and well-rotted organic matter, leaving the level a few centimetres below the surrounding soil. Alternatively you can make use of a naturally occurring damp ditch, which you won't need to line unless the soil dries out completely at the bottom in summer. Plant occasional tufts of *Iris sibirica*, curly rush, candelabra primula and hosta for an architectural effect and cover the stream bed with pebbles. Use small pebbles for the very base of the stream and line the 'banks' with larger ones plus a few bigger boulders for decoration. In a wilder ditch situation you could risk growing more rampant plants like *Iris glutinosus* 'Holden Clough', sagittaria, *Mimulus luteus* and houttuynia. Apply water in dry weather.

Tub pools
Tub pools are a popular addition on the patio. You just need a large container like a half-barrel big enough to hold at least 45 litres (10 gallons) of water (that is five standard watering cans full). This will be big enough to house one miniature waterlily or a floating plant like water hyacinths and an upright marginal or two.

Pool construction

There is nothing particularly difficult about making a pond; it need not even involve digging a hole if you choose to have a raised water feature, but you need to spend time doing the job properly and without stinting on materials like top-quality liners and underlay. If a pool springs a leak once it is established, it can take almost as long to repair as it did to make in the first place.

Preformed pond shapes

Preformed pond liners come in a range of shapes and sizes including formal and informal, and some come complete with their own mini cascade. They can be fitted into a hole in the ground in the same way as a flexible liner, but you must dig a hole that fits the shape of the preformed pond fairly snugly. Check it is level, then line it with sand or underlay and slip the pond into place. Make sure it is a good fit so that the edge is completely supported all round and fill any gaps with sand. Alternatively, you can simply stand a preformed shape on top of the ground and build a wall around it for support. Fill the gap between the two with sand and finish off with a wide rim around the edge that you can sit on, which makes a good feature for a patio.

Cascades

A cascade can be bought as a preformed shape, or you can make your own using flexible pond liner. The aim is to create a shallow mini pool which is slightly above the level of the main pond, perhaps as part of a rock garden feature. Water runs from a lip on one side of the cascade into the pond, creating a good splash. You can produce all sorts of artistic effects with cascades. Use several, each slightly higher than the next, to make what looks like rapids or a mountain stream, or place a single one about 60cm (2ft) or so above the pond to make a small waterfall. However, the more water you need to move and the higher you want to move it, the more powerful the pump you will need. Read the small print in the pump maker's instructions to find out how to calculate the power required, and don't expect a small, cheap pump to work miracles.

Pebble fountains

Pebble fountains are much easier to install than you might think. You can sometimes find ready-made

units that need only to be sunk into the ground, rather like a preformed pond. They resemble an upside-down bowler hat, but bigger. The submersible pump sits inside the crown of the hat, with a perforated cover fitting over the top. After adjusting the height of the fountain's spout, you simply pile pebbles all round it to hide the cover, and perhaps plant a few water-loving plants around the edge in the splash zone. You can make your own pebble fountain out of large plastic containers with strong mesh grids over the top to take the weight of the stones. A small submersible pump is enough for this job.

Tub pools

Don't worry that your half barrel leaks when you first fill it up. Keep refilling it and eventually the wooden slats will expand and the tub will become watertight. Banish impurities from the inside by burning it with a blow-torch before filling it with water.

Leaves have a habit of collecting in tub pools and fouling the water. Clear them out by hand when necessary (a messy job but a vital one) and replace or replant marginals growing in pots as necessary. Rather than standing them on the base of the tub, stand marginal aquatics on upturned pots so that they are in shallow water. Topping up will be necessary in hot, dry weather.

MAKING A POND WITH A FLEXIBLE LINER

♦ Mark your pond shape on the ground with hosepipe – it can be as convoluted as you like, but for economy bear in mind that flexible liner is sold in oblong strips usually 2–2.5m (6–8ft) wide. When working out how much you need, add twice the maximum depth of the pond to the width and length, plus a little bit over, to allow room for it to sink down into the shape of the hole. Buy the best liner you can; butyl lasts longest.

♦ Dig out the shape, leaving a planting shelf about 30cm (12in) deep all around the edge, to plant marginals, or gently sloping sides for a wildlife pond.

♦ To prevent stones puncturing the liner when the weight of water presses down on it, spread 2.5cm (1in) of soft sand, several layers of newspaper or proper pond underlay over the inside of the pond. Then spread the liner out over the top and start trickling in water from a hose. As the water pulls the liner down into the hole, adjust the excess material so it is distributed evenly and wrinkles all around the pond instead of forming big pleats across the bends.

♦ Hide the edge of the liner by burying it in the ground and growing pondside plants to cover the join, or by laying paving up to the rim of the pool.

OPPOSITE: A formal raised pool that is surrounded by lady's mantle.
RIGHT: Alongside a large pool I've built a wooden jetty, where I can sit and watch dragonflies skimming the water and fish coming up for midges.

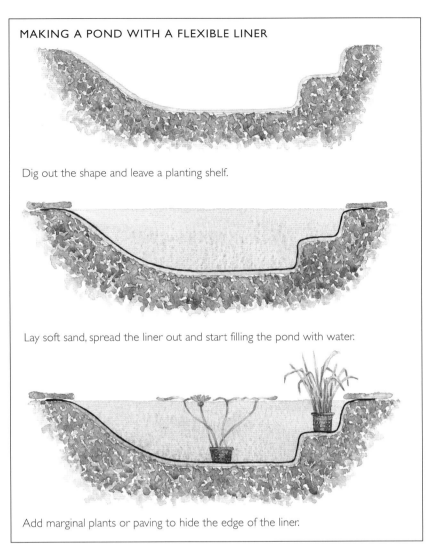

MAKING A POND WITH A FLEXIBLE LINER

Dig out the shape and leave a planting shelf.

Lay soft sand, spread the liner out and start filling the pond with water.

Add marginal plants or paving to hide the edge of the liner.

bog plants

Moisture-loving bog plants have a lifestyle and character that makes them perfect for pondsides, specially prepared bog gardens, ditches and other naturally watery places. They also provide the answer to any permanently damp places in the garden where nothing else grows.

Bog plants are those that like their feet to be wet but, unlike marginal plants, don't want to be sitting in a puddle of water all the time. Many bog plants such as lythrum and eupatorium are large, showy and spread fast, and are thus most suitable for a very natural or wild style of garden. Some, like *Gunnera manicata*, are enormous and architectural, too big for small gardens but valuable where space allows. Their summer foliage creates wonderful reflections in water and provides a good backdrop for seasonal flowers. Where space is short, there are quite a few smaller bog plants like houttuynia and mimulus that group together well to make a display with a watery theme, whether they are planted with water or not.

A bog garden is easily made in a low-lying part of the garden, with naturally damp soil, just by digging in plenty of extra organic matter to enrich it. If the ground starts drying out in a hot summer, you will need to keep it watered. Where the ground is not naturally damp, mark out a bed, excavate it to 60cm (2ft) deep and line it with pond liner or black plastic and fill it with a mixture of the original soil and lots of well-rotted organic soil matter. For a natural look, instead of planting densely as you would in a normal border, group the plants together around natural features like lichen-encrusted logs or a mossy tree stump.

TOP TO BOTTOM: Astilbe 'Venus', Iris sibirica, Osmunda regalis *RIGHT: The massive, prickly stemmed parasols of* Gunnera manicata.

Bog plants have striking foliage and spectacular flowers. They look best in bold groups: combine a good clump of foliage with a mixture of several different smaller-flowering plants for a natural look.

Darmera peltata (Umbrella plant)
1.25m (4ft) high x 2m (6ft) wide
Formerly known as peltiphyllum, this striking plant has leaves shaped just like open umbrellas that turn coppery-orange in autumn. In spring the flowers, which emerge from the mud long before the leaves, remind me of bright pink asparagus spears. Invaluable for its long season of interest, even though it does spread.

Equisetum hyemale
1m (3ft) high x 60cm (2ft) wide
Although this plant is related to the horsetail, which can be a terrible weed in

damp soil, don't be put off: this is a much better-looking and tamer version. The plump, green, quill-like stems have black rings along them; these are leaf joints, even though the plant does not have any leaves. A small clump makes a good architectural feature. It will spread in time, but is not difficult to keep under control.

Gunnera manicata (Giant rhubarb)
2.25m (7ft) high x 3m (10ft) wide
A huge, stately plant with enormous leaves and tall, thick, prickly stems – the backs of the leaves are prickly too. Despite its giant size it is a herbaceous perennial and dies back to a big, fleshy rootstock in late autumn. It is not as hardy as you might think, so collect up the dead leaves and use them with bracken or straw to protect the central mound in winter.

Houttuynia cordata 'Chameleon'
20cm (8in) high x 60cm (2ft) wide
This low-creeping plant can spread quickly in moist soil. Don't worry if it seems dead in spring; it does not emerge above the ground until much later than most herbaceous plants. The ivy-shaped, three-coloured leaves of red, cream and green make good ground cover under bigger plants or grown in drifts. It is also suitable for growing in containers.

Iris sibirica
45cm (1½ft) high x 30cm (12in) wide
A very versatile plant that is good for damp borders as well as bog gardens; it does not like the soil it is grown in to be as wet as most of the water-loving iris species prefer. However, it has the typical linear, upright foliage and characteristic three-cornered iris flowers. There are lots of named varieties in a good range of colours.

Juncus effusus 'Spiralis' (Corkscrew rush)
45cm (1½ft) high x 30cm (12in) wide
There are not many architectural bog plants but this is one of the best. The curly leaves grow in a spiral, making a large, corkscrew shape to about 60cm (2ft) high. Though the flowers are insignificant and look like little, brown tufts at the tips of some shoots in summer, the foliage is the perfect foil to upright stems of iris, smooth hosta leaves, and feathery flowers of astilbe.

Lobelia cardinalis 'Queen Victoria'
1m (3ft) high x 60cm (2ft) wide
Coloured foliage is a desirable characteristic for any plant, but it is quite unusual among bog species. The bold, reddish-purple leaves and upright stems of this plant keep their strong colour throughout the season and make a good background for the bright carmine-red flowers in mid- and late summer. It's not the hardiest of plants, so needs some winter protection. Look out for the more unusual 'Russian Princess' with its magenta-purple flowers and burgundy foliage.

Lysichiton americanus (Skunk cabbage)
1m (3ft) high x 1.25m (4ft) wide
The big, yellow, arum-like flowers of the skunk cabbage do have a bit of an odour, but planted the other side of a pond or in a big bog garden you notice only this plant's best feature without being overwhelmed by its worst. It flowers in late spring but has superb foliage that continues for the rest of the season, making a good background for colourful flowers. The leaves look particularly good reflected in water.

Osmunda regalis (Royal fern)
1.25m (4ft) high x 1.25m (4ft) wide
A large fern with upright stems of tiered foliage, some of which are topped in summer by odd-looking, brown tufts of what look like flowers, but which are actually the spores. It grows in sun or light shade, has golden tints during autumn, then dies down for the winter.

A-Z pool plants

Plants add the finishing touch to a pool, providing a fringe of flowers and foliage that blend it into the surrounding garden. The reflective surface of the water will show off their shapes and provide a good background for floating plants such as waterlilies. Plants are not only pretty, they also play a valuable part in the life of a pool. Ponds need plants to oxygenate the water, take up nutrients that would otherwise fuel algae and blanket weed, and provide shelter for fish and other water wildlife. Position your pond in full sun to help plants thrive, but avoid 'suntraps', which will cook the fish.

■ ***Aponogeton distachyos***
(Water hawthorn)
8cm (3in) high x 1m (3ft) wide
Water hawthorn provides a good alternative to waterlilies in a small pond. It has long, oval-shaped, speckled leaves that float on the water's surface. The clusters of white, waxy-looking flowers appear on their own strong stalks among the leaves from spring to late autumn and, unusually for water plants, smell strongly of vanilla.

The water hawthorn has dainty cockades of flowers that rise up above the floating leaves.

Cultivation Grow water hawthorn in planting baskets standing in water that is 30cm–1m (1–3ft) deep. Plants prefer growing in full sun in conventional ponds, but they also tolerate light shade and slow-running water (which waterlilies hate), making them particularly valuable for difficult water-garden situations. In a mild location plants may continue flowering quite well into winter and may retain their foliage all year round. In places where the weather is more severe, remove dead leaves to prevent them fouling the water.

■ ***Butomus umbellatus*** (Flowering rush)
1m (3ft) high x 60cm (2ft) wide
This is a distinctive plant with tall, upright, quill-shaped leaves and large heads of pink flowers in mid-summer. Even when it is not in bloom it is worth having for its handsome foliage. Flowering rush looks particularly good grown with sagittaria (arrowhead) due to the contrast in foliage shapes.

Cultivation A strong-growing marginal plant best kept in planting baskets and used in medium to large ponds. It grows in the margins of ponds in water up to

The marsh marigold, Caltha palustris, *is a British native that is happy with its feet in water.*

15cm (6in) deep. Lift, divide and repot into new aquatic compost every three years to prevent plants running out of vigour. Plants are rather invasive: they shed lots of seeds, which float and quickly establish new colonies all around pond margins, so be prepared for a spot of weeding.

■ *Caltha palustris* (Marsh marigold)
45cm (1½ft) high x 45cm (1½ft) wide
Marsh marigolds make a loose mound of leaves with flowers like giant, waxy buttercups in late spring at the edge of water. They do become a bit untidy later in the year, although they are fine for a wild garden pond. More compact cultivated versions with white or double flowers, such as *C. palustris* 'Flore Pleno' and *C. palustris* var. *alba* are more suited to polite garden ponds.
Cultivation These are lovers of shallow water, so grow them in planting baskets filled with aquatic soil in no more than 5cm (2in) of water at the very edge of a pond. You could also plant them in a bog garden alongside and let them spread from there. Divide and replant every three to four years when the clumps become too big or overcrowded.

■ *Eichhornia crassipes* (Water hyacinth)
23cm (9in) high x 23cm (9in) wide
A lovely, exotic-looking floating plant that forms small rafts of inflated, pale green stalks with waxy-looking leaves. Water hyacinth is mainly grown for its unusual body shapes in Britain, but if temperatures are warm enough, it will sometimes produce flowers. These are like sprays of yellow-blotched lavender flowers that resemble orchids, held just above the foliage in early autumn.
Cultivation Plants spread slowly and in warm countries can form sizeable clumps; however, they are killed by frost and in Britain they need to be overwintered indoors. Keep them through the winter in a bowl of water on a bright windowsill or in a heated greenhouse or conservatory, and transfer them back to the pond a few weeks after the last frost the following spring.

■ *Hottonia palustris* (Water violet)
25cm (10in) high x 75cm (2½ft) wide
An oxygenating plant with masses of ferny foliage that floats under the water, but unlike most oxygenators, such as Canadian pondweed, also has very attractive flowers. These exotically fringed, white flowers are tinged faintly pink around the edges and appear on spikes up to 60cm (2ft) tall in early summer.

Cultivation No need to plant, just drop a young plant into the water of an established pond. Thin out excess weed growth in time. Keep it away from pumps and fountains, which it can clog; in fact it prefers to be grown in completely still water. It dies away in winter to resting buds; remove dead foliage from the water.

■ *Iris laevigata* (Japanese water iris)
60cm (2ft) high x 30cm (12in) wide
Dense, clump-forming plants with typical sword-shaped iris foliage and three-cornered flowers in shades of blue, purple and mauve, sometimes streaked or stippled with white, in early summer.
Cultivation Plant in baskets of aquatic soil and stand in water 10–15cm (4–6in) deep around the edge of a pond. They can also be grown in a wet bog garden by the water's edge, but they cannot stand any lime in the soil. Plants spread quickly, so lift and divide large clumps every five years after flowering. Newly replanted clumps may take a year to

Iris laevigata *'Colchesterensis': handsome leaves and spectacular flowers.*

start flowering well again. If deadheaded after flowering to prevent them setting seed, they sometimes produce a few more flowers later in the year.

■ *Menyanthes trifoliata* (Bogbean)
23cm (9in) high x 60cm (2ft) wide
A wild flower that suits a very natural-style pond best; the spreading mat of leaves is a good way to blend a bog garden with a pond or hide the edges of a butyl pond liner. The plant's common name comes from the foliage and stems which look something like those of broad beans. The flowers are nothing like beans, though, and the spikes of fringed, white blooms that appear in late spring resemble water violets.
Cultivation Plant in baskets of aquatic compost and grow on planting shelves around the edge of a pond in up to 30cm (12in) of water or in a wet bog garden with rich but lime free-soil.

■ *Orontium aquaticum* (Golden club)
30cm (1ft) high x 60cm (2ft) wide
Slender, yellow-tipped white fingers of orontium that poke up out of the water in early summer always remind me of the Arthurian legend of the Lady of the Lake. (I'm still waiting for it to hand me the sword.) The thick, oval leaves float on the water's surface when the plant is grown in deep water; in shallower water they stand upright, which does not look so good but will not harm the plant.
Cultivation Grow in planting baskets filled with aquatic soil, and lower new plants into position in the pond in spring. Orontium grows in water up to 45cm (1½ft) deep and is slow-growing and non-invasive. Don't let it become swamped by larger and faster-growing water plants, or disturb it until it badly needs dividing and replanting, which probably won't be more than every four or five years.

■ *Pistia stratiotes* (Water lettuce)
5cm (2in) high x 8cm (3in) wide
The velvety, green rosettes of the water lettuce look almost unreal, as they sail majestically across the surface of a pond powered by a light breeze. This is the perfect plant for anyone who has ever played with toy boats in their bath. It also makes a pleasing feature floating in a bowl on a table in a bright conservatory.
Cultivation Simply float a few plants out over the surface of the pond any time during the summer; plants are available in water plant centres from early to late summer. In a warm season they can increase slowly by offsets. They are frost-tender, so in a cold climate they should be replaced each year or overwintered inside – put a couple into a jar of water and keep them on a windowsill or in the greenhouse.

■ *Pontederia cordata* (Pickerel weed)
75cm (2½ft) high x 60cm (2ft) wide
The only popular water plant with true-blue flowers, pickerel weed also has a very long flowering season – from early summer to early autumn or slightly later. The large, upright, rather heart-shaped leaves act as niches housing each of the upright flower spikes, making it very distinctive.
Cultivation Grow it in planting baskets submerged under 15–30cm (6–12in) of water. Plants tend to be invasive, so this is one that is best kept to a reasonably big pond. It can scramble ashore, rooting itself into the muddy edges of a pond or even a bog garden, and become quite a nuisance, but plants that are not protected by a few centimetres of water over the top in winter may not always survive. Lift and divide congested plants in spring.

■ *Sagittaria sagittifolia* (Arrowhead)
60cm (2ft) high x 45cm (1½ft) wide
Large, perfect, arrowhead-shaped leaves make this an easy plant to identify, even when it is not in flower, though the tall, upright stems of three-petalled, white flowers are very conspicuous in mid-summer. Its architectural shape makes it the perfect partner for the narrow, needle-like foliage of flowering or stripy rush.

The pickerel weed (pontederia) is valued for its blue flower spikes in summer.

Cultivation Even when confined to planting baskets, arrowhead will produce floating tubers in autumn. These spread around the pond, giving rise to new colonies which appear spontaneously in the middle of other clumps of plants the following year. Fish them out when you spot them to prevent it becoming too invasive, or use one or two to replace old plants when they outgrow their space; otherwise lift and divide the original plants every few years.

■ *Schoenoplectus lacustris* subsp. *tabernaemontani* 'Zebrinus' (Stripy rush)
1m (3ft) high x 60cm (2ft) wide
The distinctive, white-ringed foliage of this architectural rush make it a firm favourite with water gardeners. It has a bad habit of losing its variegation after a few years, so re-pot plants when this happens to restore the variegation.

Cultivation Plant three plants several centimetres apart in a large planting basket filled with aquatic soil in spring for an instant display as this plant does take time to spread. Submerge the basket in anything from 2.5–30cm (1–12in) of water in a very sunny spot. Lift and divide after three or four years when the basket is full, or re-pot plants if they have turned to plain green.

■ *Stratiotes aloïdes* (Water soldier)
30cm (12in) high x 30cm (12in) wide
An odd plant with a lifestyle that sounds like pure science fiction, as it alternately floats and sinks throughout the year, moving around like an aquatic triffid. The plant makes a rosette of spiky, evergreen leaves. It sinks after flowering, produces offsets and reappears, then sinks again to spend winter on the floor of the pond, where the foliage acts as an oxygenator.
Cultivation Float a plant on the water in late spring and from then on simply catch it towards the end of summer and remove excess offsets to prevent the pond being overrun. Hardy in all but the coldest winters.

■ *Typha minima* (Lesser reedmace)
60cm (2ft) high x 30cm (1ft) wide
A miniature version of the plant commonly, but mistakenly, called bulrush, with typical rushy stems and soft brown, cigar-shaped flower spikes. These can be cut and dried for winter arrangements indoors, but provide late-season interest if left growing in the pond.
Cultivation Grow in planting baskets placed on shelves around the pond margin in water up to 30cm (12in) deep. In a natural-looking pond, the plants look best grown about 30cm (12in) apart to form large drifts like wild reedbeds. *Typha minima* is less invasive and better proportioned for small ponds, but larger species are also available which look more in scale in a big pond.

Ferns and hostas enjoy the moist and shady sides of a waterfall.

waterlilies

With their familiar dinner-plate leaves that float on the surface and huge, cabbagy flowers in a range of colours, waterlilies are classic plants for a water garden. Their distinctive flowers adorn still waters from early summer until well into autumn and there are plants in all sizes to suit every situation, from a full-blown lake to a family pond or even a small tub on the patio.

Waterlilies do not just look good, they actually improve the condition of the water in a pond. The shade provided by their leaves deters blanket weed and prevents the water overheating in summer, as well as providing valuable cover for fish and other pond life. Water snails commonly deposit their eggs – slimy, transparent, slug-shaped 'packages' – on the undersides of the big leaves, where they provide an easy meal for fish.

Most people choose to grow waterlilies for their appearance; despite their exotic looks, they behave much like any perennial garden plant. They start growing in spring, flower all summer, then die down in autumn to overwinter as rhizomes safe from the frost in their planting baskets well below the water's surface where they cannot freeze. When the plants grow too big or their planting baskets become overgrown with roots, they need lifting and dividing in much the same way as border plants. Take the basket out of the water in April, just as the plants start making new growth. Divide up the rhizomes, throwing out old, dark or woody-looking ones, and replant a healthy section of young roots into fresh aquatic compost. Then cover the compost with 2.5cm (1in) of gravel to keep it weighted down (otherwise fish will disturb the roots by sucking and blowing at the soil around them). Water well to consolidate the compost around the roots, then lower the basket back into the water.

Choose carefully before buying a waterlily, as they range enormously in vigour and there are relatively few varieties that are compact enough to grow in shallow water or a small pond. I would recommend only a couple for growing in tub pools. The wrong plant will swamp its surroundings within a year or two. Waterlilies need a sunny situation and will not tolerate moving water or being splashed by a fountain or waterfall, so attempt them only in still ponds.

Nymphaea 'Froebelii'

A very free-flowering, blood-red waterlily for a small pond. Its flowers start out tulip-shaped before opening to the true starry waterlily shape. Grow it in 23–30cm (9–12in) of water and it will cover about 1m (3ft) square.

Nymphaea 'James Brydon'

One of the most popular varieties ever, with mauvish-red, cup-shaped flowers and purple-flecked foliage. One of the few waterlily varieties to thrive in light shade for part of the day, it is also ideal for a small to medium-sized pond. Grow it in 30–45cm (12–18in) of water; it will cover an area about 1.25m (4ft) square.

Nymphaea 'Laydekeri Lilacea'

The smallest-growing, pink-flowered waterlily, with flowers that darken in colour as they mature. The small leaves are flecked with purplish-brown. It is ideal for a very small pond or a tub pool, where it grows happily in 15–23cm (6–9in) of water. Since a small volume of water warms up quickly, this can give rise to better early and late flowering.

Nymphaea 'Marliacea Albida'

Another very popular variety, this one has large, white, scented flowers up to 15cm (6in) across with slightly wavy edges to the leaves. It is quite a big plant, more suitable for a medium-sized pond, and needs to be grown in 30–60cm (1–2ft) of water, where it will cover an area at least 2m (6ft) square.

Nymphaea 'Marliacea Chromatella'

This vigorous-growing waterlily is suitable only for a large pond, but the big, golden, chalice-shaped flowers, set off by marbled foliage, are very freely produced. Grow it in 45cm–1m (1½–3ft) of water and allow it plenty of room to develop. It needs direct sun all day long to thrive.

OPPOSITE LEFT: Nymphaea *'Froebelii'*
OPPOSITE TOP: Nymphaea *'James Brydon'*
LEFT: A Monet-style pool awash with waterlilies.

Nymphaea 'Pygmaea Helvola'

One of the real miniature waterlilies, with small-scale, yellow flowers and tiny, freckled leaves. It thrives best in 10cm (4in) of water so long as there is a large enough volume of water to prevent it heating up too much in the sun and literally cooking the plant. This makes it an ideal variety for growing in a tiny patio water feature or tub pool. However, it is also happy in a basket of aquatic compost in a normal pond: place it on a couple of bricks to keep it at the right planting depth.

Nymphaea 'Rose Arey'

A free-flowering waterlily with large, perfumed, pink flowers and attractive foliage, which has a purplish-red tinge when it first emerges. A moderate grower, it needs a medium-sized pond and water 30–60cm (1–2ft) deep. Expect it to cover an area of 2m (6ft) square or more.

Nymphaea 'Sioux'

The unusual-coloured flowers of this variety change from light buff to bright amber as they mature. A reasonably compact variety suitable for a small pond; in 30–45cm (12–18in) of water it is likely to cover about 1m (3ft) square.

Nymphaea tetragona alba

Another winner for the smallest ponds, this variety has tiny, white flowers with leaves in proportion. It enjoys the same growing conditions and situations as N. 'Pygmaea Helvola'. Avoid the red-flowered variety of N. tetragona as it does not flower very well.

Nymphaea 'Vesuve'

Mid-green leaves forming a clump 1.25m (4ft) across are decorated with bright red stars, centred with orange stamens. The blooms darken with age and are scented.

Nymphaea 'Virginalis'

The leaves are bronzed when young, becoming pale green, and the scented, starry flowers are white with yellow centres. Makes a clump up to 1.25m (4ft) across.

Pool problems solved

Some aquatic problems can be avoided by doing the right thing from the start, but others are inevitable and need tackling early to prevent them spoiling your enjoyment of the pond. Like most areas of gardening, the longer you leave them, the worse they get.

Green water

This is caused by millions of tiny, one-celled algae, and it always happens when you make a new pond. Normally it rights itself within about six months as the natural balance of the pond is established. Green water can also be caused by topping up the pond with a large amount of tap water, for instance if it leaks, or after the pond has been cleaned, or if nitrogen fertilizers or soil leach into the pond. In established ponds, water may turn green in spring before water plants cover the surface. If it is a constant problem, it may be due to too much sun on the water, so add more plants to cover up to two-thirds of the water's surface. You can also buy chemical or bacterial products for clearing the water; I'd rather get the balance right.

Blanket weed

This is another form of algae which forms filamentous strands like handfuls of green cotton wool that hang in the water. Avoid blanket weed by washing new plants, pre-used planting baskets or anything that you put in a pond before they go into the water so you don't introduce it, though it can be spread by birds. Remove blanket weed regularly by twisting a stick into the fibres and lifting it out, shake out any tadpoles and fish fry, then put it on the compost heap – it is a rich source of nutrients.

Fish problems

Don't be tempted to overpopulate the pond: 2.5cm (1in) of fish to every 30cm (1ft) square of water surface is about right. Goldfish and shubunkins are the best species for a small pond; koi need very large ponds. Check fish over carefully before buying them and reject any with white fungal spots, external parasites or obvious injuries or that appear to be sluggish. If there are existing fish in the pond, it is also a good idea to quarantine new fish, for a week or more, in a separate container of water. Use a net to remove dead, injured or sick fish as soon as they are seen; this prevents them contaminating the water and infecting the others. Keep herons away using a 'trip wire' 10cm (4in) high stretched around the edge of the pond and make sure fish have plenty of water plants for cover – even if the birds do not take the fish, they often injure them. In hot weather oxygen levels in the water drop, so if fish are seen gasping, run a fountain or a fine spray of water from a hosepipe over the surface to oxygenate the water.

A pool rimmed by the juicy, blue-grey leaves of Hosta sieboldiana, *happy left undisturbed for years.*

RENOVATING A POND

After five to 10 years you will probably find that there is a lot of silt and other debris in the bottom of the pond into which water plants root and spread fast. When this happens it is probably easier to clear the pond out completely and virtually start again. This can be done in early spring, but if frogs or fish are breeding (and they often start as early as late winter), shake the tadpoles and fish fry into a bucket or leave some water in the deepest part of the pool. Alternatively, clean out your pond in late summer or early autumn when disturbance is less critical.

♦ Remove all the planting baskets, divide overcrowded plants and repot after washing everything well in clean water. Try to remove all traces of duckweed.

♦ Empty as much water as you can out of the pond; you can often use a submersible pond pump, or create a siphon with a hosepipe, instead of bailing it out with a can.

♦ Either catch fish and put them in a bucket, or leave some water for them in the deepest part of the pond.

♦ Clean out all but 5cm (2in) of silt from the pond, removing water weeds as you work. Remove any fallen leaves and rotting vegetation.

♦ Take care not to damage the pond liner and don't stand inside the pond – work from the edges. If you have to stand in the pond, take off footwear and go barefoot!

♦ Finally, refill the pond. Make up a few bundles of Canadian pondweed, weight them with stones and put them into the water; they will sink to the bottom. Replace the planting baskets and fish.

A small formal pool with waterlilies and a Japanese maple providing shade for fish.

HOW TO AVOID PROBLEMS

♦ Use ramshorn snails to keep the pond clean. They feed on decaying plant material and fish waste and do less damage to water plants than freshwater whelks, which are the commonest water snails.

♦ Cover a pond with netting in autumn and winter. This keeps out dead leaves which rot and foul the water, and protects fish from herons – remove it in spring.

♦ Thin out excess Canadian pondweed every few weeks in summer to prevent it choking the pond, and collect up surplus floating tubers of sagittaria (arrowhead) in autumn to stop it spreading out of control.

♦ Remove spotty or decaying leaves of waterlilies and marginal plants otherwise they will foul the water.

Vegetables

The key to success in growing vegetables is not to take on more than you can comfortably manage. Choose varieties for flavour or those that are expensive or difficult to buy. With careful planning, you can pick something tasty for a meal all year round without too much work.

When I started gardening for a living, I never thought I would see the day when vegetable growing was fashionable. But now everybody is at it. Many professional people are even taking on allotments for recreation, and so-called 'designer' gardens are not complete without a potager, which is just a posh name for a decorative vegetable bed planted so that the crops make pretty patterns. This sort of fashionable garden suits fashionable vegetables, like the latest pencil beans, white onions, baby varieties such as mini leeks and those tiny patty-pan squashes that look like baby turtles.

Even small gardens can have vegetables in raised or deep beds. The beds are made deliberately narrow so you work from the paths round the edge without treading on the soil and they are incredibly high-yielding, as the crops grow in compost. This means the plants can be grown much more closely together than usual, so the crops act as ground cover and need less weeding. You can harvest twice the veg from half the space in a quarter of the time.

Even if you don't have enough room for a raised bed, you can still grow decent vegetables in containers. The secret is to grow the most productive crops possible, like runner beans, outdoor tomatoes or new potatoes. Or you can grow salads: go for compact kinds like 'Little Gem' lettuce, which you can plant as close as 10cm (4in) apart, or the cut-and-come-again sort like 'Salad Bowl', where you don't cut the whole lettuce but just pick a few leaves at a time and let the rest of the plant keep on growing.

With vegetable growing, the right technique is essential. Start by planning what you are going to grow and where. It is a good idea to divide the area into three so you can rotate crops instead of growing the same thing in the same place every year. This helps to prevent a build-up of diseases that affect certain types of plants as crops are always being moved on to fresh ground. Also, by growing together crops that need similar conditions, you will save yourself work and have a better harvest. Don't try to follow the advice on crop rotation you'll read in Grandpa's favourite vegetable-growing book. Nowadays we don't want to spend time growing tons of maincrop carrots, potatoes and onions. We want things he probably didn't grow much, like salads, courgettes, sweetcorn and outdoor tomatoes, which just do not figure in a traditional crop rotation plan.

ABOVE: Rhubarb and forcing pots LEFT: *Courgettes and tomatoes.* RIGHT: *Here's proof that a vegetable garden can be colourful as well as appetizing.*

A modern cropping plan (see mine on page 235) follows the old principles, but can be adapted to suit a more diverse vegetable selection. Here's one such option. On one plot dig in manure the winter before planting and feed with liquid tomato feed during the summer. Here plant dwarf French beans, mangetouts such as the variety 'Sugar Snap', sweetcorn and outdoor tomatoes. On another plot dig in only very well-rotted manure or use old growing-bag compost the autumn before planting, and feed with chicken manure pellets during spring and summer. Here you can grow courgettes, brassicas, lettuce, endive, radicchio, spinach and oriental leaf vegetables like Chinese cabbage and pak choi. The third plot does not need manure added to it; instead dig in blood, fish and bone fertilizer in spring before sowing. This provides suitable conditions for growing leeks, beetroot, spring onions, radishes, salad carrots and kohl rabi. If your vegetable plot is so small that it is not possible to rotate your crops, then just grow what you like

ABOVE: French marigolds grown with tomatoes can help keep them free of whitefly. BELOW: A classic 'potager'-type vegetable garden.

HOW TO GROW YOUR OWN LETTUCES

1 Any patch of ordinary soil that is in full sun can be used to produce your own fresh lettuces. Push in a taut garden line into the soil to mark the row and flick out a shallow drill with a garden cane.

2 Sprinkle the lettuce seeds into the drill quite thinly so they rest about 0.5cm (¼in) apart and then rake back the displaced soil to cover them. Water them in and don't let the soil dry out for the next two weeks.

3 Hearting varieties need thinning to around 15cm (6in) apart when they are large enough to handle, but the 'Salad Bowl' types can be left unthinned and cut as needed. Re-sow every three weeks for a succession.

where you can and hope for the best, but try to avoid planting the same thing in the same place for two years running.

There are two ways of growing vegetables: by sowing seeds where you want the crops to mature and by transplanting young plants. In both cases you need to have a good seedbed ready in advance. Dig the ground, sprinkle over a general fertilizer like chicken manure pellets or blood, fish and bone and rake thoroughly, removing any stones and big lumps of soil. After planting or sowing, water the ground well.

Sowing

Sowing seed where you want a crop to grow suits things that don't like being transplanted, particularly root crops. It is also useful in summer when you are growing crops like lettuce and other salads and French beans, as they don't transplant well in hot weather. Always sow vegetable seeds (see above step by step for how to grow lettuces) in straight rows: besides looking better, it makes it easier to hoe weeds out later. Use a straight edge, like a garden line or the handle of a hoe, as a guide. After sowing, cover big seeds like peas with about 1cm (½in) of soil, less for smaller seeds. If your soil is light and sandy or heavy clay, it is a good idea to sprinkle seed compost along the drills to cover the seed, otherwise the seed may dry out or have difficulty getting through. Then, after the seeds germinate,

you need to thin the seedlings to give those that remain room to grow. The safest way to do this is in several stages, a few at a time, until they eventually reach the right spacing.

Planting

Raising young vegetable plants under cover means you have to sow them in pots or seed trays, then plant them out and keep them watered for quite a while afterwards. This may seem time-consuming, but it has its advantages. It is very useful if you want early crops, as you can start them in the greenhouse weeks earlier than you could sow them outdoors. This is essential for crops like tomatoes, sweetcorn and courgettes that you can't plant outdoors until after the frosts are over. If you sowed seed of these straight in the garden, you would hardly have time to start eating your crops before the autumn frosts killed the plants.

Planting seedlings is also a handy way to stop birds or mice pinching your early pea and bean seeds, which is what often happens when you sow them straight into the garden. Plants like leeks, cabbages, sprouts and other brassicas, which are perfectly hardy, can be sown in an outdoor seedbed. You should concentrate your plant propagation into a small area, leaving most of the space for maturing crops. Then as crops are harvested and space becomes available, transplant your seedlings into their final growing position. And for anyone who

My own kitchen garden in Hampshire, filled to bursting with a little of everything.

does not want to grow their own, garden centres sell a good range of young plants. You can also buy baby vegetable plants as plugs (individual seedlings in a plug of potting compost) through the post.

Growing in containers

It is amazing just what can be grown in containers. The more decorative crops like runner beans, red, frilly lettuce and purple dwarf French beans are the ones to grow where they are going to be on show. Tomatoes need a warm, sunny spot, like a corner of the patio, and climbing crops like runner beans and outdoor cucumbers need trellis to scramble up.

All sorts of containers are suitable. You can use large pots or tubs, troughs or growing bags, whatever is most convenient. Do start each season with fresh compost in containers and new growing bags, though you can use the same compost several times over, for instance, if you are growing several quick crops like dwarf French beans, lettuce, spring onions and radishes. Vegetables grown in containers must be well watered. If they dry out, you will ruin the crop or possibly even kill the plants. They also need feeding regularly; I use liquid tomato food at about half-strength for everything.

Aftercare

To grow vegetables as good as the ones you buy in the shops you need to give them regular attention. This is why it is better to grow small quantities, so you get to eat the lot rather than trying to grow more than you have time to look after properly. The secret of success is to keep vegetables growing steadily without letting them dry out and without becoming choked with weeds.

Water the plants well in dry spells. I like to water in the evenings in hot weather, so that the water does not evaporate before plants have had a good drink. Top up the nutrients by liquid feeding or sprinkling a little more fertilizer along the rows and watering it in, once or twice, while they are growing. Weeds can be kept down by frequent hoeing, so they do not compete for food and water. Start picking crops like lettuce as soon as the first one is big enough to use, and work your way through the rest in the row as they reach a usable size. Sowing little and often is the best way to avoid a glut of crops that you can't freeze.

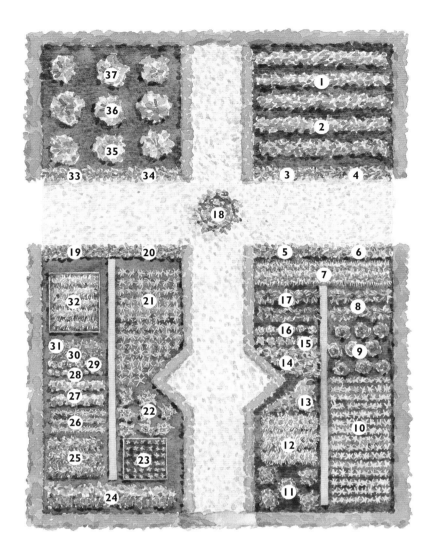

Alan's kitchen garden plan

1. Potato 'Red Duke of York'
2. Potato 'Rocket'
3. Step-over apples 'Greensleeves'
4. Step-over apples 'Fiesta'
5. Step-over apples 'Cox's Orange Pippin'
6. Step-over apples 'Egremont Russet'
7. Strawberry Eros
8. Swiss chard 'Fordhook Giant'
9. Calabrese 'Landmark'
10. Leek 'Firena'
11. Mint
12. Florence fennel 'Cantino'
13. Coriander
14. Turnip 'Snowball'
15. Lettuce 'Frillice'
16. Lettuce 'Cerize'
17. Ruby chard 'Charlotte'
18. Nasturtium 'Salmon Baby'
19. Step-over apples 'James Grieve'
20. Step-over apples 'Discovery'
21. Onion 'Red Epicure'
22. Tomato 'Gardener's Delight'
23. Brassica Seedbed
24. Climbing French bean 'Kentucky Blue'
25. Mange-tout pea 'Ambrosia' and purple-sprouting brocolli 'Claret'
26. Spring onion 'Guardsman'
27. Broad bean 'The Sutton'
28. Lettuce 'Little Gem'
29. Lettuce 'Lollo Rossa'
30. Lettuce 'Salad Bowl'
31. Rocket
32. Carrot 'Amini'
33. Step-over apples 'Blenheim Orange'
34. Step-over apples 'Bountiful'
35. Courgette 'Gold Rush'
36. Courgette 'Bambino'
37. Cabbage 'Spring Hero'

HOW TO GROW POTATOES IN POTS

1 If you have no vegetable plot but love a few early potatoes, grow some in large pots. Choose a variety such as 'Foremost' and sprout them by placing them in egg boxes or seed trays on a bright windowsill.

2 Plant them in late winter at the rate of two or three to a large flowerpot of soilless multipurpose compost. Half fill the pot, put the potatoes in and then cover with compost so that the pot is just over half full.

3 Stand the pot in a cool but well-lit greenhouse or porch. As the shoots grow, top up with more compost and water as necessary. Harvest them about ten weeks later and enjoy fresh new potatoes.

Organic gardening

Organic gardening means growing things as naturally as possible, without chemicals, artificial fertilizers, weedkillers or pesticides. In my own garden I am almost entirely organic, but I prefer, when necessary, to use chemicals rather than those that are non-selective but organically derived.

Bulky organic matter

The first essential of organic gardening is that you feed the soil, not the plants. Instead of using a bag of artificial fertilizer, you add huge amounts of organic matter to the soil which is broken down by naturally occurring soil bacteria, releasing nutrients in the process to provide plant food. Any form of bulky organic matter is fine so long as it comes from a chemical-free source – garden compost and manure are the most popular and widely available. Organic matter supplies lots of valuable trace elements which are not usually provided by bags of fertilizer. This is thought to be why organically grown crops have a better flavour. However, organic matter alone does not provide enough of the three main plant nutrients N, P and K (see pages 38–40), which is why an organic source of these important nutrients needs to be added to the soil as well, especially in high-yielding areas like a vegetable garden.

Ruby or rhubarb chard is a colourful and tasty vegetable. Cooked separately, the stalks supply one vegetable and the leaves another.

Organic feeds

Blood, fish and bone or pelleted poultry manure are the organic alternative to a gardener's general-purpose fertilizer. Use them when preparing soil before planting and to feed crops during the growing season. You can sprinkle them around fruit trees and bushes or between rows of vegetables, then water them in. For vegetarians, and anyone who prefers not to use products containing animal remains, there are also a few general fertilizers using ingredients with wholly vegetable origins. If you can't find any at your local garden centre, try an organic mail-order supplier. Use vegetable-based feed in exactly the same way as blood, fish and bone. When it comes to liquid feeds, organic gardeners have a wide choice. Liquid seaweed extract contains little N, P or K, but is a very good source of trace elements and acts as a general plant tonic. Use it mixed with other liquid feeds, or well diluted on its own as a foliar feed. Liquid feeds made from manure, comfrey or fish by-products are also available from specialist organic gardening supply firms.

Home-brew

Lots of organic enthusiasts like to make their own home-grown plant feeds. You can make a good general liquid feed by dunking a sack of well-rotted manure into a water-butt and leaving it for a few weeks. For a high-potash feed for tomatoes, and other flowering or fruiting plants, make your own comfrey brew. You will need to cultivate a few comfrey plants: I recommend Russian comfrey; *Symphytum × uplandicum*. The strain called 'Bocking 14' has especially high potash levels. A word of warning here: comfrey is very invasive and can become a rampant weed. Confine it in a small area with sunken boards to prevent its spread. Cut armfuls of comfrey leaves during the summer and push them into a water-butt; fill it to the brim with water and put the lid on. By the time the comfrey has rotted, the water looks dark brown and really smells like it would do a bit of good. You can make a similar high-nitrogen brew using nettles – a good example of natural recycling in action.

The idea is to dilute any of these home-made brews with water to the colour of weak tea before giving them to plants, but I wouldn't recommend using them for seedlings or young plants, as there's no way of telling the true strength. You can't use home-brews like a bottled liquid feed where you don't know the precise nutrient levels and dilution rate.

HOW TO AVOID PESTS AND DISEASES

◆ **Barriers** Use fine crop-protection mesh to cover crops that might be at risk, burying the edges of the mesh in the soil to prevent hard-to-tackle pests, like carrot and cabbage root fly, brassica whitefly and aphids, reaching their target crop.

◆ **Traps** Use pheromone traps to lure male codling moths to a sticky end before they can fertilize the females, causing maggoty apples and plums – hang the traps in the trees in early summer.

◆ **Hand picking** Pick off caterpillars and diseased leaves whenever you see them. To avoid a bigger outbreak of blackfly, nip out the growing tips of broad beans when a good crop has set.

◆ **Grow strong, healthy plants** Well-grown plants in organic-rich soil withstand pests and diseases better than weak plants.

A colourful vegetable plot of cabbages, parsley, borage, coriander and sweetcorn.

✎ top tip

To stop nitrogen being washed out of the soil in winter, sow crops that are known as green manures, such as grazing rye, tares or field beans, in late summer after earlier crops have been cleared. These crops are chosen because they store nitrogen in their leaves through the winter. Six weeks before you want to prepare soil for planting and sowing in spring, mow the crop to chop the foliage, then dig it in to add nitrogen to the soil. Green manuring improves the condition of the soil wonderfully. Nitrogen can also be added in the form of a high-nitrogen fertilizer, such as sulphate of ammonia, applied at the rate of 1 clenched fistful to the sq m (sq yd) in late winter.

ORGANIC SOLUTIONS

Weed control Mulching, hand weeding and hoeing are important. Also use paper mulches in the vegetable garden.

Organic pest and disease remedies Use sulphur candles for greenhouse fumigation; liquid sulphur for mildew; yellow and green sulphur powder for protecting dry onions and bulbs from storage rots; pyrethrum and derris for most common plant pests; aluminium-sulphate-based products for killing slugs.

Biological control You can control vine weevil and slugs with nematodes supplied as freeze-dried powder. Hoverflies, centipedes and spiders are beneficial; frogs and toads take slugs and bluetits feast on greenfly.

Pest- and disease-proof varieties Calabrese resistant to club root, greenfly-proof lettuce and tomatoes immune to root diseases are already available through seed firms. Check with suppliers for new varieties of fruit with built-in resistance.

Companion planting The idea of growing plants to ward off pests from vegetables works by using nectar-rich flowers to attract insect predators that feed on greenfly, and by providing distracting scents that stop pests homing in on target plants. Good companions include garlic planted with roses, onions with carrots, and marigolds with tomatoes.

Herbs

Herbs are multi-purpose plants that can keep you supplied with everything from kitchen condiments to home-made pot-pourri. Grow herbs all round the garden, with flowers in borders, as edgings around formal beds and even in pots on the kitchen windowsill.

If you are a keen cook, you already know the culinary herbs. Parsley, sage, rosemary, thyme and chives are probably the most popular, and many people have a clump of mint at the bottom of the garden to flavour new potatoes. But now, thanks to all those exotic cookery programmes on television, everyone wants to grow things like lemon grass, Thai basil and coriander leaves too.

If you are starting to grow herbs for the first time or have limited space, it is a good idea to choose the ones you know you are going to use. Most herbs are very easy to grow.

Herbs can be grown in a cook's corner in the garden, or you can keep them in a large container by the back door: after all, no one wants to grope their way down to the end of the garden in the dark just for a sprig of rosemary. It's funny the way herbs creep up on you. Once you have a few, you'll find yourself wanting to grow more, and, before you know it, you will have collected tarragon, fennel and several different types of mint too. There are many different mint varieties aside from the classic mint-sauce kind, spearmint, *Mentha spicata*, which has narrow, pointed leaves. Apple mint, *M. suaveolens*, which has fat, furry leaves, brings out the flavour of peas and spuds. Or you could grow eau-de-Cologne mint, *M. piperita citrata,* which smells exactly as the name suggests. A few sprigs in a jar of water in the kitchen make an effective air freshener and you can even have fresh mint over winter (see page 240). As you become increasingly interested in herbs you will find yourself buying the sorts that you use only occasionally, like basil and chervil, only to discover that they rapidly become kitchen essentials and you need lots more. This is when it's time to start raising your own from seed (see pages 258–61) and also to stop and think how best to house your growing collection.

The geometric shapes of traditional herb gardens originates in medieval monasteries, where the monks grew medicinal herbs in oblong beds with paths in between. This is an extremely practical arrangement, as it keeps each variety separate and provides easy access in all weathers. Today's formal herb gardens are usually based on a round or square shape divided up into segments to make a series of individual beds, each planted with a mixture of herbs. Nowadays we grow mainly culinary kinds plus a few scented plants like lavender, chamomile and the apothecary's rose, *Rosa gallica* var. *officinalis*, which was once used medicinally but is now more likely to end up in pot-pourri. The geometric shapes of this type of herb garden look even more obvious because of the gravel or paved paths running through it. Each individual bed can be outlined with dwarf clipped box or lavender hedges, or fancy edging tiles with terracotta knobs at each corner. A sundial or bird bath in the centre will complete the symmetrical look. Herb nurseries will often provide plans for a traditional herb garden, complete with planting suggestions, though it is good fun designing your own on squared paper using a pile of herb catalogues for reference.

You don't have to grow herbs in such a formal way; it is possible to keep quite a comprehensive stock outside the back door by grouping containers together to make a potted garden. A strawberry pot with planting pockets in the sides as well as the top makes a good way to grow a lot of different herbs

ABOVE: Pot marigolds and borage – two herbs that are hardy annuals. RIGHT: A garden filled with herbs is at its decorative best in early summer when flowers are opening and scents are rich. Make sure you preserve supplies for winter to capture these summer flavours.

HOW TO HAVE FRESH MINT FOR WINTER

1 Dig up an existing clump of mint. (Overcrowded clumps can be dug up, divided and replanted in autumn. Replant them in sunken bottomless buckets or pots to restrict their spread.)

2 Tease out some of the fattest and healthiest runners (stems just below the surface, which may already have roots forming). Snip them with secateurs or snap them off by hand.

3 Space out the runners in a tray of potting compost and cover with 2.5cm (1in) of the mixture. Water and stand it in a porch or cool greenhouse. Shoots will be produced all winter.

in small quantities. Strawberry pots are better than the herb pots you sometimes see, as they are bigger so they hold more compost and don't dry out so fast. It's a good idea to grow mint in a pot of its own; if you mix it with other herbs it takes over.

Some herbs, like creeping thymes and marjoram, have a natural hanging habit and are good for baskets or round the edge of a big planter.

The blue flowers of borage mix happily with ox-eye daisies and pot marigolds in a colourful herb garden; use them to float on your glass of Pimms.

Although the most useful cooking herbs tend to look very green, you can add plants like red-leaved basil, *Ocimum basilicum* 'Dark Opal', variegated pineapple mint, *Mentha suaveolens* 'Variegata', pineapple sage, *Salvia elegans* 'Scarlet Pineapple', which has spikes of red flowers and pineapple-scented leaves and nasturtiums to make a potted culinary garden look prettier. Some of the bigger herbs like rosemary, French lavender and bay look good enough to plant in normal garden beds alongside flowers or shrubs. Angelica has a bold, architectural shape that looks good in a big, perennial border or even a wild garden. Essential cooking herbs can also be housed in a corner of the vegetable garden. Grow parsley and chives, which you are likely to need a lot of, as an edging alongside the path where they are also easiest to pick. Or if your garden soil is not naturally well-drained, make a raised bed for them.

One of the prettiest ways of growing mat-forming plants like creeping thyme and the non-flowering chamomile *Chamaemelum nobile* 'Treneague' is to make a herb seat. This is just a raised bed, with a back and arms, that you can sit on. Since the herbs are gently crushed each time you sit down, they release their fragrance on demand, which is very soothing.

To grow well, most herbs need a sunny, sheltered spot with soil that is not too rich but is well-drained. The perennial herbs, like sage, pot marjoram, rosemary and tarragon, keep going for

years without needing much work. Regular picking tends to keep them compact, but if you don't cut them very often, it is a good idea to trim them back once a year to stop them getting leggy. Start trimming them the first year after planting, as evergreen herbs hate being cut back into old wood.

Chives will flower if you do not keep them regularly cut, but the mauve globes are very pretty and edible, so you can use the petals in salads. The plants die down in winter, but you can cut extra supplies in summer and freeze them chopped up in a plastic food container, or just dig up a clump, pot it and keep it on the kitchen windowsill, where it will soon start growing again.

Mint likes richer and damper soil than most herbs, but needs watching as it is terribly invasive. The best way of growing it is in a large flowerpot, sunk into the ground so that the rim is 5cm (2in) above ground level. This stops the mint creeping out over the top. Grow mint in containers and, to stop the compost drying out on hot summer days, stand the pots in large saucers of water. Annual herbs like chervil, dill, coriander, basil and parsley, which goes to seed in its second year, all need sowing each spring.

Parsley is notorious for being difficult to germinate. According to an old wives' tale you should sow it in the nude by the light of a new moon. The truth is that it germinates best in warmth, so I sow mine in a pot in the propagator where it grows happily. It germinates well on a warm windowsill indoors too. Don't believe all

Herbs are not simply plants to be grown for foliage – some of them have spectacularly colourful flower heads of great stature. Here the herb garden at Wisley is enlivened by clumps of clary sage, Salvia sclarea.

those tales about parsley not transplanting. It transplants easily while it is small. You can prick the seedlings out singly into small pots, or sow it thinly and just plant the whole clump out without breaking it up. This way you get a good-sized clump of parsley more quickly than usual. If you do have to sow parsley directly into the garden, there is one tip that really works. Pour boiling water along the drill before you sow. This warms the soil up, then, after letting it cool for a few minutes, sow the seed as usual.

Exotics like ginger and lemon grass really need a warm greenhouse or conservatory to grow in. They both make untidy plants with wide, grassy leaves that are too big for a windowsill indoors, though you could stand them outside in a warm, sheltered corner for the summer. To grow ginger, just plant a chunk of fresh root ginger from the greengrocer's; choose a large piece with a fat growth bud and put it in a pot of seed compost to take root. You can also root stems of fresh lemon grass in a glass of water. Pot them when they begin to root. Lemon grass is also easily raised from seed on the windowsill and pricked out into pots when it is big enough. Spares of this and all herbs are always popular for charity garden stalls. You may even help someone else get hooked on herbs.

Fruit

Gnarled, ancient fruit trees add a touch of character to a garden. If you don't have any old ones, plant some new ones – fruit bushes too – which you can make look very ornamental and delight in the feeling of self-sufficiency they give you. You will also enjoy some pretty delicious home-grown fruit.

I know a lot of people shy away from growing fruit because they think it takes up a lot of room and they don't have time for all the pruning and spraying. Well, nowadays you can get fruit trees growing on dwarfing rootstocks that keep them compact throughout their whole life. Not only do they take up very little room, but you don't need a ladder to pick fruit any more. You can train trees flat in a fan shape to grow against a wall or use cordons or espaliers as garden dividers to screen off a greenhouse or vegetable garden. You can even get horizontal, low-growing, 'step-over' trees, which make fruitful edgings to beds and borders, and there are exotic species that you can grow in pots on the patio.

As well as the shapes and sizes of the trees, growing techniques have changed. Now you can avoid maggoty fruit without spraying by hanging up codling moth traps in early summer. Fruit growing has never been simpler – or more fun.

Fruit cultivation

You will need suitable growing conditions for a successful crop. Choose a sunny, sheltered spot with deep, rich, fertile, well-drained soil. No fruit will do well in waterlogged ground or thin, chalky or sandy soil, and only a few kinds put up with windy or shady conditions. However good the soil, dig in lots of compost or old manure before planting. It is the only chance you will get, since most kinds of fruit live for many years. Early spring is the best time for planting, but you can plant pot-grown fruit trees and bushes in summer and autumn too. If you choose to plant in summer, you will need to keep new fruit trees well watered for the rest of the season.

Caring for fruit is not all that different from looking after trees and shrubs. Mulch and feed all fruit trees and bushes generously every spring, as they are notoriously heavy feeders. Keep the plants well watered while the fruits are swelling. This is especially important with the more shallow-rooted kinds like strawberries, redcurrants and gooseberries and for fruit in pots. If they dry out badly, you may find that the developing fruits fall off and you have wasted a whole season's work.

Apples and pears

If I could only have one fruit tree in my garden, it would be an apple. Not only do you get fantastic blossom in spring, but also reliable crops of fruit with a variety of culinary uses. Actually, it is a much better idea to grow two or three apple trees if you can. You need several different varieties to make sure they are all pollinated – otherwise you won't have a good crop. That does not mean you have to fill your garden with apple trees. Choose trees growing on dwarfing rootstocks, as they will stay small and start fruiting within a few years of being planted. If space is short, grow a family tree which has several compatible varieties grafted on to one trunk, or grow cordons, planted 60cm (2ft) apart, to make a fruiting screen. You can grow a single half-standard tree in the lawn if a neighbour has an apple tree or even a flowering crab apple that is a suitable pollinator within bee-range (about 45m/147ft).

Pears are probably the second most popular garden fruit tree. A really ripe pear must be one of the best fruits you can find but, some varieties can be tricky to grow well. You need a warm, south-facing wall and one of those melt-in-the-mouth varieties like 'Williams' Bon Chrétien' or 'Doyenné du

ABOVE: Peaches grow well against a warm and sunny wall.
RIGHT: Our 'Brown Turkey' fig tree crops well most years, but needs a good summer to ripen the fruits.

There's something comforting and very British about an apple tree laden with rosy fruits – fit one in if you possibly can.

Comice' trained flat as fans or espaliers against it. These both ripen in autumn, but they need other varieties close by for pollination or you won't have a crop. Most people opt for the old favourite, 'Conference', as it is easy to grow and does not need a pollinator. So if you want only one, or would like it to grow as a free-standing tree, this is the best choice.

Other tree fruit

Plums are always popular. My advice is stick to the tried-and-tested 'Victoria', which you can either eat fresh or cook. It gives enormous crops and, as it is self-fertile, you don't need another variety as a pollinator. Buy a tree grown on Pixy rootstock, which makes a medium-sized tree, as there is no very dwarfing rootstock available. Still, it will provide somewhere to sling your hammock.

Cherries were once suitable only for a huge garden, but now dwarfing rootstocks are available which make them viable as small garden trees. Choose a modern, self-fertile variety like 'Stella' or 'Sunburst' – and watch the adverts in gardening magazines, as new ones keep appearing all the time. The best way to grow cherries is as fan-trained trees against a wall, so you can fix bird netting over them. Put this up in plenty of time as birds will eat cherries under-ripe. Without it, you'll never taste a single one.

When buying plum or cherry trees, choose a well-shaped one, with four or five strong branches evenly spaced out all round the trunk and you should not need to do any serious pruning. If you ever need to thin out overcrowded branches, both plums and cherries should be pruned only in summer to avoid the risk of silver-leaf disease.

Figs, peaches and nectarines are worth considering only if you have a sheltered, south-facing wall, otherwise the fruit is unlikely to ripen properly. If you have, grow fan-trained plants and prepare the ground well before planting. The foundations and rubble at the foot of a wall usually mean the soil is poor, and fruit needs good ground. Dig out a trench 60cm (2ft) wide all along the wall and fill it with a mixture of well-rotted manure or compost and topsoil. In the case of figs, it is a good idea to make a bed about 100 × 60cm (3 × 2ft) lined with bricks, or old sheets of corrugated tin, to stop the roots wandering. Unless they are restricted, figs tend to grow big and leafy without producing much fruit.

Peaches and nectarines are martyrs to a disease called peach leaf curl, which makes new leaves turn red and curly. A bad case can weaken the tree so much it hardly fruits. If your trees suffer from it, the only remedy is regular spraying with a copper-based fungicide. If it is rife in your area, grow apricots instead – and they are hardier, so you can grow them as free-standing trees.

Bush fruit

There are two kinds of soft fruit, the sort that grows on bushes, which are usually nice and tidy, and the sort that grows on canes, which are not. Bush fruits like redcurrants and gooseberries are the easiest to accommodate if you don't have much space. They can be trained into cordons against a wall, grown as standards, which look pretty enough to put in a flower garden, or simply left to grow as bushes. If you want blackcurrants, grow them as bushes as they don't suit fancy training. Opt for a compact blackcurrant like 'Ben More' or 'Ben Sarek' if space is short; these varieties are also unlikely to be hit by frost, a useful bonus in a cold areas. One or two of each sort of bush fruit is probably enough for most people as long as you are not on holiday when they fruit!

ABOVE: *Autumn fruiting raspberries such as 'Fallgold' are a treat worth looking forward to at the end of the season.*
BELOW: *Damsons make wonderful jam and can be grown as part of a country hedge. This is 'Langley Bullace'.*

Cane fruit

Cane fruits like blackberries and loganberries take up an awful lot of room, but you can fit them into a modern garden by growing them along the fence. If you have chain-link fencing, tie the canes out along it to make a productive fruiting barrier to shelter the garden from wind, which these tough canes do not mind. As they are so prickly, they provide a good vandal- and pet-proof garden boundary too. Training the stems out this way makes the fruit easy and relatively painless to pick apart from the ones that do not grow on your side. If you have wooden fences, you could follow the same technique along wires and grow a thornless variety (though I think the flavour of prickly varieties is better).

Raspberries

Summer-fruiting raspberries have to be grown in rows, supported by posts and wire, which is fine if you have plenty of room. They are rather time-consuming. Each summer, just after the fruit has been picked, you need to cut down the old canes that carried fruit close to ground level and tie in the new canes to their supports as it is these that will crop next time round. Feed, mulch and dig out any canes growing up in the path and you are ready for another year.

The newer autumn fruiting raspberries are much less work and, I think, are more worthwhile, since they ripen after the summer raspberries have vanished from the shops and fresh raspberries are not available. Autumn varieties, such as 'Autumn Bliss', do not need to be grown in rows – a solid bed of them will take up less room. They grow only 1–1.25m (3–4ft) tall, so they do not need rows of posts and wire to hold them up. As for pruning, you just chop the lot down to about 5cm (2in) above ground level in early spring. Chuck a bit of mulch and some general fertilizer down round them and, apart from picking the fruit, that is all you have to do. Even the birds do not seem to go for autumn raspberries in the same way they do summer ones. As far as I'm concerned, innovations in fruit growing do not get much better.

Potted fruit

If your garden does not provide ideal conditions for growing fruit in the ground – perhaps it is on heavy clay, very shady or in a windy area – you may still be able to grow fruit in pots on the patio. In a sunny, sheltered corner surrounded by heat-reflective walls and paving, most fruit trees will do very well. This is probably the only place in the garden you can grow more exotic, warmth-loving types like lemons, which are particularly rewarding.

Big pots are essential. You can use terracotta or plastic, but they should be at least 38–45cm (15–18in) in diameter. Large half-barrels and big, decorative containers are ideal. Plant in spring or early summer. Use John Innes No. 3 potting compost and keep fruit trees well fed and watered all summer, particularly while they are carrying fruit. If you let them dry out, they have a nasty habit of dropping their crop. (An automatic watering system saves no end of work.) A shot of liquid tomato feed, diluted at normal tomato strength, at least once a week will provide enough nutrients. After the fruit has been picked, stop feeding, and reduce watering for the winter.

Hardy trees can be left on the patio all winter, though it is a good idea to secure the trunks to trellis or a fence to stop them blowing over. Raise the pots off the ground, so they are not standing in puddles of water after heavy rain – those little pot feet are ideal. If you get a long spell of freezing weather in winter, it is wise to group the trees close together and pile bark chippings over the pots for

A fair crop of strawberries can be obtained even if the plants are grown in pots, and this way the fruits are held clear of the ground and of slugs.

frost protection, or stand them temporarily in a garage or shed because, if the compost freezes solid, it can kill the roots. This does not happen when fruit trees are grown in the ground, as the soil acts as insulation so the roots stay safe. In pots, the roots are above ground and much more exposed.

Every second or third year, repot fruit trees in early spring. They can go back into the same pot after you have teased out the roots and given them some fresh compost. In the years when you don't repot, top dress by scraping away the top 2.5–5cm (1–2in) of old compost and replacing it with fresh.

Apples and pears

Apples and pears on very dwarfing rootstocks do well in pots. The specially trained columnar trees (upright cordons), that bear fruit along the length of a single vertical stem, are particularly good. These single-stemmed trees are available in many of the popular varieties, such as 'Cox's Orange Pippin', 'Fiesta' and 'Gala' apples and 'Conference' and 'Comice' pears. They are very productive and easy to look after and, because of the way they are trained, you can stand a row against a wall with the edges of the pots touching, to give you a complete potted orchard that takes up hardly any more space than a couple of hanging baskets.

Peaches and figs

Patio peaches are particularly outstanding. They have full-sized fruit, but on trees that are genetic dwarfs and don't need any pruning. If you want figs, choose 'Brown Turkey' to grow in a pot outdoors. Let it grow as a bush or make it into a standard tree. Growing a fig in a pot restricts the roots and keeps the plant much more compact than if it were planted in the ground, and you can harvest huge crops from quite a small plant. You can also move the tree into a sunroom or cold greenhouse in winter for protection, which helps ensure bigger and better crops. Keep potted figs well fed and watered in summer, but let the compost remain almost dry in winter when the trees lose their leaves.

Citrus trees

If you have space in a heated greenhouse during winter, you can grow all sorts of citrus fruit in pots to stand on the patio in summer. Lemons, oranges, kumquats and limes are attractive, evergreen trees that have scented flowers and can give quite a good crop of fruit, which usually ripens towards the end of summer. They need careful watering: let them start to dry out, then give them a thorough soaking. They hate being constantly saturated, and require a high-nitrogen liquid feed from late spring to late summer. Special citrus plant feeds are available, otherwise use general-purpose liquid feeds – not tomato feed. These trees are a bit prickly and I'm always snagging my sweater on mine, so if they grow too big, give them a light prune just before bringing them in for the winter; it helps to keep them a good shape too. As citrus plants will not stand any frost, keep them in a frost-free greenhouse or sunroom from early autumn until a couple of weeks after the last frost in spring. They'll usually start flowering while they are inside and the fragrance is a real knockout.

Strawberries

Strawberries are among the easiest and most decorative fruits to grow in pots. Forget the Ali Baba jar with planting pockets built into the sides. It is too big. Use ordinary 25-cm (10-in) half-pots instead. Fill them with John Innes No. 3 potting compost and plant them up with young, pot-grown plants in spring. Stand them in the sunniest spot on the patio. When the flowers are over and tiny green fruits start to form, cover them loosely in fine, insect-proof mesh or crop-protection fleece (not the frost-proofing sort) or make a cage out of canes and drape bird-proof netting over it.

The same plants can be left in these pots for two or three years, as long as you keep them well fed. Strawberries need plenty of potash, so give them liquid tomato feed once a week all summer. When the plants need replacing, tip everything out and start again with new plants and new compost. It's a productive way of growing strawberries and makes them much easier to pick. You'll also find that the fruits don't rot as they do on the ground, and even the slugs have to be pretty acrobatic to get a look in. A few pots brought into the greenhouse in early spring will carry early fruit.

I love growing citrus trees. Their scented blossom fills the conservatory in winter and when stood outside in summer they bring a touch of the Mediterranean to my Hampshire garden.

Undercover gardening

Gardening under cover can double the season for crops like tomatoes, show off your warmth-loving pot plants, over-winter frost-tender plants and raise young plants from seed or cuttings. A greenhouse is the most popular form of cover, but a cold frame and heated propagator are useful extras.

A greenhouse puts you firmly in charge. No longer does bad weather create complete mayhem with your gardening schedule. There is always something you can be getting on with. Inside, you have complete control over the climate. In summer, automatic ventilators and liquid shading painted on over the glass help to keep the air cool and damping down keeps it humid. In winter, an electric fan heater with a built-in thermostat keeps the temperature above freezing and a layer of bubble plastic fixed inside the roof acts as insulation, keeping heating costs down. The most economical minimum temperature for winter, that suits a wide range of normal greenhouse plants, is 4°C (40°F).

Throughout the year, not only are plants protected from rain and wind, but a greenhouse also provides shelter for gardeners when the weather is not too good outside. This is particularly useful in late winter and early spring, when there is a lot of seed sowing to be done.

Heated propagators

If you already have an electricity supply in the greenhouse for heating, invest in a heated propagator. It is as good as having your own little nursery. This useful gadget has its own independent heating system that lets you provide the high temperatures needed for seeds to germinate. You can use a heated propagator in an unheated greenhouse to keep frost-tender plants safe for the winter, without spending money heating the whole greenhouse. If you use a heated propagator in a greenhouse that is itself heated to around 4°C (40°F), the propagator is capable of keeping an even higher temperature inside, which will allow you to start tomatoes and bedding plants into growth early. I use mine virtually all the year round to raise all kinds of exotic flower and shrub seeds, along with tomato plants, peppers and cucumbers that will grow in the greenhouse for the rest of their lives, and for growing bedding plants and vegetable plants for the garden too. It also comes in very handy for rooting cuttings and providing extra heat as an occasional 'intensive care ward' for sick houseplants, or anything that needs a bit of extra care.

ABOVE: A passionflower blooms reliably in a cool greenhouse.
LEFT: The propagator is the boilerhouse of the garden, a place where you can raise masses of plants from seed and cuttings and save lots of money. RIGHT: One man and his greenhouse – divided into three sections which are heated to different temperatures. Luxury!

worthwhile investment, adding extra under–cover growing space and acting as a half-way house between greenhouse and garden conditions where young plants can acclimatize gradually – known as hardening off. To harden plants off just move the trays of biggest seedlings into the cold frame from the middle of spring until after the last frost, when it is safe to plant them outside. Open the lid for ventilation during the day and close it at night to keep plants snug. Without a cold frame, the only way to harden off seedlings is to keep moving them outside on fine days and back into the greenhouse at night. This is labour intensive and does nothing to ease congestion in the greenhouse.

When it is not being used for hardening off, a cold frame is very handy for growing summer crops like cantaloupe melons, which like a bit of warmth but don't need the height of a greenhouse. Let melons scramble over wire netting, which will keep them raised off the ground so the fruits do not rot. And in autumn, you can use a cold frame for overwintering sweet pea seedlings, or for growing winter lettuce, spring onions or corn salad. Once you have had a cold frame for a complete growing season, you will wonder how you ever managed without it.

Cold frames

By the time you have filled the propagator with pots of seed and pricked out the first crop of seedlings, it is easy to find yourself running out of greenhouse space. Trays of young plants take up far more room than pots of seed. If you grow lots of vegetables and bedding plants a cold frame is a

PROPAGATORS FOR SOWING SEEDS IN WINTER

1 The cheapest type of propagator on the market consists of a standard plastic seed tray fitted with a Perspex dome, but it lacks the bottom heat that can speed up the germination of seeds or the rooting of cuttings.

2 Larger heated propagators are fitted with a thermostat. Seed trays can be stood inside them, or the base can be filled with cuttings compost. Good ones cost only a penny or two per hour to heat.

3 A top-of-the-range, long, narrow propagator with a heated base will fit neatly on to a windowsill. Each of the small trays, fitted with transparent domes, is ideal for sowing seeds or for sheltering about half a dozen cuttings.

Edible crops

Tomatoes are the one thing almost everybody grows in their greenhouse at some time or another. Although you can grow tomatoes outdoors, you will get only about three trusses of ripe fruit even in a good summer and green tomatoes are good only for making chutney. Under glass, you should produce twice that many trusses in an unheated house and even more in one that is heated. I reckon that you average about 0.6kg (1½lb) of tomatoes per truss, which means two or three plants are about enough for most families. One of the best reasons for growing your own tomatoes is flavour. You can choose your favourite varieties, plant them in the greenhouse border soil enriched with plenty of well-composted manure, keep them fed with liquid tomato feed and seaweed extract or chicken manure pellets and leave the fruits on the plant until they are completely ripe. They have a flavour quite unlike anything you can buy in the shops.

Once you have grown tomatoes, you will find peppers and aubergines just as easy. Grow them in exactly the same way, but instead of training a single main stem up a cane and taking out sideshoots as you do with normal greenhouse varieties of tomato, treat them like bush tomatoes. Just tie the plant to a short stake to support the main stem and let all the sideshoots grow as they all carry fruit. Cucumbers are no harder, but as they grow on tall, fast-growing vines, the plants need twisting round strings tied to the roof for support. Remove any male flowers which don't have the distinctive swelling at the base, or grow an all-female variety so that cucumbers don't get pollinated. Greenhouse-grown cucumbers that have been pollinated are full of hard seeds and taste bitter.

Greenhouse pot plants

The way to get the widest possible use from the glass-to-ground type of greenhouse is to put a path along the middle, leave one side as a soil border and cover the other side with paving slabs to support staging. Two-tier staging is best as it gives you twice the amount of surface space. In spring, use the staging to park your propagator and trays of seedlings and in summer use it to display a collection of flowering pot plants. Put sun lovers like regal pelargoniums, osteospermum and heliotrope on the top tier, and use the shadier second storey for plants such as streptocarpus, fuchsias and ferns that hate too much direct sun. This is also the place to keep newly potted-up plants for a few days while they re-establish, as well as small seedlings, young cuttings and anything else that needs protection from bright sun. In late summer, take cuttings of

Not only is a greenhouse useful, but it can also look good in the garden. This Victorian-style greenhouse makes a handsome focal point.

HOW TO MAINTAIN YOUR GREENHOUSE IN SUMMER

1 Provide shading to protect plants from scorch. Whitewash can be applied to the glass, or roller blinds can be lowered during bright sunshine.

2 Ensure the greenhouse is ventilated well. Open side ventilators to allow a through flow of air, as well as ridge ventilators to allow hot air to escape.

3 Besides regular watering, pot plants need a weekly feed of dilute liquid fertilizer: tomato feed for those in flower, general food for foliage plants.

half-hardy perennials from the garden, root them in pots or trays and keep them in a frost-free greenhouse over the winter. This will save you buying new plants and preserve space as cuttings take up less room than old plants dug up to store; I always find young plants from cuttings grow and flower much better than old, woody ones too. Even a greenhouse that is left unheated in winter can be kept looking decorative by growing pots of hardy cyclamen, spring-flowering bulbs and early alpine plants like saxifrages.

Scented pelargoniums are wonderful plants for a cool greenhouse, providing rich fragrances as well as colour.

Seasonal greenhouse care

Spring is the busiest time as the propagator needs watching so that seedlings are pricked out on time and watered as necessary. In summer, take down the insulation and paint liquid shading over the glass or invest in blinds. Use capillary matting so that pot plants can be watered by running water on to it – much quicker than watering pots individually. Plants still need feeding individually. Water tomatoes, peppers and aubergines with liquid tomato feed at the normal dilution rate, and pot plants at half that strength. Alternatively mix slow-release food into the compost before potting, or push feed sticks into the pots so plants are fed automatically as they are being watered. Damp down on hot days to keep the air humid, and watch out for pests.

As the weather turns cooler in autumn, clear the greenhouse out. Pull up the old tomatoes and put pot plants outside, remove summer shading, clean the inside of the glass and wash staging. Put up bubble-wrap insulation in the roof. (You can also cover the sides, though this can create condensation.) Put your pot plants back after cleaning the pots, evicting snails and removing dead leaves. Check the greenhouse heater is working. Gradually reduce the watering. In winter, the workload is at its lowest since plants are just 'ticking over' and some are actually dormant and need only enough water to stop them shrivelling. Use a thermometer to check the heater is maintaining the correct temperature.

Portable protection

If you want to get vegetables off to an early start or keep them going late in the year, they need to be sheltered from bad weather by some form of portable cover. Besides extending the growing season, covers will also insulate plants from light frost, harden off bedding plants, save fruit from birds and protect crops from pests.

Cloches

A cloche is like a hand-held greenhouse. Instead of putting plants inside it, you place it over the plants. Modern plastic cloches are lightweight, safe and easy to move; the old glass sort, although attractive, are cumbersome and breakages can be dangerous, leaving bits of broken glass in the ground. For early vegetable crops, sit a row of cloches in place over soil at the start of spring. This warms it up ready for sowing seeds. Leave the cloches in place until the plants fill them or the weather is warm enough. Use them again in autumn to cover late crops to keep them growing as the temperature drops. Cloches are also useful in a poor summer: place them over newly sown seeds or young plants for a few weeks.

Mini greenhouses

If you don't have room for a normal greenhouse, you can buy a small, lean-to type that fits against a wall, like an upended cold frame with shelves. Plants and seed trays fit on the shelves, and you open up the front for watering and ventilation. You can get sophisticated versions in cedarwood and inexpensive plastic versions with roll-up fronts. Being very compact, they are ideal for tiny gardens, giving you enough room to harden off bedding plants or raise a few seedlings and young plants. Without the shelves, they can be used to grow tomatoes. You can even put a small heater inside to overwinter pelargoniums and other tender plants.

Poly tunnels

A cross between a cloche, a cold frame and a greenhouse, a poly tunnel is not everyone's cup of tea as it is not particularly attractive, but it is a very useful accessory for a keen vegetable gardener or plant propagator. Use it for summer crops like tomatoes, peppers and cucumbers, and for hardening off bedding plants. It is also good for growing early and late vegetables, which you plant

Cloches are tremendously useful for providing instant crop protection on the vegetable plot. This one is made from corrugated Perspex.

in the border soil of the tunnel where they remain until they are harvested. A poly tunnel makes a handy propagation unit for raising hardy annuals and vegetable plants in spring, and for rooting and growing on young hardy plants and shrubs. It is also very useful for providing winter protection for pots of patio shrubs and climbers that need shelter from wind or rain in winter.

Fleece and netting

This portable protection is available in many different guises. Woven polypropylene fibre fleeces are obtainable in different weights. The heavyweight types give a few degrees of frost protection and are used to throw over plants on cold spring nights to protect soft, young growth from frost damage. Lightweight versions are more like very fine, spun netting and provide protection for fruit and vegetable crops from pests like flea beetle and brassica whitefly; these can be put over plants immediately after planting and left on for the life of the crop for complete protection. (It is an organic alternative to spraying vegetables with chemicals.) Coarser plastic netting is used for climbers like runner beans to climb up, and a heavier-duty version to cover fruit cages. Choose small-mesh netting to cover soft fruit to protect it from birds.

✔ Do remember to water and weed plants under cloches regularly – weeds grow faster than usual and plants will dry out faster due to the warmth and better growing conditions.

✔ Do use fine insect-proof mesh to 'filter' out pests on vegetable crops. Make sure the fleece covers the crop completely and bury the edges in soil along each side of the row so nothing can creep in. Also check that vegetable plants are pest-free before covering them.

✔ Do put bird netting in place while fruit is still small and green, this discourages birds from investigating further.

✘ Don't leave cloches over crops in hot weather, and ventilate polytunnels or mini greenhouses well, otherwise plants will literally cook.

Good crops for cloches or poly tunnels

A huge range of crops thrive given an early start under cloches or grown permanently in a poly tunnel. Crops grow faster due to the extra warmth, so they need feeding and watering more often than when grown outside, but this also means you can get an extra crop or two from the same space during the growing season. To make the most of this very intensive way of growing vegetables, have another set of plants ready to put in as soon as you clear each row. Here are a few ideas for using a poly tunnel or cloches:

Spring Sow spring onions, radishes, lettuce, forcing varieties of carrots, such as 'Amsterdam Forcing', and turnip 'Tokyo Cross' for a crop of baby turnips about 8–10 weeks later. Plant calabrese; all varieties crop early and fast under cover and give huge crops.

Late spring About three weeks before the date of the last expected frost in your area you can plant early potatoes, courgettes (all varieties do well under cover) and outdoor varieties of tomato. Cover with fleece for extra protection on cold nights.

Early summer Plant greenhouse varieties of tomato, cucumbers, melons, peppers, chillies and aubergines in a polytunnel. For cloches, choose outdoor varieties.

Late summer Sow or plant oriental cabbage, pak choi and other oriental leaf crops; sow fast-maturing lettuce such as 'Little Gem'.

Early autumn Plant overwintering cauliflowers such as 'All The Year Round' or 'Alpha' for a spring crop when they are expensive in the shops; sow lamb's lettuce, overwintering spring onions and, if you take a gamble on it being a mild winter, sow early carrots and mangetout peas for an early spring crop.

✎ top tip

Sow little and often to avoid crops such as lettuce going to seed because they are all ready to eat at the same time. You'll also get sick of eating the same vegetable, so sow a few seeds of lots of different things for variety.

Conservatory

A conservatory is a living room, patio and greenhouse in one. It is the only way of enjoying a garden with guaranteed good weather all year round, without leaving home or hanging around an airport for hours. You are in complete control of the climate. Just add plants and furnishings to taste.

Conservatories are available in a range of styles, so you can choose one that complements the design of your house, whether it's Victorian, high tech or traditional. You may find it is not too expensive to have one individually designed to fit an awkward site or unusual property. Adding a conservatory to your house may also improve its value. Check with the local planning authority before you build.

Some people use their conservatory mainly as a plant room, filled with tender exotics grown in borders or on staging, with just a couple of garden seats and a table where they can sit and enjoy morning coffee in a subtropical garden atmosphere. Lots more use theirs as a spare living room, dining room or children's playroom which just happens to be decorated with plants. And some even use a conservatory to house a swimming pool, spa bath, tropical water gardens, or their collection of orchids.

A conservatory allows you to create a permanent garden-room setting using the sort of furniture and plants that would not survive if you left them permanently outdoors. So all your cushions and cane are quite safe, as well as your oleanders.

Without heat

Even without any form of heating, a conservatory tends to stay just about frost free in winter because the glass roof acts as a big solar panel and the brick walls store up heat rather like a night storage heater. The room also traps heat escaping from the house. So in winter you can grow indoor plants that enjoy cool temperatures like cyclamen, azaleas, freesias and lachenalias. You can also bring in plants in pots to add a splash of colour: try spring bulbs, early alpines like saxifrages, and camellias, tree peonies and Christmas roses. The comparative warmth of the conservatory will force flowers so you can enjoy them earlier than outdoors and unblemished by bad weather. Put them back outdoors after they have finished flowering.

In summer, patio plants like brachyscome, argyranthemum and osteospermum make up colourful containers. Take the opportunity to grow the more delicate annuals like coleus and the big, double, frilly-flowered, grandiflora-type petunias that never do very well out of doors.

OPPOSITE: Fleece will offer protection to crops early in the year.
BELOW: My conservatory is kept just free of frost in winter and is a great place in which to have lunch or supper all the year round.

Dedicated gardeners can grow a grape vine in a heated or unheated greenhouse and enjoy succulent crops for dessert.

With heat

If you want to sit in the conservatory comfortably all year round, it makes sense to put in some form of heating. A radiator connected to the domestic central heating is probably the best idea if you want to keep the conservatory at room temperature. Otherwise it is quite easy to have a power point installed so you can plug in an electric greenhouse heater.

Once you have heating, the sort of plants you can grow depends on how much heat you are prepared to provide. If you decide to keep it at room temperature, virtually any tropical plants, including houseplants, will be perfectly happy, as long as you can keep the conditions roughly the same as those indoors all year round. Tropical houseplants prefer shady conditions and reasonably steady temperatures, which can be pretty hard to provide in summer when the sun is on the glass. Keep the temperature down with a combination of shading and ventilating: make sure you have adequate ventilators, blinds and circulating fans to maintain comfortable conditions.

The easiest kinds of plants to accommodate are the true conservatory plants. These are tender flowering trees, shrubs and climbers that need a bit of background heat in winter to keep them just above freezing, about 5–10°C (40–50°F) is fine. But in summer they are happy to enjoy the warmth, with the temperature going up to 30°C (85°F) or so during the day and dropping at night. Ideal conservatory plants to grow include all the popular daturas, oleanders, bougainvillea, orange and lemon trees, and more unusual types such as tibouchina and passionflowers that you will probably have to buy from conservatory plant specialists. You can even grow unusual plants from seed and have a unique display of exotics.

Specimen plants

Large specimen plants make a good focal point in a conservatory. In a garden room they add a touch of drama to the back of a big group of plants, but if yours is the sort of conservatory that is more for people than plants, a few good-sized specimen plants growing in tubs will probably be all the greenery you need. They are certainly much easier to look after than lots of small pots.

Something big and bold such as the florists' mimosa, *Acacia dealbata*, makes a pretty indoor tree with lots of feathery foliage and scented balls of fluffy, yellow flowers in early spring. Oleander is another good, large plant; it can be grown as a tree or shrub, and has spicy-scented flowers all summer and autumn. The ones you see planted as street trees around the Mediterranean usually have pink flowers, but conservatory specialists have varieties with yellow, apricot, orange and red flowers too. There is even one with variegated leaves called *Nerium oleander* 'Variegatum'.

For a striking specimen, try datura, which we should now call brugmansia; it is especially attractive when trained as a standard. A datura grown in this way will be neat and won't take up too much room. Specialist nurseries keep a whole range of named varieties with long, trumpet-shaped flowers in various colours, but my favourite is *Brugmansia aurea* 'Grand Marnier' which has strongly scented, burnt-orange flowers well into winter.

Climbers

Climbers are the perfect way to cover the inside walls of a conservatory, but if you grow suitably vigorous ones you can also train them out along the roof timbers so they create dappled shade, which helps to keep the conservatory cool in summer. Grape vines and fan-trained figs give a conservatory an authentic Mediterranean look and, if you garden in a cold area, this is the most reliable way to grow your own fruit.

Plumbago is always popular but, left to itself, makes an untidy, sprawling sort of shrub. The best way to grow it is trained on a wall, tied to trellis. This way you can space the branches out and keep it tidy. Several slightly tender jasmines are worth growing just for their scent, though the flowers look lovely too and in a warm conservatory the perfume can be almost overpowering.

Bougainvillea really is the perfect conservatory climber. It needs a cool winter to flower well the next year, but in summer does not mind if the temperature soars. It will even put up with the odd missed watering without dropping dead. And if you don't have room on the wall, you can always train bougainvillea into a flowering pyramid by growing it in a tub with the stems fanned out over a topiary frame. There are also some naturally dwarf varieties which are ideal for growing in hanging baskets.

Shrubs

Conservatory shrubs can either be grown in large pots and tubs, or grouped together in a soil border for more of a Kew Gardens effect. Abutilons have big, vine-like leaves and lots of large, brightly coloured, bowl-shaped flowers; I like them because they flower virtually all the year round and are very easy to grow. Bottle brush is a real stunner from Australia with big spikes of bristly, red flowers. Lantana and fuchsias are also a great way to provide lots of colour, but they do attract whitefly. If you grow these, it's a good idea to stand them outside on the patio in summer. Citrus plants like oranges, lemons and kumquats can also be stood outside if you want to make space for other plants in summer, and they certainly look very glamorous on the patio. But the larger, fruiting kinds like pink grapefruit, or unusual kinds like variegated lemon, which has stripy leaves and variegated fruit, are a bit more delicate and are best kept permanently under cover.

Growing conservatory plants

The conservatory year starts in early spring, when plants in containers need repotting. Tease out some of the old compost and put them back into the same pot, or one just a size larger, using John Innes No. 3 compost. Plants growing in soil borders, or those that you don't want to repot, should be top dressed. Carefully scrape away the top few centimetres of old compost and replace it with new John Innes No. 3. Avoid repotting plants like clivia, hoya and streptocarpus, as these flower best when

they are slightly pot-bound and may not flower for several years in a container that is too big for them.

As the weather warms up and plants begin growing faster, feed and water them generously. I like to use half-strength liquid tomato feed on flowering plants, but a general indoor plant feed would be fine. The most important time to feed plants is while they are actually in flower or fruit. After flowering, cut back plants like plumbago and bougainvillea lightly, to tidy them up. As the days become shorter in autumn, reduce feeding and watering gradually so that, by the time winter arrives, plants are just 'ticking over'. A lot of conservatory plants keep their leaves in winter and should be given just enough water to stop them shrivelling. Plants like figs and grape vines that lose their leaves in winter need to be kept almost bone dry. Prune these in mid-winter when they are completely dormant so they do not 'bleed'. But bougainvillea, oleander, datura and passionflower should be pruned more closely in early spring, just before they start growing again.

In my conservatory the plants grow in soil borders to make watering easier. Here scented-leaf pelargoniums, Abutilon *'Canary Bird' and* Plectranthus argentatus, *mingle happily.*

Plant propagation

Raising your own plants from seed or cuttings is a satisfying and inexpensive way to grow stock for beds and borders. You can overwinter frost-tender plants indoors as rooted cuttings, and grow a whole catalogue of new plants from seed for very little cost.

Sowing seed

Loosely fill enough pots or seed trays with compost, level the surface 1cm (½in) below the rim of the container and firm it very lightly – the base of another pot or tray the same size makes a good tool for this task. Water well, then sprinkle your seeds very thinly; it helps to imagine each one growing into a tiny plant. Very fine seeds like begonia don't need covering with compost, but put cling film over the top of the pot to stop them drying out. Cover small- to medium-sized seeds very thinly. Big seeds like peas are best spaced 2.5cm (1in) apart over the compost, then pushed in until they just vanish from sight.

Softwood cuttings

This type of propagation consists of cutting 8–10cm (3–4 in) from the tip of a young shoot. Take off the lower leaves, leaving the bottom two-thirds of the stem bare, then use a sharp knife to trim off the bottom of the stem just below a leaf joint. Dip the cut end in rooting powder, then push five cuttings in round the edge of a 10cm (4in) pot filled with seed compost and label them. Water well and let the compost drain. Thin-leaved cuttings like fuchsias root best if the pot is stood inside a large, loosely tied plastic bag as it keeps the air around them nice and humid, but don't use this technique for plants with silver, furry or hairy leaves or they may rot. Softwood cuttings usually root in about six to eight weeks. Take them in spring and summer.

Hardwood cuttings

These are cuttings taken in autumn from woody plants. A lot of shrubs and roses root easily this way, and it is a very good method as you don't need any special equipment. Prepare a patch of spare soil by forking in lots of second-hand potting compost or the contents of old growing bags to make a seedbed. Then cut 30-cm (12-in) long stems from suitable shrubs. You can cut slightly shorter shoots from plants like box or perennial herbs which don't make so much new growth. The shoots must be reasonably straight and unbranched. Use sharp secateurs or a knife to trim the base of the cuttings cleanly just below a leaf joint. Next, snip off the top 5–8cm (2–3in) of each shoot to remove all the soft growth at the tip of the stem, leaving a slanting cut

ABOVE: Seeds can be sown direct from the packet if you have a steady hand. LEFT: When pricking out, handle seedlings by their leaves.

✏ top tip

Use vermiculite to cover seeds instead of compost. It trickles between the fingers so you can easily control the amount you put on. Being pale-coloured, it lets light reach the seeds of those plants that cannot germinate in the dark. It also keeps them moist without being too wet. Use pots of pure vermiculite to root difficult softwood cuttings, but start liquid feeding them or pot them into proper seed compost soon after they take root, since vermiculite does not contain any nutrients. Use horticultural vermiculite sold in garden centres, not the sort sold for insulating lofts.

DOS AND DON'TS OF DISEASE PREVENTION

✔ Do keep a sharp knife especially for taking cuttings and clean the blade by wiping it with methylated spirit to avoid spreading disease between plants. Otherwise use a craft knife with disposable blades.

✔ Do make sure containers are very clean and fill them with seed compost from a newly opened bag to avoid any risk of damping off (the rotting of seedlings which is caused by a micro-organism).

✘ Don't economize on seed compost: never re-use it or make your own from garden soil as you are likely to spread disease.

✔ Do clean out and disinfect your propagator every spring before use and take precautions against woodlice, slugs and snails which can wipe out young seedlings overnight.

✘ Don't take cuttings from plants that have obvious viruses or other diseases, as these will spread to the new plants.

✔ As soon as faded leaves or flowers are noticed on rooted cuttings or plants, remove them to prevent the spread of fungal diseases such as botrytis.

✘ Avoid keeping the leaves of downy or hairy plants wet as this can lead to rotting.

GERMINATING SEEDS AND ROOTING CUTTINGS

♦ After sowing, put seeds that need warmth in a heated propagator or on a warm windowsill. Check the back of the seed packet to see what temperature they need.

♦ While they are germinating, keep seeds out of direct sun, and water them just enough to keep the compost evenly moist.

♦ Use rooting powder when taking cuttings. Besides helping them to root, it contains fungicide that prevents the stems rotting. Different strengths are available for softwood and hardwood cuttings.

♦ Stand pots of cuttings out of direct sun and draughts while they root, but in a warm humid spot. Water them just enough to stop the compost drying out.

Cuttings can be rooted in all kinds of small containers; yoghurt pots are cheaper than flowerpots, even if they are not as pretty!

just above a leaf joint. Take off all the leaves except for the top two or three, and dip the bottom of each stem into rooting powder especially for hardwood cuttings. Push the cuttings into the ground about 5cm (2in) apart in a row, leaving only the top 5cm (2in) sticking out. If you have several rows, space them 30cm (12in) apart so you can run a hoe between them later. Don't forget to label the plants, so you remember what they are, and water well. Hardwood cuttings will usually root the following spring and be ready for transplanting the following autumn.

Division

Some plants, such as perennials and a few houseplants, grow into thick clumps that spread slowly. They are most easily propagated by division. Do this in autumn or early spring when the plants are not growing strongly. Dig up perennials or knock houseplants out of their pots and use a spade, knife or your fingers to divide the rootball in two. Divide each half into smaller pieces depending on the size of

the original clump, and re-plant or re-pot the best sections. Throw away the centre of an old parent plant if it has started to die out and re-use only the strong, healthy pieces from around the edge.

Growing and pricking out seedlings

Once you have raised a good crop of seedlings or cuttings, the fun is only just beginning. To turn them into successful plants ready for the garden, you need to grow them on. This demands almost as much care as the first stage, but it is very satisfying to see young plants develop. You can literally watch your investment grow.

When the seeds first germinate, most seedlings develop a pair of rounded seed leaves before starting to grow normal foliage. The best time to prick them out (transfer them to a seed tray), is while they are still small, when the first true leaf has just opened out. Use the point of a pencil or a small dibber to loosen each seedling from the compost, then lift it by a leaf – not the stem. Meanwhile have ready a seed tray filled with fresh seed compost,

LAYERING

Use layering to propagate shrubs that are difficult to root from cuttings, like rhododendrons. Choose a young shoot growing at the base of the plant and fork plenty of second-hand potting compost or the contents of old growing bags into the ground nearby, making a trench about 2.5cm (1in) deep. Make a shallow, sloping cut part-way through the stem with a knife, to help the stem to bend and encourage rooting. Dust the cut with rooting powder, then bend the stem down until it lies along the ground in the bottom of the trench. Hold it down with pegs made from bent wire or the hooks cut from wire coat hangers. Then cover most of the stem with soil, leaving just 15cm (6in) or so at the tip uncovered. It can take 12–18 months for layers to root well, but when they are visibly growing you can detach them, dig them up and you have a new plant that is ready to move to its final position.

These magnolia stems have been layered.

SOFTWOOD OR HARDWOOD CUTTINGS

♦ Don't try to take cuttings from shrubs that are expensive to buy in garden centres, like rhododendrons and magnolias, because they are usually grafted or else need special equipment like mist propagation units to root. Try layering them instead.

♦ Take softwood cuttings of box, lavender or rosemary in summer to grow your own dwarf edgings for formal flower beds.

♦ Take hardwood cuttings of shrub roses, rhus, cornus, sambucus, berberis, hypericum, cotoneaster, salix, spiraea, forsythia and privet in autumn.

♦ Some shrubs root best from softwood cuttings taken in mid-summer, including bush roses, hydrangeas, hardy hibiscus, hebe, heathers, cistus, escallonia and weigela.

♦ Take softwood cuttings of half-hardy perennials such as pelargoniums, fuchsias and argyranthemums in late summer, and root one per small pot. Keep these on a windowsill indoors or in the greenhouse. Do this instead of digging up the old plants to overwinter them as it takes up much less room.

Heel cuttings being removed from a sprig of rosemary.

levelled and firmed. Make a hole for each seedling and lower the roots into it until the seed leaves are just above the surface of the compost. Then firm the roots gently in with the point of the pencil or dibber. Space the seedlings in rows about 4cm (1½in) apart and water them well. Place newly pricked-out seedlings somewhere warm, humid and shady, to reduce stress while they form new roots, then give them really good light to prevent them becoming 'drawn' and spindly.

Potting up rooted cuttings

Softwood cuttings are ready for potting when their roots are about 5cm (2in) long. You can normally tell without tipping them out, as the new plants suddenly start looking very fresh and begin growing. Knock them out of the original pot, keeping as much compost as possible around the roots. Re-pot each plant singly into a 10-cm (4-in) pot filled with potting compost, re-planting it to the same depth it was growing before. Then water it and place in a shady, humid place for a week or so to recover. Use the same technique for potting up seed-raised houseplants and others intended for growing in pots.

Growing on

Once newly potted seedlings and cuttings have recovered from the shock of being re-potted, they are ready to move to a more open situation where they can grow into young plants big enough to

plant out. Stand them on capillary matting on the greenhouse staging, or on a bed of damp sand in a cold frame where they will receive plenty of light. Re-pot into bigger pots later as necessary. Plants grown from hardwood cuttings are transplanted outdoors. When they have rooted, dig them up in autumn and re-plant them 30cm (12in) or more apart in a nursery bed with well-prepared soil – this is what nurserymen call lining out. Wait until plants are about the same size as those you buy in a nursery before planting them out in the garden, to ensure a good survival rate. Autumn or early spring are the best times to move them to their final positions.

Aftercare

While they are growing on, young plants need regular watering to keep the compost evenly moist. Feed little and often, using a liquid or soluble feed, and make sure they have plenty of fresh air and sunlight, but avoid strong sun which may cause scorching under glass. To form nice, bushy plants, finger prune young plants regularly. Nip out the growing tip when you pot up seedlings or cuttings (except where plants are supposed to be grown on one main stem, such as tomatoes and standard fuchsias). Within a few weeks sideshoots will develop. Wait until these reach 8–10cm (3–4in) long then nip them out in the same way to create secondary branching.

Houseplants

A house becomes a home with something green living in it. Houseplants are not just part of the decoration, they are more like personalities in pots. Each one lends its particular character to the surroundings and behaves as an individual with its own likes and dislikes.

Having plants in the house is like bringing the garden indoors, especially if you grow lots of them, but most houseplants are actually a long way from home. Many come from tropical forests where they get constant shade, warmth and high humidity, protected from the breeze by the dense canopy of leaves overhead. In their natural habitat this type is kept evenly moist by the spongy tree bark they cling to or water running down branches to the 'pocket' of humus lodged in the crevice where they live. Their tolerance of low light levels is precisely what makes them good houseplants, but other aspects of domestic life are rather less to their liking, and most problems are caused by unsuitable conditions.

When you buy a new plant, the first thing to do is to read the care label that comes with it. If the label is not clear or there are no instructions, look it up in a houseplant book. Once you know what it wants, you can start to care for it properly. First, you need to find it somewhere to live. Few houseplants can stand being in sunlight during the middle of the day, which is when the sun is at its hottest and brightest. On a south-facing windowsill, where they are close to the glass, even sun-loving plants can scorch, especially if they are dry. The best plants for this situation are dwarf pelargoniums, small scented-leaved pelargoniums, cacti and gerbera, but keep them well watered. An east- or west-facing windowsill has direct sun early or late in the day, while the sun is relatively weak. This suits a lot of plants that like some sun but not scorching conditions. Tuberous begonias, jasmine, succulent plants like euphorbia and echeveria, hibiscus, shrimp plant (*Justica brandegeeana*), hoya, hippeastrum and *Campanula isophylla*, among others, all love this situation. A north-facing windowsill and other places that never have direct sun – like a tabletop inside a room – are ideal for many shade-loving houseplants. This is where tropical plants like maranta, anthurium, stephanotis, palms and philodendron as well as African violets and most foliage plants like ferns are happiest.

There is a big difference between light shade, which is what most houseplants prefer, and deep shade, which makes them grow pale and leggy. A room with pale, reflective walls, mirrors, large windows and light colours suits most shade lovers. If the heating is not left on all the time in winter, don't risk tropical plants as they need constant warmth. Instead, go for tougher shade lovers like ivy, fatshedera, aspidistra, asparagus fern, spider plant (chlorophytum) and grape ivy (rhoicissus). These are the 'old indestructibles' that put up with a lot of neglect.

Rooms with poor natural light, such as hallways without windows, or rooms with windows that are small or overlook a wall, don't usually suit houseplants. Even here you can cheat a bit, by standing plants in place for a few days at a time, then returning them somewhere brighter to recharge their batteries.

One of the problems of growing plants indoors is that central heating dries out the air badly, so instead of water vapour making up 60 per cent of the air, as it does out in the garden, the level can fall as low as 20 per cent – in nature, that is normally found only in a desert. In a tropical rainforest 100 per cent humidity is not unusual.

Houseplants grow best when grouped together because a group produces its own cloud of humidity by 'breathing out' water vapour through the leaves to make a mini microclimate.

ABOVE: The Christmas flower, poinsettia, likes a warm room.
RIGHT: A room where tender plants will thrive means that you can still be among plants and flowers even in the depths of an inhospitable winter.

HOW TO CARE FOR HOUSEPLANTS IN WINTER

1 Place geraniums on a brightly lit windowsill and water them sparingly. They are happy to be kept on the dry side in winter. Snap off faded leaves and flowers before they have a chance to rot.

2 Clean the leaves of glossy-leaved plants such as palms and weeping figs. Wipe them with kitchen paper dipped in a mixture of milk and water to give them added shine.

3 Clean the foliage of African violets (saintpaulias) by flicking over them with a stiff, dry paintbrush to remove dust. Pull off faded leaves and flowers and do not allow water to sit on the hairy leaves.

Humidity–loving plants like African violets and streptocarpus should be grouped together on a tray of damp pebbles. Fill the tray so that the water level stays about 1cm (½in) below the bottom of the pots – its purpose is to increase humidity, not moisten the compost.

African violets flower best if fed dilute liquid tomato food fortnightly.

There are a few plants that really must have rainforest conditions, or they will wither away. Club moss (selaginella), fittonia and pilea need high humidity and are best grown in a terrarium – a sort of indoor mini greenhouse. A terrarium will also show these plants off nicely. Stand it on the coffee table, right out of the sun, or the plants will cook.

Houseplant care

Most pot plant troubles are caused by watering: either too much, or too little. You know what happens. You put a plant on the windowsill. One day you notice it is drooping over the edge of the pot. You feel guilty because you have forgotten to water it, so you give it a drink. Water runs out through the bottom of the pot because the compost is bone dry and can't absorb it. Alternatively the plant is wilting, not because it is too dry, but because it is too wet. The additional watering is the last straw and the plant dies.

It would be easy if you could water all your houseplants once a week. You could make a note on your kitchen calendar and it would get done on time. But plants have different requirements. Some grow faster, some need wetter conditions, some need extra watering while they are flowering or because are standing in a sunnier spot than others. So you have to treat them all individually, which means checking them every few days by poking a finger into the compost or having a look to see which needs a drop of water and which doesn't. The ideal technique is to water plants thoroughly,

let the surplus drain away, then empty out pot-covers or saucers. Wait until the compost is just starting to dry out before watering again. It really doesn't matter if you water from the top or the bottom, so long as you don't leave plants standing in water afterwards.

If you really have problems with watering, I'd suggest getting hold of a water meter. This is an inexpensive gadget with a probe you push into the compost and a meter that tells you the moisture level. If you still have difficulties, grow fewer plants but use self-watering pots. These have a store of water built into the base, from which the plant draws up what it needs. All you need to do is top up the reservoir every week or so.

Houseplants need more than just a drop of water to survive. Because they grow in such small amounts of soil, they need their nutrients topped up regularly. Adding a few drops of liquid feed to the can each time you water is a good idea: you can't forget it. If you rely on feeding once a week, or at every third watering, you may lose track of where you are. There is another way of making sure plants are properly fed. Just mix slow-release feed granules into the compost when you pot or repot plants, or push feed sticks in the compost around the side of the pot. That way, each time you water, the plants automatically get fed too, as long as you remember to replace the feed sticks or granules every few months.

Most houseplants live happily in the same pot for a year or more. The way to tell when they need

Bright windowsills are the perfect home for cacti and other succulents. Provided they are not overwatered, they are easy to grow.

larger premises is when the roots start to grow out through the drainage holes in the bottom – lift the plant up to have a look. The best time to repot is in spring, at the start of the growing season, but most plants can be lifted out of one pot and into a slightly bigger one without damaging the rootball so, with care, you can repot at any time of year. If you need to divide clump-forming plants, such as ferns, the job should be done in spring. Some plants, like clivia, hoya and stephanotis, should only be put into a pot barely bigger than the old one, or they won't flower again until they fill the new pot with roots – they flower well only when they are slightly pot-bound and this can take years if the pot is too big.

Pests can be a bit of a problem, even indoors. Keep an eye out for them each time you water. It's much easier to wipe the odd greenfly off by hand instead of waiting for an epidemic and having to resort to an insect spray. Greenfly are the commonest indoor plant pest, though scale insects can be a problem on tough evergreen plants. Pests usually arrive as stowaways when you buy new plants, so always check them over and, if in doubt, spray to stop anything spreading to the rest of your plants. And if you stand cyclamen and Christmas cactus outdoors in summer, which I always do because it's good for them, give them a good spray before you bring them back in. It saves a lot of messing about later.

LOCATION GARDENING

No two gardens are identical. Some have extremes of climate and others have problem soils. Alternatively, you may wish to create a certain type of garden. This section caters for all these eventualities, so whether you garden on an exposed site, one where the ground is chalky, or if you want to make a scented garden, you'll find useful information here.

Wildlife gardens

Wildlife plays a vital role in my garden. You can't beat the sight of bluetits methodically clearing the roses of greenfly, or blackbirds teaching their babies how to pinch your redcurrants. One of my favourite summer sports is spotting caterpillars and looking them up to see what sort of butterfly they are going to turn into. If you're lucky enough to find hedgehogs, frogs and toads, they are not only entertaining but also good for the garden – between them they eat no end of slugs and snails that would otherwise make a meal of your plants. Look out, too, for bats which will often swoop down on summer evenings to take moths feeding on night-scented flowers; the latter are also attracted by lights left on outside at night when you are having a barbecue. More and more, gardens are becoming a haven for wildlife, and you will often find more unusual creatures like dragonflies, colourful beetles and slow-worms.

A birdbath outside the kitchen window – or any window – provides year-round interest.

Attracting wildlife

There is no need to worry about attracting wildlife; it will find you. Wildlife likes gardens that are left fairly undisturbed – unfussy ones with lots of trees, shrubs and grass to hide in, not immaculate borders and pristine lawns.

If you want birds in your garden, food is, naturally, a big attraction. Birds also need places to perch and take cover from predators so, as well as putting out nut feeders and seed on the bird table, grow plenty of trees and shrubs. The right types of plant will also provide a source of nourishment. Even an ordinary apple tree attracts lots of blackbirds and redwings to feed on windfalls in autumn, but grow plants that provide a range of berries for birds to eat at different times of year. Birds leave the ones they don't like much until last.

Ornamental thistles, grasses and other plants with seed-filled heads, like teasel and sunflowers, are a great way to attract finches, which will hang upside down and perform extraordinary antics dangling at the end of amazingly frail-looking stems. And anything that gets greenfly, like roses and fruit trees, is a big draw for bluetits. They can strip bushes of greenfly in a few days, which is a good reason for not using pesticides. What's more, bluetits can reach all the high branches you would never be able to reach with a spray.

You can help even more by providing nest boxes in safe, sheltered places – old teapots lodged on their sides in thick hedges (spout down) make good homes for robin families.

One thing all wildlife needs is water. A big, shallow bowl, filled regularly with water and placed on the lawn, will attract birds to drink and bathe. If you're lucky, you'll also spot hedgehogs there at night. If you have space, a pond is even better, and also provides a breeding place for frogs, toads, newts and dragonflies. All sorts of birds will use mud from round the edge to build their nests, plus the fibrous debris from marginal plants as nest lining.

Nectar-rich flowers are the key to attracting insects like butterflies and bees. The best kinds are herbs, wildflowers and old-fashioned cottage garden flowers such as hardy annuals. If you can, leave a clump of nettles as it is an excellent food source for caterpillars.

Encourage natural forms of pest control such as the hedgehog – a great slug eater!

It is not just in summer you need to think about wildlife. In winter, many animals need somewhere safe to go even if they do not actually hibernate. Hedgehogs, slow-worms and shrews tend to hide up in compost heaps. So spread your compost in early autumn, before hibernation time, or in late spring when they have moved on, to avoid disturbing them.

Many insects and spiders, which are beneficial in the garden, need a place to rest. A fringe of wildflower or perennial plant debris round the edge of the garden is the ideal place for insects. Better still, put off clearing your borders until spring. If you grow lots of wildlife-friendly plants, such as ornamental grasses and berrying shrubs, you'll find that the frost on the dead heads and late berries makes a dazzling garden display.

Wildlife will visit any garden that provides a few of the things it needs, particularly food. But if you really want animals, birds and insects to feel at home, you can create the kind of garden that has a bit of everything, where they can stay relatively undisturbed in a natural setting. This type of garden is fairly low-maintenace, giving you more time to sit back and enjoy the wildlife.

Wild garden

The most natural of all the wildlife-friendly gardens is a wild garden, which looks just like an improved chunk of natural countryside. You do not need a huge area. Just sow a mixture of grass and wildflowers instead of normal lawn grass and plant native trees and shrubs, such as elder, dog rose, blackthorn and hazel, in borders or as a hedge or shelter belt.

Grow your own wildflowers from seed, raising them just like hardy annuals, but leaving them in the ground to set seed after flowering so they

HOW TO MAKE A BIRD TABLE

1 Make your own bird table from old timber. A piece of external-quality plywood will make the top and 2.5-cm (1-in) square battens can be fixed to the rim to keep food in place.

2 Screw the table top to a stout wooden post driven into the ground. A height of 1.5m (5ft) keeps it out of reach of prowling cats and still allows it to be filled up with ease.

3 As well as scattering food on the top of the table, suspend squirrel-proof nut feeders from hooks around the edges. Make sure that fresh water is provided daily, too.

BEST WILDLIFE PLANTS

Buddleia	Teasel	Sweet rocket
Cotoneaster	Sunflowers	Night-scented stock
Rosa rugosa	*Limnanthes douglasii*	Elder
Marjoram	*Phacelia tanacetifolia*	Apple
Lavender	Nepeta	Hawthorn
Borage	Honesty	Nettle
Bronze fennel	*Sedum spectabile*	Honeysuckle
Ornamental grasses	Michaelmas daisy	

ARTIFICIAL SHELTER

If your garden does not naturally provide enough facilities for wildlife, you can add some artificial ones.

◆ A range of bird nesting boxes is available in shops and mail-order catalogues of organizations like the Royal Society for the Protection of Birds (RSPB).

◆ You can also get bat roosting boxes, which have slots like letter boxes instead of round entrance holes.

◆ Lacewing hotels, which are open-fronted boxes filled with hollow plant stems designed to shelter these beneficial insects in winter.

◆ There are even hedgehog houses, rather like small dog kennels, that you part-bury in dead leaves after putting some suitable nesting material inside.

◆ A pile of logs in a corner of the garden will provide a shelter for insects.

◆ Make a small pool as a refuge for frogs, toads, dragonflies and damsel flies.

ABOVE: The gardener's favourite bird – the robin. LEFT: A cottage garden is much more of a welcoming haven for wildlife than one which is tidied to within an inch of its life.

provide their own replacements naturally. They are ideal for banks and borders.

A natural-style pond is a big bonus in an area like this. Dig out the pond shape with gently shelving 'beaches' around the edge, so that hedgehogs can get out and birds can bathe in the shallows. Line it with pond liner and plant clumps of wild waterside plants like *Iris pseudacorus* and arrowhead (sagittaria) round the edge. Surrounded with drifts of moisture-loving wildflowers, like figwort and purple loosestrife, your pond will be a natural-looking attraction for wildlife and a highlight of your garden.

Cottage garden

An old-fashioned cottage garden can be just as wildlife friendly because of the types of plants grown. Typical cottage garden favourites include hardy annuals, semi-wild plants like teasels and foxgloves, and the sort of perennials that attract bees and butterflies, such as marjoram, lavender, *Sedum spectabile* and Michaelmas daisies.

In my view, the best cottage gardens have an ancient and gnarled apple tree hung with climbing roses and honeysuckle, which besides adding bags of character to the garden, provides lots of food and safe nesting places for whole families of birds. If you have a pair of trees, they are pretty good for slinging a hammock between, too.

A real old cottage garden would also be surrounded by a mixed fruiting hedge yielding damsons, crab apples, elderberries, blackberries and rosehips, though nowadays we would probably settle for *Rosa rugosa* instead – birds enjoy the huge, tomato-shaped hips.

Bird or butterfly garden

In only a small space you can make a mini garden designed to attract one particular type of wildlife. A bird garden needs to include a bird table and nut feeders. You may find that your local hawks have discovered that bird tables provide them with easy pickings too, so site the bird table close to the house or a wall where you get a good view but hawks cannot manoeuvre easily. Also, hang feeders up in big, twiggy shrubs so that the songbirds have plenty of cover. This will make them stay longer as they feel safe.

If squirrels are a problem, invest in a squirrel-proof feeder as the normal sort will get chewed to bits in no time. Exotic weeds can sometimes

A painted lady drinks nectar from a buddleia, but lays her eggs on stinging nettles along with red admirals, small tortoiseshells and peacock butterflies.

be a nuisance around bird tables where spilt seed falls on to grass or flower beds and germinates. You can avoid this quite easily by standing the bird table on paving slabs so that spilt seed can be swept up. It's a good idea to surround your bird table with plants that provide natural bird seeds, fruit and berries.

To attract butterflies and bees, plant a bed containing lots of nectar-rich plants, like the old-fashioned cottage-garden flowers or a collection of herbs and lavenders in a sunny but sheltered part of the garden. This looks particularly attractive as a double border with a path running through it so you can walk among the flowers.

You can also encourage white clover, bugle and other low-growing wildflowers to flower in your lawn by not using weedkiller on it. The bees will love it. Sow a small clover lawn if you like. You can buy seed in some garden centres and from specialist seedsmen. In fact, one of the most effective and fastest ways to encourage a whole range of fascinating butterflies, dragonflies, bees, hoverflies and flying beetles is simply to stop using pesticides anywhere in the garden. It's something I've done and never regretted and, after an initial settling down period, severe outbreaks of pests are rare indeed.

Shade gardening

Many gardeners think that if part of their plot is in shade, they might just as well forget about it. What a waste! Gardening in the shade can be every bit as interesting as gardening in the sun, and the range of plants that can be used is surprisingly wide.

It is true that many bright flowers need the sun to perform well and that summer bedding plants are not successful in the gloom. The secret of success is to choose those plants that are native to woodland, or whose natural habitat occurs where light intensity is low; that way you can grow plants that will positively enjoy the conditions in which sun lovers languish.

The thing to remember is that shade-loving plants usually grow in earth which is rich in organic matter. Nobody sweeps up in woodland: fallen leaves are allowed to rot down and turn into wonderful leaf mould, which holds on to moisture and improves any kind of soil. Add plenty of leaf mould or well-rotted garden compost or manure to your shady patch so that it provides your plants with food and a vital reservoir of moisture.

Where shade gardening does become tricky is in a tidy garden where the ground is riddled with roots, as is frequently the case immediately below established trees and shrubs. Here all fallen leaves will have been swept up and the grey dust exposed to view. In these circumstances it really is asking too much to stick in a few woodland plants and expect

Japanese maples enjoy shade from scorching sun, and ferns are excellent choices for heavy shade.

them to thrive. The competition for nutrition and moisture will be just too severe to enable them to establish themselves. Dry shade, such as this, is the hardest place in which to grow anything.

However, there are one or two plants that will grow even here if they are given a bit of encouragement at the start. Varieties of ivy (hedera) will make good ground cover, especially the Irish ivy (*Hedera hibernica*), which will grow into a thick and glossy, green rug that runs right up to tree trunks. Snip off any stems that look like legging it up the trunk.

Consider lightly thinning out canopies of trees that cast heavy shade, or employ a tree surgeon to do so.

The rose of Sharon, *Hypericum calycinum*, will often cope with dry shade and knits together to form a thick mat of stems. The leaves are evergreen or semi-evergreen, and the yellow flowers are carried from summer to autumn.

Add organic matter to the soil before you plant these obliging ground coverers and water them well with a sprinkler after planting, making sure that they don't go short of water in their first season. Thereafter, they should cope on their own.

Native woodland plants
Britain's flora is rich in demure woodlanders which can easily be raised from seed and planted out where they will feel at home. Legislation now protects many of these native plants, including bluebells, which must not be dug up from the wild. If you find a source of bulbs, make sure that they have been raised in cultivation.

If you want to plant up native British plants, the following are among those suitable for shady spots. Being British natives, they are listed under their common names with Latin names in brackets.

Bluebell (*Hyacinthoïdes non-scripta*)
Cuckoo pint (*Arum maculatum*)
Dog's mercury (*Mercurialis perennis*)
Foxglove (*Digitalis purpurea*)
Herb Paris (*Paris quadrifolia*)
Male fern (*Dryopteris filix-mas*)
Primrose (*Primula vulgaris*)

Solomon's seal (*Polygonatum x hybridum*)
Wood anemone (*Anemone nemorosa*)
Wood sorrel (*Oxalis acetosella*)
Wood spurge (*Euphorbia amygdaloïdes*)
Wood violet (*Viola odorata*)

top tip

In areas that are shaded by deciduous rather than evergreen trees, try planting spring-flowering bulbs which will grow and flower before the leaf canopy opens and cuts out the light. Suitable types include hardy cyclamen, *Anemone blanda*, erythronium (dog's tooth violet), dwarf narcissus, snowdrop, bluebell and crocus.

BEST SHADE PLANTS

Dry shade
Alchemilla
Asplenium
Astrantia
Bergenia
Brunnera
Calamintha
Convallaria
Corydalis
Digitalis
Dryopteris
Euphorbia
Geranium
Lamium
Viola

Damp shade
Ajuga
Alchemilla
Anemone
Asplenium
Astilbe
Astrantia
Brunnera

Calamintha
Cimicifuga
Dicentra
Digitalis
Epimedium
Euphorbia
Geranium
Geum
Gunnera
Helleborus
Hemerocallis
Heuchera
Hosta
Kirengeshoma
Lamium
Liriope
Lysimachia
Matteuccia
Meconopsis
Milium
Mimulus
Polemonium
Polygonatum
Polygonum

Primula
Pulmonaria
Rheum
Rodgersia
Smilacina
Thalictrum
Trollius
Viola
Zantedeschia

Heavy shade
Aucuba
Buxus
Fatsia
Gaultheria
Hedera
Ilex
Pachysandra
Prunus laurocerasus
Ruscus
Sarcococca
Skimmia
Symphoricarpos
Vinca

There is no shortage of plants for shade. Hostas and forget-me-nots are both happy there and very easy to grow.

Chalk gardening

In Hampshire I garden on chalk, but there are relatively few plants that do not thrive here.

Gardeners who have acid soil that can grow strapping rhododendrons, azaleas and camellias would probably rather die than own a garden with the alkaline soil that these plants hate. But a garden on chalk or limestone need not be the disaster area that some people fear. I have gardened on flinty soil overlying solid chalk for nearly 20 years now, and the range of plants that thrive is vast.

Almost half of Britain's gardens have alkaline soil, which may be due to underlying chalk or limestone, and while the cultivation of some species is made impossible, the situation is not without its advantages.

In parts of my own garden the solid bed of chalk is barely 8cm (3in) below the surface. This shallow soil overlying chalk is recognized as being the most inhospitable soil of all, but the solid wodge of chalk has two big advantages: it drains well, yet acts as a dense sponge which holds on to moisture in times of drought, allowing plants to tap into its resources.

Some soils over limestone are so free-draining that they are among the first to suffer from drought, so provision must be made to boost their water-retaining capacity. Other areas possess limy clay soils that are hard to work – rock-like in dry weather and sticky in the wet – or calcareous silts or sands that may contain large deposits of calcium-rich seashells.

All alkaline soils are 'hungry' soils in terms of plant nutrients, but there are ways of improving things. For a start, be generous with supplies of bulky organic matter, in the form either of well-rotted garden compost or manure, leaf mould, spent hops or even spent mushroom compost. I know that the latter also contains bits of chalk, but if your soil has great lumps of the stuff in it already, a few more chippings are not going to make a lot of difference.

Peat is thought of by some as being a great conditioner for chalky soils. It can be, but not all peats are acidic, none of them contains nutrients (unlike manure and compost) and peat can be very expensive to use in quantity. You may also feel that peat is a non-renewable resource that must be conserved (see pages 40).

Where the soil is shallow, add the compost and manure to the surface to increase its depth and plant directly into this. Regular applications over the years can produce a soil that is rich above and which has that valuable reservoir of moisture below.

When planting trees and shrubs, dig a larger hole than you think is necessary and use a pick-axe to break up the chalky substrate. Work in plenty of organic matter, and before returning the earth to the hole, mix more organic matter with it so that the new plant really has a good start. An organic mulch will complete the operation.

Limy clay soil can be improved by adding sharp grit as well as organic matter, and the effect of the two combined will last much longer than organic matter alone.

Fertilizer is vital to plants on chalky soil; apply a good sprinkling of general fertilizer in early spring and again in summer, lightly working it into the soil.

Many plants take off from the word go, but I've found that some trees and shrubs need a year or two really to settle in before growing away lustily. Don't give up on them, but wait and see how they respond.

The reason why plants such as rhododendrons and camellias do not thrive on chalky ground is that they do not have the ability to extract the vital plant food iron from alkaline soils. As a consequence of this, their leaves turn yellow and growth becomes stunted due to their deficiency in this important nutrient. It can be supplied to them in the form of diluted sequestered iron (see page 40), but this is something that should be thought of as an occasional boost for lime-hating plants growing in containers, not as a permanent solution when cultivating them in the garden. In the open ground it is less effective and far too costly to use on a regular basis.

PLANTS TO AVOID ON ALKALINE SOIL

This list shows those plants that will generally not enjoy growing in soil containing limestone or chalk. Some gardeners can get away with one or two of them, but not many.

Andromeda
Calluna
Camellia
Corylopsis
Crinodendron

Cytisus
Daboecia
Desfontainia
Embothrium
Enkianthus
Erica (except *E. carnea*, *E. darleyensis* and *E. mediterranea*)
Eucryphia (except *E. nymansensis* and *E. cordifolia*)
Exochorda
Fothergilla

Gaultheria
Gentiana
Halesia
Iris kaempferi
Kalmia
Leptospermum
Liquidambar
Lupinus
Magnolia (except 'Merrill')
Meconopsis
Pieris
Rhododendron and azalea
Vaccinium

In this border, solid chalk is about 15cm (6in) below the surface, but plenty of compost and manure helps a wide range of plants to grow. Sweet rocket is very happy here.

WHICH TYPE OF SOIL?

Indicator plants

The type of wild plants growing in your locality can indicate whether your soil is overlying chalk. If old man's beard (*Clematis vitalba*) grows up through the hedgerows, you are almost certainly on chalk. Similarly, the wayfaring tree (*Viburnum lantana*) and the common yew (*Taxus baccata*) also grow well here.

Test your soil

When you move into a new house and garden, it is always a good idea to find out if your soil is acid or alkaline. Use a soil-testing kit, which will reveal the pH (acidity or alkalinity) of your soil (see page 41).

Containers

The simplest way to grow plants that really hate alkaline soil is to cultivate them in large pots or tubs containing lime-free or ericaceous compost. Water them with rainwater if possible and give them an occasional feed using proprietary sequestered iron. I have had dwarf rhododendrons growing in pots for nearly 10 years in my chalky garden and they have done really well.

*ABOVE: Old man's beard (*Clematis vitalba*) is an indicator of chalky soil.*

Seaside gardening

A garden by the sea seems a wonderful prospect, but, as anyone who has grown plants on the coast will tell you, it isn't all beer and skittles. There are two big problems – wind and salt spray. Combined, they can reduce a healthy, green plant to a blackened, soggy mass overnight. Couple these with drought and a sandy soil and the problem is intensified.

But I still dream of having a garden by the sea. The light intensity is wonderful, the soil is usually well-drained and the days seem longer. Even if every day is not a holiday, the coastal air makes you feel better and temperatures by the sea seldom fall as low in winter as they do further inland.

The most important factor in any seaside garden is a windbreak or shelterbelt to cut down the force of the wind before it hits your plants. Such screen planting needs to be carried out with care so that you don't lose your view, but its erection is essential if plants are to be able to establish themselves on its leeward side.

ABOVE: *Coastal gardens suffer from salt spray as well as wind.*
BELOW: *My own seaside garden – the pleasure without the pain!*

top tip

Plant small specimens rather than large ones in a seaside garden. This means that by the time the plants are large enough to be hammered by wind, they have a strong and fully developed root system which will give them good anchorage.

PLANTS FOR SEASIDE GARDENS

Shrubs		Eryngium
Atriplex	Rosmarinus	Euphorbia
Bupleurum	Santolina	Festuca
Choisya	Senecio	Geranium
Cordyline	Tamarix	Gypsophila
Corokia	Ulex	Heuchera
Cytisus	Yucca	Iris
Elaeagnus		Kniphofia
Escallonia	**Perennials**	Lathyrus
Fuchsia	Achillea	Linaria
Genista	Agapanthus	Lychnis
Hebe	Alstroemeria	Morina
Helianthemum	Anemone	Oenothera
Hydrangea	Artemisia	Penstemon
Ilex	Bergenia	Physostegia
Lavandula	Centaurea	Polygonum
Lavatera	Centranthus	Potentilla
Leycesteria	Crambe	Salvia
Olearia	Crocosmia	Sedum
Phlomis	Dianthus	Tradescantia
Phormium	Dierama	Veronica
Pittosporum	Echinops	Zantedeschia
	Erigeron	

The siting of your windbreak will depend on the direction of the prevailing wind. In Britain it is usually from the south-west, and the windbreak itself will often need some kind of screen for the first few years to allow it to become established. There are many plastic netting materials on the market which are sold specifically to provide shelter, but they don't look particularly attractive. Woven wattle or willow hurdles 2m (6ft) high are a more appealing alternative and can be bought from local craftsmen or garden centres. Make sure they are held in place with stout stakes, knocked into the ground for at least 60cm (2ft).

When the fence-like windbreak is in position, suitable shrubs can be chosen to make a shelterbelt. Look around the area and choose those that do well.

Suitable seaside shelterbelts
In severe on-shore gales all plants will suffer to a certain degree, but some of the following trees and shrubs are among the toughest.

D = deciduous   E = evergreen
* These are slightly tender plants, more suitable for growing on south and west coasts of Britain than further inland due to the heat-storing effect of the sea.

Betula pendula (Silver birch) **D**	*Euonymus japonicus* **E**
Crataegus monogyna (Hawthorn) **D**	*Fraxinus excelsior* (Ash) **D**
Cupressus macrocarpa (Monterey cypress) **E**	*Griselinia littoralis* **E**
x *Cupressocyparis leylandii* (Leyland cypress) **E**	*Hippophaä rhamnoïdes* (Sea buckthorn) **D**
Elaeagnus x *ebbingei* **E**	*Olearia traversii* **E**
Escallonia rubra var. *macrantha* (for mild areas only) **E** *	*Pinus mugo* (Mountain pine) **E**
Eucalyptus (Gum – many species) **E**	*Pittosporum crassifolium* **E** *
	Quercus ilex (Evergreen oak) **E**
	Salix caprea (Goat willow) **D**
	Tamarix ramosissima (Tamarisk) **D**
	Ulex europaeus (Gorse) **E**

The soil
As in any garden, before you plant anything carry out a pH test to determine soil acidity or alkalinity (see page 41). Many seaside gardens have alkaline soil due to the high calcium content caused by the presence of crushed seashells. In such cases it is a waste of time planting lime-hating plants.

Soil in seaside gardens is often poor and sandy, so it is essential to add to it as much organic matter as possible to retain moisture and add nutrients. Go for the usual well-rotted garden compost and manure, leaf mould and spent mushroom compost.

Once the soil has been enriched and your plants put in, mulch the surface with chipped bark or compost to seal in the available moisture.

The plants
Choose your plants sensibly. Those with tough, leathery leaves, or those that are spiny or grey and hairy, will usually have more resistance to drying winds than those that are soft and sappy. Join the local gardening club and don't be afraid to ask about which plants do well and which do not. You don't need to have a garden that looks identical to your neighbours', but listening to their advice will save you time and money on plants that are non-starters. Finally, plant closely. In seaside gardens, plants benefit from the proximity of their neighbours in reducing wind rock.

A series of walls and screens will help reduce the strength of the wind in seaside gardens and widen the range of plants that can be grown.

Windy gardens

Gales make me bad-tempered: I cannot bear to see plants that I have spent years nurturing being battered by strong winds. It seems so destructive. Does wind have any benefits from the gardener's point of view? Only one: it does help to dry out the soil for spring sowings, but that's about it. Greenfly still manage to cling on in the teeth of a gale, or are simply redistributed by it, so it doesn't even blow away pests and diseases.

We can do nothing about gales, but some gardeners live in exposed places where there is almost always a breeze, and often quite a strong wind. Gardens on high ground and around the coast (see pages 276–7) are at the mercy of winds on more days than those of us in lower-lying areas, so something has to be done to reduce the strength of the wind and make gardening more pleasurable and more rewarding as far as plant growth is concerned.

Windbreaks are the answer. It may be tempting (if expensive) to surround the garden with a high brick or stone wall, but if this is the only measure taken, it can create as many problems as it solves.

When a strong wind hits an impenetrable barrier, it is forced over the top, but its activity does not end there. It then tumbles into a kind of forward somersault, causing tremendous turbulence some metres further on. The effect on plants is that those growing in the immediate lee of the wall may be protected, but those at some distance from it will suffer even more than if the wall were not there.

If you have, or intend to make, a walled garden on an exposed site, the wind must be further controlled inside the enclosure with a smaller network of hedges that dissipate its force. This is brilliantly illustrated in the Queen Mother's garden at the Castle of Mey in Caithness. Here is a garden right on the north coast of Scotland, where Arctic winds come in with great force for much of the year. A tall stone wall surrounds the castle garden, but inside the wall smaller hedges divide the area into patches designated for fruit, flowers and

Cupressus macrocarpa, *the Monterey cypress, is an excellent windbreak, even in coastal areas where salt-laden winds are a problem.*

Especially at home by the sea, the tamarisk has feathery foliage and delicate pink flowers that belie its tough constitution.

whereas smaller gardens must rely on shrubs to do the same job. Here you need to select the tough cookies – plants that can grow in soil which may be poor and in conditions which make the going tough.

In exposed gardens it is even more important than elsewhere to improve the soil so that it offers the best possible sustenance at the roots. A plant clinging on by the skin of its teeth in impoverished soil is likely to give up the ghost more readily than one that has ample resources of organic matter to call upon. You might think that too much soil enrichment would produce soft and sappy growth less able to resist wind, but the presence of a good root system, which gives the plant an ability to absorb moisture readily, far outweighs this consideration. The biggest problem presented to a plant by wind is desiccation. Leaves that dry out turn brown. Anything you can do to reduce this moisture loss will make plant growth less vulnerable to drying out, and soil preparation is an important factor here.

Shelterbelts for exposed gardens

As a rough guide, a windbreak will offer protection to plants at a distance roughly equivalent to five times its height. For example, a 3m- (10ft-) tall hedge on the windward side of a garden will provide shelter for plants growing a distance of up to 15m (50ft) away.

vegetables. The result is a garden that tames the wind to a tremendous degree and makes it possible to grow plants that would otherwise perish.

For most of us building a 3-m (10-ft) wall is out of the question, so we must look for other means of protecting our plants. Willow or hazel hurdles 2m (6ft) tall are good, but interwoven softwood fencing is less successful, not only because it is impermeable to wind and may cause turbulence, but also because it puts up such resistance that it is often blown down in high winds.

If you would rather not gaze at a fence, you can rely on plants to make windbreaks and shelterbelts. In much of Britain the prevailing wind is from the south-west, and it is on this side of the garden that a windbreak is often most useful. Consult with local gardeners to check that your part of the country is not an exception to this rule due to the lie of the land.

Large areas of land can be protected by rows of trees planted to intercept the prevailing wind,

H = also useful as hedges	E = evergreen
Trees	*Tilia cordata*
Acer pseudoplatanus (Sycamore)	(Small-leaved lime)
Betula (Birch)	**Shrubs**
Crataegus (Hawthorn) **H**	*Cornus alba* (Dogwood)
Fagus (Beech) **H**	*Hippophaä rhamnoïdes* (Sea buckthorn)
Fraxinus (Ash)	Juniperus (Juniper) **E**
Larix (Larch)	*Mahonia aquifolium* **E**
Pinus sylvestris (Scots pine) **E**	Philadelphus (Mock orange)
Populus (Poplar – no closer than 40m (130ft) to a house)	*Prunus spinosa* (Blackthorn)
Quercus (Oak)	*Rhododendron ponticum* **E**
Sorbus (Mountain ash and Whitebeam)	Salix (Willow)
Taxus baccata (Yew) **H/E**	Tamarix (Tamarisk)
Thuja occidentalis (White cedar) **H/E**	Ulex (Gorse) **E**
	Viburnum opulus 'Roseum' (Snowball tree)

Scented gardens

Mrs Beeton once cautioned against using hyacinths on the table at dinner parties, lest the overpowering perfume should cause fainting fits in ladies with tight stays. Fortunately there's not much risk of that happening out in the garden. Fragrance adds an invisible extra to your borders, turning a quiet afternoon in the hammock into a complete workout for your nose.

It is amazing just how many scented plants there are. Some, like cowslips, have a fragrance so delicate you would need to sit in the middle of a good-sized patch of them to get the full benefit. But others are positively powerful, like Mrs Beeton's hyacinths. These need placing carefully. I like to put a tub of hyacinths by the front door, so the perfume trickles in each time someone goes in or out. But most perfumed plants come somewhere between the two extremes. With these, the trick is to dot different sorts all around the garden so you can pick up a new scent at every bend in the path. Some perfumes blend nicely together, but a strong smell, such as lavender, simply dominates a group and spoils the effect, so be firm and keep heavier scents separate.

ABOVE: Catmint (Nepeta mussinii) makes an aromatic edging to a path, provided your cats will let it grow. BELOW: A cottage-garden mixture, rich in fragrances.

Flower fragrances tend to be strongest on summer evenings, when the air is warm and humid, without any breeze to waft it away. You can't beat an evening stroll in the garden inhaling the fragrance of

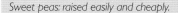

Sweet peas: raised easily and cheaply.

night-scented stocks and nicotiana. A lot of plants actually step up their perfume production at night to attract moths to pollinate them. *Datura stramonium,* for instance, has almost no scent during the day, but at night gives out a musky perfume so strong you can almost hear it. And the old-fashioned flowering tobacco, *Nicotiana alata,* actually folds up its petals during the day and comes to life only at night. Modern dwarf nicotianas may look better during the day, but they don't have as much scent.

Although spring and summer are the peak times for scent in the garden, there are quite a few unusual winter-flowering shrubs with scented flowers, including the shrubby honeysuckles *Lonicera fragrantissima* and *L. × purpusii.* Since you probably don't spend as much time wandering round the garden in winter, it is a good idea to plant these close to a doorway or at the side of a frequently used path.

Not all scented plants, of course, have scented flowers. The ones with scented leaves are even better value, since you get their fragrance whether they are flowering or not. Unfortunately they are not always very spectacular plants, but by growing things like lemon-scented verbena, eau de Cologne mint and pineapple sage in your borders as foliage plants among unscented flowers, you can have the best of both worlds. My all-time favourites are scented-leaved pelargoniums. Don't go away with the idea of a zonal geranium with a dab of scent behind the leaf joints. These plants are more like herbs, but with leaves perfumed with a combination of pot-pourri bowl and spice rack – cinnamon,

lemon, orange, pine, rose, balsam and even extra-strong peppermints. Unlike scented flowers, which blast their scent out into the air without any help, plants with scented leaves need assistance. You have to bruise the leaves very slightly to release the aromatic oils. These are the plants to grow in tubs next to your garden seat, where you can run your hand through them, or close to a path where they will get disturbed every time someone brushes past. Fill in cracks between paving slabs with thymes – the result is like grow-it-yourself aromatherapy.

PLANTS FOR SCENTED GARDENS

Aloysia triphylla (Lemon verbena)	*Matthiola incana* (Brompton, ten week and East Lothian stocks)
Choisya ternata (Mexican orange blossom)	*Narcissus jonquilla* (Wild jonquil)
Convallaria majalis (Lily of the valley)	Philadelphus (Mock orange)
Cosmos atrosanguineus (Chocolate-scented cosmos)	*Reseda odorata* (Mignonette)
Crambe cordifolia	*Ribes odoratum* (Clove currant)
Daphne mezereum	
Heliotropium arborescens (Cherry pie, Heliotrope)	*Salvia microphylla*
Iris graminea (Plum tart iris)	*Salvia rutilans* (Pineapple sage)
Matthiola longipetala subsp. *bicornis* (Night-scented stock)	Syringa (Lilac)
	Zaluzianskya ovata (Night stock)

Damp gardens

Damp soil can be a blessing or a burden. Some gardens are damp because they are in a wet part of the country. In the Lake District, for instance, it is unusual for more than two weeks to go by without any rain, so the soil stays permanently moist, despite being over rocks which let surplus water run away quickly. This sort of moist but well-drained soil provides very good growing conditions for a wide range of plants. In fact, it is probably the soil most garden plants prefer.

Other gardens are damp because the soil is heavy clay, or because rainwater is unable to run away. This is problem damp. The obvious solution, if you find yourself in this situation, is to grow only those plants that are happy in such conditions. Rose species, ornamental elders, bog myrtle, *Myrica gale,* and shrubby willows grow happily on unimproved clay soil, and the wilder waterside plants thrive

where drainage is especially poor. The trouble is, this does limit your choice of plants.

With both clay and boggy soil, digging in lots of grit is the long-term solution as this opens up the texture and introduces air spaces. But you also need to keep adding organic matter. Dig it in when preparing a new bed for the first time, add more whenever you put in a new plant, and apply a layer about 5cm (2in) thick as a mulch every spring. Use this technique to upgrade naturally boggy soil, turning it into a proper bog garden suitable for a wide range of moisture-loving plants.

You can raise the soil level by making a low retaining wall of logs or walling blocks, then filling it up with topsoil to improve drainage.

There are many traditional remedies for clay soil that actually do more harm than good, such as adding lime. This works only on ground that is acid

SOIL IMPROVERS

♦ Grit should look rather like muesli, a mixture of large and small particles. Make sure it is lime and salt-free, the sort that nurseries use to mix their own potting composts. Builders sand contains lots of lime and is too fine, and sand or grit dredged from seawater channels is full of salt. Use a barrowload per square metre (yard), forked into the top spade's depth. It is cheapest bought in bulk direct from quarries or builders' merchants, but is also available in bags from garden centres as washed horticultural grit.

♦ Use whatever organic matter you can get in useful quantities cheaply and easily (see pages 38–9). Farmyard manure, old growing bags, spent hops or mushroom compost are all suitable, or you can make you own compost. If all else fails, the smallest sort of bark chippings can be dug in and, though more expensive, last longer than most other forms of organic matter.

OPPOSITE: *Bold foliage plants such as darmera (peltiphyllum) and gunnera love boggy soil.* ABOVE: *Beth Chatto's garden in Essex shows off bog and moisture-loving plants to perfection.*

in the first place and many clay soils are already quite alkaline. Additives like lime and gypsum need to be used regularly, so they are not a quick fix. Deep digging is also recommended as a remedy, but when you dig a hole, if you hit nasty blue or yellow clay, the last thing you want to do is bring it to the surface and mix it with good topsoil. It will be years before anything much grows as this sort of subsoil is infertile. If you take a bit of trouble to improve clay topsoil only, you should end up with a fertile, moisture-retentive bit of ground.

Moisture-loving plants

Once problem damp has been turned into good, retentive soil, you will be able to grow a huge number of delightful, moisture-loving plants. Hostas and astilbes, hardy ferns, brunnera, pulmonaria, Solomon's seal, foxgloves, polemonium and dicentra enjoy light, dappled shade. Coloured primroses and the charming gold-laced polyanthus do well towards the front of this type of border. In sun go for phlox, monarda, schizostylis, *Macleaya microcarpa* 'Kelway's Coral Plume' and *Rheum palmatum* 'Atropurpureum', which looks like rhubarb with high blood pressure.

Some grasses, including Bowles' golden grass, miscanthus and hakonechloa, enjoy moist borders. In damper conditions still, choose the sort of plants you associate with pondsides such as candelabra primulas, rodgersia and lythrums. For something slightly more unusual, look out for *Sanguisorba obtusa*, which has leaves like a giant salad burnet but with tall spikes of rose-pink, bottle-brush flowers in late summer.

TREES AND SHRUBS FOR DAMP GARDENS	
On improved clay soil	**On badly drained soil**
Berberis	*Carpinus* (Hornbeam)
Chaenomeles	*Cornus* (Dogwood)
Cotoneaster	*Corylus avellana* 'Contorta'
Japanese maple	(Contorted hazel)
Kerria	Hydrangea
Pyrus	*Miscanthus sinensis*
Ribes	Pterocarya
Roses	(Caucasian wingnut)
Rubus	*Salix*
Sambucus racemosa	*Sambucus nigra*
(Ornamental elder)	(Ornamental elder)
Symphoricarpos	*Taxodium distichum*
Vinca	(Swamp cypress)
	Viburnum opulus

Dry gardens

The sort of gardens where dry conditions are a permanent problem are those where the soil drains a bit too quickly for horticultural comfort: those with sandy, gravelly or chalky soils. You'll know if your garden is dry if, within 10 minutes of a downpour, all your puddles have disappeared. It does have its benefits. There is no need to choose your moment to do the winter digging and the soil is always in a fit state to cultivate.

On the down side, it can be quite difficult to get new plants established in a dry garden. The trick is to do all your new planting in autumn, so winter rains can keep everything watered for you. New plants will have had time to find their feet before the next drought turns up and are much better placed to take care of themselves than ones planted in spring or summer. The real key to success is to make the most of the conditions and plant a drought garden with gravel, cobblestones and paving instead of lawns, and drought-proof plants instead of normal perennials. Try to avoid annuals except in containers,

as they need fiendish amounts of water in dry soil. If you want to grow vegetables, cultivate deep beds filled to a depth of 60cm (2ft) with pure garden compost, to keep them from drying out.

Soil improvement

If you can add enough organic matter, you will be able to grow most normal garden plants that enjoy good drainage. The problem is keeping the level topped up. Dry soils are notoriously hungry and organic matter decomposes very much faster than on normal soil, so in no time you are back to raw sand. Sandy, gravelly or chalky soils are the only ones in which it is permissible to dig in undecomposed organic matter. Bury fresh manure, unrotted garden waste, seaweed, straw or whatever you can get in autumn. By the time you come to plant in spring, it will have decomposed to just the

Drought-tolerant plants grown attractively in the gravel garden by Beth Chatto at White Barn House in Essex.

The most efficient way to keep annual flowers and vegetables watered is to use perforated hosepipe or special porous flexible pipes along the rows. Each covers about a 60-cm (2-ft) width of bed.

PLANTS SUITABLE FOR DRY SOIL	
Agapanthus	Junipers
Alchemilla mollis	Kniphofia
Allium	Liatris
Alstroemeria	*Linaria purpurea*
Artemesia	Nepeta
Bearded iris	Penstemon
Buddleia	Perovskia
Ceanothus	Phormium
Centranthus ruber (Valerian)	Pinks
Cistus	*Romneya coulteri*
Convolvulus cneorum	Santolina
Cytisus	Sedum
Euphorbia	Sempervivum
Genista	Sisyrinchium
Hebe	*Spartium junceum*
Hibiscus syriacus	Verbascum
Hypericum	Yucca

right point for planting, without taking up space in the compost heap. And just think of all the barrowing you'll have avoided.

Water-retaining gel crystals, sold to put in your hanging baskets, will also help a dry soil. Just sprinkle the dry crystals over the ground at about a handful per square metre (square yard) and fork them in. You can buy large, economy-size packs by mail order. Or simply tip out your old hanging-basket compost on to the beds when the flowers are over and dig it in. The same crystals keep working for several years.

Mulching is essential on dry soil and should be undertaken in both spring and autumn, since the material will vanish faster than usual. Choose a time when the soil is moist and free of weeds in the first place and spread your compost or manure mulch as thick as you can – at least 5cm (2in). It does not need to be completely rotted and lasts a bit longer if it is not. In any areas that are hidden, such as the bottom of the garden, under a hedge, or around trees and shrubs, you can mulch with grass mowings. In theory these will use nitrogen from the soil to decompose, but on a dry soil the clippings break down so fast, releasing their own nitrogen as they do so, that it does not make much difference.

Drought-proof plants

The appearance of some plants gives you a good clue to their drought tolerance. Anything with thick, waxy foliage, silver leaves or tough, needle-like leaves is a good bet. Plants whose leaves have been replaced by green stems, such as broom, genista and gorse, are also suitable since the stems do the work of leaves without the water loss. Aromatic foliage is naturally waterproofed by the oils and resins; good examples of this type of plant are eucalyptus and evergreen herbs like rosemary and thyme. The Mediterranean region, where winters are mild and wet, with hot, dry summers, is home to countless drought-tolerant candidates. But, besides these, self-sown seedlings of a huge range of plants, such as *Eschscholzia californica, Euphorbia characias,* hellebores, *Linaria purpurea, Verbascum bombyciferum, Verbena bonariensis* and wallflowers, are extremely drought-proof. Letting seed germinate where it falls, and leaving seedlings to grow on the spot without being transplanted, means that the roots are never disturbed so they dig deep to find their own water supply.

Watering

You can make good use of all available water by installing several water-butts, and a water diverter that allows you to store rainwater from the roof and even bathwater. There are also extra gadgets that allow you to connect several water-butts together for extra storage. Keep water-butts clean by emptying them once or twice a year and scrubbing them out well, and keep the lids on so that algae cannot grow inside and turn the water green.

Ground-cover gardening

Establishing a low-growing carpet of plants to reduce labour is very appealing. This type of gardening was a popular style during the 1960s when the idea was to make a complete garden out of nothing but shrubs and woody ground-cover plants like *Cotoneaster horizontalis*. This was intended to look good all year without needing much work, since ground-cover plants would smother out weeds. A popular variation on the theme was the heather and conifer garden. As low-maintenance gardens they certainly worked, but the trouble was they never changed from one season to the next, and people soon got fed up with looking out over the same view.

Ground-cover gardens today look much more varied because we have plants like ground-cover roses, ornamental grasses and all sorts of low-spreading perennials that were either very rare or non-existent in the 1960s. There are also new materials for mulching, like the woven plastic sheet mulches you plant through when making a new bed. Nowadays you can get out of weeding altogether.

Most of us have been using ground cover for years under different names. Depending on the situation, you'll find it referred to as a living mulch, underplanting, or a carpet of plants. Each time you plant carpets of spring bulbs or interlocking mats of perennials under shrubs, it is a form of ground-cover planting. A mixture of old-fashioned or shrub roses underplanted with a mixture of spreading perennials like campanula, pulmonaria or hardy cranesbills in a cottage garden is also a form of ground cover. Thickset, tuft-forming grasses like *Festuca glauca* make ideal ground cover for hot, dry borders.

Even clematis can be used for ground cover. Use the normal climbing clematis to ramble over ground or scramble across a bank or over the top of spring-

Dense planting is one of the keys to success with ground cover.

flowering perennials. This is a very good way to hide the untidy foliage of daffodils naturalized in a border. Use *Clematis viticella* varieties or large-flowered hybrids that bloom from mid-summer onwards and prune them back hard, to about 15cm (6in) high, in early spring so you can see the spring flowers before the new clematis stems cover the ground.

Ground-cover roses are a wonderful way to cover the soil in front of normal rose bushes. They also look good grown over a bank or cascading down over the steep sides of a terraced slope. You can even partner them with a ground-cover rose grown on a standard stem: 'Nozomi' is a real winner grown this way and looks like a flowering waterfall. Do plant ground-cover roses through a mulch of plastic sheeting to smother out weeds. The stems of roses don't make a sufficiently dense cover to do the job, and believe me it is murder trying to weed between prickly, not-quite-ground-covering stems.

Make the most of plants such as vincas and some hardy cranesbills like *Geranium* 'Ann Folkard', which will scramble up into shrubs as well as covering the ground for a natural-looking effect.

Hardy geraniums are among the most effective ground covers. Here are Geranium psilostemon *(left) and* G. magnificum *(right).*

And when using woody plants like creeping cotoneasters, peg them down to the soil with wire pins to encourage them to root at intervals; you will get much stronger, faster-spreading ground cover as the plants layer themselves. So next time you have a situation vacant in your garden, there's probably a ground-cover plant poised to fill it.

Ground-cover solutions

If you have a grassy bank that is too steep to mow safely, plant it with a mixture of dwarf spring bulbs and drought-tolerant, low, spreading perennials, such as hebe, *Genista lydia* and cistus, and you'll never need bother about it again. Or in shade go for a mixture of ivies, winter jasmine and euonymus.

On a really steep slope where the soil gets washed away when it rains, or if you need to prevent rabbits burrowing, plant through holes cut in small-mesh wire netting pegged down firmly all over the soil.

To help stabilize the steep banks of a stream, grow a mixture of spreading waterside plants like creeping Jenny (*Lysimachia nummularia*), water mint, and houttuynia with *Cornus stolonifera* 'Flaviramea'.

PERENNIALS FOR GROUND COVER	
Ajuga	Festuca
Alchemilla mollis	Geranium species
Anthemis punctata subsp.	Hosta
cupaniana	Lamium
Artemisia 'Powis Castle'	Nepeta
Brunnera	Potentilla
Campanula muralis	Pulmonaria
Epimedium	*Stachys byzantina*
Euphorbia dulcis 'Chameleon',	Thyme – creeping
E. cyparissias and *E. robbiae*	

Mediterranean gardens

Remember all those jokes about the British weather? They may have died out for a while but probably not for ever. Whether it was due to climate changes or a blip in meteorological history, the mild, rainy winters and the long, hot, dry summers akin to those of the Mediterranean that we have experienced over the last few years seem to have ended. The traditional wetness – April showers, summer thunderstorms, autumn downpours and winter snow melting to produce spring floods – remains. The wet weather is the reason Britain is such a green country. Although fine weather and sunshine are enjoyable, they do make things very difficult for gardens, especially when they are accompanied by the inevitable water shortages and hosepipe bans.

This sort of weather is nothing new for people who already garden in dry spots such as East Anglia, where the rainfall is naturally low, and anywhere with fast-draining sandy or gravel soils. People who garden in these conditions have been coping with distinctly Mediterranean-like conditions for a good many years. They'll tell you normal gardening is virtually out of the question. You just cannot keep up with the watering, so bedding plants are a waste of time and even lawns spend half the year looking brown and crisp. The solution is to take a few tips from real Mediterranean gardeners.

Instead of fighting the climate, go along with it. You can use paving or gravel to make a patio or courtyard-style garden instead of one based around a grass lawn. Substitute naturally drought-proof plants for the traditional water guzzlers. It is a good idea to avoid things like bedding plants as they are so shallow-rooted. Instead grow more shrubs, especially evergreens (whose thick leaves do not lose so much water as those of deciduous shrubs) like phormium, olearia and pittosporum. Grasses and perennial plants with silvery or waxy-coated leaves, such as artemisia, euphorbia and sedum, which are all adapted to life in hot, dry places, are a good choice. Grow climbers that thrive in heat and sun, like grapevines and trumpet vine (campsis). For containers, choose heat-loving, drought-tolerant, half-hardy perennials like pelargonium, gazania and osteospermum. They won't drop dead the first time you miss a watering, and they actually do better given plenty of heat and sun.

My own Mediterranean garden in Hampshire utilizes such plants as lavender and cannas positioned next to a Cretan pithos.

Take advantage of the better summers to grow unusual half-hardy perennials like shrubby salvias and solanums, datura and anisodonta – new ones I've never heard of are popping up on nursery stands at shows all the time and they are well worth looking out for.

If you want to grow vegetables, forget the traditional large-scale plot where your lettuces bolt at the first sniff of a hosepipe ban. Choose a small, very intensive, deep vegetable bed instead, where the roots can go down deep and you have only a small area to water. If water shortages are a regular summer problem in your area, try to recycle your own waste household water to use on the garden. When water is short, use it where it counts most, on vegetables, containers and anything newly planted. Established trees, shrubs and roses can fend for themselves. Even though the lawn may turn brown, it will recover at the end of the summer when the autumn rains start, so don't waste water trying to keep it green.

GRAVEL GARDENS

A gravel garden is a good way to grow naturally drought-proof plants, as it gives them an attractive setting and saves you time. The gravel surface acts as a permanent mulch that prevents weed seedlings from germinating and also saves water by reducing evaporation.

◆ Choose a hot, sunny spot and prepare the soil well. Finish off by raking the soil level, then spread a 5-cm (2-in) layer of gravel all over the surface.

◆ Plant your gravel garden in autumn if possible so that plants have all winter for their roots to establish; it will also reduce the amount of watering you will have to do while plants settle in. Alternatively plant in spring and water until plants become established. Avoid summer planting if you possibly can as you will need to do a lot of watering.

◆ Plant through the gravel, so the rootballs go down into the soil, leaving a collar of gravel all around the plants.

◆ There is no need to try to plant a complete carpet of plants over the area. A gravel garden looks best when sparsely planted and where large chunks of stone or piles of smooth, rounded pebbles for decoration.

◆ Add a few terracotta containers planted with permanent plants such as agapanthus, or a mixture of hardy evergreen herbs, and plunge the base of each container a few centimetres into the gravel. This encourages the plants to root through into the soil underneath, which will cut down on watering.

The sloping ground in my garden makes it relatively easy to use streams of gravel as ground cover to show off drought-tolerant plants.

PLANTS FOR A MEDITERRANEAN OR GRAVEL GARDEN

Agapanthus	Galtonia	Penstemon
Centranthus (Valerian)	Genista	Phormium
Cistus	Hardy hibiscus	Rosmarinus (Rosemary)
Crocosmia	Hebe	Salvia (Sage)
Dierama	Helianthemum	Sedum
Echinops	Lavandula (Lavender)	Sempervivum
Eryngium	Allium (Ornamental	Thymus (Thyme)
Euphorbia	onion)	Yucca

GARDENERS' DIARY

I've been gardening all my life but I still find a gardening calendar useful to remind me which seeds need sowing, what needs planting and what needs pruning at a particular time of year. This section is an *aide-memoire* that should help you sleep more easily, safe in the knowledge that you won't forget anything!

Diary **Early Spring**

✳ flowers

- Dig up and divide overcrowded snowdrops.
- Divide border perennials.
- Prune roses.
- Sow sweet peas outdoors in favourable weather.
- Plant out autumn-sown sweet peas.
- Plant lily of the valley crowns.
- Protect hostas and other susceptible plants from slugs.
- Scatter rose fertilizer around bushes and fork it into the soil.
- Scatter fertilizer among border perennials and fork it into the soil.
- Prepare ground for summer bedding.
- Sow hardy annuals outdoors when the soil is in a fit condition.
- Plant gladiolus corms.
- Thin out autumn-sown annuals.
- Take cuttings from border perennials and root them in sandy compost in a cold frame.
- Plant new border perennials.
- Construct rock gardens and plant alpines.

🍎 fruit

- Plant fruit trees and bushes.
- Mulch raspberry canes with compost or manure.
- Plant strawberries on well-prepared soil.
- Pollinate outdoor peaches, nectarines and apricots and protect the blossom with muslin or old net curtains.
- Firm in newly planted fruit trees and bushes after frost.
- Soak the soil around wall-trained fruit trees and mulch with manure.

The dry riverbed of pebbles makes an attractive year-round feature.

- Prune raspberries.
- Spray outdoor peaches, nectarines and apricots to control peach leaf curl.
- Sprinkle general fertilizer around strawberries and fork it into the soil.
- Mulch fruit trees with well-rotted manure or garden compost.
- Tie in wayward branches on wall-trained fruit trees.

✎ vegetables

- Sow broad beans, broccoli, Brussels sprouts, cabbages, carrots, cauliflowers, leeks, lettuces, onions, parsnips, peas, radishes, spinach and turnips outdoors if weather permits.
- Plant rhubarb.
- Prepare celery trenches.
- Protect plants from slugs.
- Prepare soil on the vegetable plot.
- Plant early potatoes.

- Plant shallots and onion sets.
- Sow mustard and cress indoors.
- Sow herbs in a cold frame.
- Plant autumn-sown cauliflowers.
- Plant out cabbages raised under glass in January.
- Plant mint in a bottomless bucket to restrict its spread.
- Net brassicas to protect them from pigeons.

▥ lawns

- Make new lawns from turf.
- Spike and scarify lawns to improve surface drainage and remove thatch.
- Mow with the blades set no lower than 2.5cm (1in).

The plank walkway through my woodland garden makes it easy to admire the plants, which often look best in spring.

Helleborus orientalis has welcome spring flowers, useful for growing in dappled shade.

⌂ greenhouse

- Hand pollinate peaches, nectarines and apricots.
- Pot on foliage plants.
- Pinch out shoot tips of fuchsias as they grow.
- Take cuttings of chrysanthemums, pelargoniums, fuchsias and other pot plants.
- Sow half-hardy and tender annuals in a heated propagator.
- Dry out freesias and cyclamen after flowering.
- Pot up begonia tubers, achimenes and sinningia tubers.
- Water and ventilate with care.
- Pot up rooted cuttings.
- Start dahlia tubers into growth in a warm greenhouse and take cuttings from those already producing shoots.
- Thin early grapes growing in heated greenhouses.
- Sow celery and celeriac.
- Sow tomatoes, cucumbers, melons, aubergines and peppers for greenhouse growing.
- Cover seedlings with single sheets of newspaper on sunny days to prevent them from being scorched.
- Repot houseplants and give them a week or two in the greenhouse as convalescence.

Diary Mid-spring

✳ flowers

- Take cuttings from sturdy, young shoots on border perennials and root them in pots of cuttings compost in a garden frame.
- Complete the dividing up and re-planting of overcrowded border perennials.
- Continue planting gladiolus corms in a sunny spot in well-drained soil.
- Continue constructing rock gardens and planting alpines for instant spring colour.
- Continue sowing hardy annuals in vacant spaces in beds and borders.
- Plant evergreen shrubs and trees.
- Transplant evergreens that need moving.
- Continue sprinkling rose fertilizer around rose bushes and lightly fork it into the soil.
- Prune forsythia after flowering, cutting out a portion of old, flowered wood.
- Propagate rhododendrons by layering suitable branches.
- Continue planting out greenhouse-raised sweet peas.
- Prune *Buddleja davidii* by cutting it hard back.
- Construct garden pools and plant aquatics and waterlilies.
- Where aphids become a problem, spray with a specific aphicide.
- Remove faded flowers from spring-flowering bulbs and give the plants a sprinkling of general fertilizer.
- Start dahlia tubers into growth in trays of compost in a garden frame.
- Harden off bedding plants in a garden frame before they are planted out in late spring.

ABOVE: *The headily fragrant spring flowers of* Viburnum × burkwoodii. BELOW: *The great white cherry,* Prunus *'Tai Haku'.*

🍎 fruit

- Strawberries need to be planted as soon as possible now.
- Pollinate outdoor peaches, nectarines and apricots by hand.
- Prick over the ground among established strawberries with a fork and remove weeds.
- Prune damaged branches from fruit trees and bushes.
- If you haven't done so already, sprinkle general fertilizer around fruit trees and bushes and lightly fork it into the soil.
- Keep down weeds between fruit bushes by light hoeing.
- Start vines into growth in unheated greenhouses.
- Pinch out badly placed shoots on wall-trained fruit trees as they start to grow.
- Place cloches over a few strawberry plants to produce an early crop.
- Spray gooseberries with a systemic fungicide if mildew is a problem.
- Thin out the fruits of peaches, nectarines and apricots being grown under glass to leave one fruit every 15cm (6in) or so.
- Tie in lengthening growths on greenhouse-grown grape vines to the support wires.

🔨 vegetables

- Sow broad beans, beetroot, broccoli, Brussels sprouts, cabbages, carrots, cauliflowers, kale, kohlrabi, leeks, lettuces, onions, parsnips, peas, radishes, rocket, spinach, swedes, Swiss chard and turnips outdoors.
- Scatter general fertilizer around spring cabbages and hoe it into the soil.
- Protect young vegetable plants with netting if birds are a problem.
- Plant early, second early and maincrop potatoes.
- Plant globe artichokes.
- Continue preparing trenches for celery and runner beans by manuring a strip of ground for each.

- Plant onion sets.
- Plant asparagus crowns in rich, well-drained soil.
- Harden off greenhouse-raised vegetables in a garden frame.
- Protect the growing shoots of early potatoes by earthing up round plants.
- Sow celery in trays in a garden frame.
- Thin out overcrowded vegetable seedlings.
- Sow parsley in soil that has been enriched with compost or manure.

🪟 lawns

- Mow fortnightly now, still setting the blades high – to around 2.5cm (1in).
- Sow new lawns on well-prepared, weed-free ground.
- Make new lawns from turf.
- Re-turf or re-seed bare patches.

🏠 greenhouse

- Sow half-hardy and tender annuals for summer bedding and greenhouse displays.
- Sow tomatoes to be grown outdoors.
- Prick out seedlings from earlier sowings.
- Shade seedlings in spells of bright sunshine.

- Plant tomato plants, peppers and aubergines in a heated greenhouse.
- Pot on flowering and foliage pot plants that have outgrown their containers.
- Allow freesias and cyclamen to dry off in their pots after flowering.
- Plant cucumbers and melons in a heated greenhouse.
- Sow sweet peppers, cucumbers, melons and aubergines for growing in an unheated greenhouse.
- Take cuttings of flowering and foliage pot plants.
- Sow French beans at the rate of five to a 20cm (8in) flowerpot to provide an early crop under glass.
- Sow marrows and courgettes for planting out in late spring.
- Pot up begonia and gloxinia tubers for greenhouse decoration.
- Ventilate your greenhouse well in sunny spells – an automatic ventilating arm is a great investment.
- Pot up overwintered cuttings of geraniums, fuchsias and other half-hardy perennials.
- Sow broad beans, runner beans, peas, onions, lettuces and leeks for planting out later.

An old, cottage-garden favourite, aubrieta looks at home tumbling over walls.

Diary Late spring

✷ flowers

- Push in twiggy pea sticks around border perennials to give support.
- Continue to harden off bedding plants in a garden frame.
- Protect susceptible plants against slugs.
- Plant out greenhouse-raised sweet peas.
- Plant waterlilies and other aquatics in garden pools.
- Plant dahlia tubers at the foot of stout stakes in rich, well-drained soil.
- Risk sowing a few half-hardy annuals outdoors.
- Thin out hardy annuals to prevent overcrowding.
- Once danger of frost is past, plant out summer bedding.
- Dig up, divide and replant polyanthus after flowering.
- Clear spring bedding from beds and borders as soon as it fades, and lightly fork in general fertilizer before summer bedding is planted.

- Remove faded flower heads from daffodils, but do not cut down the foliage just yet.
- Plant up hanging baskets but do not put them outdoors until all danger of frost is past.
- Introduce fish to garden pools.

🍅 fruit

- Where aphids are a problem, spray with a specific aphicide that will not harm beneficial insects.
- Work straw among strawberry rows, or lay black polythene to act as a mulch and prevent the fruits from being soiled.
- Make sure that newly planted fruit trees and bushes do not go short of water.
- Keep part of a row of strawberries covered with cloches or a polythene tunnel to harvest an earlier crop.
- Pick off and burn any peach, nectarine and apricot leaves that show signs of leaf curl. Give the plants a foliar feed.

- Protect strawberries from slug damage by tucking straw underneath them.
- Spray gooseberries with a systemic fungicide if mildew is a problem.
- Thin out raspberry canes to leave about half a dozen new ones per plant. Tie these in to the support system.
- Cover strawberries with plastic netting to prevent birds from eating their fill.
- Thin the fruits of outdoor peaches, nectarines and apricots to leave one fruit every 15cm (6in) or so.
- Harvest rhubarb regularly.
- If there are runners on strawberries, remove them unless you want to make new plants from them.
- Thin out gooseberries and use these early pickings in a pie.

✎ vegetables

- Sow broad beans, French beans, runner beans, beetroot, broccoli, Brussels sprouts, cabbages, carrots, cauliflowers, endives, kale, kohlrabi, leeks, lettuces, onions, parsley, parsnips, peas, radishes, rocket, salsify, scorzonera, spinach, spring onions, swedes, sweetcorn, Swiss chard and turnips outdoors if weather permits.
- Plant maincrop potatoes.
- Erect supports for runner beans.
- Hoe between vegetable rows to keep down weeds.
- Support peas with twiggy pea sticks or canes and twine.
- Plant out greenhouse-raised broad beans, runner beans, peas, onions, lettuces and leeks.
- Plant out celery and celeriac.

A waterfall of flowers from Cytisus *'Minstead', growing alongside* Deutzia *'Mont Rose'.*

The horizontal branches of Viburnum plicatum *'Mariesii' are a spectacular highlight of the spring garden.*

- Harvest asparagus from established beds.
- Earth up potatoes.

▥ lawns

- Apply a combined weedkiller and fertilizer dressing to the lawn.
- Sow new lawns.
- Spot treat lawn weeds if no general lawn weedkiller is to be applied.
- Mow lawns once a week now, reducing the height of the cut to 2cm ($^3/_4$in).

▣ greenhouse

- Take cuttings of chrysanthemums for growing in pots.
- Remove sideshoots from greenhouse-grown tomatoes.
- Sow seeds of cinerarias, cyclamen and greenhouse primulas for winter flowers.

- Sow marrows, courgettes, melons and sweetcorn individually in small pots for planting out later.
- Continue to prick out seedlings of half-hardy and tender annuals.
- Pinch out sideshoots of cucumbers and melons when two sideshoots have been formed.
- Pot on begonia and gloxinia tubers when they outgrow their containers.
- Tie in lengthening growths of grape vines.
- Ventilate well and damp down the floor of the greenhouse on sunny days.
- Plant tomatoes in an unheated greenhouse.
- Feed all plants in active growth once a week from now on.
- Take cuttings from flowering and foliage pot plants and root them in a propagator.
- Pot up rooted cuttings.
- Remove male flowers from cucumber plants before they open – male flowers, unlike female flowers, don't have a small swelling at their base.
- Continue to dry off freesias and cyclamen in their pots.

- Introduce insect predators as biological control for red spider mites and whitefly, or fumigate to keep on top of these pests.
- Apply some form of shading to the outside of the greenhouse or add blinds.

Spring-flowering red campion seeds itself happily among shrubs in my garden.

Diary Early summer

The giant bellflower, Campanula latifolia, makes a stately show in early summer with its blue or white flowers.

✳ flowers

- Plant summer bedding.
- Sow wallflower, forget-me-not, Canterbury bell and sweet William seeds outdoors in drills.
- Prune shrubs that flowered in spring.
- Clip hedges.
- Plant up window boxes and troughs.
- Keep newly planted beds and borders watered in prolonged dry spells,
- Support taller annuals and perennials with twiggy pea sticks pushed into the soil.
- Dig up and divide overcrowded clumps of large-flowered irises once they have finished flowering.
- Spray roses to control pests and diseases, if necessary.
- Dig up and dry off tulip and hyacinth bulbs for replanting in autumn.
- Remove suckers from rose bushes as soon as they are seen.
- Remove faded flowers from roses and border plants.

🍎 fruit

- Tie in extending shoots of blackberries and loganberries to the support wires.
- Summer prune gooseberries and currant bushes by shortening sideshoots by one third.
- Harvest rhubarb regularly and remove any flower spikes that form.
- Plant melons in a garden frame.
- Remove damaged branches from plum trees.
- Protect strawberries from slugs by tucking straw underneath the fruit.
- Space out and tie in the stems of wall-trained fruit trees.
- Pick raspberries and strawberries.
- Mulch raspberry canes with well-rotted manure, garden compost or grass clippings when the soil is moist.

🔧 vegetables

- Sow broad, French and runner beans, beetroot, carrots, chicory, endives, herbs, kohlrabi, lettuces, marrows and courgettes, peas, radishes, salsify, scorzonera, spinach, swedes, sweetcorn, Swiss chard and turnips.
- Complete the harvesting of asparagus, leaving all remaining shoots to grow.
- Thin vegetable seedlings in the row to prevent overcrowding
- Make sure onions do not go short of water or the bulbs will stop fattening.
- Stake peas with twiggy branches or canes and twine.
- Protect susceptible plants from birds.
- Pull up soil around leeks to blanch the stems, and earth up potatoes.
- Pinch shoot tips from broad beans once the plants are 45cm (1½ft) high to discourage blackfly.
- Plant tomatoes outdoors in a sunny spot in well-drained soil.
- Harvest early potatoes.

▥ lawns

- Mow once a week with the blades set at around 1cm (½in).
- Give tired lawns a liquid feed for a quick pick-me-up.
- Apply a combined weedkiller and fertilizer dressing if you have not already done so this year.
- Irrigate lawns in dry weather, provided a hosepipe or sprinkler ban is not in force. If water *is* in short supply, remember that the lawn will be the first thing to suffer but the first thing to recover. Drought does not kill lawns, it just turns them brown.

⌂ greenhouse

- Prick out seedlings and pot on rooted cuttings.
- Make sure the greenhouse is shaded and well ventilated on sunny days.
- Feed all plants in active growth once a week.
- Thin out the fruits on greenhouse grapes.
- Feed tomatoes once a week as soon as fruits have formed.
- Train and feed cucumbers and melons (continuing to pick male flowers from cucumber, and making sure that female melon flowers are pollinated).
- Use biological control or fumigate if pests are a problem.
- Damp down the floor and staging of the greenhouse morning and evening.

- Sow seeds of greenhouse primulas, calceolarias, cyclamen and cinerarias for flowers next spring.
- Continue to train vines.
- Take cuttings from pot plants such as pelargoniums and fuchsias.

ABOVE: These old paeonies were growing in my garden when it was a rough orchard twenty years ago, and they still bloom well each year. BELOW: The 'teahouse', framed by early summer flowers, is a great place to sit in the afternoon sun.

Diary Mid-summer

✳ flowers

- Remove faded flowers from roses, annuals and perennials regularly.
- Sprinkle fertilizer around perennials and shrubs and hoe it into the soil.
- Disbud dahlias and roses being grown for exhibition.
- Control pests and diseases on roses.
- Thin out the shoots of *Clematis montana* if they look like a disembowelled mattress.
- Water hanging baskets at least once a day.
- Cut faded foliage from spring-flowering bulbs six weeks after the blooms have faded.
- Hand weed between border plants and annuals.
- Make sure bedding plants do not go short of water.

- Shorten long shoots on wisteria, cutting them back to around 30cm (12in).
- Stake gladioli.
- Prune weigela and philadelphus, cutting out completely a portion of older wood.
- Clip hedges, especially privet and box. Yew can wait until the end of the summer.
- Take semi-ripe cuttings of shrubs and root them in a propagating frame with bottom heat.
- Transplant wallflowers and other spring bedders, spacing them 15cm (6in) apart in rows 45cm (18in) apart on the vegetable plot or a spare patch of ground.
- Plant madonna lilies in good soil and a sunny spot.
- Take cuttings of pinks and border carnations.

- Train in young and extending shoots of climbing and rambling roses and clematis.

🍎 fruit

- Net raspberries and strawberries to protect them from birds.
- Peg down strawberry runners into pots of compost to produce new plants.
- Cut foliage and remove straw from strawberries that have finished fruiting.
- Remove flower spikes from rhubarb and mulch the plants with manure or compost.
- Thin out fruits on trained fruit trees.

Yew and box hedges give year-round form to a garden and act as a perfect foil for summer flowers.

*The Mediterranean garden comes into its own, with pencil cypresses (*Cupressus sempervirens *'Stricta') surrounded by summer flowers.*

- Pick raspberries regularly.
- Cut back the sideshoots of gooseberries and currants by one third if you have not already done so.
- Summer prune trained apple trees by cutting back sideshoots.
- Dig up and replant strawberry beds that are more than three years old.
- Sprinkle rose fertilizer around soft fruit bushes and hoe it into the soil.
- Cut out branches of plum trees that are affected with silver-leaf disease or prune to reduce overcrowding.
- Pot up strawberry plants for forcing in the greenhouse next spring.
- Prune blackcurrants by cutting out three or four older branches as soon as the fruit has been harvested.

vegetables

- Sow broad beans, beetroot, spring cabbages, carrots, endives, kohlrabi, lettuces, radishes, spinach, Swiss chard and turnips.
- Plant out leeks raised from a spring sowing.
- Make successional sowings of vegetables to keep up a constant supply of fresh produce.
- Plant out winter-maturing cabbages.
- Water crops thoroughly in dry spells.
- Thin vegetable seedlings to prevent overcrowding.
- Apply liquid feed to onions.
- Cut and dry herbs for winter use.
- Earth up celery to blanch the stems.
- Mulch runner beans with grass clippings when the soil is moist.
- Continue to harvest early potatoes.
- Harvest globe artichokes.
- Lift and dry off shallots under cloches or in a frame.
- Cover peas with netting to protect the crop from birds.

lawns

- Raise the height of cut on the mower to 2.5cm (1in) if the weather is very dry.
- Irrigate the lawn, if possible, in dry weather.
- Apply a liquid feed in damp weather to give the lawn a boost.

greenhouse

- Take cuttings of flowering and foliage pot plants and root them in a propagating frame.
- Spray peaches, nectarines and apricots with tepid water every day.
- Introduce predators to effect biological control.
- Feed all plants in active growth once a week with liquid fertilizer.
- Damp down the floor and staging of the greenhouse morning and evening.
- Pot up rooted cuttings.
- Pick faded flowers and foliage from all plants.
- Arrange for someone to water your plants while you are on holiday.
- Take leaf cuttings of African violets, *Begonia rex*, streptocarpus and gloxinias.
- Continue to remove sideshoots from tomatoes and male flowers from cucumbers.
- Remove small side buds on tuberous begonia plants to encourage full development of the central flower.
- Remove one or two leaves around ripening tomato fruits to improve air circulation.
- Support melons in nets as they ripen.

Diary Late summer

❄ flowers

- Plant colchicums, autumn-flowering crocuses and hardy cyclamen.
- Remove faded flowers from roses, annuals and perennials.
- Clip yew and other hedges.
- Remove the side flower buds from dahlias and chrysanthemums, leaving only the centre one on each stem, if you want large flowers.
- Take cuttings of border carnations and pinks and tender perennials such as penstemons.
- Water hanging baskets daily and feed them every two weeks.
- Spray roses to control severe outbreaks of pests and diseases.
- Water newly planted container-grown plants in dry weather.
- Sow hardy primulas outdoors in moist ground.
- Cut and dry everlasting flowers for decoration.
- Take cuttings of flowering shrubs and root them in a heated propagator.
- Trap earwigs among dahlias by inverting straw-filled flowerpots on garden canes among the plants.
- Take cuttings of rock and alpine plants.
- Prune rambling roses when the flowers have faded.

🍅 fruit

- Cut out raspberry canes at ground level after harvesting fruit.
- Cut out two or three older stems from blackcurrants after harvesting the fruit.
- Dig up old strawberry beds and make a new one on a different site.
- Pick early apples as soon as they will part easily from the tree.
- Propagate blackberries and loganberries by tip layering.
- Prepare the ground for fruit trees and bushes to be planted in autumn, and order your chosen varieties now.
- Pot up strawberries for forcing in the greenhouse next spring.
- Support plum branches that are heavily laden and pick the fruits as soon as they are ripe.
- Summer prune wall-trained fruit trees.

🥕 vegetables

- Sow spring cabbages, endives, kohlrabi, lettuces, radishes, spinach and turnips.
- Harvest crops while they are small and tender.
- Hoe between vegetable rows to keep down weeds.
- Dry off shallots under cloches or in a frame.
- Blanch leeks and celery by drawing up soil towards the stems. Blanch endives by covering the centre of the plants with an upturned flowerpot and blocking the hole to exclude light.
- Feed marrows and courgettes with liquid fertilizer once a week.
- The leaves of onions should be bent over to hasten ripening of the bulbs. Once they have begun to dry off and the bulbs have stopped growing, they can be lifted and further ripened in a greenhouse or garden frame.
- Mulch runner beans with grass clippings or compost if not done.

A plant 'theatre', filled with potted auriculas in spring and pelargoniums in summer.

- Make sure no developing crops go short of water.
- Make a new compost heap.

⚏ lawns

- Mow lawns weekly, raising the height of cut in dry weather.
- Irrigate lawns in dry weather, provided a sprinkler or hosepipe ban is not in force.
- Apply a selective lawn weedkiller if weeds are getting out of hand.
- Prepare ground to be sown with grass seed.
- If you are making a new lawn from turf, make sure it does not dry out after laying.

⬛ greenhouse

- Pot up freesia corms for winter flowers.
- Ventilate the greenhouse well and damp down the floor and staging morning and evening.

- Pinch sideshoots from tomatoes and remove a few leaves around developing fruits to improve air circulation.
- Feed all plants in active growth once a week.
- Introduce biological control or fumigate if pests are a problem.
- Remove faded flowers and foliage from all plants.
- Pot up rooted cuttings.
- Sow cyclamen and schizanthus.

A summer mixture of annuals: eschscholzia, mallows, coreopsis and limnanthes.

- Take cuttings of flowering and foliage pot plants.
- Stop watering melons as soon as they start to ripen.

By mixing conifers and shrubs, annuals and perennials, the garden scene is ever changing.

Diary **Early autumn**

ABOVE: Rosa rugosa *in autumn* BELOW: *The burnished leaves of maples in Hampshire.*

✳ **flowers**

- Take cuttings of roses and root them outdoors in a sheltered spot.
- Plant spring-flowering bulbs such as daffodils, narcissi and crocuses outdoors where they are to flower.
- Take cuttings of conifers and evergreen trees and shrubs and root them in a propagator.
- Sow hardy annuals outdoors for flowers next summer.
- Continue to disbud dahlias and chrysanthemums.

- Remove faded flower heads from annuals, perennials and roses.
- Plant lily bulbs in beds and borders or in large pots.
- Pull out and compost faded hardy annuals.
- Prune rambling roses.
- Protect the blooms of outdoor chrysanthemums with special white paper bags.
- This is a good time to move evergreens and conifers growing in the wrong place.
- Sow sweet peas outdoors in a sheltered spot.

🍎 fruit

- Continue to harvest and store apples and pears.
- Tie in the new growths on raspberry canes to the support wires.
- Prepare the ground for fruit trees and bushes to be planted this autumn and order your chosen varieties now.
- Harvest plums and damsons as soon as they are ripe.
- Complete the planting of new strawberry beds.
- Propagate gooseberries by rooting cuttings outdoors.
- Check fruit tree ties and stakes to make sure they are secure.
- Remove any runners that form on newly planted strawberries.
- Complete the pruning of raspberries and loganberries.
- Cut out blackberry canes when they have finished cropping and tie in new ones.

🏹 vegetables

- Sow lettuces, spinach and turnips.
- Plant out spring cabbages.
- Continue to blanch endives.
- Net brassicas to prevent bird damage.
- Take precautions against slugs to prevent lettuces and other crops from being damaged.
- Hoe regularly between vegetable rows to keep down weeds.
- Cut and dry herbs for winter use.
- Remove dead leaves from brassicas and other crops.
- Water growing crops in dry weather.
- Dig up and store potatoes, carrots and beetroot.
- Store onions in a dry, bright place.
- Pick any unripened fruit from outdoor tomatoes and then compost the plants.
- Fork over and clean up ground vacated by harvested vegetables.
- Protect the developing curds of cauliflowers by bending a few leaves over them.

One of the best shrub roses for colourful hips is Rosa moyesii *'Geranium'.*

🏛 lawns

- Make new lawns by sowing seed or laying turf.
- Raise the height of cut on the mower to around 2.5cm (1in) and reduce the frequency of mowing.
- Do not apply any more fertilizer or weedkiller to the lawn now.

🏠 greenhouse

- Plant spring-flowering bulbs such as hyacinths and narcissi in pots and bowls and keep them cool and dark for a couple of months.
- Sow winter lettuces in a vacant greenhouse border.
- Dry off begonia and gloxinia tubers to rest them for the winter.
- Sow annuals in pots for a spring greenhouse display.
- Prick out seedlings of flowering pot plants sown earlier.
- Remove all remaining fruits from cucumbers, melons, tomatoes and peppers and compost the plants.
- Use biological control or fumigate to control pests and diseases.
- Take cuttings of pelargoniums and fuchsias.
- Pot up rooted cuttings.
- Remove faded leaves and flowers from all pot plants.
- There is no longer any need to damp down now that temperatures are lowering and the air is becoming damper.
- Continue to ventilate the greenhouse in sunny spells.
- Pot up hippeastrum bulbs for winter flowers, but give them very little water until the flower spike is well clear of the bulb.
- Pot up freesia corms for a winter display.
- Bring late-flowering chrysanthemums into a cool greenhouse.

Diary Mid-autumn

A guinea fowl sculpted by Dennis Fairweather perches on top of my old garden fork.

❋ flowers

- Clear faded summer bedding plants from beds and borders.
- Sweep up and stack fallen leaves to rot down into leaf mould.
- Propagate deciduous shrubs by hardwood cuttings.
- Dig up and store gladiolus corms.
- Plant out wallflowers and other spring bedding plants.
- Plant new herbaceous perennials on light soils.
- Plant conifers and evergreen trees and shrubs.
- Plant winter- and spring-flowering bulbs.
- Plant lily bulbs outdoors and in pots.
- Take hardwood cuttings of roses and root outdoors.
- Sow sweet peas in pots in a cold frame.
- Dig up and store dahlia tubers once their foliage is blackened by frost.

- Cut down faded border perennials and lightly fork the soil between them.
- Dig up, divide and replant overcrowded clumps of lily of the valley.
- Deadhead roses.
- Protect tender plants such as gunnera with a layer of bracken or straw.

🍅 fruit

- Pick and store any remaining apples and pears.
- Cut out blackberry and loganberry canes that have finished cropping and tie in new ones to the support framework.

- Check that stakes on fruit trees are secure and that ties are not constricting growth.
- Cut out fruited raspberry canes and tie in new ones to support wires.
- Order fruit trees and bushes to be planted this autumn; prepare ground.
- Remove runners from newly planted strawberries.
- Check fruits in store and remove any that show signs of rotting.
- Shelter pot-grown strawberries from heavy rain.
- Take hardwood cuttings of currants and gooseberries.

Larches look stunning in autumn.

The Persian ironwood, Parrotia persica, *provides wonderful colour through the season.*

- Examine pears in store every couple of days and eat them as soon as they are ripe.

vegetables

- Sow cauliflowers and lettuces, as well as broad beans ('The Sutton') and peas ('Meteor') under cloches in a sheltered spot.
- Cut down and remove foliage of asparagus.
- Dig up and store any remaining potatoes.
- Protect cauliflower curds by bending two or three leaves over them.
- Cut down globe artichokes and protect the crowns with straw.
- Pick and store any remaining marrows or runner beans.
- Plant winter lettuces in a cold frame.
- Remove any faded leaves from vegetables and hoe between the rows to keep down weeds.
- Dig up and store carrots and beetroots in boxes of dry sand.
- Cover brassicas with plastic netting to protect them from pigeons.
- Stake large Brussels sprout plants on exposed sites.
- Dig over ground as it becomes vacant.
- Cut down the stems of Jerusalem artichokes.
- Check onions and potatoes in store to make sure they are not rotting.
- Plant spring cabbages.

lawns

- Make new lawns from turf.
- Scarify lawns with a wire-toothed rake to remove dead grass and spike the surface with a fork if drainage is poor.
- Mow much less frequently now, and with the blades set high. When the weather turns cold, send the machine off for servicing.

greenhouse

- Heat may be needed to protect tender plants at night if frost threatens.
- Box up a few mint roots for winter supplies.
- Fumigate if pests and diseases are a problem.
- Prick out cyclamen and other seedlings sown in summer.
- Remove faded leaves and flowers from all plants.
- Sow winter lettuces in greenhouse border soil.
- Pot up winter- and spring-flowering bulbs but keep cool and dark for eight weeks.
- Sow French beans in pots for a winter crop.
- Pot up freesia corms for winter flowers.
- Wash pots and trays and store for use next spring.
- Remove any greenhouse shading.
- Sow mustard and cress for winter salads.
- Carry out all watering in the morning so that foliage does not remain wet at night.
- Pot up rooted cuttings.
- Pot up annuals sown in late summer and which are being grown for early colour in the greenhouse.
- Clean the glass both inside and out to make maximum use of winter sun.
- Ventilate the greenhouse with care.

Diary **Late autumn**

✳ flowers

- Plant bare-root roses, trees and bushes.
- Heel in plants that arrive before you are ready to plant them in their final positions.
- Pull up and compost faded annuals and bedding plants.
- Rake up leaves from beds and borders and rot them in a wire-netting bin.
- Plant tulips and lily bulbs.
- Remove faded foliage and fallen leaves from garden ponds.
- Check that climbers and wall plants are securely fastened to their support framework.

- Cut back faded border perennials.
- Provide food and water for garden birds.
- Protect tender plants from frost by covering them with straw or bracken.
- Take hardwood cuttings and root them outdoors.
- Plant hedges.
- Make a new compost heap.
- Plant new herbaceous perennials and dig up, divide and replant those that are overcrowded or in need of a move.

A stone lion (LEFT) and herons (BELOW) made of steel take on extra prominence in my garden in autumn.

◉ fruit

- Dig over and manure ground that is to be planted up with fruit trees and bushes later in the season.
- Plant fruit trees and bushes.
- Prune apple and pear trees.
- Check that tree ties are not constricting the trunks of young trees.
- Check fruits in store and discard any that are rotting.
- Order fruit trees and bushes for planting in late winter.

✎ vegetables

- Sow broad beans outdoors for an early crop. Cloche protection will be helpful.
- Dig or fork over vacant ground on the vegetable plot, working in well-rotted compost or manure.
- Compost faded vegetable plants.

- Check vegetables in store and discard any that are rotting.
- Protect cauliflower curds by bending a few leaves over them.
- Cut back globe artichokes and protect them with straw.
- Stake tall Brussels sprout plants to prevent wind rock.
- Send off for seed catalogues.

▥ lawns

- Dig or fork over ground where lawns are to be sown next spring, removing all thick-rooted perennial weeds.
- Apply an autumn lawn feed.
- Spike the surface of badly drained lawns to improve drainage, and rake with a wire-toothed rake to remove dead grass if you have not done so already this autumn.
- Give the lawn a final cut with the blades set high – about 2.5cm (1in) – then send the mower off for servicing.
- Lay turf when the ground is neither too wet nor frozen.

A last burst of autumnal colour in my garden before the advent of winter.

◼ greenhouse

- Ventilate the greenhouse with care and avoid splashing water on the foliage of plants.
- Knock out begonia, gloxinia, achimenes and smithiantha tubers from their pots once the foliage has died back and store them in dry, soilless compost.
- Water carefully and in the morning rather than the evening to reduce the likelihood of fungus diseases.
- Wash the greenhouse windows to admit as much light as possible.
- Pick faded leaves and flowers from all plants.
- Pot up rooted cuttings.
- Cut back the shoots of tender fuchsias.
- Fumigate to control pests, unless you are using biological control.
- Bring in bulbs that were potted in late summer but keep them cool and in a brightly lit spot.

Diary **Early winter**

✳ **flowers**

- Plant new rose bushes, cutting them hard back afterwards.
- Prune hybrid tea and floribunda roses.
- Tidy up beds and borders, cutting down faded perennials and pulling up and composting faded annuals.
- Dig up, divide and replant herbaceous perennials and plant new ones, except on heavy soils.
- Examine gladiolus corms and dahlia tubers in store and discard any that are rotting.
- Pot up lily bulbs for flowers next summer. Stand the pots outdoors in a sheltered spot.
- Send off your seed order.
- Remove fallen leaves from beds and borders.
- Carefully melt ice on garden pools so that fish can breathe.
- Provide food and water for garden birds.
- Repair broken gates and fences.
- Plant trees and shrubs lifted from the open ground.
- Knock snow from evergreens as soon as possible after it falls.
- Re-firm the earth around newly planted trees, shrubs, roses and perennials after frost.
- Plant hedges.
- Check that tree ties are not constricting saplings.
- Bring pots of bulbs into the house.

A greater-spotted woodpecker tucks in.

- Stand container-grown plants against the house wall in cold weather, and when severe frosts threaten, lag clay pots with old sacking or hessian.
- Drain fountains and water features that do not contain fish.
- Move garden ornaments that will be susceptible to frost into a shed.

fruit

- Plant new fruit trees and bushes on prepared ground.
- Prune apple and pear trees.
- Give trees that have been troubled by woolly aphid and other pests a tar-oil winter wash.
- Order fruit trees and bushes for planting later in the season.
- Prune newly planted raspberries, gooseberries and currants.
- Shelter pot-grown strawberries from heavy winter rains.

ABOVE: Garden ornaments, however humble, take on additional importance in winter. LEFT: Pebbles and stone give a garden form and texture, even in winter.

vegetables

- Send off your vegetable seed order soon.
- Dig or fork over vacant ground and work in well-rotted manure or compost where necessary.
- Stake tall Brussels sprouts to prevent wind rock.
- Check vegetables in store and discard any that are rotting.

lawns

- Keep off lawns in frosty weather.
- If you haven't already done so, send off the mower for servicing.
- Lay turf when the ground is workable.
- Prepare ground to be sown with grass seed in spring.

greenhouse

- Water cautiously in the morning, taking care not to splash foliage.
- Ventilate the greenhouse on warm days.
- Pick faded leaves and flowers from all plants.
- Bring in pots of bulbs planted in early autumn.
- Feed Christmas-flowering pot plants once every two weeks.
- Wash pots and seed trays that are not being used.
- Keep an eye open for slugs and snails and control them where necessary.
- Fumigate to control pests, unless you are using biological control (which will be less effective at low temperatures).
- Keep greenhouse glass clean to admit as much light as possible.
- Use a thermometer to check that the heating system is working.
- Invest in a heated propagator for sowings in the months ahead.

Diary Mid-winter

Windfall fruits are valued by birds at this time of year.

❋ flowers

- Tidy up beds and borders, cutting down faded foliage on herbaceous perennials.
- Clean all tools and oil the blades, rubbing down wooden handles with raw linseed oil.
- Firm in newly planted perennials and shrubs lifted by frost.
- Send off your seed order, and when the seeds arrive, store them in a cool place.
- Plant new rose bushes.
- Check dahlia tubers in store and remove any that are rotting.
- Repair paths, fences and gates.
- Fork or dig over vacant ground in beds and borders to prepare it for planting.
- Make a new compost heap.
- Plant deciduous trees and shrubs lifted from open ground.
- Take root cuttings of Oriental poppies, verbascum, romneya and phlox.
- Prune wisteria.
- Knock snow from the branches of evergreen trees and shrubs.

- Carefully melt ice on garden pools so that fish can breathe.
- Prune summer-flowering deciduous shrubs.

🍎 fruit

- Prune fruit trees and bushes.
- Plant new fruit trees and bushes when the ground is in a fit condition (not too wet or frozen solid).
- Check fruits in store and remove any that are rotting.
- Heel in trees and bushes that arrive before you or the ground are ready for planting.
- Prune outdoor vines.
- Tie in wayward branches on wall-trained fruit trees.
- Renew broken tree ties.
- Position rabbit guards around the trunks of young trees if damage is likely.
- Firm back newly planted trees and bushes lifted by frost.
- Prune newly planted raspberries and currants.
- Cover outdoor peaches, nectarines and apricots with old curtains or sacking to protect them from frost.

🍃 vegetables

- Protect young pea and bean plants with cloches.
- Mulch asparagus beds and clumps of rhubarb with manure or compost.
- Dig vacant ground and work in manure or compost.
- Discard any stored vegetables that are rotting.
- Bend leaves over cauliflower curds to protect them from the weather.

- Place cloches over ground where early sowings are to be made.
- Add lime to acid soil that is to be occupied by brassicas.
- Remove faded leaves from cabbages and Brussels sprouts.
- Plant lettuces under cloches.
- Net brassicas to protect them from pigeons.
- Force rhubarb outdoors under straw.
- Plant Jerusalem artichokes when the soil is neither frozen nor too wet.
- Send off your seed order.

Snow on my peacocks, but not enough to do any harm.

- Stand seed potatoes in trays with eyes uppermost to encourage them to sprout. Place them in a bright, frostproof place.

lawns

- Lay turf in mild spells and when the ground is not too wet.
- Send off the mower for servicing.
- Keep off grass in frosty weather.

greenhouse

- Bring in batches of winter- and spring-flowering bulbs.
- Plant grape vines.
- Sow exhibition onions.
- Sow French beans in pots for an early crop and lettuces in vacant border soil.

- Water carefully and always in the morning.
- Start peaches, nectarines and vines into growth in heated greenhouses.
- Provide daffodils and narcissi with some support as they flower.
- Force rhubarb under the staging in a warm greenhouse.
- Pot up rooted cuttings if you can give them a little warmth.
- Remove faded leaves and flowers from all plants.
- Plant potatoes in large pots for an early crop.
- Fumigate if pests are a problem.
- Bring in pots of strawberry plants for forcing.

RIGHT: Euonymus *'Red Cascade'*, whose *shocking pink fruit cases split open in winter to reveal bright orange berries. All this and autumn colour, too.*

Diary Late winter

✳ flowers

- Plant trees and shrubs lifted from nursery rows.
- Plant lily bulbs in beds and borders.
- Prune summer-flowering shrubs.
- Prune roses.
- Feed garden birds and provide them with water.
- Renovate and replant herbaceous borders.

- Lightly trim winter-flowering heathers with shears as soon as the flowers fade.
- Make new rock gardens.
- Carefully melt ice on pools so that fish can breathe.
- Prune winter jasmine as the flowers fade.
- Dig up, divide and replant snowdrops if you want to increase their number.
- Plant lily of the valley crowns.

🍅 fruit

- Cut back autumn-fruiting raspberries to within 15cm (6in) of the ground and trim the canes of summer fruiters to within 15cm (6in) of the topmost wire of their support system.
- Spray outdoor peaches with fungicide to control peach leaf curl.
- Protect outdoor peaches, nectarines and apricots from frost by covering them with old curtains or sacking on frosty nights.
- Feed fruit trees with a fertilizer high in nitrogen.
- Tie in wall-trained fruit trees and bushes.
- Check fruits in store and discard any that are rotting.
- Plant fruit trees and bushes when the ground is workable.
- Prune out stems of blackcurrants infested with big bud mite.
- Cut back tips of blackberry canes and tie the stems into the support wires.
- Complete the pruning of fruit trees.
- Prune figs.

🛠 vegetables

- Sow parsnips, spinach and broad beans when soil is workable.
- Plant shallots and garlic.
- Plant rhubarb and lift, divide and replant established clumps that need rejuvenating.
- Dig up and store remaining parsnips in dry sand.
- Plant Jerusalem artichokes.
- Dig vacant ground.
- Continue to force rhubarb outdoors under buckets of straw.

Rhododendron 'Praecox' is one of the first to flower in late winter.

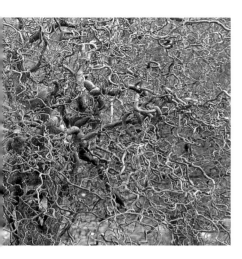

ABOVE: *The corkscrew hazel (*Corylus avellana *'Contorta') produces its catkins on twisted, bare stems.* RIGHT: *Few stems are brighter than those of* Cornus sanguinea *'Midwinter Fire'.*

- Protect brassicas with a net if pigeons are a problem.
- Unless you are on alkaline soil, add lime to any plot that is to be occupied by brassicas.
- Dig a trench for runner beans and fill it with organic matter.

lawns

- Keep off lawns in frosty weather.
- Make sure the mower is serviced ready for spring.
- Lay turf when the ground is workable.
- Spike lawns with a fork if surface drainage is poor.

greenhouse

- Sow broad beans, Brussels sprouts, cabbages, cauliflowers, celery, leeks, lettuces, onions and peas for planting out later.
- Plant tubers of achimenes and smithiantha in pots of soilless compost and keep them warm.
- Bring potted strawberries into the greenhouse for an early crop.

- Pot up rooted cuttings.
- Plant new grape vines.
- Take cuttings from flowering and foliage pot plants.
- Water and ventilate cautiously in the greenhouse.
- Pollinate flowers of peaches, nectarines and apricots.
- Sow sweet peas in pots for planting out later.

- Sow half-hardy annuals such as antirrhinums, begonias and salvias.
- Dry off cyclamen after flowering.
- Clean up the greenhouse before spring sowings begin.
- Prick out seedlings from earlier sowings.
- Pot up begonia and gloxinia tubers for early flowers.
- Pot up hippeastrum bulbs.

Index

Page numbers in *italics* refer to illustrations.

PICTURE CREDITS

BBC Worldwide would like to thank Jo Whitworth, who has taken most of the photographs in this book. All photographs are the copyright © of BBC Worldwide, with the exception of the researched ones (below) and the following, which are the copyright © of Jo Whitworth: pages 72 *top, middle and bottom*, 97 *bottom*, 99 *bottom*, 101, 102, 115 *top*, 136 *top*, 140, 141 *bottom*, 142 *top*, 145, 150–1, 151 *top*, 155 *top and bottom*, 156, 157, 159, 160 *top*, 162 *top and bottom*, 164 *bottom*, 165 *top and bottom*, 171 *top*, 189 *bottom*, 191 *top*, 207, 244, 248 *top*, 262.

BBC Worldwide would like to thank the following for providing photographs and for permission to reproduce copyright material. While every effort has been made to trace and acknowledge all copyright holders, we would like to apologize should there have been any errors or omissions.

BBC/JONATHAN BUCKLEY pages 5 *bottom*, 23, 25 *top*, 64–5 *left*, 95, 126–7 *both*, 139, 249, 301, 303 *top*, 304 *top*, 306–7 *all*, and 308–9 *all*; BBC GARDENERS' WORLD MAGAZINE page 291 *right* (Justyn Willsmore); GARDEN & WILDLIFE MATTERS pages 270 *right* and 310 *top* (*both* Maurice K. Walker); GARDEN PICTURE LIBRARY pages 6 *top* (Brian Carter), 45 (John Glover), 51 (Philippe Bonduel), 114 (Howard Rice), 117 (Lamontagne), 160 *bottom* (David England), 176–7 *centre* (Chris Burrows), 185 *top* (John Glover), 220 *centre left* (Mark Bolton), 231 (John Glover), 259 (Brian Carter), 263 (John Glover), 264 *bottom* and 265 (Frederich Strauss), 271 (Brian Carter) and 280 *bottom* (John Glover); HOLT STUDIOS pages 42 *top* (Len McLeod), 42 *bottom*, 43, 44, 46 (*all* Nigel Cattlin), 47 *left* (P. Peacock) and 47 *right* (Nigel Cattlin); PHOTOS HORTICULTURAL pages 4 *centre*, 91 *bottom*, 109 *top*, 110 *both*, 111 *bottom*, 112 *both*, 116 *both*, 117, 163 *top*, 195, 258 *both*, 260, 261, 268, 269 *top*, 275 *right* and 312 *left*; RADIO TIMES TIM SANDALL pages 32 *bottom*, 52, 56 *all*, 58 *all*, 72–3 *right*, 93 *all bottom*, 103 *all top*, 104 *all*, 118, 144 *all*, 168 *all bottom*, 183, 184 *all*, 188, 233 *all*, 235 *all*, 240 *all top*, 250 *all bottom*, 252 *all top*, 264 *all top*, 269 *all bottom* and 285; HARRY SMITH HORTICULTURAL COLLECTION page 36; ROB WHITWORTH page 96–7 *centre*.

BBC Worldwide would also like to thank the owners of the following gardens for allowing their gardens to be photographed:

p10 *left*: Little Court, Crawley, Hants; p12 *bottom*: Steve Jordan and Sarah Morgan, St. Mary Bourne, Hants; p13 Catherine Smith, London (Designer: Jennifer Harkins); p24 Croylands, Romsey, Hants; p39 Meadow House, Ashford Hill, Berks; p53 *right*: 2 Warren Farm Cottages, W.Tytherley, Hants; p57 Mrs D. Hucker, Dulwich, London; p60 Lt Colonel J. Ellicock, Hants; p63 Scypen, Ringmore, Devon; p66 Revd R. Legg, Whitchurch, Hants; p71 Valentine Cottage, Newnham, Hants; p74 RHS Gardens, Wisley; p75 Croylands, Romsey, Hants; p76 Mrs J. Blount, St Mary Bourne, Hants; p77 Chilworth Manor, Surrey; p78–9 *bottom*: 22 Springvale Road, Kingsworthy, Hants; p80 *bottom*: G. and M.J. Darrah, Hants; p81 Scypen, Ringmore, Devon; p83 Exbury Gardens, Beaulieu, Hants; p84 Meadow House, Ashford Hill, Berks; p85 Somerset Lodge, Petworth, W. Sussex; p86 Savill Gardens, Windsor; p87 *top*: Savill Gardens, Windsor *and bottom*: RHS Gardens,Wisley; p88 *bottom*: RHS Gardens, Wisley; p89 22 Springvale Road, Kingsworthy, Hants; p91 *top*: RHS Gardens,Wisley; p93 Valentine

Cottage, Newnham, Hants; p94 *top*: Manor Lodge, Crawley, Hants; p97 RHS Gardens, Wisley; p99 *top and bottom*: Hilliers Arboretum, Hants: p101 Frith Hill, W.Sussex; p102 Frith Hill, W.Sussex; p103 *bottom*: Frith Hill, W.Sussex; p105 Meadow House, Ashford Hill, Berks; p106 Frith Hill, W.Sussex; p107 *bottom*: 2 Warren Farm Cottages, W. Tytherley, Hants; 108 *top*: Mrs D Hucker, Dulwich, London; p109 *bottom*: Hollingtons Herb Garden, Newbury, Berkshire; p115 *top and bottom*: Valentine Cottage, Newnham, Hants; p129 Longstock Park Nursery, Hants; p130 RHS Gardens, Wisley; p131 Little Court, Crawley, Hants; p132 RHS Gardens, Wisley; p134 RHS Gardens, Wisley; p135 Meadow House, Ashford Hill, Berks; p136–7 *bottom*: Mrs Gunner, Crawley, Hants; p138 RHS Gardens,Wisley; p141 *top*: Little Court, Crawley, Hants; p143 Fairfield House, Hants; p145 RHS Gardens, Wisley; p146 RHS Gardens, Wisley; p147 *right*: RHS Gardens, Wisley; p150–1 RHS Gardens, Wisley; p152 Beth Chatto Gardens, Elmstead Market, Essex; p153 Exbury Gardens, Beaulieu, Hants; p154 RHS Gardens, Wisley; p158 2 Warren Farm Cottages, W. Tytherley, Hants; p159 Loseley Park and Gardens, Surrey; p161 Little Court, Crawley, Hants; p163 *bottom*: Savill Gardens, Windsor; p165 *top*: RHS Gardens, Wisley; p166 Lt Colonel J. Ellicock, Hants; p172 Longstock Park Nursery, Hants; p172–3 *bottom*: RHS Gardens, Wisley; p175 RHS Gardens, Wisley; p178 *top*: Lt Colonel J. Ellicock, Hants *and bottom*: RHS Gardens, Wisley; p186 RHS Gardens, Wisley; p187 Little Court, Crawley, Hants; p189 *top and bottom*: RHS Gardens, Wisley; p191 *top*: Loseley Park and Gardens, Surrey; p192 *top*: G. and M.J. Darrah, Hants; *bottom*: Beth Chatto Gardens, Elmstead Market, Essex; p193 *top and bottom*: RHS Gardens, Wisley; p196–7 Longstock Park Nursery, Hants; p198 Meadow House, Ashford Hill, Berks; p200 Meadow House, Ashford Hill, Berks; p201 Valentine Cottage, Newnham, Hants; p202 Lt Colonel J. Ellicock, Hants; p203 Valentine Cottage, Newnham, Hants; p205 Meadow House, Hants; p207 Little Court, Crawley, Hants; p208 Test Cottage, Hants; p209 Little Court, Crawley, Hants; p210 *top*: Scypen, Ringmore, Devon; *bottom*: Hayden Barn Cottage, Warnford, Hants; p211 Scypen, Ringmore, Devon; p212 Longstock Water Gardens, Hants; p213 RHS Gardens, Wisley; p214 G. and M.J. Darrah, Hants; p215 Longstock Water Gardens, Hants; p218 Frith Hill, W. Sussex; p220 *top and bottom*: Longstock Water Gardens, Hants; p220–1 *bottom*: Longstock Water Gardens, Hants; p222 Exbury Gardens, Beaulieu, Hants; p223 *top*: RHS Gardens, Wisley; *bottom*: Longstock Water Gardens, Hants; p226 *top and centre*: Longstock Water Gardens, Hants; p226–7 Longstock Water Gardens, Hants; p228 Longstock Water Gardens, Hants; p229 Little Court, Crawley, Hants; p230 *top and bottom*: Little Court, Crawley, Hants; p232 *top*: 2 Warren Farm Cottages, W. Tytherley, Hants; *bottom*: Somerset Lodge, Petworth, W. Sussex; p237 RHS Gardens, Wisley; p238 Test Cottage, Hants; p239 Hollingtons Herb Garden, Newbury, Berks; p240 *bottom*: Test Cottage, Hants; p241 RHS Gardens, Wisley; p242 22 Springvale Road, Kingsworthy, Hants; p244 RHS Gardens, Wisley; p245 *top*: G. and M.J. Darrah, Hants; *bottom*: RHS Gardens, Wisley; p248 *top*: Secretts Garden Centre, Milford, Surrey; p251 Little Court, Crawley, Hants; p256 Little Court, Crawley, Hants; p270 *left*: Test Cottage, Hants; p273 *bottom*: Beth Chatto Gardens, Elmstead Market, Essex; p276 *top*: Headland, Polruan, Cornwall; p277 Headland, Polruan, Cornwall; p278 Headland, Polruan, Cornwall; p280 *top*: Hollingtons Herb Garden, Newbury, Berks; p282 Beth Chatto Gardens, Elmstead Market, Essex; p283 Beth Chatto Gardens, Elmstead Market, Essex; p284 Beth Chatto Gardens, Elmstead Market, Essex; p286–7 Croylands, Romsey, Hants; p287 *top*: RHS Gardens, Wisley: p293 *top*: Beth Chatto Gardens, Elmstead Market, Essex; p295 Chilworth Manor, Surrey; p296 Frith Hill, W. Sussex; p297 Meadow House, Ashford Hill, Berks; p302 *bottom*: White Windows, Longparish, Hants.